AF478148

Determinants of Innovative Behaviour

Determinants of Innovative Behaviour

A Firm's Internal Practices and its External Environment

Edited by

Cees van Beers, Alfred Kleinknecht,
Roland Ortt and Robert Verburg

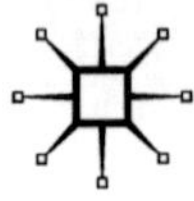

First published 2008 by
PALGRAVE MACMILLAN
Houndmills, Basingstoke, Hampshire RG21 6XS and
175 Fifth Avenue, New York, N.Y. 10010
Companies and representatives throughout the world

PALGRAVE MACMILLAN is the global academic imprint of the Palgrave Macmillan division of St. Martin's Press, LLC and of Palgrave Macmillan Ltd.
Macmillan® is a registered trademark in the United States, United Kingdom and other countries. Palgrave is a registered trademark in the European Union and other countries.

ISBN-13: 978–0–230–20632–8   hardback
ISBN-10: 0–230–20632–8   hardback

This book is printed on paper suitable for recycling and made from fully managed and sustained forest sources. Logging, pulping and manufacturing processes are expected to conform to the environmental regulations of the country of origin.

A catalogue record for this book is available from the British Library.

Library of Congress Cataloging-in-Publication Data

Determinants of innovative behaviour : a firm's internal practices and its external environment / edited by Cees van Beers ... [et al.].
    p. cm.
  Includes bibliographical references and index.
  ISBN-13: 978–0–230–20632–8 (alk. paper)
1. Technological innovations—Management. 2. Diffusion of innovations. I. Beers, Cees van, 1960–
  HD45.D37 2008
  658.4′063—dc22
                                           2008020589

10 9 8 7 6 5 4 3 2 1
17 16 15 14 13 12 11 10 09 08

Printed and bound in Great Britain by
CPI Antony Rowe, Chippenham and Eastbourne

Contents

Tables

Figures

Boxes

Notes on the Contributors

Amal Amarouch is a PhD candidate at Ecole Polytechnique de Montréal, Canada.

Spyros Arvanitis is Senior Researcher at the KOF Swiss Economic Institute of the ETH Zurich. He is head of the Research Division 'Structural Change' of this institute and lecturer in economics at the ETH Zurich. He has published extensively on the economics of innovation, technology diffusion, technology transfer and market dynamics.

Torsten Brodt holds a business degree from the University of Mannheim, received his PhD in innovation research from the University of St Gallen in Switzerland and is currently employed at Swisscom. His thesis reported on applied research projects with leading mobile operators, media and high-tech companies in Europe. His research interest is on experience design and new-product development in digital media industries as well as on global collaborative work environments.

Luc Cassivi is an associate professor in the Department of Management and Technology at the Université du Québec à Montréal. He received his PhD from École Polytechnique de Montréal and École Centrale de Paris. His research interests include information systems, innovation management and supply-chain management.

Vittoria Chiesa is a full professor of R&D strategy and organisation at Politecnico di Milano. He is member of the Management Council of MIP Business School, where he is responsible for the Technology Strategy Area. He is author of several books and more than 50 publications in international refereed journals in the fields of R&D management and technology strategy.

Doris Fay is a full professor of work and organisational psychology at University of Potsdam, Germany. She was awarded her PhD in psychology from the University of Amsterdam, after which she lectured at the University of Giessen, Germany and Aston University, UK. Her research interests revolve around questions of individual, team and organisational creativity and innovation, work and health, and HRM.

Federico Frattini is PhD candidate in management, economics and industrial engineering at Politecnico di Milano. He was lecturer in business economics and organisation at Università Vita-Salute San Raffaele, and previously at Università Carlo Cattaneo – LIUC. His research interests concern R&D management and organisation, R&D performance measurement, and the commercialisation of innovation in high-tech markets.

Michael Fritsch is Professor of Economics and Chair of Business Dynamics, Innovation, and Economic Change at the Friedrich Schiller University, Jena, Germany. He is also Research Professor at the German Institute for Economic Research (DIW-Berlin) and at the Max-Planck Institute for Economics, Jena. His main fields of research are entrepreneurship and new business formation, innovation systems, and economic development strategies.

Alfred Kleinknecht is Professor of Innovation Economics at Delft University of Technology. Previously he was Professor of Industrial Economics at Amsterdam University. Since 1978 he has been affiliated to the Berlin *Wissenschaftszentrum*, the University of Maastricht, the Free University and the University of Amsterdam.

Sebastian Knoll holds a degree in industrial management and engineering from the Technical University of Berlin and received his PhD in corporate strategy research from the University of St Gallen in Switzerland. His thesis explored strategies and related organization designs for the realization of cross-business growth synergies in multi-business firms. He worked as an independent corporate strategy consultant and as a project manager at General Electric and is currently employed by Fresenius Medical Care.

Elisabeth Lefebvre is a professor in the Department of Mathematics and Industrial Engineering at École Polytechnique in Montréal. She received her PhD in business administration from the University of Montréal. Her current research interests are in the area of technology management, supply-chain management and interorganizational collaboration.

Louis A. Lefebvre is a professor in the Department of Mathematics and Industrial Engineering at École Polytechnique in Montréal and invited professor in the Department of Management Studies at the University of Wageningen. He received his PhD in business administration from the University of Montréal. His current research interests are in the area of technology and innovation management, supply-chain management and RFID technologies.

Gaël le Hen is in the Department of Mathematics and Industrial Engineering at École Polytechnique in Montréal. He is also an engineering practitioner.

Hans Lööf is Director of Economic Studies in the Division of Economics, Department of Transport and Economics, Royal Institute of Technology in Stockholm. His fields of expertise are econometrics, industrial organization, economics of innovation and international trade. He has published various articles in, among others, the *Journal of Technology Transfer, Economics of Innovation and New Technology, Journal of Evolutionary Economics, World Economic Review* and *Annals of Regional Science.*

Jonathan Michie is Director of the Department for Continuing Education and President of Kellogg College, University of Oxford. Previously he was Director of Birmingham Business School. Before that Dr Michie was the Sainsbury Professor of Management at Birkbeck College, University of London, and Head of the School of Management and Organizational Psychology there. He was also previously at the Judge Business School, University of Cambridge.

Pierre Mohnen is Professor of Microeconometrics of Technical Change at Universiteit Maastricht, a professorial Fellow at MERIT, Maastricht, and an associate fellow at CIRANO, Québec. He carries out research on applied econometrics in the areas of R&D, innovation and technological change.

Roland Ortt is an associate professor of technology and R&D management at Delft University of Technology. He teaches in both areas. His current research interest includes different paths of technology development and diffusion with a special focus on methods of market and technology analysis in order to assess the potential of new technologies. Previously he worked as an R&D manager for a telecommunications company. He is the author of various articles in many journals, including the *Journal of Product Innovation Management,* the *Market Research Society* and the *International Journal of Technology Management.*

Franz Palm has been a professor of econometrics at Universiteit Maastricht since 1985. In 2005 he was awarded the Royal Academy Professorship for his contributions to the theory of econometric time series models. He is currently interested in panel data econometrics with applications to finance and innovation.

Mariacristina Piva is an associate professor in economic policy at the Università Cattolica del Sacro Cuore, Piacenza and Milan. Her main topics of interest are in the economics of innovation and labour economics, with specific emphasis on the role of human capital and organizational practices in the innovative process. She has published in various refereed journals.

Sybrand Schim van der Loeff is an associate professor of econometrics at Universiteit Maastricht. His research interests are in applied (micro)econometrics.

Maura Sheehan is a reader in human resource management at the University of Brighton Business School. She was previously an associate professor at the Graduate School of Management, University of Dallas and a senior lecturer in economics at Queen's University, Belfast. She has researched and published extensively on management and business issues, including on the link between human resource management practices on the one hand and organizational outcomes and corporate performance on the other.

Helen Shipton is a senior lecturer at Aston Business School. Her research is on the contribution of effective people management practice to organizational effectiveness and she has explored the relationship between HRM and organizational innovation within SMEs. More recently, she has been examining organizational learning and change in a qualitatitive, longitudinal study of an electronics company based in the UK. Dr Shipton has published in a variety of journals, including *Human Resource Management Journal*, the *European Journal of Work and Organizational Psychology* and the *International Journal of Management Reviews*.

Viktor Slavtchev is research assistant at the Chair of Business Dynamics, Innovation, and Economic Change at the Friedrich Schiller University in Jena. He studied economics at the Georg August University, Göttingen. His main fields of research are innovation systems and economic development. Particular topics of interests include economic growth, generation and transfer of knowledge, and the role of public research.

Amaresh Tiwari is a research assistant and a PhD student at Universiteit Maastricht. His thesis is on the financing of innovation in Dutch firms.

Paul Trott is Reader in Innovation Management at the Business School, University of Portsmouth. He holds a PhD from Cranfield University. His research focuses on aspects of how firms manage innovation. His book *Innovation Management & New-Product Development* (Prentice Hall), is currently in its 4th edition. Recently he was appointed as visiting Professor of Innovation and Entrepreneurship at Delft University of Technology.

Cees van Beers is currently associate professor of innovation economics at Delft University of Technology. Before this he was at the University of Leiden and the Free University Amsterdam. His published work is on international trade and environment, and more recently technology and firm performance.

Robert Verburg is associate professor of organizational behaviour at Delft University of Technology (TUD). Prior to joining TUD, he conducted senior-level executive search assignments for advanced technology companies. He has a PhD in organizational psychology from the Free University Amsterdam. His current research addresses HRM, innovation and leadership within knowledge-intensive organizations. He is the author of numerous articles in academic journals, chapters and books.

Marco Vivarelli has PhDs in economics and science and technology policy, is Full Professor at the Catholic University of Piacenza and senior scientist at the European Commission-JRC-IPTS, Seville. He is Research Fellow at IZA-Bonn; External Research Fellow at the Max Planck Institute, Jena, External Associate at the CSGR, Warwick University, and associate editor of *Small Business Economics*. He has extensively published in the fields of industrial organization, labour economics and economics of innovation.

1
Introduction

Cees van Beers, Alfred Kleinknecht, Roland Ortt and Robert Verburg

1.1 Background

1.1.1 Organizational background

This book is the result of a workshop on innovation systems at Delft University of Technology in October 2006. All chapters in this volume were presented and discussed at the workshop. After the workshop all chapters were critically judged in an additional anonymous review procedure. The main aim of the workshop was to provide an overview of the growing body of knowledge on innovation systems and their influence on the performance of firms. This book presents a multidisciplinary overview of research in the area of innovation with contributions from economics, management, marketing and psychology.

1.1.2 Scientific background

Research on determinants of innovative behaviour have developed at high speed over the past 25 years. Many contributions are interdisciplinary, drawing from economics, history, sociology and management sciences (Nieto, 2003). Most of the papers in this volume draw from economics, management and psychology.

The idea that technological change is important for economic growth and human development had been recognized much earlier by Adam Smith, Karl Marx and Joseph Schumpeter. Systematic research on innovation and technological change arose after Solow's 'A Contribution to the Theory of Economic Growth' in 1956. It received an important new impulse from the seminal work of Romer (1986, 1990) on endogenous economic growth. Solow investigated the impact of labour and capital input on long-run economic growth in the US and found an unexplained residual of more than 80 per cent, which he attributed to 'technical change'. Arrow (1962) argued that the production of knowledge, which is essential for technical change, has characteristics different from the production of tangible goods. Production of knowledge involves incomplete appropriation of benefits (that is, positive externalities), indivisibilities and uncertainty, leading to underinvestment in knowledge production by private producers.

Incomplete appropriability of new technological knowledge means that knowledge developed in a firm leaks to other firms which do not pay for it. Indivisibilities imply huge setup costs (high fixed and often sunk costs) which can only be recouped if the innovating firm gets a (temporary) monopoly position. Uncertainty refers to both technical and commercial uncertainty in developing new technologies and innovations. Romer (1986, 1990) incorporated these knowledge characteristics into Solow's growth model and revealed how policies can be formulated to increase economic growth.

In recent years, theoretical as well as empirical contributions have attempted to deal with innovation and technical change. Empirical analyses range from estimating production functions with macro-data (for example, Mankiw, Romer and Weil, 1992) up to investigations that analyse determinants of innovative behaviour at the firm level, using 'direct' measures of innovation (see, for example, contributions in Kleinknecht, 1996; Kleinknecht and Mohnen, 2002).

This book fits in the latter strand of research, drawing from economics, management and human resource management (HRM) literature. Contributions to this volume partly draw from the innovation systems literature (for example, Freeman 1995; Lundvall, 1992; Malerba 2004), which focuses in a conceptual way and through case studies on innovation policies that encourage innovations in both the private and the public sector. In the field of technology and innovation management, research focuses on the internal organization of the firm and deals with issues such as organizational design, marketing, financing of innovations and human resource management (see contributions in Verburg et al., 2006).

Figure 1.1 shows external and internal influences on firm performance. It shows how the internal organization affects innovativeness and firm performance. The internal organization of the firm concerns several functions such as the management of R&D, HRM or marketing.

A firm's innovativeness can be measured in various ways. Traditionally, innovation research was very much confined to using R&D and (admittedly

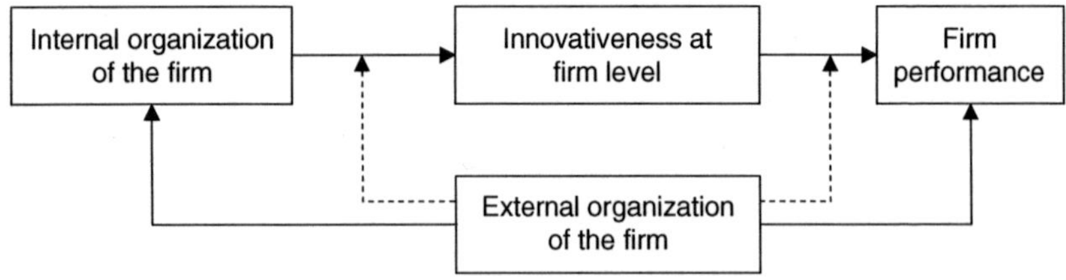

Figure 1.1   Innovation systems and firm performance: a model

deficient) patent data as indicators of innovation. The development of the Community Innovation Survey (CIS) has widened our options for empirical innovation research, firstly by providing large micro-databases on innovation all over Europe and secondly by developing new types of innovation indicators. The CIS provides information on R&D and non-R&D innovation expenditures as well as indicators of the output side of the innovation process such as sales of innovative products, as well as information on such things as R&D collaboration, bottlenecks to innovation or motives behind the innovation process. All this adds to traditional measures of firm performance such as sales, profits or client loyalty.

A firm's external organization affects firm performance directly but also indirectly by influencing adaptations of the internal organization of the firm (dashed lines in Figure 1.1). It consists of R&D networks between firms, between firms and universities, regional networks and related spillovers (that is, Marshallian versus Jacobian externalities), or the impact of market structure or government policies on firm performance.

This book provides an overview of current research on determinants of innovation at the firm level from the perspective of innovation economics, HRM and technology management. It is organized along two dimensions. The first dimension is along the lines sketched in Figure 1.1 and covers internal as well as external factors. The second dimension deals with the method of analysis, that is, conceptual versus empirical analyses. Within the latter, a distinction between case studies and samples with small and large numbers of observations is made.

Following the classification in Table 1.1 this book is organized in three parts. In Part I three chapters deal with a firm's internal organization, using empirical methods. Part II consists of six chapters in the category that links the internal to the external organization of innovating firms. These use

Table 1.1 Overview of contributions to this book

	Conceptual	Empirical		
		Case-study	**Small sample**	**Large sample**
Internal organization			Michie & Sheehan; Shipton & Fay;	Piva & Vivarelli
Linking internal to external organization	Chiesa & Frattini; Trott	Brodt & Knoll; Lefebvre, Lefebvre, Amarouch, Cassivi & le Hen	Lefebvre, Lefebvre, Amarouch, Cassivi & le Hen	Arvanitis; Tiwari, Mohnen, Palm and Schim van der Loeff
External organization				Lööf; Fritsch & Slavtchev

the broadest range of methodologies, conceptual and empirical (both case-studies and samples). Part III pays attention to the external organization of the innovating firm in two chapters using large samples.

1.2   Internal organization

In Chapter 2 Jonathan Michie and Maura Sheehan investigate whether the impact of HRM on small firms' performance depends upon their business strategy. The central idea is that use of 'high' HRM practices aimed at enhancing employees' motivation and commitment to the organization are likely to be translated into personnel initiatives and increased productivity. This seems particularly relevant in firms that work with skilled personnel. The paper tests three hypotheses. First, the 'contingency hypothesis' stating that the strength of the correlation between HRM practices and business performance depends on the business strategy of the firm, that is, cost-cutting versus innovation/quality enhancement. Second, it tests the 'universal relevance' hypothesis, that is, 'high' HRM innovation/quality enhancers outperform the other categories ('high' HRM and cost-cutting, 'low' HRM and cost-cutting, 'low' HRM and innovation/quality enhancement). Third, they test the 'configuration hypothesis' that implies that firms introducing HRM practices in an institutionally supported coherent package perform better than firms that introduce these practices in an ad hoc manner.

They analyse firms in the United Kingdom and show that HRM practices of innovators/quality-enhancers indeed outperform cost-cutters on measures of labour productivity, financial performance and customer retention (contingency hypothesis). Moreover, innovators/quality-enhancers achieve a higher level of performance when adopting 'high' HRM practices (universal relevance hypothesis) and it also appears that firms introducing HRM practices in a systematic and strategic way perform better than firms that introduce these ad hoc. Although no causal relationships have been investigated, the correlations suggest a (mutual) relationship between HRM practices aimed at increasing motivation and commitment of workers and firm performance in small firms in the UK and the USA.

In Chapter 3 Helen Shipton and Doris Fay also focus on HRM and argue that people are central to innovation performance. HRM practices play a vital role in stimulating behaviour towards learning and empowerment of the workforce. Their methodological focus is empirical and inductive. Based on datasets from 1993 and 1995 their study investigates how employee feelings and attitudes work out on HRM practices and work-design features, and how these promote innovation. The empirical analysis relates three different innovation indicators to the size and profitability of the firm and to either one of the following variables: a measure for HRM practices sophistication, the learning climate through teamwork, and an appraisal scheme. Both the sophistication of HRM practices and the learning climate affect product and process innovations positively. Appraisal schemes also show a positive effect unless they are related to remuneration schemes. In the latter case, the effect turns out negative. Employee feelings such as job satisfaction and the ability to be active and controlling towards the working environment appear to be more important than remuneration.

In Chapter 4, Mariacristina Piva and Marco Vivarelli investigate whether the macro-economic relationship between skills and R&D investments is also valid at the micro level. At the macro level the idea is that the increasing level of college-educated workers in Western economies after the Second World War led to 'skill-biased technological change' (SBTC). This leads to a dominant SBTC trajectory as it also requires more skilled workers, who push for further STBC. At the micro level this would mean that firms with *ex-ante* skill endowment would show higher profitability of R&D investment and hence higher R&D expenditures. They create a model explaining R&D expenditures out of lagged R&D expenditures (path dependency), sales (demand pull), and the ratio of white-collar to blue-collar workers, the latter being a proxy for a firm's skill endowment.

In their econometric estimates from a balanced panel of 215 manufacturing firms in Italy over the period 1995–2000 they find evidence in favour of this relationship.

1.3   Linking internal to external organization

The next six chapters analyse the link between the internal and external organization, sketching conceptual frameworks and applying empirical methods. Vittoria Chiesa and Federico Frattini provide a conceptual framework in Chapter 5. They argue that changes in the external environment have forced companies to adopt different combinations of organizations that enable both internal and external innovation activities. In their discussion of an organization's innovation activities, they focus on several strategic issues. Examples are whether innovating and operating activities and R&D activities in a company should be combined or separated. A contingency approach in describing the organization for innovation is adopted. First, they describe general trends in the external environment and how these trends have an impact on technology management in general and the appropriate organization for innovation in particular. Second, when describing alternative choices for an innovative organization, they indicate the conditions under which specific choices are more appropriate. For example, more decentralized R&D at division or business unit level makes sense in markets where incremental innovation is most important and time-to-market is essential. In contrast, when similar basic research is needed for all divisions of a corporation, then a more central organization of R&D makes sense.

Chapter 6 comprises a literature review by Paul Trott. He illustrates how the 'open-innovation' paradigm of Chesbrough (2003) builds on previous research and that it is a realistic opportunity for innovation management. While emphasizing that accessing and utilizing knowledge flows are a fundamental part of the innovation process, Trott also points at some threats of 'open innovation' for the innovating firm: information leakage and counterfeiting. Future research should focus on how best to protect valuable information and knowledge, in particular if they concern core competencies.

In Chapter 7 Torsten Brodt and Sebastian Knoll emphasize the importance of early-stage integration mechanisms in the success of mergers and acquisitions (M&As) aimed at acquiring the R&D capabilities of a target firm. They present a testable model that is based on constructs that describe the codification of knowledge (observability) and the extent to which knowledge is embedded in a physical setting (mobility). Combinations of high and low knowledge codification with high and low knowledge mobility lead to three relevant archetypes of R&D centres whose organizational characteristics are related to two integration mechanisms – task and human integration. If knowledge mobility is low, a higher level of task integration in the early integration period can be expected. If knowledge mobility is high and codification of knowledge low, much tacit knowledge is the result and a positive association with human integration can be expected. A case study in the telecommunications sector illustrates the model.

In Chapter 8, Elisabeth and Louis Lefebvre investigate the value and effectiveness of e-collaboration tools. They focus on the supply chain of a multinational firm in the automotive industry and how e-collaboration affects the performance in new-product development. The data make this research unique as they are based on a questionnaire set out among members of global virtual teams that work together on the development of new products. This system of 'open innovation' uses several e-collaboration tools, which are governed by several determinants. The most important determinant that multinational firms find hard to influence is the language barrier. Differences in languages of the global virtual team members result in more frequent use of e-collaboration tools that use graphics as a means of communication. Among the determinants that can be influenced by the multinational firm, training is the most important. E-collaboration between global virtual members significantly enhances communication and hence more effective new-product development in the supply chain. The results suggest that the 'open-innovation' paradigm is useful in analysing innovation processes in the supply chain.

In Chapter 9 Spyridon Arvanitis investigates the impact of innovation on productivity in the Swiss manufacturing sector in the second half of the 1990s. Several innovation indicators are used to test how determinants of innovation affect 1) the basic decision to engage in innovation; 2) innovation intensity; and 3) labour productivity. Favourable demand conditions enhance innovation, the latter being measured by the introduction of product or process innovations by R&D or by patenting. This supports Schmookler's (1966) 'demand-pull' hypothesis, implying that effective demand has more implications than has traditionally been assumed by Keynesians. As expected, the estimates by Arvanitis confirm that favourable conditions for appropriation of innovation benefits are beneficial to innovation.

In Arvanitis' analysis, the role of 'free competition' versus market power is not clear-cut. While competitive pressure appears to be quite important for innovation intensity, the basic decision to innovate seems to be favoured by a certain degree of market concentration. According to his estimates, innovation is affected positively by a low number of competitors. Particularly, working in a niche market with up to five competitors shows a positive relationship with innovation while higher numbers of competitors have a negative impact. The eight innovation variables used by Arvanitis are positively related to productivity increases. A firm's shifting from no innovation towards undertaking some innovation activities is related to productivity increases of between 21 and 46 per cent. Moreover, a 1 per cent increase in a firm's R&D intensity is related to a 0.054 per cent productivity increase, controlling for other influential factors. Strong negative effects on innovation can be found for lack of internal finance. Similar conclusions are drawn by Tiwari, et al. in this volume. Lack of qualified personnel in general and of R&D-personnel in particular are also ranking high as barriers to innovation in Switzerland; this underlines the importance of HRM policies for innovation (see also Michie and Sheehan in this volume).

In Chapter 10 Amaresh Tiwari, Pierre Mohnen, Franz C. Palm and Sybrand Schim van der Loeff deal with the impact of financial constraints on innovation. Innovation processes are risky and financial constraints can reduce innovation activity. Using Dutch CIS data for the period 1998–2002 they address two questions. First, what is the impact of financial constraints on R&D investments?; and second, what are determinants of financial constraints? As to the first question, they do not rely on balance sheet data (as was done in previous studies), but on qualitative information about bottlenecks to innovation as reported in the CIS. From their semi-parametric model estimation, they conclude that binding financial constraints to innovation activities in the Netherlands are relevant. The financial constraints are less binding when other constraints such as market uncertainty, regulation and organizational rigidities are considered, but they do remain significant. This suggests that financial restrictions are an important barrier to innovation in the Netherlands and that they should be addressed by policy-makers.

The second research question on determinants of financial constraints leads to two findings that are important to those concerned about promotion of innovative entrepreneurship: 1) firm age matters for financial constraints. Older firms have fewer problems with financial constraints than their younger counterparts; 2) firms that belong to a group of firms experience fewer financial constraints than do independent firms. This suggests that policies for the promotion of young and independent entrepreneurial firms should definitely address the working of capital markets and investigate ways of repairing market failures.

1.4   External organization

In Chapter 11 Hans Lööf investigates the relationship between technology spillovers and innovation output. He investigates three international mechanisms which, along with knowledge spillovers, can be channelled to firms to influence their innovative sales per employee in Sweden: 1) foreign direct investment; 2) imports; 3) R&D collaboration between foreign and domestic partners.

Using data from the Swedish Community Innovation Survey, covering the years 2002–4, the author constructs a model that corrects for sample selection bias and simultaneity. Lööf finds no robust evidence that foreign direct investment (FDI) plays a positive role for innovative output (that is, sales of innovative products). In other words, there is little difference between foreign-owned multinationals and domestically owned multinationals with respect to sales of innovative products. International knowledge spillovers to firms in Sweden mainly come in through imports and no evidence of a role for technology spillovers from foreign direct investment can be found. Second, as far as R&D collaboration is concerned, weak evidence is reported of knowledge transfer from foreign subsidiaries to local firms in Sweden or of bilateral R&D collaboration agreements. This comes close to findings by Brouwer and Kleinknecht (1996) from the Netherlands, reporting that sales of innovative products hardly differ between firms that engage in (various forms of) R&D collaboration and those that do it alone. The impact of technology transfer on innovative output increases, however, when foreign firms co-operate with a scientific partner or when (local) firms engage in multiple forms of collaboration simultaneously. In general, Lööf's estimates suggest that international spillovers by foreign firms are of limited relevance in Sweden, except when Swedish universities are involved.

In the final chapter, Michael Fritsch and Viktor Slavtchev deal with the question of whether the geographical environments in German regions affect patenting at the regional level. The central issue is whether regional specialization in certain industries improves the relative efficiency of regional innovation systems in Germany. They estimate a knowledge production function in the Marshall-Arrow-Romer (MAR) tradition and calculate the relative efficiency of regional innovation systems by the quotient of the patent elasticity of R&D employees of a region relative to the region with the highest patent elasticity (benchmark). These relative elasticities are explained in a regression analysis using regional characteristics as independent variables. It appears that both Marshallian and Jacobian externalities exist. This corresponds with other recent findings in the literature (see, for example, van der Panne and van Beers, 2006).

An important additional insight from the econometric exercise of Fritsch and Slavtchev relates to the non-linear nature of the relationship: while higher degrees of sectoral concentration in a region appear to be more favourable to innovation than lower degrees of concentration, very high degrees of concentration appear to be negative to innovation.

All this needs to be interpreted in light of the caveat that patents are a somehow deficient indicator of innovation. Arundel and Kabla (1998) as well as Brouwer and Kleinknecht (1999) have shown that an innovator's propensity to patent can differ considerably across sectors. Given that innovation performance in a region can be driven heavily by the sectoral composition of industry in a region, sectoral differences in the propensity to patent an innovation might bias estimates using patent data. The challenge is therefore to replicate such findings, using newly available innovation data from the Community Innovation Survey.

References

Arrow, K. (1962) 'Economic Welfare and the Allocation of Resources for Invention', in National Bureau of Economic Research, *The Rate and Direction of Inventive Activity* (Princeton: Princeton University Press).

Arundel, A. and I. Kabla (1998) 'What Percentage of Innovations is Patented?' *Research Policy*, 27, pp. 127–41.

Brouwer, E. and A. Kleinknecht (1999) 'Innovative Output and a Firm's Propensity to Patent. An Empirical Investigation', *Research Policy*, 28, pp. 615–24.

Chesbrough, H. (2003) *Open Innovation. The New imperative for Creating and Profiting from New Technology* (Cambridge, MA: Harvard Business School Press).

Freeman, C. (1995) 'The "National System of Innovation" in Historical Perspective', *Cambridge Journal of Economics*, 19, pp. 5–24.

Kleinknecht, A. (ed.) (1996) *Determinants of Innovation: The Message from New Indicators* (London: Macmillan).

Kleinknecht, A. and P. Mohnen (eds) (2002) *Innovation and Firm Performance: Econometric Explorations of Survey Data* (Basingstoke: Palgrave Macmillan).

Lundvall, B-A. (ed.) (1992) *National Systems of Innovatio: Towards a Theory of Innovation and Interactive Learning* (London: Pinter).

Malerba, F. (ed.) (2004) *Sectoral Systems of Innovation, Concepts, Issues and Analyses of Six Major Sectors in Europe* (Cambridge: Cambridge University Press).

Mankiw, N. G., D. Romer and D. N. Weil (1992) 'A Contribution to the Empirics of Economic Growth', *The Quarterly Journal of Economics*, 107, pp. 407–37.

Nieto, M. (2003) 'From R&D Management to Knowledge Management. An Overview of Studies of Innovation Management', *Technological Forecasting & Social Change*, 70, pp. 135–61.

Romer, P. M. (1986) 'Increasing Returns to Scale and Long-Run Growth', *Journal of Political Economy*, 94, 1002–37.

Romer, P. M. (1990) 'Endogenous Technological Change', *Journal of Political Economy*, 98, S71–S102.

Schumpeter, J. A. (1942) *Capitalism, Socialism and Democracy* (New York: Harper & Brothers)

Solow, R.M. (1956), 'A Contribution to the Theory of Economic Growth', *The Quarterly Journal of Economics*, 70, pp. 65–94.

Tidd, J., J. Bessant and K. Pavitt (2005) *Managing Innovation* (Chichester: Wiley).

van der Panne, G. and C. van Beers (2006) 'On the Marshall-Jacobs Controversy: It Takes Two to Tango', *Industrial and Corporate Change*, 15: 5, pp. 877–90.

Verburg, R. M., J. Ortt and W. M. Dicke (eds) (2006) *Managing Technology and Innovation: An Introduction* (London: Routledge).

Part I
Internal Organization

2
Business Strategy, Human Resource Management and Corporate Performance: Evidence from Small Firms in the UK and US

Jonathan Michie and Maura Sheehan[1]

2.1 Introduction

There is a large and growing literature on the relationship between the use of human resource management practices on the one hand, and corporate performance on the other (see for example Appelbaum et al., 2000; Guest et al., 2000; Huselid and Becker, 1996; Ichniowski et al., 1994, 1997; Mac-Duffie, 1995; Way, 2002; Wood and de Menezes, 1998). This literature has mostly found some degree of positive association between the use of such human resource practices on the one hand and organizational outcomes and corporate performance on the other. However, the strength and significance of the associations found varies across studies. Thus the general claim from the HR literature – of a positive association between what might be termed 'progressive' human resource management practices on the one hand, and organizational outcomes and corporate performance on the other – is precisely that: a *general* claim that may not apply to any given firm, since that firm may not exhibit the specific characteristics – such as pursuing an innovating rather than cost-cutting strategy – that are found to be particularly associated with these positive outcomes.

The recognition of these sorts of patterns has contributed to a consensus in the HR literature that a better understanding of the interaction between business strategy and HRM – strategic human resource management (SHRM) – will be key to gaining a better understanding of why the relationship between HRM and corporate performance varies across firms (see Delery and Shaw, 2001, for a review). Indeed, some papers have found explicitly that the associations between HR and performance do vary according to specified characteristics, such as the corporate strategies pursued by the firms in question (Aragon-Sanchez and Sanchez-Marin, 2005; Michie and Sheehan, 2005; Khatri, 2000; and Hoque, 1999).

We would therefore argue that to make further advance, three avenues of research are required. Firstly, as argued by Wall and Wood (2005), large-scale studies enable the construction of the sort of time-series data covering a sufficient number of firms to allow an analysis of causal processes. Secondly, studies analyse firms according to particular characteristics, to determine whether the general results from the literature hold equally in these more specific investigations, and if not, why not. And finally, following on from point two, as argued by Becker and Huselid (2003), there needs to be a better understanding of how effectively strategy is actually implemented, with a particular focus on the idiosyncratic dimension of HR's strategic fit. The current chapter contributes to both the second and third of these three research avenues, by analysing the relationship between business strategy, human resource management (HRM) and performance specifically within small firms.

The majority of studies on HRM in small firms are descriptive in nature, reporting the types of HR practices used (see, for example, Chandler and McEvoy, 2000; Ciavarella, 2003; Curren et al., 1996; DeKok and Uhlaner, 2001; Deshpande and Golhar, 1994; Duberley and Walley, 1995; Hayton, 2003; Heneman, 2000; Heneman et al., 2000; Heneman and Tansky, 2002; Hornby and Kuratko, 1990; Leung, 2003; McElwee and Warren, 2000; McEvoy, 1984; Marlow, 2002; Marlow and Patton, 2002; Rocha and Khan, 1985; Rutherford et al., 2003; Storey, 1995, 2004; Storey and Westhead, 1997; Vickerstaff, 1993; Wagar, 1998; Wagner, 1997; Williamson, 2001). The literature on the relationships between strategy, HRM and corporate performance in small firms is relatively underdeveloped compared to the work done in this area in relation to large firms referred to above. This is argued in detail by, for example, Cardon and Stevens (2004) who also make a distinction between small and emerging (new) firms.

This chapter therefore builds upon our previous work on the links between business strategy, human resources and competitive advantage in large UK companies by examining these relationships in small firms (employing 10–100 employees), and also in comparing this with the situation in US firms. Our previous work for large firms found, firstly, positive correlations between the use of HR practices and corporate performance ('internal fit'); secondly, that the relationship between HR and performance is dependent upon business strategy and that companies pursuing an integrated approach to HR coupled with an innovator/quality-enhancer focus within their business perform best ('external fit'); and that these relationships were strengthened further when HR practices were 'strategic' – that is where both internal and external fit occurred (see Michie and Sheehan 2001, 2003, 2005).

In particular, this chapter examines: firstly, the types of business strategies found in UK and US small firms; secondly, the relationship between business strategy, HRM and firms' performance; and thirdly, the similarities and differences between these relationships across small and large firms.[2]

2.2   Theoretical background

Economists, industrial sociologists and organizational theorists will look at and interpret the behaviour of employees at work and the role that management and work organization plays in this in quite different ways. They will have different assumptions and expectations and will be interested in different aspects of the process. Insofar as it is possible to set out a theoretical background that all would understand, it is that HR practices can influence corporate outcomes such as productivity in a number of ways. Firstly, if employees are more skilled and have competencies better tailored to the challenges they will face at work, then other things being equal those employees are likely to be more productive. Secondly, though, there is an element of discretionary effort, since monitoring is not costless. Thus if HR policies can enhance the employees' motivation and commitment to the organization then this is likely to be translated into greater discretionary effort and hence increased productivity. Such an effect may also be fostered through appropriate reward systems so that where discretionary effort is expended the employee receives a financial reward for the resultant improvement in performance, whether this is through performance-related pay or some other mechanism. Finally, though, the degree to which motivated and skilled employees can influence variables such as productivity will depend on the nature of work organization. There may be potential innovations in work organization that have yet to be identified, let alone applied. HR practices such as consultation and participation may allow such potential innovations to be identified, articulated, assessed and implemented.

Thus, HR policies can improve employee skills and motivation which will lead to discretionary effort that enhances productivity. If that productivity gain results in a reward, then the expectation of such rewards reinforces this virtuous cycle.

2.2.1   The link between strategy and HR management

Three theoretical perspectives dominate the SHRM literature: contingent, universalistic and configurational. The contingency approach argues that to be effective, an organization's HR policies must be consistent with other aspects of the organization. The organization's strategy is generally considered to be the primary contingency factor. This literature both hypothesizes that, and finds empirical evidence to support the hypothesis that, human resource policies and practices are generally consistent with the organization's strategy and that top management emphasizes different philosophies of HRM depending on the organizational strategy (Miles and Snow, 1978, 1984; Guthrie et al., 2002; Zahra and Pearce, 1990). Business performance will be improved when there is consistency (often referred to in the literature as 'fit') between business strategy and HR policies.

The best-practice, or universalistic approach, considers employees as one of the most important resources of the firm, and that investment in this resource – use of HR practices – will improve the performance of the firm (see for example Becker and Huselid, 1998; Kochan and Osterman, 1994; Pfeffer, 1994, 1998; Delery and Doty, 1996). Our previous research – which used a modified version of Delery and Doty's and Pfeffer's 'best-practice' policies – found support for this hypothesis in large firms (see Michie and Sheehan, 2001) and using the same database used in this chapter, we found evidence supporting the 'best-practice' or universalistic hypothesis in relation to small firms in the UK and US (Michie and Sheehan, 2008).

The traditional universalistic perspective suggests there is a 'best-practice' approach to SHRM, with a set of HR policies to be identified which will improve performance (Osterman, 1999, 1994; Pfeffer, 1994, 1998; Delery and Doty, 1996). These 'best-practice' policies may be embodied in a variety of concrete and detailed HR techniques or practices; for example, there may be many techniques that will encourage the sharing of information within an organization (Richardson and Thompson, 1999). This traditional approach to universalism has been modified and broadened by authors such as Hoque (1999) and Wood (1999). Hoque, for example, argues: 'When testing universalism, it is important to acknowledge the difference between the *universal effects* that HRM might have, and the *universal relevance* of HRM as an approach. Where universal effects are concerned, the implication is that contrary to external fit arguments, HRM has performance effects irrespective of circumstances, or irrespective of the business strategy adopted. Most tests of universalism have focused on this issue (Hoque, 1999, p. 422). Given that we have already found evidence of the *universal effects* of HRM for this set of firms (that is, that there is a positive relationship between HR policies and performance), in this chapter we test for the *universal relevance* of HRM – which can be regarded as a test for internal consistency, placed in an overall context of external fit. We therefore examine specifically if, and how, the relationship between HRM and performance is related to the business strategy that the firm is pursuing.

The configurational approach differs from the contingency and universal relevancy theories by being guided by a holistic approach to inquiry and by adopting the systems assumption of 'equifinality': 'In general, configurational theories are concerned with how the pattern of multiple independent variables is related to a dependent variable rather than with how individual independent variables are related to the dependent variable' (Delery and Doty, 1996, p. 804). Configurational SHRM is concerned with 'the pattern of planned human resource deployments and activities intended to enable an organization to achieve its goals' (Wright and McMahon, 1992, p. 298). The configurational approach suggests that an organization must develop HR as a *system* so that both horizontal and vertical fit can be achieved.

2.2.2 Internal and external fit

Horizontal fit implies there must be internal consistency of the organization's HR practices – as HR 'bundles' or 'systems'. Internal fit emphasises the interdependency between individual HR practices, with the use of one HR practice enhancing the effectiveness of others – a synergy between practices. Our previous work on this database found statistically significant evidence of horizontal/internal fit (see Michie and Sheehan, 2008).

Vertical fit refers to the consistency of the organization's HR system with other organizational characteristics such as the firm's strategy. External fit suggests that HR practices must 'fit', or be congruent with, the firm's policy choices outside the area of HR.

The presence of these two fits implies that specific combinations of HR practices can be identified which improved performance, but these combinations will vary according to organizational context, such as firm strategy. Different notions of 'fit' underlie the three theoretical perspectives in the literature. The traditional universalistic approach suggests that only internal fit matters, so that 'best-practice' policies work in all contexts, albeit with variation in terms of the actual HR techniques used. The contingency perspective suggests that to be effective an organisation's HR practices must be consistent with other organisational factors, primarily its strategy – there needs to be external fit. The configurational perspective suggests that improved performance will only occur when 'vertical' or external fit *and* 'horizontal' or internal fit are achieved. We use a modified approach toward 'horizontal' or internal fit that does not exclude key aspects of the firm's behaviour – its competitive strategy.

2.2.3 Competitive strategies

Porter (1985) describes competitive advantage as the 'essence of competitive strategy' and proposes three strategies that companies can use to achieve this advantage: innovation, quality-enhancement and cost reduction. Schuler and Jackson (1987) link these three strategies with the associated behaviours of employees and HR practices that a firm should adopt. They argue that HR practices will prove effective only where the firm emphasizes the importance of either quality enhancement or innovation within its business strategy. In organizations pursuing a cost-based strategy, the logical approach to HR strategy would be to emphasize wage-cost minimization and low levels of formal training: 'In such a situation, the values and goals imbued within HR would be consistent with the organization's primary cost reduction goals' (Hoque, 1999, p. 421). In organizations pursuing the innovation/quality-enhancer strategies, the logical approach to HR strategy would be to emphasize training and education and to offer above-average rates of compensation to help retain and motivate employees. Most of this literature has studied these relationships in the context of large firms. A notable exception is a study by Aragon-Sanchez and Sanchez-Marin (2005) of Spanish SMEs. Their findings are broadly consistent with the findings for large firms. Specifically, the authors found that firms with a prospector (innovator) strategy generally outperform firms pursuing the other three strategy typologies (defenders, analysers and reactors) 'because of their great capacity for management and adaptation to the current environment' (p. 306).

2.3   Hypotheses tested

2.3.1   The contingency hypothesis

Following Hoque (1999), three business strategy typologies are used to test the contingency hypothesis: 'innovators/quality-enhancers', 'cost-reducers', and 'others'. The contingency ('external fit') hypothesis tested is as follows:

> *Hypothesis 1: Any correlation found between the use of HR on the one hand and performance on the other will be contingent upon business strategy; in other words, if we find such a correlation, we would expect any such correlation to vary between firms as a result of firms pursuing different strategies.*

2.3.2   The universal relevance of HRM

The universal relevance hypothesis is tested by categorizing the firm's business strategy and the number of HR practices it uses. The following hypothesis is tested:

> *Hypothesis 2: The level of performance is dependent on the approach taken to HR and to business strategy; 'high-HR innovators/quality-enhancers' outperform the other categories within the sample.*

2.3.3   The configurational hypothesis

The final hypothesis concerns the introduction of HR as a synergistic package of mutually supporting practices. According to bundling theory, companies that adopt their HR practices as a coherent, institutionally supported synergistic package – strategic HRM – should outperform establishments within which HR has been introduced in an ad hoc manner.

> *Hypothesis 3: Firms that introduce HR practices within an institutionally supported, coherent package outperform those that introduce similar numbers of HR practices in an ad hoc manner rather than as part of an overall strategy.*

If the coupling of internal and external fit is important (the configurational hypothesis), the 'strategic HR' companies (see below for discussion) should outperform the other establishments within the sample.

2.4   Methods

2.4.1   The sample

The data used in the analysis were derived from a stratified sample of firms from the Dun & Bradstreet databases in the UK and US respectively. Two dimensions were used to stratify the sample: organizational size and the primary sector of business activity. In relation to size, the selection criterion was that the firms employ between 10 and 100 employees. Nine sectors were identified – five in manufacturing and four in services – using the 1992 UK and US Standard Industrial Classification (SIC) codes. The matched SIC codes are as follows:

Manufacturing – medical

    2833 – Medicinal chemicals and botanical products
    2834 – Pharmaceutical preparations
    3827 – Optimal instruments and lenses
    3841 – Surgical and medical instruments and apparatus
    3844 – Radiology/electrical medical equipment

Services – health

    8071 – Medical and scientific laboratories
    8072 – Dental laboratories
    8051 – Skilled nursing facilities

Services – other

    5411 – Grocery stores/supermarkets

Dun & Bradstreet supplied a total of 1281 firms with the above characteristics in the UK and 1470 in the US (see Appendix 2.1 for sample details). The medical manufacturing and health-service SIC codes were selected because these represent industries of significant growth – both current and expected – in the UK and US, and are generally associated with high skill and training levels (see, for example, United Kingdom Department of Health, 2004; US Bureau of Labor Statistics, 2008: www.bls.gov/iag/tgs/iag65.htm). The grocery-store industry was selected to serve as a comparative industry. This is a large industry with a high expected rate of growth, although not known for high skill or training levels.[3]

It was felt that by focusing on specific industries, we would reduce the problem of firm heterogeneity that bedevils small-firm research, especially since this study is in an international context. The motivation for the current chapter is to test the HRM-performance link in as specific a context as possible. The inclusion of the grocery-store industry enables us to explore, preliminarily, whether the nature and strength of reported outcomes show sensitivity to the type of industry analysed. That is, to examine the contextual conditions that moderate the extent to which human resource management systems contribute to organizational effectiveness (see Datta et al., 2005 for a detailed examination of how industrial characteristics moderate the effectiveness of high-performance work systems).

The data collected are cross-sectional. It is important to stress therefore that what is being investigated is the possible correlation between variables such as the use of various work practices, on the one hand, and the firm's performance on the other. We are not arguing that such correlations represent simple one-way causal processes. Indeed, we would expect any correlations we found to be the result of complex causal relationships between variables. It is also important to recognize the limits of the survey approach to inform on the very complex relationships between people and processes within the 'black box' of the firm. To fully illuminate the inner workings of the firm, such survey work needs to be combined with detailed case-study analysis.

Perhaps the most significant limitation in relation to such research is response bias. This is a problem inherent in almost any study of HR, but given the very different educational backgrounds (plus language-barrier and immigration-status issues) among owners of small firms, there may be additional response bias, since the most disorganized, worst, 'bleak house' (Sisson, 1993) firms may tend not to respond. On the other hand, several of those interviewed did ask for our advice in tackling management problems, so this may represent an incentive for poorly performing firms to participate.

Given that the firms employed fewer than 100 people, it was unlikely that the majority of firms would have an HR department or HR director/specialist; so letters and faxes were sent to the company's CEO/owner/director – the most senior person that could be identified from the Dun & Bradstreet database. Given low responses to postal surveys, in particular from SMEs (Dennis, 2003), it was decided to conduct a telephone survey of the selected companies. The following protocol was followed:

- The main contact person identified from the Dunn & Bradstreet databases was sent a one-page briefing on the objectives of the survey and the expected length of the interview (around 40 minutes). Confidentiality was emphasized.
- The person was then contacted to see if they would agree to the telephone interview and if agreeable, a date and time was set. They were then faxed a 'glossary' of HR terminology and definitions of the financial variables that would be asked about. It was found, however, that this fax seemed to have a negative effect on people actually completing the telephone survey. This was a particular problem in the US. It is likely that small business owners did not wish to reveal financial information, despite the assurances of confidentiality. Once this problem was identified, the financial variable information was dropped.

Interviews were conducted by telephone with the company's CEO/owner/director in 87 per cent of cases in the UK and 83 per cent of cases in the US. The remaining interviews were carried out with the director of human resources/personnel/employee relations. Many of the interviewees appeared extremely interested in the research and the survey questions. Thus, in around half of the interviews, quite lengthy discussions – almost 'mini case studies' – took place between the interviewee and the research team members conducting the interviews. Summaries of these discussions, comments, and feedback were entered into the final databases which were used in the analysis and which helped to provide an understanding of the processes and rationales behind the quantitative data. Some of this informal feedback is reported below.

In total, 1173 companies were asked (holding companies and companies where it was clear that they had been categorized in the wrong SIC were excluded) to participate in the survey in the UK. Of these, 1051 declined, 31 agreed but subsequently failed to complete the interview, and 91 interviews were completed successfully (a response rate of 7.8 per cent). In the US, 1221 companies were asked to participate, 1066 declined, 56 agreed but subsequently failed to complete the interview, and 98 interviews were completed successfully (a response rate of 8 per cent). Based on response rates to the pilot telephone interviews, the sampling aim was to obtain a total quota of 5 per cent of the 'population' and to achieve representation within the stratified sample cells.[4] Where possible, potential interviewees were asked why they declined to participate: the main reason was 'time constraints'. Many of the business owners commented that they worked long hours, often seven-day weeks, and even though many stated that the study seemed interesting and that they *did* need to learn more about 'personnel management' and how to 'manage their employees more effectively', they simply could not 'spare the time'. The other main reason for not participating in the study was 'confidentiality concerns', particularly for the US firms.

2.4.2 The measures

i) Performance variables

Three questions were asked concerning performance outcomes, with respondents asked to rate each on a scale of one (much worse) to five (much better):

1. How well does labour productivity at your company compare with other companies in the same industry?
2. How has financial performance – that is, profitability – at your company compared with other companies in the same industry over the past financial year?
3. How does the ability to retain existing customers at your company compare with other companies in the same industry?[5]

While there is a perception that small business owners may have difficulty gauging how well their company performs relative to other companies in the industry, this appeared not to be the case: companies seemed acutely aware – at least in relation to the relative/subjective measures used – where their company ranked compared to others in the same industry. Indeed, 63 per cent and 74 per cent of UK and US companies respectively had benchmarked (examined the way things are done at other workplaces and compared them with their own company) in the past two years.

For the majority of sample companies (60.4 per cent in the UK and 60.2 per cent in the US respectively), we were able to obtain financial data from Dun & Bradstreet. These data allowed us to address the issue of convergent validity between the subjective and objective measures of performance (see Appendix 2.2 for a detailed discussion on how we tested these relationships). The findings on convergent validity for the subjective and objective measures of company performance for firms in the study is consistent with our previous research that demonstrated a relatively high degree of consistency between 'subjective' performance measures and their 'objective' counterparts in large companies (Wall et al., 2004).

ii) Control variables

The following control variables were included in the analysis (see Appendix 2.1 for descriptive statistics on the variables)[6], with the name used to identify them in the results tables given in parentheses:

1. The number of employees (Size). The relationship between firm size and some of the performance variables was often nonlinear, thus the quadratic of size is also used ($Size^2$).
2. The age of the company (Age) where age was 2005 (the year of the study) minus the founding year.
3. Sector dummies for 'Industry (Manufacturing)' comprise companies in the 2833, 2834, 3827, 3841, 3844 SIC codes; companies in the 8051, 8071 and 8072 SIC codes were placed in the 'Industry (Services)' category; and companies in the 5411 SIC code in the 'Industry (Other)' category. The omitted category is 'Industry (Other)'.
4. Whether the company has a large-firm affiliation (34 per cent and 41 per cent for UK and US companies respectively) (Large Firm Affiliation),
5. The market environment ($1 =$ declining; $2 =$ turbulent; $3 =$ stable; $4 =$ growing; and $5 =$ growing rapidly) (Market Conditions).
6. Trade union presence (18.5 per cent and 14 per cent for UK and US companies respectively) (Trade Union Presence).
7. ISO 9000 series recognition (41.1 per cent and 49.5 per cent for UK and US companies respectively) (ISO Recognition) (yes $= 1$, no $= 0$). Surveys of ISO 9000 recognition in small firms indicate that installing such a system is a major exercise; is costly, especially in the short-run; must be

well planned; and usually requires an 'internal champion', especially the CEO (McAdam and McKeown, 1999; McTeer and Dale, 1996; Porter and Rayner, 1991; and Taylor, 1995). Thus, similar to investment in HRM practices, ISO recognition in small firms requires significant investment and recognition by management that this type of investment will improve the company's performance, at least in the medium to long-term. There is also overlap between requirements for ISO recognition and formalization of HRM practices, especially in relation to training and education of the workforce. Indeed, the pilot interviews found that firms with ISO recognition were more likely to have more formalized HRM systems in place and thus recognition is used as a control variable.

8. Whether the company received external assistance from organizations such as Business Links/Small Business Advisory Service, the small firms loan guarantee scheme, or the European Union in the UK; or the Small Business Administration, Chambers of Commerce, or Business Administration Centres in the US (38 per cent and 19 per cent of UK and US companies respectively) (External Assistance).

iii) Measurement of HR practices

Human resource management was measured through 17 items placed within five broad categories. These are outlined in Table 2.1. The practices cover the areas of recruitment and selection, performance appraisals, performance-based pay, training and development, employee participation (voice) and participation. The items and categories were drawn from the existing literature (see, for example, Becker and Gerhart, 1996; Dyer and Reeves, 1995; Guest and Hoque, 1994; Pfeffer, 1994, 1998; Wood and Albanese, 1995) rather than from a specific *a priori* definition of HRM. However, most of the HRM literature pertains to large firms and the pilot interviews revealed that HRM practices such as 'employment security/internal labour market', and 'single status and harmonization' were not generally applicable to small firms and were thus not included. The mean number of practices used within the UK sample is 11.1 and 12.7 for the US sample.

iv) Measures of business strategies

We build upon the business strategy typologies from Schuler and Jackson (1987) and Hoque (1999). The classifications are based on both subjective responses to questions on strategy and on objective data. In terms of the subjective responses, companies were asked to rank the importance of various business strategies for their company's competitive success (where 1 = insignificant; 2 = not very significant; 3 = moderately significant; 4 = very significant; and 5 = crucial).

Additional data used to formulate the strategy classifications were collected on how the company's remuneration rate for the overall workforce compared

Table 2.1 HR practices used in the analysis

HR Practices	Mean SD UK n = 91		Mean SD US n = 98		Mean SD All firms n = 189	
A. Recruitment and selection						
a. Use of at least one of the following selection methods: formal application form; formal interview; work sample; test of job skills; assessment of job skills	0.889	0.812	0.913	0.803	0.901	0.782
b. Written employment contract	0.934	0.856	0.615	0.549	0.768	0.687
c. Written job description	0.553	0.412	0.592	0.567	0.572	0.541
B. Performance appraisal						
Formal appraisal of majority (>50%) of managerial and non-managerial employees on a regular basis, or at least annually	0.605	0.487	0.721	0.688	0.665	0.532
C. Performance-based compensation						
a. Individually based performance related pay	0.521	0.322	0.605	0.513	0.563	0.496
b. Profit sharing (or some other type of company-based reward system)	0.100	0.233	0.152	0.337	0.126	0.268
c. Employee stock options	0.022	0.011	0.053	0.048	0.037	0.025
d. Team-based performance	0.208	0.338	0.285	0.207	0.249	0.300
e. Training-education achievement linked bonus	0.199	0.245	0.152	0.197	0.175	0.204
D. Training and development						
a. Formal induction programme for new employees	0.912	0.887	0.936	0.900	0.926	0.885
b. The majority (>50%) of managerial and non-managerial employees received formal (NVQ and/or 'off-the-job') training in the past 12 months	0.612	0.608	0.489	0.415	0.550	0.516
c. The majority (>50%) of managerial and non-managerial employees received informal ('on-the-job') training in the past 12 months	0.802	0.652	0.785	0.477	0.794	0.532
E. Employee voice and participation						
a. Employee representation at board/senior management meetings	0.462	0.388	0.412	0.466	0.434	0.392
b. Joint consultative committees (JCCs)	0.203	0.268	0.221	0.193	0.211	0.203
c. Employees are surveyed on a regular basis, at least annually	0.788	0.605	0.792	0.773	0.794	0.730
d. Employees consulted about new hires	0.332	0.389	0.255	0.228	0.291	0.267
e. Where financial targets are set (59% of UK firms; 68% of US firms), employees are informed about the status of these targets (i.e., whether targets were exceeded, met, or not met)	0.205	0.168	0.153	0.166	0.180	0.170

Table 2.2   Business strategies: UK and US firms

Business strategy	UK firms	US firms	All firms
A. *Cost-based*	21%	26%	23%
B. *Innovator-based*	22%	36%	29%
C. *Quality-based*	40%	24%	32%
D. *'Other'*	17%	14%	15%

Note: percentages may not sum to 100% due to rounding.

to its main competitors' (where 5 = well above average; 4 = above average; 3 = average; 2 = below average; 1 = well below average); and whether the company had introduced a new product or process innovation in the past three years; if it had a system of Total Quality Management (TQM) in place; and if it had ISO recognition (or other industry-specific certificates/awards).

Companies were classified as having a *cost*-based strategy if they ranked 'offering the best price'/'value for money' as the main source of their competitive advantage (4 or 5 on the scale described above) *and* paid low remuneration rates to their employees compared to their main competitors (1 or 2 on the scale described above) *and* if *at least one* of the following applied: no innovations were introduced in the past three years, no TQM system was in place, and there was no ISO recognition (21 per cent of UK companies, 26 per cent of US companies, and 23 per cent of all companies in the sample).

Companies were classified as having an *innovator*-based strategy if they ranked 'frequently innovating their product or service' and/or 'frequently implementing process innovations' as the main source of their competitive advantage (4 or 5 on the scale described above) *and* if they had introduced either a product or process innovation over the past three years (22 per cent of UK companies, 36 per cent of US companies, and 29 per cent of all companies in the sample).

Companies were classified as having a *quality*-based strategy if they ranked 'offering the highest quality product or service' as the main source of their competitive advantage (4 or 5 on the scale described above) *and* if they paid high remuneration rates to their employees compared to their main competitors (4 or 5 on the scale described above) *and* if *at least one* of the following applied: at least one product or process innovation was introduced in the past three years, a TQM system was in place, and there was ISO recognition (40 per cent of UK companies, 24 per cent of US companies, and 32 per cent of all companies in the sample).

The *innovator*-based and *quality*-based (*innovator/quality-enhancer*) strategies are combined for this analysis because of the similarities in the outcomes both groups achieved. For example, all but four UK companies and all but three US companies that had introduced an innovation had either higher than average remuneration rates, a TQM system in place, or had achieved ISO recognition.

Companies were classified as 'other' if they did not meet any of the criteria outlined above. These companies placed no significant emphasis on cost, quality or innovation in terms of their competitive success (17 per cent of UK companies, 14 per cent of US companies, and 15 per cent of all companies in the sample). These companies appeared to run their businesses in a rather ad hoc manner.

In terms of UK-US comparisons, it can be seen that US companies were more likely to emphasize a *cost*-based strategy (26 per cent) compared to their UK counterparts (21 per cent); US companies were more likely to emphasize an *innovator*-based strategy (36 per cent) compared to their UK counterparts (22 per cent); and UK companies were more likely to emphasize a quality-based strategy (40 per cent) compared to their US counterparts (24 per cent).

Comparing the strategies of UK small firms to a survey of large UK firms (employing more than 100 people), the breakdown of strategy categories for the large firms was as follows: 15 per cent *cost*-based, 25 per cent *innovator*-based, 50 per cent *quality*-based (75 per cent combined innovator/quality-based) and 10 per cent 'other' (see Michie and Sheehan, 2005). The main difference appears to be that small firms were more likely to have a *cost*-based approach (21 per cent compared to 15 per cent of large firms) and they were also more likely to have no identifiable strategy (17 per cent compared to 10 per cent of large firms). These results are not surprising since strategy tends to form and evolve as companies grow and mature, and many small firms attempt to enter the market based on the price competitiveness of their product or service.

2.4.3   Hypothesis testing

i) Testing the contingency theory

Following Hoque (1999), the measure of HR used in the analysis is cumulative, with each company being ranked according to the extent to which it adopted the 17 individual HR practices (see Table 2.1). The aim of this variable is to measure the extent to which HRM practices have been adopted. By splitting the sample by strategy typologies, and then regressing the aggregate HR variable on each of the performance variables, we can assess the effectiveness of HR in the context of 'cost-reducer', 'innovator/quality-enhancer', and 'other' business strategies. Hypothesis 1 is therefore tested for whether HRM is most effective, in terms of performance outcomes, when there is external fit. By splitting the sample based on the type of strategy the firm is pursuing, the HRM variable is then regressed on each of the performance variables. This enables us to assess the effectiveness of HRM in the context of the business strategy being pursued by the companies.

ii) Testing the universal relevance of HRM

Having split the sample three ways to perform the external fit tests, discussed above, the sample is reclassified and dummy variables created, to enable comparisons between business strategy categories as follows:[7]

1. 'Low-HR cost reducers', using eight or fewer HR practices: five UK companies and 11 US.
2. 'Medium-HR cost reducers', using more than eight but fewer than 13 HR practices: 10 UK companies, seven US.
3. 'High-HR cost-reducers', using 13 or more HR practices: four UK companies, five US.
4. 'Low-HR innovators/quality-enhancers', using eight or fewer HR practices: nine UK companies, 10 US.
5. 'Medium-HR innovators/quality-enhancers', more than eight but fewer than 13 HR practices: 16 UK companies, 14 US.
6. 'High-HR innovators/quality-enhancers', 13 or more HR practices: 32 UK companies; 32 US.
7. 'Low-HR others', using eight or fewer HR practices: four UK companies, seven US.
8. 'Medium-HR others', more than eight but fewer than 13 HR practices: seven UK companies, six US.
9. 'High-HR others', 13 or more HR practices: four UK companies; six US.

This series of dummy variables enables comparative analysis between the level of performance dependent on the approach taken to HR *and* business strategy. Category 6 is held constant which allows us to examine whether the 'high-HR innovator/quality-enhancer' establishments outperform the other categories.

iii) Testing the configurational hypothesis

The final test is for the configurational hypothesis: whether it is important to introduce HRM as a synergistic package of mutually supporting practices (in other words, are internal *and* external fit important?). Of the firms using a higher than average number of HRM practices, based on Hypothesis 3, we would expect that the firms that introduce these practices strategically should outperform the firms where HRM has been introduced in a more ad hoc manner.

Consistent with other studies of small firms (Storey, 1994; Cassell et al., 2002) it was found that a low percentage (5.9 per cent) had an HR department or specialist (3.3 per cent in the UK and 7.3 per cent in the US). The company's CEO/owner/director almost always reported that he/she felt HR and personnel issues were their responsibility. Despite the absence of HR departments or specialists, we did find evidence of 'strategic' HR practices and use evidence of these practices to determine whether companies had strategic HRM in place.

The firm is categorized as having 'strategically integrated' its HR practices if it had at least two of the following 'strategic' HR policies in place: 1) analysis of recruitment methods at least annually (33 per cent of UK firms; 39 per cent of US firms; and 36 per cent of all firms in the sample); 2) a recruitment plan for the next year (31 per cent of UK firms; 44 per cent of US firms; and 37 per cent of all firms in the sample); and 3) a training and development plan for the next year (53 per cent of UK firms; 48 per cent of US firms; and 51 per cent of all firms in the sample). This led to the following categorization:

1. *Strategic HR establishments*: above-average usage of HR practices,[8] strategically integrated with each other: 31 per cent of UK companies; 38 per cent of US companies and 35 per cent of all companies in the sample.
2. *Non-strategic HR establishments*: above-average usage of HR practices, but not strategically integrated: 24 per cent of UK companies; 20 per cent of US companies; and 22 per cent of all companies in the sample.
3. *Low-HR establishments*: below-average usage of HR practices: 44 per cent of UK companies; 43 per cent of US companies; and 43 per cent of all companies in the sample.

2.5   Results

The results from the testing of the hypotheses were as follows.

2.5.1   The contingency ('external fit') hypothesis

Table 2.3 reports strong correlations between strategy and the cumulative HR variable (Hypothesis 1). In UK and US firms, and in the combined sample, the correlation between the HR index and all three performance measures is significant: at the 5 per cent level in each sample for labour productivity and customer retention, and at the 10 per cent level for financial performance. (For reasons of space, the separate tables for the UK and US results respectively are not reported here but are available from the authors on request.) The correlation between the cumulative HR variable and all three performance measures is particularly strong for *the innovator/quality-enhancer* firms (1 per cent significance levels in each sample). However, for the *cost-reducer* firms and 'other' firms, the statistical significance of this relationship disappears for financial performance and customer retention, although remaining significantly positive in each sample for labour productivity (but only at the 10 per cent level in the UK and for the combined sample, and at the 5 per cent level for US firms). This suggests that a higher use of HR practices will be generally associated with higher labour productivity, but to be associated with relatively high values for the other performance variables, HR practices need to be combined with an innovator/quality-based strategy.

Table 2.3 Results for Hypothesis 1: all firms (UK and US)

Variables	All firms	Cost-reducers	Innovators/ quality enhancers	Others
(i) Labour productivity				
HRM	0.235 (0.090)**	0.117 (0.055)*	0.320 (0.090)***	0.250 (0.126)*
Size	0.219 (0.115)*	0.066 (0.055)	0.099 (0.039)**	0.234 (0.109)*
Size^2	0.187 (0.080)**	0.122 (0.058)*	0.188 (0.098)*	0.066 (0.030)**
Age	0.015 (0.113)	−0.033 (0.016)*	0.112 (0.057)*	0.228 (0.114)*
Industry (Manuf)	0.289 (0.119)**	0.106 (0.096)	0.296 (0.088)***	0.216 (0.083)**
Industry (Services)	0.203 (0.109)*	0.079 (0.049)	0.198 (0.097)*	0.122 (0.063)*
Large firm affiliation	0.244 (0.107)**	0.078 (0.036)*	0.223 (0.069)***	0.147 (0.064)**
Market conditions	0.172 (0.070)**	0.104 (0.065)	0.156 (0.064)**	0.119 (0.058)*
Trade union presence	0.058 (0.035)	−0.019 (0.215)	0.092 (0.078)	0.042 (0.038)
External assistance	0.155 (0.082)*	0.091 (0.055)	0.160 (0.082)*	0.111 (0.047)**
n	186	42	115	29
Pseudo R^2	0.132	0.120	0.123	0.115
(ii) Financial performance				
HRM	0.188 (0.094)*	0.072 (0.046)	0.198 (0.059)***	0.177 (0.145)
Size	0.101 (0.055)*	0.099 (0.060)	0.053 (0.025)*	0.095 (0.072)
Size^2	0.092 (0.039)**	0.126 (0.061)*	0.111 (0.045)**	0.107 (0.051)*
Age	0.099 (0.040)**	−0.112 (0.060)*	0.123 (0.048)**	0.033 (0.023)
Industry (Manuf)	0.130 (0.053)**	0.102 (0.052)*	0.095 (0.032)***	0.093 (0.038)**
Industry (Services)	0.118 (0.046)**	0.097 (0.059)	0.162 (0.070)**	0.085 (0.044)*
Large firm affiliation	0.139 (0.043)***	0.109 (0.050)*	0.203 (0.066)***	0.140 (0.057)**
Market conditions	0.144 (0.044)***	0.075 (0.036)*	0.199 (0.062)***	0.098 (0.039)**
Trade union presence	0.003 (0.009)	−0.040 (0.400)	0.026 (0.020)	−0.059 (0.044)
External assistance	0.060 (0.025)**	0.044 (0.035)	0.143 (0.061)**	0.109 (0.033)***
n	181	41	112	28
Pseudo R^2	0.110	0.127	0.119	0.103
(iii) Customer retention				
HRM	0.203 (0.085)**	0.107 (0.101)	0.246 (0.062)***	0.211 (0.171)
Size	0.111 (0.033)***	−0.060 (0.032)*	0.096 (0.031)***	0.103 (0.044)**
Size^2	−0.088 (0.037)**	−0.099 (0.031)***	0.022 (0.018)	−0.112 (0.044)**
Age	0.077 (0.040)*	−0.090 (0.049)*	0.120 (0.049)**	0.096 (0.088)
Industry (Manuf)	0.134 (0.082)	0.097 (0.058)	0.172 (0.075)**	0.119 (0.060)*
Industry (Services)	0.146 (0.057)**	0.103 (0.052)*	0.192 (0.083)**	0.123 (0.069)
Large firm affiliation	0.120 (0.049)**	0.116 (0.071)	0.203 (0.068)***	0.120 (0.048)**
Market conditions	−0.098 (0.047)*	−0.111 (0.053)*	0.221 (0.118)*	−0.131 (0.054)**
Trade union presence	0.023 (0.023)	−0.005 (0.008)	0.060 (0.035)	−0.053 (0.054)
External assistance	0.130 (0.058)**	0.082 (0.051)	0.155 (0.075)*	0.111 (0.044)**
n	185	43	114	28
Pseudo R^2	0.101	0.118	0.131	0.120

Notes: 1. Ordered probit analysis.
2. Coefficients given (standard errors in brackets).
3. ***significant at 1%; ** significant at 5%; * significant at 10%.

The type of strategy pursued by firms is also related to many of the control variables. In relation to cost-reducers, age is significantly negatively correlated with all of the performance variables. This may be because older firms that have acquired higher costs over time are attempting to cut costs to survive and/or regain competitiveness. Firm size is generally positively and significantly correlated with labour productivity and financial performance, but is negatively and often significantly correlated with customer retention, especially for those firms pursuing a cost-reducer strategy. Operating in the health-care manufacturing and health-services industries is positively and often significantly correlated with performance. Significant positive correlations are found for companies operating in the health-services industry with the customer retention variable, and, in particular, for those firms pursuing an innovation/quality-enhancer strategy.

The coefficient for a rapidly growing market and customer retention is significantly negative for all firms except those pursuing an *innovator/quality-enhancer* strategy, perhaps reflecting the fact that the emphasis placed by these firms on quality helps to keep customers coming back. The other case where patterns differ in relation to the *innovator/quality-enhancer* firms and the 'other' firms is in relation to UK trade union presence where there is a significantly positive relationship (at the 10 per cent level) with the presence of trade unions for firms pursuing an *innovator/quality-enhancer* approach to strategy and customer retention, whereas for the 'other' firms this relationship is not significant. A final significant difference between the two strategy types exists in relation to external assistance. External assistance is more positively correlated (higher coefficient significance rates) with labour productivity and financial performance for the 'other' firms compared to the *innovator/quality-enhancer* firms. Interestingly, for firms pursuing a cost-reducer strategy, while the correlations between external assistance and all of the performance measures are positive, none are significant.

These results give support to the external fit hypothesis, that is, that the effectiveness of HR is strongly dependent upon the business strategy pursued. As hypothesized, there is little evidence that the adoption of HR leads to improved performance where companies emphasize cost control in their business strategies. In contrast, where HR is coupled with strategies that emphasize quality-enhancement and innovation, performance is positively affected.

2.5.2   The universalistic ('internal fit') hypothesis

The results reported in Table 2.4 suggest that the 'high-HR innovators/quality-enhancers' are the highest performing establishments in terms of all the performance variables. The negative signs on the HR-strategy coefficients show that establishments not following the 'high-HR innovator/quality-enhancer' approach perform less well than those establishments that follow

Table 2.4 Results for Hypothesis 2: all firms (UK and US)

Variables	Labour productivity	Financial performance	Customer retention
'Low-HRM cost reducers'	−0.407 (0.155)**	−0.372 (0.258)	−0.414 (0.129)***
'Medium-HRM cost reducers'	−0.255 (0.166)	−0.245 (0.125)*	−0.255 (0.132)*
'High-HRM cost reducers'	−0.411 (0.252)	−0.299 (0.092)***	−0.220 (0.146)
'Low-HRM innovator/ quality enhancers'	−0.018 (0.015)	−0.193 (0.089)*	−0.278 (0.090)***
'Medium-HRM innovator/ quality enhancers'	−0.176 (0.129)	−0.271 (0.169)	−0.226 (0.140)
'Low-HRM others'	−0.133 (0.055)**	−0.296 (0.121)**	−0.400 (0.124)***
'Medium-HR others'	−0.118 (0.073)	−0.130 (0.084)	−0.276 (0.142)*
'High-HRM others'	0.197 (0.123)	−0.166 (0.100)	−0.198 (0.119)
Size	0.130 (0.065)*	0.224 (0.102)*	0.117 (0.052)**
Size^2	0.249 (0.107)**	0.302 (0.101)***	−0.266 (0.100)**
Age	0.134 (0.086)	0.119 (0.054)**	0.088 (0.076)
Industry (Manuf)	0.306 (0.129)**	0.185 (0.058)***	0.246 (0.177)
Industry (Services)	0.255 (0.128)*	0.196 (0.082)**	0.221 (0.094)**
Large firm association	0.349 (0.104)***	0.414 (0.127)***	0.305 (0.129)**
Market conditions	0.150 (0.078)*	0.276 (0.113)**	−0.119 (0.048)**
Trade union presence	0.027 (0.023)	−0.060 (0.049)	0.075 (0.061)
External assistance	0.098 (0.045)*	0.142 (0.061)**	0.212 (0.091)**
n	186	181	97
Pseudo R^2	0.131	0.123	0.127

Notes: 1. See Table 2.3.
2. Omitted category = 'High-HR innovators/quality-enhancers'

this approach. The exception to this appears in relation to labour productivity for 'high-HR other' (where the signs are positive but not significant); even where a firm does not have a clear strategy, HR practices do seem to enhance productivity (providing support for the traditional universalistic hypothesis). But the results suggest that the return from this HR investment for these firms would be higher if they introduced HR practices within the context of an *innovator/quality-enhancer* strategy.

Finally we examine whether establishments that introduce HR practices as a strategically integrated package of mutually supporting practices outperform establishments that introduce their practices in a more ad hoc manner (Hypothesis 3). The results reported in Table 2.5 show that 'strategic HR' companies outperform the 'low-HRM' firms across all performance measures. The 'non-strategic HRM' companies outperform the 'low-HRM' companies on only one of the performance measures – customer retention, where the fact that these practices are at least in place appears to be correlated with the delivery of service to customers. The size and statistical significance of

Table 2.5   Results for Hypothesis 3: all firms (UK and US)

Variables	Labour productivity	Financial performance	Customer retention
'Strategic HRM'	0.448 (0.115)***	0.492 (0.111)***	0.633 (0.146)***
'Non-strategic HRM'	0.293 (0.221)	0.226 (0.145)	0.325 (0.151)*
Size	0.133 (0.068)*	0.176 (0.088)*	0.140 (0.065)*
Size^2	0.243 (0.105)**	0.279 (0.094)***	−0.255 (0.098)**
Age	0.160 (0.149)	0.229 (0.093)**	0.102 (0.077)
Industry (Manuf)	0.331 (0.129)**	0.195 (0.081)**	0.104 (0.083)
Industry (Services)	0.228 (0.108)*	0.166 (0.071)**	0.211 (0.083)**
Large firm association	0.322 (0.104)***	0.336 (0.113)***	0.176 (0.063)**
Market conditions	0.144 (0.058)**	0.344 (0.110)***	−0.152 (0.077)*
Trade union presence	0.037 (0.042)	−0.113 (0.093)	0.047 (0.035)
External assistance	0.183 (0.092)*	0.146 (0.075)*	0.134 (0.064)*
n	186	181	185
Pseudo R^2	0.113	0.123	0.125

Notes: See Table 2.3 for estimation techniques and Table 2.4 for Hypothesis 3 estimation techniques

the coefficients on the performance variables are, however, unambiguously greater across the board for those firms pursuing *strategic* HRM.

2.6   Conclusions

The results reported here for small firms are consistent with results we have found previously for large firms in relation to strategic HRM (Michie and Sheehan, 2005). Thus, investing in 'progressive' HR practices appears to pay dividends in terms of corporate performance. This is also consistent with the findings of Way (2002). However, the results reported in this chapter suggest that the degree to which this is true – in statistical terms, the size and significance of the effect – will vary according to a range of factors. One of these factors is the strategy that the firm adopts. Broadly, it may pursue a 'high-road' strategy of investing in progressive HR practices that tend to be associated with a greater degree of commitment and motivation amongst the workforce, plus an increased ability and greater opportunities to work more productively. Hence such HR investment will tend to be associated with higher productivity and customer retention, and thus also profitability. Alternatively, the firm may choose a 'low-road', cost-cutting strategy. This appears to be especially so for 'older' small companies, who may turn to this approach as a 'strategy of last resort'. The effectiveness of HR policies and practices therefore will depend, in part at least, on the strategy being pursued by the company.

If a 'high-road' strategy is consciously chosen, then the costs of investing in HR practices can be expected to be recouped through improved performance. However, for this to happen, HR practices need to lead not just to higher levels of commitment and motivation amongst staff, but also for this to be matched firstly by the skills to work more productively, and also by the opportunities to put those skills and motivation to good effect. For these three factors to be present – motivation, skills and opportunities – HR practices are best introduced and implemented as a coherent 'bundle', and combined with appropriate organizational design.

It might be thought that while these results have been reported previously for firms in general, they are unlikely to apply to small firms, where there is less scope for implementing the whole range of policies and practices that such an approach involves. The results reported above suggest that such an assumption would be incorrect. The importance of introducing HR practices in appropriate combinations appears to be equally important for small firms as for larger companies. And the benefits of combining this with an appropriate company strategy is likewise confirmed by the results reported above for small firms.

Different legal, institutional and cultural contexts mean that we cannot generalize such results from one country to another. However, the results we derived from testing the above hypotheses were remarkably consistent across the firms in both the UK and the US. It is true that the likelihood of pursuing a particular company strategy varied somewhat between the two countries, as reported above, but the way in which such strategies appeared to interact with the use of HR practices, and the correlations between these interactions on the one hand, and the company's productivity, customer retention and profitability on the other, were quite consistent between the UK and US firms.

The HR-performance literature tends to look at productivity and profitability. However, in previous work we have taken innovation as an alternative outcome, and we found similar results, namely that an appropriate mix of HR policies will be associated with organizations that are more likely to innovate (Michie and Sheehan, 2003). One of the reasons may be that if 'progressive' HR policies such as consultation and communication are combined with 'no redundancy' guarantees – as is often the case in 'high-commitment work systems' that aim to enhance corporate performance through implementing an appropriate mix of HR policies – then employees may be more willing to propose process innovations that will allow the process to be undertaken with fewer employees. Thus, trust becomes central. The 'no redundancy' guarantee is introduced to reinforce the psychological contract that such gains will not be used to benefit management to the detriment of the employee.

Trust is also important for companies in their dealings with other firms – whether suppliers, customers or competitors. It facilitates cooperation, which also tends to be associated with the propensity to innovate.

Thus while this chapter has focused on management practices within the firm, the HR practices analysed, and the outcomes of improved levels of commitment and trust, may also have broader implications in facilitating and enhancing cooperation across organizations as well as within them. And both forms of cooperation may facilitate enhanced levels of product and process innovation.

Finally, the greatest weakness with the research reported in this chapter is the low response rate we got from firms. We did manage to interview our target number of firms in both countries (the US and the UK) – almost 100 companies in each country, making almost 200 in all. However, this was only achieved by surveying a larger number than we would have liked, given that the response rate – defined as those that not only responded but also did go on to complete the required interview in full, was only around 8 per cent in each country. The danger with such a low response rate, or in other words with having to survey such a large number of companies in order to secure the desired number of interviews, is that the sample of interviewed firms might be unrepresentative of the company sector in general. We were therefore alert to this possibility and were on the lookout for any signs that this might be the case. We were not able to identify any likely biases. However, this does not mean that they were not present. The results need to be considered alongside this important caveat. This also means that further research along these lines could provide valuable additional evidence that might inform the HRM-performance literature and the SME research agenda. Such research would of course need to be mindful of the difficulties of getting high rates of return for requests for interviews – or even for requests for data – from the small-firm sector.

Appendices

Appendix 2.1: Sample details

Table 2.A1   Sample details

	UK companies		US companies		Total sample	
	count	%	count	%	count	%
Establishment size:						
10–25	35	38.5	37	37.8	72	38.1
26–50	32	35.2	30	30.6	62	32.8
51–75	10	10.9	12	12.2	22	11.6
76–100	14	15.4	19	19.4	33	17.5
Total sample:	91	100.0	98	100.0	189	100.0
Age:						
Mean	25.1 years*		20.3 years		23.2	
Range	491–1.5 years		114–1.1 years		491–1.1 years	

(Continued)

Table 2.A1   (Continued)

	UK companies count %		US companies count %		Total sample count %	
Industrial activity:						
Manufacturing – medical						
2833 – Medicinal chemicals and botanical products	6		7		13	
2834 – Pharmaceutical preparations	7		9		16	
3827 – Optimal instruments and lenses	4		5		9	
3841 – Surgical and medical instruments and apparatus	9		11		20	
3844 – Radiology/electrical medical equipment	4		5		9	
Total manufacturing	30	33.0	37	40.7	67	35.4
Services – medical and health related						
8071 – Medical and scientific laboratories	9		10		19	
8072 – Dental laboratories	8		7		15	
8051 – Skilled nursing facilities	25		23		48	
Services – other						
5411 – Grocery stores/supermarkets	19		21		40	
Total services	61	67.0	61	62.2	122	64.6
Total:	91	100.0	98	100.0	189	100.0
Large firm affiliation	31	34.0	40	40.8	71	37.6
Trade union members	17	18.5	14	14.3	31	16.4
ISO recognition, and/or industry-specific quality recognition	32	35.2	54	55.1	86	45.5
External assistance	35	38.5	19	19.4	54	28.6

Appendix 2.2: Spearman rank-order correlations between subjective and objective performance measures

Method

Subjective performance was measured as: 'How does financial performance, that is, profitability, at your company compare with other companies in the same industry over the past financial year?' and 'How does your labour productivity compare with that other companies in the same industry?' Responses were obtained on a five-point response scale running from 'much worse' to 'much better'. The mean and standard deviation for these variables for UK companies were: $M = 3.33$, $SD = .65$; and $M = 3.96$, $SD = .58$ for profitability and productivity respectively; and for US companies they were: $M = 3.51$, $SD = .79$; and $M = 4.02$, $SD = .68$ for profitability and productivity respectively.

Objective financial performance was measured using financial data supplied by Dun & Bradstreet as part of the original sample framework (the 'population') and then supplemented with additional data from its Comprehensive Financial Reports for the sample companies where data was not supplied with the original sample. Financial data was obtained for a subsample of 55 of the 91 sample firms in the UK and 59 of the 98 sample firms in the US (the both samples, the least amount of financial data were available for skilled nursing home facilities and grocery stores).

Objective measures were constructed from these data. Productivity was calculated as gross sales per employee. Profit was calculated as the pre-tax financial value of sales divided by number of employees (that is, profit per employee) because costs-per-employee data were not available. To control for price movements, the profit variable was deflated by the producer price index in which the company belonged. To deal with the non-normal deviations of the data, we used the logarithm of the raw scores. The means and standard deviations for UK companies were: $M = 4.89$, $SD = 3.01$ and $M = 6.85$, $SD = 2.25$ for profitability and productivity respectively; and for US companies were: $M = 5.14$, $SD = 3.41$ and $M = 7.77$, $SD = 3.16$ for profitability and productivity respectively.

Results

Even after logarithmic transformations the data were not normally distributed, so the appropriate non-parametric, Spearman rank-order correlation was used. We conducted the analysis for each sample as a whole and by sector (manufacturing, services (both health-care related) and services (other), and grocery stores) and did find differences in the patterns of results; we thus present these results by sector.

Before the results are presented, an important caveat must be given. While objective financial data were available for the majority of firms in the sample, the overall subset does become small (55 companies in the UK and 59 in the US) and when broken down by sector, the cell sizes become smaller. In addition, all of the analysis presented here is cross-sectional, so only convergent validity can be tested and not discriminant analysis. Having said this, the results are remarkably consistent for both the US and UK subset of firms and the overall results are broadly consistent with our previous work that utilized larger samples in this area for large firms (Wall et al., 2004).

Our findings (available from the authors on request) show that the relationships between the directly corresponding subjective and objective performance measures are the strongest in both the UK and US samples. The relationships are strongest in the manufacturing sector, then services and weakest (although all of the direct measures are significant) for the Services 'other' sector (grocery stores). These patterns are not surprising, especially since it is well recognized that productivity is generally easier to measure in the manufacturing sector compared to the service sector. An additional financial performance variable, 'current ratio' (current ratio indicates a firm's liquidity and is measured by its liquid assets (current assets) relative to its liquid debt (short-term or current liabilities)), was available for this same sub-sample of companies. The correlation between profitability and the current ratio was .82** for UK companies and .73** for US companies. These high correlations imply that the current ratio, an asset-based measure, is also a good proxy for a firm's financial performance. We next tested the correlations between subjective financial performance and the objective current ratio. For UK firms, this correlation was .58** and for US firms .63**

Notes

1. This research was funded by the ESRC as part of their 'Human Resource Management and Performance in Small & Medium Sized Enterprises' project (Grant RES-000-22-1142). We would like to thank our researchers Linda Mapp and Alesha Aljeffri at the University of Birmingham and Mahsa Asil and the 'Research Team' at the University of Dallas. We would also like to acknowledge the support of Deans Lynch (deceased) and Whittington, and Professor John Watters, all of the University of Dallas. Finally, we are indebted to Alfred Kleinknecht and two anonymous referees for making a number of helpful suggestions.
2. Related work using the same database has examined: firstly the types of HR practices found in UK and US firms; secondly, how the use of these practices vary in relation to different characteristics of these firms; and thirdly, the relationship between HR practices and firm performance (see Michie and Sheehan, 2006). We find firstly a wide *range of usage* of HR practices, including some degree of strategic HR; secondly, a *positive relationship* between HR policies and performance; and thirdly, that HR is more likely to contribute to competitive success when introduced strategically as part of an integrated and coherent package, that is, as part of a *bundle* of innovative work practices.
3. For details on the grocery store industry in the US and UK see: www.connexions.gov. uk/jobs4u/furtherdetails.cfm?id=605&parentID=594 (2004) and www.collegegrad. com/industries/trade03.shtml (2004).
4. To check for response bias, t-test comparisons of the size and SIC category of the responding firms with the same data for the non-responding firms were made. No significant differences (i.e., $p > 10$) between these two subgroups were found for size. Firms in manufacturing industries were significantly (i.e., $p > 10$) more likely to respond than firms in the service industries. Firms in the grocery-store industry were the least likely to participate in the study.
5. The measure 'customer retention' is not standard in the HRM-performance literature but was adapted for this study on small firms. The use of this measure was informed by the pilot interviews where the issue of customer retention was flagged up very frequently as a factor that interviewees viewed as key to the performance and, indeed, the survival of their firm. Customer retention was mentioned frequently by interviewees, even before they were prompted about this variable.
6. These control variables have been used in previous performance-HRM research and SME research (e.g., Aragon-Sanchez and Sanchez-Marin, 2005; Bacon et al., 1996; Cassell et al., 2002; Guest et al., 2003; and Huselid, 1995).

7. Companies that use less than 50 per cent of the possible HR practices (eight or fewer practices out of a possible 17) are placed in the 'low HRM category'; companies that use between nine and 12 practices are placed in the 'medium HRM category', and companies that use 75 per cent or more of the possible HR practices (13 or more) are placed in the 'high HRM category'.

References

Appelbaum, E., T. Bailey, P. Berg and A. L. Kalleberg (2000) *Manufacturing Advantage: Why High-Performance Work Systems Pay Off* (Ithaca: Cornell University Press).

Aragon-Sanchez, A. and G. Sanchez-Marin (2005) 'Strategic Orientation, Management Characteristics and Performance: A Study of Spanish SME's', *Journal of Small Business Management,* 43: 3, pp. 287–309.

Bacon, N., P. Ackers, D. Storey and D. Coates (1996) 'It's a Small World: Managing Human Resource Management in Small Businesses' *International Journal of Human Resource Management,* 1: 1, pp. 82–98.

Becker, B. and D. Gerhart (1996) 'The Impact of Human Resource Management on Organizational Performance: Progress and Prospects', *Academy of Management Journal,* 39: 4, pp. 779–801.

Becker, B. E. and M. A. Huselid (1998) 'High Performance Work Systems and Firm Performance: A Synthesis of Research and Managerial Implications', in G. R. Feffis (ed.) *Research in Personnel and Human Resources,* Vol. 16 (Stanford,: JAI Press), pp. 53–101.

Becker, B. and M. Huselid (2003) 'Value Creation Through Implementation: The "Black-Box" in SHRM Theory', Rutgers: mimeo.

Cardon M. S. and C. E. Stevens (2004) 'Managing Human Resources in Small Organizations: What Do We Know?' *Human Resource Management Review,* 14, pp. 295–323.

Cassell, C. S., M. Nadin Gray and C. Clegg (2002) 'Exploring Human Resource Management Practices in Small and Medium Sized Enterprises', *Personnel Review,* 31: 5/6, pp. 671–92.

Chandler, G. N. and G. M. McEvoy (2000) 'Human Resource Management, TQM, and Firm Performance in Small and Medium-Size Enterprises', *Entrepreneurship: Theory & Practice,* 25: 1, pp. 43–57.

Ciavarella, M. (2003) 'The Adoption of High-involvement Practices and Processes in Emergent Developing Firms: A Descriptive and Prescriptive Approach', *Human Resource Management,* 42: 4, pp. 337–56.

Cully, S., S. Woodland, A. O'Reilly and G. Dix (1998) *Britain at Work as Depicted by the 1998 Workplace Employee Relations Survey* (London: Routledge).

Curren, J., R. A. Blackburn, J. Kitching and J. North (1996) *Establishing Small Firms' Training Needs, Difficulties and Use of Industry Training Organisations* (London: Department of Education and Employment, HMSO).

Datta, D., J. Guthrie and P. Wright (2005) 'Human Resource Management and Labor Productivity: Does Industry Matter?' *The Academy of Management Journal,* 48: 1, pp. 135–45.

Delery, J. and D. H. Doty (1996) 'Models of Theorizing in Strategic Human Resource Management: Tests of Universalistic, Contingency, and Configurational Performance Predictions', *Academy of Management Journal,* 39: 4, pp. 802–35.

Delery, J. and J. D. Shaw (2001) 'The Strategic Management of People in Work Organizations: Review, Synthesis and Extension', in G. R. Ferris (ed.) *Research in Personnel and Human Resources Management,* Vol. 20 (Amsterdam: JAI Press), pp. 165–97.

Dennis, W. J. (2003) 'Raising Response Rates in Mail Surveys of Small Business Owners: Results of an Experiment', *Journal of Small Business Management*, 41, pp. 278–95.

Deshpande, S. P. and D. Y. Golhar (1994) 'HRM Practices in Large and Small Manufacturing Firms: A Comparative Study', *Journal of Small Business Management*, 32: 2, pp. 49–56.

de Kok, J. and L. M. Uhlaner (2001) 'Organization Context and Human Resource Management in the Small Firms', *Small Business Economics*, 17: 4, pp. 273–91.

Duberley, J. P. and P. Walley (1995) 'Assessing the Adoption of HRM by Small and Medium-sized Manufacturing Organizations', *International Journal of Human Resource Management*, 4: 4, pp. 891–09.

Dyer, L. and T. Reeves (1995) 'Human Resource Strategies and Firm Performance: What We Know and Where Do We Need to Go?' Paper to the 10th IIRA World Congress, Washington, 31 May–4 June.

Guest, D. and K. Hoque (1994) 'The Good, the Bad and the Ugly: Human Resource Management in New Non-union Companies', *Human Resource Management Journal*, 5: pp. 1–14.

Guest, D., J. Michie, M. Sheehan and N. Conway (2000) *Employee Relations, HRM and Business Performance: An Analysis of the 1998 Workplace Employee Relations Survey* (London: Chartered Institute of Personnel and Development).

Guest, D., J. Michie, N. Conway and M. Sheehan (2003) 'A Study of Human Resource Management and Corporate Performance in the UK', *British Journal of Industrial Relations*, 41: 2, pp. 291–314.

Guthrie, J., C. Spell and O. Nyamori (2002) 'Correlated and Consequences of High Involvement Work Practice: The Role of Competitive Strategy', *International Journal of Human Resource Management*, 13: 1, pp. 183–97.

Hayton, J. (2003) 'Strategic Human Capital Management in SMEs: Am Empirical Study of Entrepreneurial Performance', *Human Resource Management*, 42: 2, pp. 375–91.

Heneman, R. L. (2000) 'Human Resource Management Practices in Small and Medium-Sized Enterprises: Unanswered Questions and Future Research Perspectives', *Entrepreneurship: Theory & Practice*, 25: 1, pp. 11–26.

Heneman, R. L. and J.W. Tansky (2002) 'Human Resource Management Models for Entrepreneurial Opportunity: Existing Knowledge and New Directions', in J. A. Katz and T. M. Welbourne (eds) *Managing People in Entrepreneurial Organizations: Learning from the Merger of Entrepreneurship and Human Resource Management* (Greenwich: JAI Press), pp. 55–81.

Heneman, R. L., J. W. Tansky and S. M. Camp (2000) 'Human Resource Management Practices in Small and Medium-Sized Enterprises: Unanswered Questions and Future Research Perspectives', *Entrepreneurship: Theory & Practice*, 25: 1, pp. 11–26.

K. Hoque (1999) 'Human Resource Management and Performance in the UK Hotel Industry', *British Journal of Industrial Relations*, 37: 3, pp. 419–43.

Hornby, J. S. and D. F. Kuratko (1990) 'Human Resource Management in Small Business: Critical Issues for the 1990s', *Journal of Small Business Management*, 28: 2, pp. 9–18.

Huselid, M. (1995) 'The Impact of Human Resource Management on Turnover, Productivity and Corporate Financial Performance', *Academy of Management Journal*, 38: 3, pp. 635–72.

Huselid, M. and B. Becker (1996) 'Methodological Issues in Cross-Sectional and Panel Estimates of the Human Resource-Firm Performance Link', *Industrial Relations*, 35: 3, pp. 400–22.

C. Ichniowski, K. Shaw and G. Prennushi (1997) 'The Effects of Human Resource Management on Productivity: a Study of a Steel Finishing Line', *American Economic Review*, 87: 3, pp. 291–313.

Ichniowski, C., K. Shaw and G. Prennushi (1994) *The Effects of Human Resource Management Practices on Productivity* (New York: Columbia University Press).

Khatri, N. (2000) 'Managing Human Resource for Competitive Advantage: A Study of Companies in Singapore', *International Journal of Human Resource Management,* 11: 2, 336–65.

Kochan, T. and P. Osterman (1994) *Mutual Gains* (Boston: Harvard Business School).

Leung, A. (2003) 'Different Ties for Different Needs: Recruitment Practices of Entrepreneurial Firms at Different Phases of Development', *Human Resource Management,* 42: 4, pp. 303–20.

McAdam, R. and M. McKeown (1999) 'Life after ISO 9000: An Analysis of the Impact of ISO 9000 and Total Quality Management on Small Businesses in Northern Ireland', *Total Quality Management,* 10: 2, pp. 229–41.

McTeer, M. M. and B. G. Dale (1996) 'The Process of ISO 9000 Series Recognition: an Examination in Small Companies', *International Journal of Production Research,* 34: 9, pp. 2379–92.

MacDuffie, J. (1995) 'Human Resource Bundles and Manufacturing Performance: Organizational Logic and Flexible Production Systems in the World Auto Industry', *Industrial and Labour Relations Review,* 48: 2, pp. 197–221.

Marlow, S. (2002) 'Regulating Labour Management in Smaller Firms', *Human Resource Management Journal,* 12: 3, pp. 5–25.

Marlow, S. and D. Patton (2002) 'Minding the Gap: the Challenges of Managing Employment Relations in Small Firms', *Employee Relations,* 24: 5, pp. 523–39.

McElwee, G. and L. Warren (2000) 'The Relationship between Total Quality Management and Human Resource Management in Small and Medium Sized Enterprises', *Strategic Change,* 9: 7, pp. 427–35.

McEvoy, G. M. (1984) 'Small Business Personnel Practices', *Journal of Small Business Management,* 22: 4, pp. 1–8.

Michie, J. and M. Sheehan-Quinn (2001) 'Labour Market Flexibility, Human Resource Management and Corporate Performance', *British Journal of Management,* 12: 4, pp. 287–306.

Michie, J. and M. Sheehan (2003) 'Labour Market Deregulation, Flexibility and Innovation', *Cambridge Journal of Economics,* 27: 1, pp. 123–43.

Michie, J. and M. Sheehan (2005) 'Business Strategy, Human Resources, Labour Market Flexibility and Competitive Advantage', *International Journal of Human Resource Management,* 15: 3, pp. 445–64.

Michie, J. and M. Sheehan (2008) 'Human Resource Management Practices and Performance: Evidence from Small Firms in the UK and US', Academy of Management (2006) and forthcoming in R. Barrett and S. Mayson (eds) *An International Handbook on Human Resource Management* (Cheltenham: Edward Elgar).

Miles, R. and C. Snow (1978) *Organizational Strategy, Structure, and Processes* (New York: McGraw Hill).

Miles, R. and C. Snow (1984) 'Designing Strategic Human Resource Systems', *Organizational Dynamics,* 13: 1, pp. 35–52.

Osterman, P. (1994) 'How Common is Workplace Transformation and Who Adopts It?', *Industrial and Labor Relations Review,* 47, pp. 173–88.

Osterman, P. (1999) *Securing Prosperity* (Princeton: Princeton University Press).

Pfeffer, J. (1994) *Competitive Advantage through People* (Boston: HNS Press).

Pfeffer, J. (1998) *The Human Equation* (Boston: HBS Press).

Porter, L. and P. Rayner (1991) 'BS 5750/ISO 9000 – the Experience of Small and Medium-sized Businesses', *International Journal of Quality and Reliability*, 18: 6, pp. 16–29.

Porter, M. (1985) *Competitive Advantage: Creating and Sustaining Superior Performance* (New York: Free Press).

Porter, M. (1980) *Competitive Strategy: Techniques for Analysing Industries and Competitors* (New York: The Free Press).

Richardson, R. and M. Thompson (1999) *The Impact of People Management Practices on Business Performance: A Literature Review* (London: Institute of Personnel and Development).

Rocha, J. R. and M. R. Khan (1985) 'The Human Resource Factor in Small Business Decision Making', *American Journal of Small Business*, Fall: pp. 53–62.

Rutherford, M., P. Buller and P. McMullen (2003) 'Human Resource Management Problems over the Life Cycle of Small to Medium-sized Firms', *Human Resource Management*, 42: 4, pp. 321–35.

Schuler, R. and S. Jackson (1987) 'Linking Competitive Strategies with Human Resource Management Practices,' *Academy of Management Executive*, 1: 3, pp. 207–19.

Sisson, K. (1993) 'In Search of HRM', *British Journal of Industrial Relations*, 31: 2, pp. 201–10.

Small Business Service (2003) *The Annual Small Business Survey 2003* (London: Department of Trade and Industry).

Storey, D. J. (1994) *Understanding the Small Business Sector* (London: Routledge).

Storey, D. J. (1995) *Human Resource Management: A Critical Text* (London: Thompson International).

Storey, D. J. (2004) 'Exploring the Link, among Small Firms, between Management Training and Firm Performance: a Comparison between the UK and other OECD Countries', *International Journal of Human Resource Management*, 15: 1, pp. 112–30.

Storey, D. J. and P. Westhead (1997) 'Managing Training in Small Firms – a Case of Market Failure?' *Human Resource Management Journal*, 7: 2, pp. 61–71.

Taylor, W. (1995) 'Organizational Differences in ISO 9000 Implementation Practices', *International Journal of Quality and Reliability*, 12: 7, pp. 10–38.

Tichy, N., C. Fombrun and M. Devanna (1982) 'Strategic Human Resource Management', *Sloan Management Review*, 11: 3, pp. 47–61.

Truss, C. and L. Gratton (1994) 'Strategic Human Resource Management: A Conceptual Approach', *International Journal of Human Resource Management*, 5: 3, pp. 663–86.

United Kingdom Department of Health (2004) *National Standards, Local Action: Health and Social Care Standards and Planning Framework* (London: Department of Health).

United States Bureau of Labor Statistics (2008): Health and Education, at: www.bls.gov/iag/tgs/iag65.htm

Unites States Small Business Office of Advocacy (2004). *The Small Business Economy: A Report to the President* (Washington, DC: US Government Printing Office).

Vickerstaff, S. (1993) 'The Training Needs for Small Firms', *Human Resource Management Journal*, 2: 3, pp. 1–15.

Wagar, T. H. (1998) 'Determinants of Human Resource Management Practices in Small Firms: Some Evidence from Atlantic Canada', *Journal of Small Business Management*, 36, pp. 13–23.

Wagner, J. (1997) 'Firm Size and Job Quality: A Survey of the Evidence from Germany', *Small Business Economics*, 9: 5, pp. 411–25.

Wall, T. D., J. Michie, M. Patterson, S. J. Wood, M. Sheehan, W. C. W. Clegg and M. A. West (2004) 'On the Validity of Subjective Measures of Company Financial Performance', *Personnel Psychology,* 57, pp. 95–118.

Wall, T. D. and S. J. Wood (2005) 'The Romance of HRM and Business Performance, and the Case for Big Science', *Human Relations*, April, 58: 4, pp. 429–62.

Way, S. A. (2002) 'High Performance Work Systems and Intermediate Indicators of Firm Performance within the US Small Business Sector', *Journal of Management*, 28, pp. 765–85.

Williamson, I. O. (2001) 'Employer Legitimacy and Recruitment Success in Small Businesses', *Entrepreneurship: Theory & Practice*, 25: Fall, pp. 27–42.

Walton, R. (1985) 'From Control to Commitment in the Workplace', *Harvard Business Review,* 62: 2, pp. 77–84.

Wood, S. and M. Albanese (1995) 'Can We Speak of High Commitment Management on the Shop Floor?', *Journal of Management Studies,* 32, pp. 215–47.

Wood, S. and L. de Menezes (1998) 'High Commitment Management in the UK: Evidence from the Workplace Industrial Relations Survey, and Employers' Manpower and Skills Practices Survey', *Human Relations*, 51, pp. 485–515.

Wood, S. (1999) 'Getting the Measure of the Transformed High-Performance Organization', *British Journal of Industrial Relations*, 37, 3, pp. 4391–417.

Wright, P. and G. McMahon (1992) 'Theoretical Perspectives for Strategic Human Resource Management', *Journal of Management,* 18: 2, pp. 295–310.

Zahra, S. and J. Pearce (1990) 'Research Evidence on the Miles-Snow Typology', *Journal of Management,* 16, pp. 751–68.

3

Where People Provide the Impetus: HRM Practices, Employee Job Satisfaction and Innovation

Helen Shipton and Doris Fay

3.1 Introduction

Successful organizations almost invariably exhibit an ability to change, adapt and on occasions reinvent themselves in order to survive in challenging circumstances. What does this intense commitment to innovation mean for the employment systems of these organizations? What is the logic behind assertions that certain HRM practices and work design features promote innovation while others suppress and constrain this result? And what is the impact of employee feelings and attitudes on an organization's propensity to operate in this way? It is with these and other questions that we are concerned in this chapter. Our assertions are necessarily tentative, since there have been few empirical studies examining this topic. Nonetheless, there is a burgeoning literature concerned with understanding what organizations can do internally to promote innovation. Some of the studies that we describe below offer new empirical insights into this area.

Pfeffer (2000) argues that organizational success frequently depends on innovation and flexibility, and that such attributes are derived from the human resources of the business and the way in which they are managed. He posits a number of important practices; rigorous selection, internal merit procedures (such as paying for performance), cross-functional teams, high levels of training, participatory mechanisms, job security, group-based rewards and skill-based pay. Other practices that have been examined include human resource planning (Koch and McGrath 1996), profit sharing and results-oriented appraisals (Delery and Doty, 1996) and selectivity in staffing, training and incentive compensation (Delaney and Huselid, 1996).

Researchers such as Delery (1998) argued that HRM practices should be mutually supportive. In other words, each single HR practice should convey the same or similar signals to the workforce so that employees are clear about what performance outcomes are anticipated by the organization and how desirable behaviours are recognized and rewarded. For example, if an organization introduces team working, its reward systems should recognize collective as well as individual achievement and performance. According to these arguments, what is important is the combined effect of inter-related practices rather than the effect any one specific variable (Bae and Lawler, 2000; Guthrie, 2001; Huselid, Jackson and Schuler, 1997).

Overall, the argument is that high-performance HRM systems may influence organizational-level performance outcomes (including innovation) in several ways:

1. Through developing workforce skills, thereby providing a sound platform for the future learning required to meeting changing external challenges.
2. Through designing an appropriate structure to draw upon employee knowledge and skills. This includes teamwork as well as individual job design considerations such as job empowerment and variety. The argument is that through such arrangements, external demands can be dealt with more rapidly and effectively than in highly centralized structures.
3. Through developing the commitment and satisfaction of employees, so that working for the organization is valued (and employees therefore are less likely to leave) and there is a willingness to endorse change and to go 'beyond contract' (that is, to put in extra effort to achieve important goals).

This chapter falls into three sections; the first examines research specifically addressing HRM/innovation relationships, the second section considers the role of work-design features such as team-working, and the third presents research investigating the association between employee feelings at work and innovation. The chapter concludes by summarizing the main findings of the chapter. We begin by providing brief background on definitions, methodology and measures.

3.2 HRM and innovation

Innovation is defined as the development (or the adaptation) and implementation of an idea that is useful and new to the organisation at the time of adoption (Amabile et al., 1996; Damanpour and Evans, 1984; van de Ven, 1986). Innovation relates to new products and services, production methods and procedures, production technologies, and to administrative changes. In the studies described here, we focus on innovations which pertain to products and technical systems (that is, production processes and procedures). The two key factors for a successful innovation are an organisation's ability to be creative and its ability to successfully manage the complex process of turning creative ideas into reality (Damanpour, 1991; van de Ven, 1984; Zaltman, Duncan and Holbek, 1973).

3.2.1 Methodology and measures

Data presented in this section and indeed for all the empirical results described in this chapter were gathered via a postal questionnaire survey sent to senior managers and technical specialists, who were the respondents to this questionnaire. Innovation was assessed twice, in 1993 and 1995. Respondents were asked to provide information on organizational change, relating to changes in products made by the organization, and changes in production technology and procedures. Information was collected with open questions and rating scales. Based on this information, researchers provided ratings of product innovation and innovation in technical systems using a seven-point answering scale from 1 = not at all innovative to 7 = extremely innovative (see Shipton et al., 2006a).

The item *product innovation* is based on the following information: estimates of the number of entirely new and adapted products developed in the last two years; percentage of production workers involved in making the new products; current sales turnover accounted for by the new products; and the extent to which production processes had been changed to accommodate the new products (Shipton et al., 2006a).

The item *innovation in technical systems* is based on information collected with regard to changes in product innovation *and* production technology, production methods and products. Specifically, the research took account of the number of newly introduced technologies (i.e., CNC, robots, self-feeding machines, etc); how different the change was for the organization, the magnitude of change. It also took account of the number of changes in production procedures (for example, just-in-time management, TQM, or information scheduling and planning systems; and the novelty and magnitude of those changes (Shipton et al., 2006a). This measure incorporates all aspects of change (products and technology), and is thus a very comprehensive measure.

Control variables: size and profitability could be confounding variables affecting both independent and dependent variables; they are therefore controlled for in the analyses. Size was assessed in these studies by the number of full-time equivalent employees; profitability was measured with real profits per employee for the period 1991–3 (Shipton et al., 2006a).

3.2.2 Main results

In a study focusing on 30 manufacturing organizations in the UK, Shipton et al. (2005) showed that a combination of sophisticated HRM practices was significantly and positively associated with organizational innovation in products and production processes. The HRM practices related to recruitment and selection procedures, and procedures for staff induction, training and performance management; the researchers also explored the existence or otherwise of an HRM strategy. The results suggested that the more sophisticated these HRM practices, the higher the innovation (see Table 3.1). This means that the more organizations had systems in place that would help their staff to *understand* what was expected of them, to

Table 3.1 Results of regression analyses showing effects of sophistication of HRM, learning climate and appraisal linked to remuneration on innovation

Dependent variables (Time 2)	Innovation in products			Innovation in production technology			Innovation in production progress		
	β	ΔR^2	Δ adj. R^2	β	ΔR^2	Δ adj. R^2	β	ΔR^2	Δ adj. R^2
Control varibles [1]		0.05	−0.02		0.01	−0.06		0.03	−0.03
Sophistication of HRM (Time 1, n = 35)	0.47*	0.20*	0.18	0.52**	0.25**	0.24	0.27	0.07	0.05
Control varibles [1]		0.04	−0.04		0.00	−0.08		0.08	0.01
Learning climate (Time 2, n = 27)	0.46*	0.20*	0.18	0.53**	0.26**	0.22	0.00	0.00	−0.05
Control varibles [1]		0.05	−0.04		0.01	−0.08		0.16	0.09
Appraisal linked to remuneration (Time 2, n = 25)	−0.32	0.10	0.07	0.21	0.04	0.00	−0.39*	0.15*	0.11

Note: *$p < 0.05$; **$p < 0.01$; 1. Control variables = organisational size; profitability. Adapted from Shipton et al. (2005).

Table 3.2 Results of regression analyses showing moderating effects of HR variables on the relationship between exploratory learning and innovation in technical systems

Dependent variable		Innovation in technical systems		
		β	R^2	Adjusted R^2
	Control variables*	0.31	0.10	0.05
1.	Exploratory learning	0.58**	0.40	0.34
	Appraisal	0.32	0.50	0.42
	Interaction	0.28	0.56	0.46
2.	Exploratory learning	0.58**	0.40	0.34
	Training	0.54**	0.59	0.53
	Interaction	0.38*	0.70	0.63
3.	Exploratory learning	0.58**	0.40	0.34
	Induction	0.37	0.50	0.42
	Interaction	0.40*	0.61	0.52
4.	Exploratory learning	0.60**	0.37	0.29
	Contingent reward	−0.01	0.38	0.25
	Interaction	0.50*	0.57	0.45
5.	Exploratory learning	0.57**	0.41	0.27
	Extent of team working	0.33	0.48	0.32
	Interaction	0.34	0.57	0.39

Notes: $p < 0.05$; **$p < 0.01$; ***$p < 0.001$. Control variables = prior innovation; profitability. Adapted from Shipton (2006b).

successfully *perform* those tasks, and to *understand and manage* the wider context of their work, the better they were in developing new products and introducing new production processes. Research by the authors also demonstrated that organizations that have practices in place that enhance a learning climate (say, through a mentoring system) are more likely to innovate (see Table 3.1).

Further analysis of the same data set (presented in Table 3.2) revealed that organizations that had an appraisal scheme were more likely to be innovative (Shipton et al., 2006a). It is, however, a truism that not *any* appraisal scheme will benefit the organization. For appraisals to be effective, to enhance learning and motivation, and to help people to fill skill gaps, they must be performed with care. Our analyses showed that when appraisals were linked to remuneration, this actually impaired innovation (see Table 3.2). Combining appraisals with remuneration is unfortunately a common practice, which perverts the idea of openly exploring strengths and weaknesses and initiating employee growth.

We cannot rule out the possibility that the associations we depict are attributable to extraneous factors. To mitigate this possibility, we measured innovation at two points in time, controlling for prior innovation. If the variance had been attributable to a third variable not considered in our study, it is probable that in controlling for prior innovation neither exploratory learning nor the other independent variables highlighted in Table 3.2 would have been significant, since unidentified variables would have explained the outcomes. The fact that our findings were significant strengthens, without of course proving, that case for causality.

One organization in particular, Electroco, a market leader manufacturing components for the telecommunications industry, attributed success to the ongoing learning opportunities that were offered. Staff would pursue part-time academic study at a local business school; secondments to different parts of the company were encouraged; there was an established mentoring scheme; employees were expected to visit suppliers and customers regularly in order to gain further insights into the production process and their role within it. As one middle manager stated: 'a trained and educated workforce is likely to be more willing and able to respond positively to change.'

3.2.3   Theoretical overview

Although the studies highlighted above appear to demonstrate that HRM plays an important, perhaps crucial role in enabling innovation, the challenge has been to establish a theoretical case. One possibility is that HRM promotes innovation to the extent that people and the networks to which they belong are enabled to create, transfer and institutionalize knowledge. This links in with the idea that innovation is a two-stage process, involving both the generation of a creative idea and its implementation (West, 2002), and also builds on the notion that change and innovation frequently fall outside the remit of technical specialists such as R&D professionals, involving those who have most knowledge of the task and the technology required to ensure its effective completion (see, for example, Paton and McCalman, 2000; Senior, 1997).

Following through this argument, for the first stage – that is, to promote creativity – it is important that people are recruited who have the skills and knowledge required to generate ideas (Song, Almeida and Wu, 2003; MacDuffie, 1995). This can be achieved where organizations use relatively sophisticated practices such as psychometric tests, assessment centres and work-sampling activities. Extensive training in a variety of jobs or skills can create the breadth of knowledge required to make connections between divergent stimuli (Bae and Lawler, 2000; Guthrie, 2001). Such activities can give rise to less entrenched perspectives and greater willingness on the part of employees to be adaptable and to take on board varied interpretations of problems (Clark, Amundson and Cardy, 2002).

These are essentially individual activities; transferring knowledge, by contrast, requires individuals to work collaboratively with those around them and involves developing shared understanding between individuals and work groups. Nahapiet and Ghoshal (1998) showed that knowledge has a collective, tacit dimension; therefore, according to one scholar '… it is the most secure and strategically significant kind of organizational knowledge' (Spender, 1996, p. 52). HRM systems can help to reinforce the transfer of knowledge between individuals so that it assumes a collective dimension. Where organizations focus on team-based activity and horizontal processes that require reciprocal interdependence, employees can develop a frequency of contact with others that promotes effective coordination (see Gittel, 2000). Performance management systems that emphasize collective attainment can highlight the value attached group achievement (Leana and van Buren, 1999). Extensive induction and socialization can help employees understand how they fit into the collective dimension of the workplace (Feldman, 2000; Feldman and Rafaeli, 2002). Mentoring activities (whereby senior members provide support and guidance to others on general career development matters) enable employees to build networks across the organization, thereby facilitating knowledge transfer (Collins and Clerk, 2004; Laursen and Foss, 2003).

The final stage of the organizational learning cycle represents the point at which innovations are enacted. This implementation stage involves organizations making efforts to codify learning and to articulate the unconscious thinking which informs practice (Argote and Epple, 1990; Cummings and Worley, 1997). Reward and performance management systems need to offer appropriate recognition for the successful application of ideas. Training activities will have to be designed to offer the necessary guidance for employees in conducting new routines. Employees will frequently have to discard ways of working that have become outdated and embrace new approaches, ways of working that have implications for recruitment and selection and the ongoing management of performance.

In sum, innovation will be promoted and sustained where HRM practices are in place to manage the three stages of the organizational learning cycle – the creation, transfer and implementation of knowledge. This does not mean that a particular practice is only linked to one stage; indeed, some practices such as training are likely to promote creativity, whilst simultaneously enhancing the transfer and indeed the implementation of knowledge.

An alternative way of understanding HRM/innovation relationships proposes that HRM directly facilitates both the creation and innovation implementation phases (see Table 3.2). The first stage (creativity) involves 'exploration' – employees taking risks, experimenting and being flexible in their quest to discover new and different ideas, while to achieve the second stage (implementation), employees need to work within an environment where 'exploitation' is valued, and where they are encouraged to follow prescribed rules to enhance efficiency (see March, 1991). According to this argument, HRM practitioners have two main responsibilities. Firstly, to establish the framework whereby employees are clear about their tasks and have the basic skills necessary to perform effectively (Boxall, 1996; Purcell, 1999). A number of HRM practices are important: appraisal and performance management systems, for example, clarify where responsibilities lie and offer support to individuals as they acquire the skills necessary to work effectively (Armstrong and Baron, 1998; Bach, 2000). Secondly, HRM practitioners instigate the mechanisms necessary to promote an exploratory learning focus (Scarborough and Swann, 1999). Through project working, job rotation and visits to parties external to the organization, employees can achieve the attitudinal change required to question and challenge existing ways of operating (Cross et al., 2001). Broadly speaking, the first approach involves developing the knowledge, skills and attitudes required to promote performance, while the second represents a concern with exploration, and with identifying new and different opportunities for the future. The argument holds that each set of practices will directly promote organizational innovation, and that the effect will be amplified where mechanisms designed to promote exploratory focus are used in conjunction with those intended to develop knowledge, skills and attitudes.

HRM practices promoting exploratory learning focus: Exploratory learning involves generating new ideas through actively searching for alternative viewpoints and perspectives (Danneels, 2002; McGrath, 2001). Exposure to different experiences and points of view makes individuals more willing to examine their own mental models and to make any necessary adjustments, thereby avoiding the tendency to become locked in to limited perceptual frameworks (Tushman and Anderson, 1986; Henderson, 1991). For example, engagement with customers and suppliers can lead employees to question the perceptual model that they hold and to embrace opportunities for change (MacKenzie and van Winkelen, 2004; Thompke and von Hippel, 2002). Similarly, intra-organizational secondments may facilitate the transfer of knowledge internally and enrich individuals' perceptions of the challenges faced by other organizational members (Tsai 2001; Amabile et al., 1996; West, 2002). In our studies we found that organizations who promoted exploratory learning through, for example, visits to external suppliers or customers, through internal secondments, or through supporting learning skills not directly necessary for the current job, are better innovators (Shipton et al., 2006a).

Promoting 'on job' development may be a more effective strategy for this type of learning than endorsing external training events (Stern and Sommerlad, 1999). Through experiential learning, employees gain knowledge that is relevant for the tasks for which they are responsible. They are also likely to anticipate knowledge transfer issues, so the learning acquired has the potential to be applied. This process is facilitated where organizations have developed systems for managing the transfer of knowledge (Kogut and Zander, 1992; Nonaka and Takeuchi, 1995). Such systems formally legitimize the value of learning from others within the organization and, where operated effectively, encourage disparate groups to share their learning.

HRM practices designed to develop knowledge, skills and attitudes: We argued above that HR practitioners establish the framework required to facilitate the 'exploitation' of existing knowledge, whereby employees have the knowledge, skills and attitudes required to perform effectively. This involves providing guidance and support to employees about what behaviours are valued, recognized and rewarded. Given that a typical HRM 'system' encompasses training, appraisal/performance management and sophisticated socialization as well as practices designed to promote participation and involvement, such as teamwork and reward (Bae and Lawler, 2000; Huselid, 1995; MacDuffie, 1995), these are amongst the variables to be considered here.

According to this argument, there is conceptually a distinction between mechanisms designed to promote exploratory learning and those intended to exploit existing skills. Training, for example, does not necessarily promote the exposure to new and different experiences to which we make reference to in our depiction of 'exploratory learning'. Training interventions and other HR activities will impact upon organizational innovation to a greater extent where they are implemented in conjunction with practices designed to promote exploratory learning.

Either of these models – the first taking an organizational learning perspective and the other investigating the potential synergy that occurs where HRM successfully manages two competing agendas – we believe provide a useful starting point for researchers investigating HRM/innovation relationships. We now turn to the second section of the chapter, where we consider structural and work-design features.

3.3   Structural and work-design features

In the introductory section we raised the idea that HRM systems elicit innovation through enabling employees to work collaboratively in teams. Many would define HRM as encompassing structural and work-design features (Bae and Lawler, 2000; Huselid, 1995; MacDuffie, 1995); we have chosen to devote a section to the topic because in our view its remit extends beyond the HR function and has wider implications for the way work is managed across the organization. We consider below research highlighting the role of teamwork for innovation, and further examine work-design features – in particular job variety – as potential antecedents of organizational innovation. We also examine a factor rarely considered within the organizational psychology literature – harmonization or single-status arrangements.

3.3.1   Results

The role of teamwork for innovation has received relatively little research attention. Shipton et al. (2006b) started to fill this gap; they showed that there is a significant and positive relationship between the extent of teamwork and innovation in products and in technical systems for the manufacturing organizations covered in their study. The effect of working in teams also depends on the organizational context in which the teams are embedded.

Team-working seems to benefit innovation most when teams operate within a framework of sophisticated and effective HRM practices. The wider organizational context needs to support team-working to reap its full benefit. Furthermore, the way individual jobs are designed will have an influence on how effectively teamwork operates.

One company that we visited in our research had discovered that teamwork offered better productivity outcomes, with higher quality and less waste produced. This organization, manufacturing wire and cabling for the electronics industry, had made a concerted effort a year before our visit to implement team-working and supported the initiative through careful selection of team leaders and ongoing training. Team leaders we spoke to described some of the innovations that they had brought about. One team decided of its own volition to run short batches – requiring frequent set-up changes – during the day shift when there were more people available to assist with the process. The night shift was set aside for longer runs, since there were fewer personnel available to carry out the necessary set-up changes. Another decided to video its members in action on the production line, and then to scrutinize the video in order to look for ways of improving the process. The next stage in their development, according to the production manager, would be to increase their contact with suppliers and customers, an initiative that was starting to be addressed at the time of our visit.

Two job-related attributes likely to influence teamwork/innovation relationships are job variety and the extent of harmonization. Focusing for a moment on job variety, a wide literature holds that both the variety and responsibility of jobs will influence effort (including creative endeavour) (Hackman and Oldham, 1980; Locke, 1997). Those experiencing variety may be more inclined (relative to those whose roles are constrained) to engage in the sustained effort necessary to promote innovation because they have a stronger sense of the meaning of and the interconnection between tasks. Further, it is possible that exposure to different experiences and points of view makes individuals more willing to examine their own mental models and to make any necessary adjustments (Eisenhardt and Tabrizi, 1995; McGrath, 2001; Tushman and O'Reilly, 1997). Through experiencing variety, employees may be less inclined to resist new ideas and willing to at least to consider their potential benefits, with positive results for innovation. Job variety also presents opportunities for skill development. It is likely that that operators experiencing variety are better at resolving quality issues, for example, than those whose jobs are more narrowly defined.

A recent study by Shipton et al. (2006b) revealed that although job variety itself was not significantly associated with innovation in production processes/technology, the combination of job variety together with high aggregate job satisfaction was significant and positive for this dependent variable (see the third section below). Furthermore, the study reveals that high job variety in conditions of low job satisfaction is detrimental to innovation (see Figure 3.2). It suggests that the extent to which job variety facilitates innovation may be contingent upon existing employee attitudes. Thus, job satisfaction may be the crucial factor determining whether or not variety is an enabling rather than a debilitating experience. It should be noted that this study draws upon a small sample size (n = 24).

Single status/harmonization is factor that is frequently overlooked in the organizational behaviour literature. The term depicts a willingness to embrace ideas regardless of the hierarchical status of the initiator, where there is free and open communication across the various levels of the organization (Cully et al., 1999). In single-status organizations (where there are high levels of harmonization), reward distribution is more likely to be based upon relevant job criteria (such as task performance) than upon arbitrary factors such as status differentials (for example, whether individuals are 'blue' or 'white'-collar workers). Such equal and just treatment of employees may lead to their making more discretionary effort (Fahr, Podsakoff and Organ, 1990; Niehoff and Moorman, 1993), which is likely in itself to promote organizational innovation. A positive and significant association was found between this variable and innovation in production technology/processes in a study reported by Shipton et al. (1996b), and this relationship was moderated by aggregate job satisfaction. As we reported in the case of job variety, the converse was also the case; high harmonization in an environment where people reported low satisfaction appears to inhibit innovation, perhaps because people are unlikely to exhibit the positive behaviours described above where they feel demotivated and possibly resentful about work activity.

We stated in the introductory section that through developing the commitment and satisfaction of employees, working for the organization is valued and there is a willingness to endorse change and to go 'beyond contract'. The following and final section of this chapter examines the potential role of employee feelings – and highlights empirical evidence addressing this point.

3.4   Job satisfaction and innovation

Research addressing this topic has for many years been concerned with the relationship between job satisfaction and performance, defined in performance and productivity terms. Indeed, the idea that satisfied employees will perform their work more effectively underpins many theories of performance, leadership, reward and job design (for example, Batt, 2002; Hackman and Oldham, 1976; Morrissey, Cordery and Girardi, 2005). In a recent meta-analysis, Judge et al. (2001) demonstrated that employees' overall job satisfaction is on average correlated .30 (after corrections for measurement unreliability) with their work performance or role-prescribed behaviour. At the level of the organization, Ostroff (1992), for example, found that there were significant and positive correlations between teachers' average job satisfaction and several measures of school performance.

Any relationship between employee attitudes and innovation is complicated because innovation is a multifaceted process involving both the generation of a creative idea and its implementation (West, 2002). Some employees will be required to initiate innovation (at the creativity stage) while others will be expected to provide the support necessary to implement the ideas within their organizations. For the creativity phase, early work by Isen and colleagues revealed that those experiencing a positive frame of mind respond more warmly to others and also score more highly on creativity tests than those who feel less happy and less optimistic (Isen, Daubman and Nowicki, 1987; Isen and Baron, 1991).

For the second phase, innovation implementation, we draw upon Staw et al.'s (1994) framework, which suggests that there are a number of possible mechanisms to be considered. Firstly, there are direct effects on task activity, persistence and functioning. Positive feelings can increase both the expectancy that one's effort will lead to high performance and the belief that sustained effort will lead to desirable outcomes, such as innovation. The second intervening process in Staw et al.'s model (1994) is interpersonal: it is likely that positive affect and its manifestations yield more favourable responses from other people and greater influence over them. Third, Staw and colleagues reviewed evidence that employees with more positive emotion react favourably to others, resulting in greater altruism and task cooperation. Thus employees experiencing positive affect will be open and responsive to change, so that where new ideas are put forward, they are endorsed rather than rejected or embraced less than enthusiastically.

There is also likely to be a relationship between *aggregate* job satisfaction and organizational innovation. We suggest that measuring job satisfaction at the organizational level may capture components that are not salient at the individual level. Ryan, Schmit and Johnson (1996), for example, suggested that because organizational performance is not simply a sum of individual performance, it must be influenced by factors other than those affecting individual level performance – such as shared values. Given that innovation in any areas requires the cooperation of most in the organization (for example R&D, production workers, sales, marketing) we argue that aggregate firm-level satisfaction will predict innovation in this area.

A recent study by Shipton et al. (2006b), based on the manufacturing companies dataset portrayed in the first section, revealed significant and positive relationships between aggregate job satisfaction (measured at Time 1) and innovation in production technology/processes ($\beta = 0.68$, $p < 0.001$). Indeed,

Table 3.3 Summary of hierarchical regression of innovation in processes/technology on to job satisfaction

Independent variables[b]	Innovations in processes/technology Time 2		
	β	ΔR^2	Adjusted ΔR^2
Controls *	0.15	0.11	0.03
Job satisfaction	0.68***	0.36***	0.37***

Notes: *$p < 0.05$; **$p < 0.01$; ***$p < 0.001$; $n = 28$. Control variables = prior innovation; profitability. Adapted from Shipton et al. (2006b)

aggregate job satisfaction explains around 36 per cent of the variance for this dependent variable (see Table 3.3). Although the sample size is small ($n = 28$), the study has significant strengths: data are longitudinal, making it possible to control for prior innovation as well as organizational profitability, and data representing the independent and dependent variables are drawn from distinct and separate sources.

Recent research conducted by the authors in a company manufacturing office equipment suggests that, at times, employee job satisfaction may inhibit, rather than enhance innovation. This organization was highly dependent on its parent company. Traditionally, many important decisions concerning investment and R&D options had been made arbitrarily away from the local plant, creating a sense of powerlessness and a belief that employees would be supported regardless of the economic situation. Thus, although there was substantial investment in training, quality systems and continuous improvement, there was limited opportunity or support for radical learning and engagement with the customer. The company was in danger of losing manufacturing capacity to China and Taiwan and had indeed become less central in its contribution to the global operation – and yet there appeared to be relatively little awareness of the threat they faced. It was clear that employees appreciated the job security they had been offered over the years, as well as the generous sick pay and pension arrangement. This situation reveals that employee job satisfaction alone cannot compensate for a lack of strategic vision and an unwillingness to reflect critically upon past performance and future success.

3.5 Discussion

Evidence presented in each section of this chapter suggests that the way people are managed in the workplace is a crucial factor in determining whether organizations exhibit high or low innovation. The logic is that there are three alternative and/or complementary routes whereby innovation is sustained in organizations. The first, covered in section one, holds that HRM practices develop the necessary skills. An alternative pathway or route examines structural arrangements, arguing that teamwork represents a way of drawing upon diverse perspectives and facilitating a rapid and effective response to customer demands. Thirdly, innovative organizations have to take account of employee feelings. Job satisfaction – especially where experienced by the majority of the workforce – may promote a change orientation, so that where new ideas are put forward, they are endorsed rather than rejected or embraced less than enthusiastically. The main findings are summarized as follows.

3.5.1 Developing skills

According to evidence presented in Shipton et al. (2006a) 'exploratory learning' may determine whether practices such as appraisal enable employees to acquire the necessary competence to promote organizational innovation. This variable, entered into a regression with training, and again with appraisal and induction, explained more of the variance for the type of innovation being examined in this study (innovation in technical systems) than either set of practices applied independently. Our argument holds that because innovation encompasses the implementation of an idea as well as its initial conception, successfully managing the process involves achieving a balance – engaging in exploratory learning whilst simultaneously enabling people to acquire the skills necessary to exploit and implement the knowledge. Some sets of HRM practices may be better than others at creating the competence to enable employees to see an innovation through to completion, as opposed to devising the initial idea.

Future research could usefully explore whether exploratory learning does indeed trigger creativity and highlight what activities are likely to shape an individual's competence in terms of challenging existing ways of operating. Visits to customers are likely to be important, for example, but in addition the number and frequency of interactions with those outside the immediate work sphere could be analysed in this regard. The role of other HRM practices such as appraisal, induction and more equitable working arrangements (such as a commitment to single status) could be analysed in terms of the role that these activities may play in enabling knowledge transfer and/or securing innovation implementation.

As well as examining the synergistic effects of implementing a combination of mutually supportive HRM practices, future research could examine whether there are specific HR mechanisms likely to promote innovation. One aspect that deserves further attention is the learning orientation of the organization. An organization supports learning when mentoring is endorsed and supported, when there is high commitment towards the career development of shop-floor as well as managerial and supervisory staff, and when there is a strong strategic vision for employee development. We assert that these HRM practices are important in determining whether and how knowledge is transferred throughout the organization. Through career development meetings, for example, employees have the opportunity to prepare themselves for internal promotion or for lateral career moves, thereby transferring the knowledge that they have acquired into other areas. Furthermore, research shows that mentoring practices are extremely effective in developing individuals' networking skills, thereby facilitating the flow and transfer of knowledge both laterally and vertically through organizational hierarchies (Collins and Clerk, 2004). Results from the study by Shipton et al. (2005) have shown that there are significant and positive relationships between the learning environment and innovation in the manufacturing organizations studied.

3.5.2 Structural arrangements

Little is known about the effect of using team-working as a work-design strategy on the innovativeness of organisations. Much of the rhetoric of teamwork argues that the more widespread team-working is in an organisation, that is, the higher the extent to which the workforce is organised in teams, the higher is the level of organizational innovation (Mohrman et al., 1995; West and Markiewicz, 2004). Empirical underpinning for this assumption, however, is still scarce.

One study that looked at the role of team-working for organizational innovation found that the higher the extent to which staff was organized in teams, the higher the level of innovation (Shipton et. al. 2006a). Team-working was assessed in terms of the extent to which staff were organized in teams. The results of this study demonstrated that the extent of team-working – ranging from organizations not using team-working at all to having 100 per cent of staff organized in teams – was related to innovation in products and technical systems.

We assume that the team-working–innovation link is based on several processes. Firstly, people organized in teams have different experiences and attitudes in comparison to people in traditional structures, both of which amplify creativity. Secondly, the implementation of team-working is associated with higher organizational flexibility and adaptability (Mohrman et al., 1995). When an organization implements self-directed team-working, much of the traditional organization, which is characterized by hierarchical decision-making, goal-setting and rule-making, needs to be jettisoned. Furthermore, the flow of information and knowledge is increased because teams provide the vertical linkages relevant to this (Mohrman et al., 1995). Finally, teamwork–innovation relationships are likely to be moderated by individual job-design elements. We suggest that job variety and the extent of 'single status' arrangements may be significant here; other variables that deserve further consideration are task autonomy, meaning and significance (see Hackman and Oldham, 1976).

3.5.3   Employee feelings

The third route whereby people may influence organizational innovation is through the emotional/feeling aspects, in particular peoples' attitudes towards work. The study reported here (Shipton et al. 2006b) focused on satisfaction across the organization as a whole, rather than satisfaction as experienced by individuals. For innovation *implementation*, it may be especially important for employees at all levels of the business to work collaboratively in order to endorse the ideas proposed by others. Those experiencing job satisfaction are likely to maintain sustained effort over time, believing that they will be ultimately successful, and to be more effective at an interpersonal level than those not experiencing this state, exerting a positive influence on those around them. We argue similarly that, faced with challenging tasks and expectations, employees in highly innovative organizations have to work together to sustain momentum in order to endorse rather than reject proposals for change. Such momentum is facilitated where the majority or employees enjoy work; indeed, through examining aggregate job satisfaction, we capture components that are not salient at the level of the individual (Ryan, Schmit and Johnson, 1996).

We further speculate that aggregate job satisfaction will promote the cognitive flexibility associated with creativity. Our conclusions here are tentative, since we have no direct measure of creativity, and the pattern that we report refers to the extent to which organizations have, over the course of time, successfully *implemented* creative ideas. Nonetheless, a persuasive literature holds that creative potential is amplified as groups develop mental models endorsing the value of creativity (for example, George, 1996; West, 2002) and it is possible that the results that we report can be explained in part in terms of the enhanced capacity of individual employees to devise creative ideas where they operate within an environment high on collective satisfaction.

3.6   Conclusion

People are central to innovation performance, and the findings we report in this chapter suggest that relatively high levels of innovation can be achieved where people are empowered to make changes at local levels through effective HRM practice. We believe that HRM practices – effectively designed and synchronized – enhance learning and empower people at all levels to instigate change and innovation. Managing people to promote innovation is necessary if we are to release the full creative potential of our work organizations. Understanding the factors that may influence innovation is necessary to achieve the same goal, so that work organizations and those who work within them will advance and thrive in years to come.

References

Amabile, T., R. Conti, H. Coon, J. Lazenby and M. Herron (1996) 'Assessing the Work Environment for Creativity', *Academy of Management Journal,* 39, pp. 1154–84.

Argote, L. and D. Epple (1990) 'Learning Curves in Manufacturing', *Science,* 247, pp. 920–24.

Armstrong, M. and A. Baron (1998) *Performance Management; the New Realities* (London: CIPD).

Bach, S. D (2000) 'From Performance Appraisal to Performance Management', in S. Back and K. Sisson (eds) *Personnel Management,* 3rd edition (Oxford: Blackwell).

Bae, J. and J. J. Lawler (2000) 'Organizational and Human Resource Management Strategies in Korea', *Academy of Management Journal,* 43, pp. 502–17.

Batt, R. (2002) 'Managing Customer Services: HR Practices, Quit Rates and Sales Growth', *Academy of Management Journal,* 45, p. 587.

Boxall, P. F. (1996) 'The Strategic HRM Debate and the Resource-based View of the Firm', *Human Resource Management Journal,* 6: 3, pp. 59–75.

Clark, K. B., S. D. Amundson and R. L. Cardy (2002) 'Cross-functional Team Decision-making and Learning Outcomes: A Qualitative Illustration', *Journal of Business and Management,* 8, pp. 217–36.

Collins, C. and K. Clerk (2004) 'Strategic Human Resource Practices, Top Management Team Social Networks and Firm Performance: The Role of Human Resource Practices in Creating Organizational Competitive Advantage', *Academy of Management Journal,* 46, pp. 740–51.

Cross, R., A. Parker, L. Prusak, and S. P. Borgatti (2001) 'Knowing What We Know: Supporting Knowledge Creation and Sharing in Knowledge Networks', *Organizational Dynamics,* 30, 2, pp. 100–20.

Cully, M., S. Woodland, A. O'Reilly and G. Dix (1999) *Britain at Work; as Depicted by the 1998 Workplace Employee Relations Survey* (London: Routledge).

Cummings, T. G. and C. G. Worley (1997) *Organization Development and Change,* 6th edition (Cincinnati: South-Western College Publishing).

Damanpour, F. (1991) 'Organizational Innovation: A Meta-analysis of Effects of Determinants and Moderators', *Academy of Management Journal,* 34, 3, pp. 555–90.

Damanpour, F. and W. M. Evan (1984) 'Organizational Innovation and Performance: The Problem of "Organizational Lag"', *Administrative Science Quarterly,* 29: 3, pp. 392–409.

Danneels, E. (2002) 'The Dynamics of Product Innovation and Firm Competences', *Strategic Management Journal,* 23, pp. 1095–121.

Delaney, J. E. and M. A. Huselid (1996) 'The Impact of HRM Practices on Perceptions of Organizational Performance', *AMJ,* 8, pp. 289–309.

Delery, J. E. (1998) 'Issues of Fit in Strategic Human Resource Management: Implications for Research', *HRM Review,* 8: 2, pp. 89–309.

Delery, J. E. and D. H. Doty (1996) 'Modes of Theorizing in Strategic Human Resource Management: Tests of Universalistic, Contingency, and Configurational Performance Predictions', *Academy of Management Journal,* 39: 4, pp. 802–35.

Eisenhardt, K. and B. Tabrizi (1995) 'Accelerating Adaptive Processes: Product Innovation in the Global Computer Industry', *Administrative Science Quarterly,* 40, pp. 84–110.

Fahr, J. L., P. M. Podsakoff and D. W. Organ (1990) 'Accounting for Organizational Citizenship Behavior: Leader Fairness and Task Scope Versus Satisfaction', *Journal of Management,* 16, pp. 705–22.

Feldman, M. S. (2000) 'Organizational Routines as a Source of Continuous Change', *Organization Science,* 11, pp. 611–29.

Feldman, M. S. and A. Rafaeli (2002) 'Organizational Routines as Sources of Connections and Understandings' *Journal of Management Studies,* 39: 3, pp. 309–31

George, J. M. (1996) 'Group Affective Tone', in M. A. West (ed.) *Handbook of Work Group Psychology* (London, Wiley).

Gittell, J. H. (2000) 'Organizing Work to Support Relational Co-ordination', *International Journal of Human Resource Management,* 11, pp. 517–539.

Guthrie, J. (2001) 'High Involvement Practices, Turnover and Productivity', *Academy of Management Journal,* 44, pp. 180–90.

Hackman, J. R. and G. R. Oldham (1976) 'Motivation through the Design of Work: Test of a Theory', *Organizational Behavior and Human Performance,* 16, pp. 250–79.

Hackman, J. R. and G. R. Oldham (1980) *Work Re-design* (Reading, MA: Addison Wesley).

Henderson, R. (1991) 'Technological Change and the Management of Architectural Knowledge', in M. D. Cohen and L. S. Sproull (eds) *Organizational Learning* (London: Sage Publications).

Huselid, M. A. (1995) 'The Impact of Human Resource Management Practices on Turnover, Productivity, and Corporate Financial Performance', *Academy of Management Journal,* 38: 3, pp. 635–72.

Huselid, M. A., S. E. Jackson and R. S. Schuler (1997) 'Technical and Strategic Human Resource Management Effectiveness as Determinants of Firm Performance', *Academy of Management Journal,* 40: 1, pp. 171–88.

Isen, A. M. and R. A. Baron (1991) 'Positive Affect as a Factor in Organizational Behavior', *Research in Organizational Behavior,* 13, pp. 1–53.

Isen, A. M., K. A. Daubman and G. P. Nowicki (1987) 'Positive Affect Facilitates Creative Problem Solving', *Journal of Personality & Social Psychology,* 52: 6, pp. 1122–31.

James, L. R., R. G. Demaree and G. Wolf (1984) 'Estimating Within-group Interrater Reliability with and without Response Bias', *Journal of Applied Psychology,* 69: 1, pp. 85–98.

Judge, T. A., C. J. Thoresen, J. E. Bono and G. K. Patton (2001) 'The Job Satisfaction–Job Performance Relationship: A Qualitative and Quantitative Review', *Psychological Bulletin,* 127: 3, pp. 376–407.

Koch, M. and R. McGrath (1996) 'Improving Labor Productivity: Human Resource Management Policies Do Matter', *Strategic Management Journal,* 17: 5, pp. 335–54.

Kogut, B. and U. Zander (1992) 'Knowledge of the Firm, Combinative Capabilities and the Replication of Capabilties, and the Replication of Technology', *Organization Science,* 3: 3, pp. 383–97.

Laursen, K. and N. K. Foss (2003) 'New Human Resource Management Practices, Complementarities and the Impact on Innovation Performance', *Cambridge Journal of Economics,* 27, pp. 243–63.

Leana, C. and H. van Buren (1999) 'Organizational Social Capital and Employment Practices', *Academy of Management Review,* 24, pp. 538–56.

Locke, E. A. (1997) 'The Motivation to Work: What We Know', in M. M. Maihr and P. R. Pintrich (eds) *Advances in Motivation and Achievement,* 10, pp. 375–412.

MacDuffie, J. P. (1995) 'Human Resource Bundles and Manufacturing Performance', *Industrial and Labor Relations Review,* 48: 2, pp. 197–221.

March, J. G. (1991) 'Exploration and Exploitation in Organizational Learning', *Organization Science,* 2, pp. 71–87.

McKenzie, J. and C. van Winkelen (2004) *Understanding the Knowledgeable Organization* (Padstow: Thomson).

McGrath, R. G. (2001) 'Exploratory Learning, Innovative Capacity and Managerial Oversight', *Academy of Management Journal,* 44, pp. 118–31.

Mohrman, S. A., S. G. Cohen and A. M. Mohrman (1995) *Designing Team-based Organizations* (San Francisco: Jossey-Bass).

Morrissey, D., J. Cordery, A. Girardi and R. Payne (2005) 'Job Design and Opportunities for Skill Utilization and Intrinsic Job Satisfaction,' *European Journal of Work and Organizational Psychology,* 14: 5, pp. 9–79.

J. Nahapiet, J. and S. Ghoshal (1998) 'Social Capital, Intellectual Capital and the Organizational Advantage', *Academy of Management Review,* 23, 242–66.

Niehoff, B. P. and R. H. Moorman (1993) 'Justice as a Mediator of the Relationship between Methods of Monitoring and Organizational Citizenship Behaviour', *Academy of Management Journal,* 36, pp. 527–56.

Nonaka, I. and H. Takeuchi (1995) *The Knowledge Creating Company* (Oxford: Oxford University Press).

Ostroff, C. (1992) 'The Effects of Climate and Personal Influences on Individual Behavior and Attitudes in Organizations', *Organizational Behavior & Human Decision Processes,* 56: 1, pp. 56–90.

Paton, R. A. and J. McCalman (2000) *Change Management. A Guide to Effective Implementation* (2nd ed.) (Thousand Oaks, CA: Sage).

Pfeffer, J. (2000) *The Knowing–Doing Gap: How Smart Companies Turn Knowledge into Action* (Boston, MA: Harvard Business School Press).

Purcell, J. (1999) 'Best Practice or Best Fit: Chimera or Cul-de-sac?', *Human Resource Management Journal,* 9: 3, pp. 26–41.

Ryan, A. M., M. J. Schmit and R. Johnson (1996) 'Attitudes and Effectiveness: Examining Relations at Organizational Level', *Personnel Psychology,* 49, pp. 853–82.

Scarborough, H. and J. Swann (1999) *Knowledge Management: a Literature Review* (London, CIPD).

Senior, B. (1997) *Organizational Change* (London: Pitman).

Shipton, H., D. Fay, M. A. West, M. Patterson and K. Birdi (2005) 'Managing People to Promote Innovation', *Creativity and Innovation Management,* 14: 2, pp. 118–28.

Shipton, H., M. A. West, J. Dawson, K. Birdi and M. Patterson (2006a) 'HRM as a Predictor of Innovation', *Human Resource Management Journal,* 16: 1, pp. 3–27.

Shipton, H., M. A. West, C. Parkes, J. Dawson and M. Patterson (2006b) 'When Promoting Positive Feelings Pays: Aggregate Job Satisfaction, Work Design Features and Organizational Innovation In Manufacturing Organizations', *European Journal of Work and Organizational Psychology,* 15: 4, pp. 404–30.

Song, J., P. Almeida and G. Wu (2003) 'Learning by Hiring: When is Mobility More Likely to Facilitate Interfirm Knowledge Transfer?', *Organization Science,* 49, pp. 351–65.

Spender, J. C. (1996) 'Making Knowledge the Basis of a Dynamic Theory of the Firm', *Strategic Management Journal,* 17, pp. 45–62.

Staw, B. M., R. I. Sutton and L. H. Pelled (1994) 'Employee Positive Emotion and Favorable Outcomes at the Workplace', *Organization Science,* 5, pp. 51–71.

Stern, E. and E. Sommerlad (1999) 'Workplace Learning, Culture and Performance', *Issues in People Management* (London: CIPD).

Thompke, S. and E. von Hippel (2002) 'Customers as Innovators: a New Way to Create Value', *Harvard Business Review,* 80: 4, pp. 74– 81.

Tsai, W. (2001) 'Knowledge Transfer in Intraorganizational Networks: Effects of Network Position and Absorptive Capacity on Business Unit Innovation and Performance', *Academy of Management Journal*, 44, pp. 996–1004.

Tushman, M. L. and P. Anderson (1986) 'Technological Discontinuities and Organizational Environments, *Administrative Science Quarterly*, 31, pp. 439–65.

Tushman, M. L. and C.A. O'Reilly (1997) *Winning through Innovation: Leading Organizational Change and Renewal* (Boston: Harvard Business School Press).

van de Ven, A. H. (1986) 'Central Problems in the Management of Innovation', *Management Science*, 32: 5, pp. 590–607.

West, M. A. (2002) 'Sparkling Mountains or Stagnant Ponds: An Integrative Model of Creativity and Innovation Implementation in Work Groups', *Applied Psychology: An International Review*, 51: 3, pp. 355–387.

West, M. A. and L. Markiewicz (2004) *Building Team-based Working* (Oxford: BPS Blackwell).

Zaltman, G., R. Duncan and J. Holbek (1973) *Innovations and Organizations* (New York: Wiley).

4

Skill Endowment and R&D Investment: Evidence from Micro Data

Mariacristina Piva and Marco Vivarelli

4.1 Introduction

History has seen periods of change biased in favour of the unskilled: this was the case during the transition from the artisan-based to the factory-based system of production (Marx, 1961, Book I, Chap. XIII; Goldin and Katz, 1998), and of the massive introduction of Tayloristic methods in the 20th century (Braverman, 1974).

Nevertheless, there is now overwhelming empirical evidence showing that the information and communication technologies (ICT) paradigm (see Dosi 1988; Freeman and Soete, 1994) is mainly and persistently biased against the unskilled. Evidence supporting the skill-biased technological change (SBTC) hypothesis was first provided with regard to the US (Berman et al., 1994; Doms et al., 1997), then to the UK (Machin, 1996; Haskel and Heden, 1999), continental Europe (Machin and van Reenen, 1998) and more recently even to the middle-income developing countries (Berman and Machin, 2000, 2004). Hence, the general consensus is that computerization and ICT have led to an increase in the demand for white-collar workers, and in their relative wages.

While the dominant approach has seen skill bias as a consequence of an exogenous technological change, some authors (Acemoglu, 1996, 1998; Kiley, 1999; Funk and Vogel, 2004) have put forward the idea that *'endogenous* skill-bias' may in fact have induced a dominant SBTC trajectory. In such a view, which is basically macroeconomic and falls within an endogenous growth framework, it is the significant increase in the excess supply of college-educated workers in Western economies during the second half of the 20th century that has induced SBTC. In other words, the attractiveness of investing in SBTC would seem to be related to the supply of the factor which complements that technology; in particular, a large number of educated workers would raise the incentive to invest in that technology which is intensive in the production factor having become more abundant and cheaper, that is, skilled labour.

The basic idea of this paper is that this kind of inducing mechanism may work at the micro as well as at the macro level. When deciding the amount to invest in R&D, a firm can well predict that R&D, after a certain time-lag and with a high degree of uncertainty, will generate skill-biased innovation (either process innovation, increasing the complementarity between capital and skilled workers, or product innovation, requiring more skilled labour). If such is the case, the initial skill endowment may increase the *ex ante* expected profitability of R&D investment and so also increase the amount of a firm's R&D expenditure.

The novelty of this study is precisely the attempt to investigate the missing link in the triangle skills–innovation–performance at the microeconomic level, that is the possible role of current skills in determining corporate R&D investment. Hence, the basic research question of this paper can be summarized as follows: is a firm's larger *ex ante* skill endowment a good predictor of higher R&D investment? In other words, the hypothesis put forward in the next sections is that a better workforce skill endowment may increase the *ex ante* expected profitability of R&D investment and so increase a firm's R&D expenditures.

Although specific literature explicitly discussing the possibility that upskilling can induce R&D investment does not exist (at least to the best of our knowledge), there is a considerable number of managerial and economic studies that propose arguments which indirectly support the hypothesis investigated in this study. In section 4.2 of this chapter, we will try to examine these different strands of literature critically.

Section 4.3 will describe the micro data used in this study and will introduce the least-squared-dummy-variable-corrected (LSDVC) estimator used in the econometric estimates, the results of which will be discussed in the following section; finally, section 4.5 will propose some conclusions.

4.2   Theoretical framework

Before motivating the skill-augmented specification of the firm's decisions as regards R&D, we briefly introduce the baseline equation. Traditionally, R&D investment is modelled as a path-dependent process related to demand evolution.

As far as demand is concerned, we will check for the so called '*demand pull*' hypothesis which underlines the following aspects: 1) a positive demand evolution can increase the expected profitability from innovation; 2) an increase in market share increases the degree of innovation appropriability; and 3) a higher cash flow can alleviate possible credit constraints in financing the R&D investment (see Schmookler, 1966; Scherer, 1982; Brouwer and Kleinknecht, 1999; Kleinknecht and Verspagen, 1990; Hall et al., 1999; Piva and Vivarelli, 2006, 2007).

Moreover, R&D activities are highly localized (Atkinson and Stiglitz, 1969) and path-dependent (David, 1985; Rosenberg, 1982; Arthur, 1988; Ruttan,

1997; Antonelli, 1998). These considerations open the way to a dynamic specification of the R&D investment decision.

Finally, sectoral peculiarities in terms of different technological opportunities may be important in affecting R&D investment (Pavitt, 1984; Malerba and Orsenigo, 1996; Breschi et al., 2000; Malerba, 2005).

Taking all these considerations into account, we can put forward a dynamic specification of the R&D decision of the type:

$$RD_t = \alpha + \beta RD_{t-1} + \gamma Sales_t + v_t \tag{1}$$

where the lagged dependent variable takes into account the path-dependent and localized nature of technological change within a firm, and the *Sales* regressor is a way to represent the *demand-pull* hypothesis. Finally, sectoral technological opportunities will be taken into account through the insertion of two-digit sectoral dummies (see section 4.4).

Given this baseline equation, there are some interrelated lines of reasoning which support the choice to augment (1) with a variable indicating a firm's skill endowment. For the sake of simplicity, we discuss these interactive arguments separately in the following four points.

1. Complementarity between new technologies and skills

When investing in R&D, a firm's management can well predict that the likely final outcome, although uncertain and delayed, of the R&D decision will be a SBTC reinforcing the capital-skill complementarity (Griliches, 1969). This means that the firm's present skill endowment increases the expected profitability from innovation and so the amount of current R&D expenditure. Analytically, this means that there is a profit function characterized by super modularity in innovation and skills.[1] The fact that 'the whole is more than the sum of its parts' (Milgrom and Roberts, 1990, 1995; Topkis, 1998) makes the more highly skill-endowed firm more inclined to invest in R&D.

For instance, Dunne and Troske (2005), using data from US manufacturing plants, found that the likelihood of adopting a computer-aided design (CAD) machine was highly correlated with the proportion of skilled labour within the plant (p. 2); by the same token, plants with a greater share of investment in computing equipment in 1992 experienced skill upgrading in the period 1977–92 (p. 7).

Moreover, skilled labour has been found to be a direct complement to R&D activities: in the UK 2001 innovation survey, 88 per cent of firms that were engaged in R&D on a continuous basis employed graduates, while this percentage dropped to 57 per cent for the no-R&D firms (see CRIC, 2005, Table 4.5, p. 64).

On the whole, firms that possess high skills should perceive R&D investment as being more profitable, while initially low-skilled firms should be less likely to recognize profitable R&D investment opportunities (see Leiponen, 2000).

2. *Endogenous skill bias*

Reflecting what happens at the macro level (see previous section), a large endowment of skills within the firm may well induce investment in current R&D. Following the 'induced bias' theory (see Hicks, 1932; Vivarelli, 1995, Chap. 2) a large *ex ante* endowment of skilled workers acts as an incentive to invest in R&D, and this in turn develops into innovation which will be intensive in the internally abundant and cheaper factor of production (see Acemoglu, 1998; Kiley, 1999). In other words, those firms which are already well-endowed with the proper skills will be less reluctant to invest in R&D and will not be afraid to incur any skill shortage or rising wages, once R&D has generated skill-biased innovation.

For instance, using UK data on the relative wages of the relevant occupational categories and on skilled labour shortages, Nickell and Nicolitsas (1997) found that a permanent 10 per cent increase in the number of companies reporting skilled labour shortages in the industry to which a firm belongs would lead to a permanent 10 per cent reduction in the industry's fixed-capital investment and a temporary 4 per cent reduction in its R&D expenditure. Vice versa, a large internal endowment of skills should facilitate R&D expenditures at the firm level.

3. *Absorptive capacity*

It is well known that firms invest in R&D not only to *produce* innovation, but also in order to create internal capacity (see Cohen and Levinthal, 1989) able to *absorb* external knowledge coming from other firms and scientific institutions such as universities and public laboratories. In other words, firms that conduct their own R&D are better able to identify, assimilate and exploit externally available knowledge. However, 'an organisation's absorptive capacity will depend on the absorptive capacities of its individual members' (Cohen and Levinthal, 1990, p. 131). In this framework, skilled labour is a necessary complement to R&D activities in reinforcing the absorptive capacity of a given organisation.

This is the third channel that renders R&D investment *ex ante* more profitable for those firms which are well endowed with skilled labour. Leiponen (2005) underlines the fact that skills are an important component of absorptive capacity, being complementary to internal R&D, collaborative R&D joint ventures and a firm's implementation of external knowledge; her results clearly indicate that internal skills (proxied by educational levels) complement external collaboration strategies in positively affecting a firm's operating profit margin. Thus, employees' skills also reinforce the expected profitability of the indirect by-products of internal R&D investment such as the absorption of external knowledge (spillovers[2]) and the occurrence of collaborative R&D agreements with other firms.

On the whole, the entire firm's innovation strategy may benefit from a strong skill base, and employees' skills are expected to complement the effect of innovation on the firm's profitability. In particular, interactions and synergies between activities within the firm (points A and B) as well as between the firm's internal and external sources of knowledge (point C) may have a great impact on profitability from innovation, and so on the expected returns from R&D expenditure. Hence, points A to C motivate the main purpose of this paper, which is to test an augmented version of equation (1):

$$RD_t = \alpha + \beta RD_{t-1} + \gamma Sales_t + \vartheta \left(\frac{WC}{BC} \right)_t + \kappa \left(\frac{WC}{BC} \right)_{t-1} + v_t \qquad (2)$$

where the ratio between white (WC) and blue (BC) collars is taken as a proxy of the skill endowment within a given firm[3]; the lagged term is inserted to control for delayed effects and to make the computing of long-term coefficients possible.

4.3 Data and econometric methodology

The dynamic specification (equation (2)) will be tested using a unique longitudinal database, suitable for panel data analysis. This new database is derived from questionnaire surveys collected by the Italian investment bank Mediocredito Centrale (MCC, now Capitalia) and involving representative samples of Italian manufacturing firms with no fewer than 11 employees. The original MCC database comes from two different questionnaire waves, each of them collecting contemporary and retrospective (previous two years) data from samples of more than 4000 firms.[4] In order to obtain a balanced panel dataset, we merged the two waves (1995–2000) and kept only the overlapping firms declaring continuous data on R&D expenditure, sales and skill endowment. We ended up with a panel of 215 firms over a six-year period.

Monetary variables are expressed at 1995 constant prices; some descriptive statistics are given in Table 4.1.

Table 4.1 Descriptive statistics (monetary values at 1995 Italian lire, in millions)

	Mean (1995)	Standard deviation	Average growth rate (1995–2000)
Log (Sales)	9.38	1.26	0.41%
Log (R&D)	4.74	1.70	2.39%
Log (White collar/ blue collar)	−0.67	0.87	0.02%
Employees	168	344.236	1.06%

As can be seen, our sample is made up of relatively large (168 employees on average) and successful firms, showing increasing sales and employment over the examined period. Interestingly enough, on average the sample has been affected by an overall upskilling of its workforce.

Estimates will test the following specification for firms (i) over time (t):

$$\log RD_{i,t} = \alpha + \beta \log RD_{i,t-1} + \gamma \log Sales_{i,t} + \vartheta \log \left(\frac{WC}{BC}\right)_{i,t}$$

$$+ \kappa \log \left(\frac{WC}{BC}\right)_{i,t-1} + (\eta_i + \lambda_t + \nu_{i,t}) \tag{3}$$

$$i = 1, \ldots, N; t = 1, \ldots, T$$

where variables are expressed in natural logarithms, η is the idiosyncratic individual and time-invariant firm's fixed effect and ν the usual error term.[5] In addition, λ, the unobservable time effect, has been inserted to check for possible macroeconomic and business cycle effects.[6]

The reasons for taking the lagged dependent variable into consideration as a first regressor are both interpretative (see previous section) and econometrical: in fact, the revealed persistence of the R&D variable ($\rho = 0.79$) also calls for a necessary AR(1) check.

Once we have checked for lagged R&D, sales are considered in order to check for the demand-pull hypothesis.

Finally, our main determinant (WC/BC) is considered in its contemporaneous and lagged impact.[7] Here, a possible endogeneity problem may arise. Indeed, the two theoretical hypotheses, that technological change increases the demand for skills and that skills endowment can induce SBTC, are not mutually exclusive. Rather, at the corporate level, one can well imagine a sort of virtuous circle where skill endowment induces SBTC and the latter then further increases the demand for skilled workers (see Finegold and Soskice, 1988; Wilson and Hogarth, 2003). However, our dependent variable measures an initial, pre-innovation investment in R&D, with R&D expenditure having an uncertain and delayed outcome in terms of subsequent skill-biased technological change. Since only subsequent successful innovation can have an impact on skill distribution, the possible reverse effect is not between present R&D expenditure and present skill endowment, but between future successful SBTC and future skill proportions. Indeed, it is reasonable to assume that the final skill-bias effect of current R&D expenditure will be detected well over the short time dimension of the panel used in this study. Consistently with this conclusion, the Arellano-Bond estimator used for initializing the adopted econometric procedure (see below) on the overall sample of 215 firms does not accept the assumption of endogeneity of WC/BC; in fact, the corresponding Sargan test rejects the null hypothesis of validity of instruments under the assumption of the endogeneity of WC/BC ($\chi^2 = 33.79^{***}$). Taking these theoretical and statistical arguments into account, we can exclude the insurgence of endogeneity with regard to our main regressor.

However, the need for considering the lagged dependent variable implies another obvious problem of endogeneity. A natural solution for first-order dynamic panel data models is to use GMM (General Method of Moments; see Anderson and Hsiao, 1981; Arellano and Bond, 1991; Arellano and Bover, 1995; Blundell and Bond, 1998). Unfortunately, this method is only efficient asymptotically and turns out not to be suitable for small samples (such as the one used in this study).

Therefore, we have implemented a rather new methodology, suitable for small panels, proposed by Kiviet (1995 and 1999), Judson and Owen (1999), Bun and Kiviet (2001, 2003), and extended by Bruno (2005a, 2005b) to unbalanced panels. In Appendix 4.1, we briefly reconsider the properties of the adopted methodology: the so-called Least Squared Dummy Variables Corrected (LSDVC) estimator.

In the next section estimates are run using OLS, LSDV and LSDVC estimates. The first are affected by both fixed effects and endogeneity; the second wipe out fixed effects;[8] the third also take the endogeneity of the lagged R&D variable into account. While OLS and LSDV are reported for completeness, the more reliable outcomes are those from the LSDVC estimate.

4.4   Estimation results

Table 4.2 presents the OLS, LSDV and LSDVC outcomes: both OLS and LSDV estimates exhibit a satisfactory fit (see R squared and F test respectively). As discussed in the appendix, LSDVC estimates are initialized by the Arellano-Bond estimator to get accuracy of approximation of bias B_3 and are characterized by bootstrapped standard errors. Estimates are checked both for time (in order to take possible aggregate and cyclical effects into account) and sectoral dummies (two-digit sectoral dummies have been included). For computational reasons, it was impossible to insert sectoral dummies into the LSDVC estimates; however, their inclusion in the OLS and LSDV estimates affects the values and the significance of the relevant coefficients only negligibly.[9]

As is immediately clear, estimates are affected by a strong path-dependence in R&D expenditure; as expected, the coefficients of the lagged dependent variable are all significant to a 99 per cent degree of confidence. This confirms the presence of innovative persistence at the corporate level.

As far as sales are concerned, they turn out to positively affect R&D investment. In all the three estimates, the relevant coefficient is significant to a 99 per cent level of confidence and in the LSDVC regression the related elasticity is 0.43, meaning that doubling a firm's own demand should imply an

Table 4.2   Empirical results: dependent variable: log(R&D)

	(1) OLS	(2) LSDV	(3) LSDVC	
Constant	−1.53***	(3.22)		
log(R&D-1)	0.62***	0.35***	0.60***	
	(28.44)	(11.82)	(14.01)	
log(Sales)	0.33***	0.56***	0.43***	
	(10.74)	(4.62)	(3.23)	
log(WC/BC)	0.34***	0.20*	0.23**	
log(WC/BC-1)	−0.17*	−0.03	−0.09	(1.33)
	(1.68)	(0.29)	(0.79)	
R^2 and F test	0.72	149.63***		
Observations	1075	1075	1075	

Notes: – t-statistics in brackets for OLS and LSDV estimates; z-statistics for LSDVC estimates (bias correction initialised by Arellano-Bond estimator and bootstrapped standard errors): *significant at 10%; **significant at 5%; ***significant at 1%.
– R^2 is reported for OLS estimates, F test is reported for LSDV estimates together with its significance level.
– Time dummies are always included and not reported; sectoral dummies are included in the OLS and LSDV specifications and not reported.
– LTE is the Long-term Elasticity; z-statistics in brackets.

increase in R&D investment of about 43 per cent. These outcomes can be seen as further confirmation of the demand-pull hypothesis (see section 4.2).

Turning our attention to the main focus of this analysis, the impact of skill endowment is positive, as expected, with a degree of statistical significance ranging from 90 to 99 per cent, according to the different estimates. While remaining positive, the long-run elasticity does not turn out to be significant.[10] On the whole, and considering the conservative and cautious methodology adopted,[11] these results give support to the hypothesis that current skill endowment may significantly influence a firm's current R&D decision. As reported in the last, more reliable, estimate, an increase of 100 per cent in the white-collar/blue-collar ratio would imply an increase of 23 per cent in R&D investment. This micro-econometric evidence is in accordance with the endogenous skill bias macroeconomic hypothesis and with the other theories discussed in section 4.2.

4.5   Summary and conclusions

This paper tests the role of skill endowment in increasing a firm's R&D investment. Its micro-econometric results are not in contrast with this hypothesis and pave the way for further studies based on other samples across different sectors and different countries.

In particular, the positive and significant link between *ex ante* available skills and R&D investment suggests a new way to look at the alleged complementarity between skills and innovation. In other words, the co-evolution of the two dimensions has to be thought of not solely as a consequence of SBTC, but also the other way round: an adequate *ex-ante* endowment of skills may accelerate R&D investment and so assure innovation *ex-post*.

In terms of managerial implications, this means that HRM can also be seen as a strategy to improve a firm's R&D efforts and ultimately to improve its performance through innovation.

In terms of policy implications, our results suggest that education and training policies can act as indirect subsidies for R&D investment.

Appendix 4.1

In the case of an autoregressive panel data model, the LSDV estimator is the following:

$$LSDV = (W'AW)^{-1}W'Ay \tag{A1}$$

where y is the vector of observations for the dependent variable, W is the matrix of the explanatory variables including the lagged dependent variable and A is the within-transformation which wipes out the individual effects. However, in the case of first-order dynamic panel data models, the LSDV estimator turns out to be not consistent and its bias has to be corrected.

In their Monte Carlo simulations, Bun and Kiviet (2003) and Bruno (2005a) consider three possible nested approximations of the LSDV bias:

$$c_1(T^{-1}) + c_2(N^{-1}T^{-1}) + c_3(N^{-1}T^{-2}) + O(N^{-2}T^{-2}) \tag{A2}$$

Where T is the number of time-series observations and N the number of cross-section units (for the derivation of the shorthand notation reported here, see Bun and Kiviet, 2003, p. 147). In particular, with an increasing level of accuracy, it is possible to identify different levels of bias:

$$B_1 = c_1\left(T^{-1}\right); \ B_2 = B_1 + c_2\left(N^{-1}T^{-1}\right); \ B_3 = B_2 + c_3\left(N^{-1}T^{-2}\right) \tag{A3}$$

In this study we corrected for the most comprehensive and accurate one (B_3). Therefore, the LSDV corrected estimator (LSDVC) is equal to:

$$LSDVC = LSDV - B_3 \tag{A4}$$

Again through their Monte Carlo experiments, Kiviet (1995), Judson and Owen (1999) and Bun and Kiviet (2001) have shown that the LSDVC estimator outperforms GMM estimators such as the Anderson-Hsiao and the Arellano-Bond for small samples.

However, the procedure has to be initialized by a consistent estimator to make the correction feasible, since the bias approximation depends on the unknown population parameters. Three possible options for this purpose are the Anderson-Hsiao, Arellano-Bond and Blundell-Bond estimators (these alternative procedures are asymptotically equivalent; (see Bruno, 2005b). In this study, we have initialized bias correction with the Arellano-Bond estimator.

Finally, the small size of the sample poses a problem in evaluating the variability of the coefficients. Indeed, Bun and Kiviet (2001) derived the asymptotic variance of the LSDVC estimator for large N. However, the estimated asymptotic standard errors may provide poor approximations in small samples, generating possibly unreliable t-statistics; in these cases, a possible solution is to use bootstrap methods, which generally provide approximations to the sampling distributions at least as accurate as approximations based upon first-order asymptotic assumptions (see also Bruno, 2005b). Accordingly, in this study the statistical significance of the LSDVC coefficients has been tested using bootstrapped standard errors (100 iterations).

Notes

1. In a standard framework, complementarity between innovation and skills means that the marginal expected return on innovation (in this case R&D expenditures) is increasing with the level of skills internal to the firm, or more formally that the cross-partial derivatives of the expected profitability function are positive.
2. In a related stream of literature (Katsoulacos and Ulph, 1998; Kultti and Takalo, 1998; Kamien and Zang, 2000) spillovers are 'endogenised' within the firm's overall innovation strategy.
3. An alternative possible measure of skills is the percentage of college graduates within a firm's workforce; unfortunately our dataset provides longitudinal data only for white and blue collars and not for education levels. This prevents the use of this variable in the following panel data analysis. However, the two ratios are generally highly correlated; in fact, the correlation coefficients in the two years (1997 and 2000) where education data are available turn out to be 0.90 and 0.88 respectively.
4. Although they are apparently very attractive for research purposes, these surveys are characterized by some shortcomings, the most important of which is that the sample overlapping across waves is unfortunately rather small.
5. Under the assumption that the disturbances are independent across firms.
6. Accordingly, in the following econometric analysis, regressions will include time dummies (see section 4.4).
7. Of course, it would have been better to take higher-degree lags of our main impact variable (WC/BC) into account; unfortunately, when dealing with short panels, a trade-off exists between the implementation of further lags and the acceptable extension of the time dimension of the dataset used.
8. In our analysis we wipe out all the firms' time-invariant fixed effects that might influence a firm's incentive to engage in R&D investment and which may explain

why only some firms are innovative (see Veugelers, 1997; Cassiman and Veugelers, 2002). While this is an important stream of literature in explaining both R&D and cooperative R&D decisions in a static, cross-sectional framework (see Colombo and Garrone, 1996; Piga and Vivarelli, 2003, 2004), in our dynamic analysis only innovative firms are considered and fixed effects are excluded through the LSDVC estimator.

9. Results are available from the authors upon request.
10. In our context 'long-run' elasticity takes into account the impact of both current and lagged WC/BC according to the formula $\frac{\vartheta + \kappa}{1 - \beta}$ (long-run multiplier, see Verbeek, 2004, p. 311).
11. With regard both to the sets of controls and dummies and to the adopted econometric method.

References

Acemoglu, D. (1996) 'A Micro Foundation for Social Increasing Returns in Human Capital Accumulation', *Quarterly Journal of Economics*, 111, pp. 779–804.

Acemoglu, D. (1998) 'Why Do New Technologies Complement Skills? Directed Technical Change and Wage Inequality', *Quarterly Journal of Economics*, 113, pp. 1055–90.

Anderson, T. W. and C. Hsiao (1981) 'Estimation of Dynamic Models with Error Components', *Journal of the American Statistical Association*, 76, pp. 598–606.

Antonelli, C. (1998) 'The Dynamics of Localized Technological Changes. The Interaction between Factor Costs Inducement, Demand Pull and Schumpeterian Rivalry', *Economics of Innovation and New Technology*, 6, pp. 97–120.

Arellano, M. and S. Bond (1991) 'Some Tests of Specification for Panel Data: Monte Carlo Evidence and an Application to Employment Equations', *Review of Economic Studies*, 58, pp. 277–97.

Arellano, M. and O. Bover (1995) 'Another Look at the Instrumental Variables Estimation of Error-components Models', *Journal of Econometrics*, 68, pp. 29–51.

Arthur, B. W. (1988) 'Competing Technologies: An Overview', in G. Dosi, C. Freeman, R. Nelson, G. Silverberg and L. Soete (eds) *Technical Change and Economic Theory* (London: Pinter), pp. 590–607.

Atkinson, A. B. and J. E. Stiglitz (1969) 'A New View of Technological Change', *Economic Journal*, 79, pp. 573–78.

Berman, E. and S. Machin (2000) 'Skill-biased Technology Transfer around the World', *Oxford Review of Economic Policy*, 16, pp. 12–22.

Berman, E. and S. Machin (2004) 'Skill-Biased Technological Change and Labour Demand', in E. Lee and M.Vivarelli (eds) *Understanding Globalization, Employment and Poverty Reduction* (New York: Palgrave Macmillan), pp. 39–66.

Berman, E., J. Bound and Z. Griliches (1994) 'Changes in the Demand for Skilled Labor Within US Manufacturing Industries: Evidence from the Annual Survey of Manufacturing', *Quarterly Journal of Economics*, 109, pp. 367–97.

Blundell, R. and S. Bond (1998) 'Initial Conditions and Moment Restrictions in Dynamic Panel Data Models', *Journal of Econometrics*, 87, pp. 115–43.

Braverman, H. (1974) *Labour and Monopoly Capital* (New York: Monthly Review Press).

Breschi, S., F. Malerba and L. Orsenigo (2000) 'Technological Regimes and Schumpeterian Patterns of Innovation', *Economic Journal*, 110, pp. 388–410.

Brouwer, E. and A. Kleinknecht (1999) 'Keynes-plus? Effective Demand and Changes in Firm-level R&D: An Empirical Note', *Cambridge Journal of Economics*, 23, pp. 385–91.

Bruno, G. S. F. (2005a) 'Approximating the Bias of the LSDV Estimator for Dynamic Unbalanced Panel Data Models', *Economics Letters*, 87, pp. 361–66.

Bruno, G. S. F. (2005b) 'Estimation and Inference in Dynamic Unbalanced Panel Data Models with a Small Number of Individuals', *The Stata Journal*, 5, pp. 473–500.

Bun, M. J. G. and J. F. Kiviet (2001) 'The Accuracy of Inference in Small Samples of Dynamic Panel Data Models', *Tinbergen Institute Discussion Paper* TI 2001-006/4.

Bun, M. J. G. and Kiviet, J. F. (2003) 'On the Diminishing Returns of Higher Order Terms in Asymptotic Expansions of Bias', *Economics Letters*, 79, pp. 145–52.

Cassiman, B. and R. Veugelers (2002) 'R&D Cooperation and Spillovers, Some Empirical Evidence from Belgium', *American Economic Review*, 92 , pp. 1169–84.

Cohen, W. M. and D. A. Levinthal (1989) 'Innovation and Learning: the Two Faces of R&D', *Economic Journal*, 99, pp. 569–96.

Cohen, W. M. and D. A. Levinthal (1990) 'Absorptive Capacity: A New Perspective on Learning and Innovation', *Administrative Science Quarterly*, 35, pp. 128–52.

Colombo, M. G. and P. Garrone (1996) 'Technological Cooperative Agreements and Firms' R&D Intensity: a Note on Causality Relations', *Research Policy*, 25, pp. 923–32.

CRIC (2005) *A Literature Review on Skills and Innovation. How Does Successful Innovation Impact on the Demand for Skills and How Do Skills Drive Innovation?*, CRIC report for the Department of Trade and Industry, Centre for Research on Innovation and Competition, University of Manchester.

David, P. (1985) 'Clio and the Economics of QWERTY', *American Economic Review Proceedings*, 75, pp. 332–37.

Doms, M., T. Dunne and K. Troske (1997) 'Workers, Wages and Technology', *Quarterly Journal of Economics*, 112, pp. 253–90.

Dosi, G. (1988) 'Source, Procedure and Microeconomic Effect of Innovation', *Journal of Economic Literature*, 26, pp. 1120–71.

Dunne, T. and K. Troske (2005) 'Technology Adoption and the Skill Mix of US Manufacturing Plants', *Scottish Journal of Political Economy*, 52, pp. 387–405.

Finegold, D. and D. Soskice (1988) 'The Failure of Training in Britain: Analysis and Prescription', *Oxford Review of Economic Policy*, 4, pp. 21–51.

Freeman, C. and L. Soete (1994) *Work for All or Mass Unemployment* (London: Pinter).

Funk, P. and T. Vogel (2004) 'Endogenous Skill Bias', *Journal of Economic Dynamics and Control*, 28, pp. 2155–93.

Goldin, C. and L. F. Katz (1998) 'The Origins of Technology-skill Complementarity', *Quarterly Journal of Economics*, 113, pp. 693–732.

Griliches, Z. (1969) 'Capital–Skill Complementarity', *Review of Economics and Statistics*, 51, pp. 465–68.

Hall, B., J. Mairesse, L. Branstetter and B. Crépon (1999) 'Does Cash Flow Cause Investment and R&D? An Exploration Using Panel Data for French, Japanese, and United States Scientific Firms', in D. Audretsch and R. Thurik (eds) *Innovation, Industry Evolution and Employment* (Cambridge: Cambridge University Press), pp. 129–56.

Haskel, J. E. and Y. Heden (1999) 'Computers and the Demand for Skilled Labour: Industry and Establishment-level Panel Evidence for the UK', *Economic Journal*, 109, pp. C68–C79.

Hicks, J. R. (1932) *The Theory of Wages* (London: Macmillan).

Judson, R. A. and A. L. Owen 'Estimating Dynamic Panel Data Models: a Guide for Macroeconomists', *Economics Letters*, 65: 1, pp. 9–15.

Kamien, M. I. and I. Zang (2000) 'Meet Me Halfway: Research Joint Ventures and Absorptive Capacity', *International Journal of Industrial Organization*, 18, pp. 995–1012.

Katsoulacos, Y. and D. Ulph (1998) 'Endogenous Spillovers and Research Joint Ventures', *Journal of Industrial Economics*, 96, pp. 333–57.

Kiley, M. T. (1999) 'The Supply of Skilled Labour and Skill-biased Technological Progress', *Economic Journal*, 109, pp. 708–24.

Kiviet, J. F. (1995) 'On Bias, Inconsistency, and Efficiency of Various Estimators in Dynamic Panel Data Models', *Journal of Econometrics*, 68, pp. 53–78.

Kiviet, J. F. (1999) 'Expectation of Expansions for Estimators in a Dynamic Panel Data Model; Some Results for Weakly Exogenous Regressors', in C. Hsiao, K. Lahiri, L. F. Lee and M. H. Pesaran (eds) *Analysis of Panel Data and Limited Dependent Variables* (Cambridge: Cambridge University Press), pp. 199–225.

Kleinknecht, A. and B. Verspagen (1990) 'Demand and Innovation: Schmookler Reexamined', *Research Policy*, 19, pp. 387–94.

Kultti, K. and T. Takalo (1998) 'R&D Spillovers and Information Exchange', *Economics Letters*, 61, pp. 21–3.

Judson, R. A. and A. L. Owen (1999) 'Estimating Dynamic Panel Data Models: A Guide for Macroeconomists', *Economics Letters*, 65, pp. 9–15.

Leiponen, A. (2000) 'Competencies, Innovation and Profitability of Firms', *Economics of Innovation and New Technology*, 9, pp. 1–24.

Leiponen, A. (2005) 'Skills and Innovation', *International Journal of Industrial Organization*, 23, pp. 303–23.

Machin, S. (1996) 'Changes in the Relative Demand for Skills in the UK Labor Market', in A. Booth and D. Snower (eds) *Acquiring Skills: Market Failures, Their Symptoms and Policy Responses* (Cambridge: Cambridge University Press), pp. 129–46.

Machin, S. and J. van Reenen (1998) 'Technology and Changes in the Skill Structure: Evidence from Seven OECD Countries', *Quarterly Journal of Economics*, 113, pp. 1215–44.

Malerba, F. (2005) 'Sectoral Systems of Innovation: A Framework for Linking Innovation to the Knowledge Base, Structure and Dynamics of Sectors', *Economics of Innovation and New Technology*, 14, pp. 63–82.

Malerba, F. and L. Orsenigo (1996) 'Schumpeterian Patterns of Innovation', *Cambridge Journal of Economics*, 19, pp. 47–65.

Marx, K. (1961) *Capital* (Moscow: Foreign Languages Publishing House) (first edition: 1867).

Milgrom, P. and J. Roberts (1990) 'The Economics of Modern Manufacturing: Technology, Strategy, and Organization', *American Economic Review*, 80, pp. 511–28.

Milgrom, P. and J. Roberts (1995) 'Complementarities and Firms: Strategy, Structure and Organisational Change in Manufacturing', *Journal of Accounting and Economics*, 19, pp. 179–208.

Nickell, S. and D. Nicolitsas (1997) 'Human Capital Investment and Innovation: What Are the Connections'? Paper CEPDP0370 (London: Centre for Economic Performance).

Pavitt, K. (1984) 'Sectoral Patterns of Technical Change: Towards a Taxonomy and a Theory', *Research Policy*, 3, pp. 343–73.

Piga, C. A. and M. Vivarelli (2003) 'Sample Selection in Estimating the Determinants of Cooperative R&D', *Applied Economics Letters*, 10, pp. 243–46.

Piga, C. A. and M. Vivarelli (2004) 'Internal and External R&D: A Sample Selection Approach', *Oxford Bulletin of Economics and Statistics*, 66, pp. 457–82.

Piva, M. and M. Vivarelli (2006) 'Is Demand-Pulled Innovation Equally Important in Different Groups of Firms?', IZA Discussion Paper no. 1982, February (Bonn: IZA).

Piva, M. and M. Vivarelli (2007) 'Demand-Pulled Innovation under Liquidity Constraints', *Applied Economics Letters*, forthcoming.

Rosenberg, N. (1982) *Inside the Black Box: Technology and Economics* (Cambridge: Cambridge University Press).

Ruttan, V. W. (1997) 'Induced Innovation, Evolutionary Theory and Path Dependence: Sources of Technical Change', *Economic Journal*, 107, pp. 1520–29.

Scherer, F. M. (1982) 'Demand-pull and Technological Invention: Schmookler Revisited', *Journal of Industrial Economics*, 30, pp. 225–37.

J. Schmookler (1966) *Invention and Economic Growth* (Cambridge, MA: Harvard University Press).

Topkis, D. M. (1998) *Super Modularity and Complementarity* (Princeton: Princeton University Press).

Verbeek, M. (2004) *A Guide to Modern Econometrics*, 2nd edition (Chichester: Wiley).

Veugelers, R. (1997) 'Internal R&D Expenditures and External Technology Sourcing', *Research Policy*, 26, pp. 305–15.

Vivarelli, M. (1995), *The Economics of Technology and Employment: Theory and Empirical Evidence* (Cheltenham: Edward Elgar), reprinted 1997.

Wilson, R. and T. Hogarth (2003) *Tackling the Low Skills Equilibrium: A Review of Issues and some New Evidence* (London: Department of Trade and Industry).

Part II
Linking Internal to External Organization

5
Designing the Organization for Innovation

Vittorio Chiesa and Federico Frattini

5.1 Introduction

The external environment in which firms have been competing in the last decades has profoundly changed, both in high-technology and in more mature industries. Accordingly, a significant evolution in the way in which the technological innovation process is managed has occurred as well. Since innovation is often the single most important driver of economic value creation, most innovative and successful firms have adapted their approach to innovation management to the changing external environment, in an attempt to protect or nurture their competitive advantage.

What are the organizational implications of these changes? How do most innovative and successful firms organize themselves for innovating efficiently and effectively in their rapidly evolving external environment? This paper attempts to answer to these questions, according to the following conceptual model (Figure 5.1).

We define *organization for innovation* as the set of organizational dimensions that influence a firm's capability to manage technological innovation efficiently and effectively. Adopting the standpoint of the contingency theory (Galbraith, 1973; Birkinshaw et al., 2002), this paper tries to answer the following research question: how can a firm design an organization for

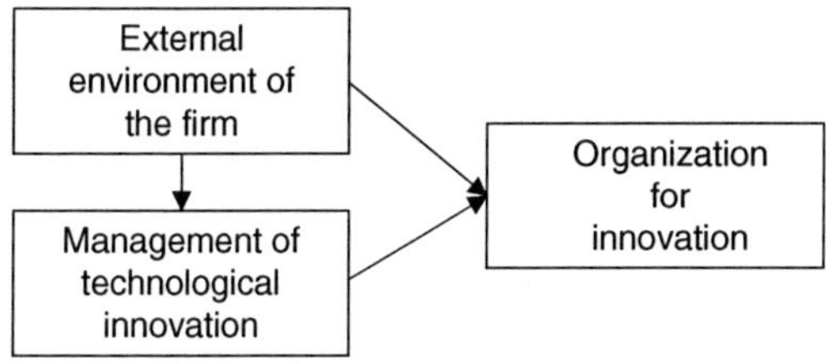

Figure 5.1   The conceptual model

innovation that fits with its external environment and with the approaches it employs for managing technological innovation? (see Figure 5.1).

The paper is structured as follows: in the next two sections we describe the major trends that have characterized the external environment of the firm and their implications for the way in which technological innovation is managed. In the fourth and fifth sections we briefly review literature about organization for innovation and describe the research standpoint adopted in the paper. The sixth and seventh sections, which represent the core of the paper, address the problem of designing the structural dimensions of the organization for innovation. Finally, we draw some conclusions and outline future directions of research.

5.2 The external environment of the firm

The major trends that have characterized the external environment of the firm in the last decades, and that have influenced the way in which companies manage technological innovation, can be synthesized as follows (see Ortt and Smits, 2006, for a comprehensive review):

- *Dynamicity and turbulence*. Market arenas are getting more and more turbulent and dynamic: customer needs, competitors, business models and the set of competencies necessary to compete in a definite industry change over time with a frequency much higher than ever (Wolf, 2006; Mohr et al., 2005);
- *Globalization of markets and business activities*. Globalization has fostered homogeneity in customer needs but, at the same time, has renewed companies' interest toward the satisfaction of local demand (Gupta and Wilemon, 1996);
- *Increased competition*. Globalization, liberalization and convergence of markets and technologies have increased competition in several industries, both at a domestic and at a global level (Gupta and Wilemon, 1996);
- *Rapid advances in technology*. New knowledge is developed and applied to products and services faster and faster (Bayus, 1994; Wind and Mahajan, 1997). Consequently, life-cycles are shortening in some product categories (Nevens et al., 1990), a greater number of new products and services are being introduced over time, and the time between subsequent innovations is decreasing (Bayus, 1998).

5.3 The management of technological innovation

5.3.1 Major trends in technology management

The evolutionary patterns we described pose significant challenges for companies and influence the way in which they manage technological innovation. The major trends in technology management that have emerged with the abovementioned changes of the external environment can be synthesised as follows:

- *End of the linear model of innovation.* Traditionally, technological innovation was conceived as a sequential process that linearly proceeded from idea generation, through development, prototyping and testing, manufacturing and market launch. The input of this process was either a technology advancement (the *technology push* approach), the identification of a market need (the *market pull* approach), or a combination of the two (the *interactive* or *coupling* model) (Rothwell and Zegveld, 1985). This point of view has radically changed in the last decades; technological innovation has become a flexible, iterative process, contemporarily involving R&D and other functions, characterized by a strong participation of both suppliers and lead users and by a systemic nature (Ortt and Smits, 2006; Rothwell, 1994; Nelson, 1993);
- *Increased reliance upon external sources of technology.* Firms generally lack the financial and technical resources to build the whole range of competencies they need and hence move towards a higher level of technical specialization, concentrating internal R&D efforts on core activities where they are more likely to excel. Contemporarily, they rely strongly on external sources of technology to access the other required competencies and to feed their innovation pipeline with higher frequency and continuity (Chatterji, 1996; Howells, 1999; Roberts, 2001; Jones et al., 2000; Chatterji and Manuel, 1993);
- *Leverage on multiple channels for technology exploitation.* Traditionally, firms have exploited innovations, incorporating them into products or services that were internally developed and launched in the final market. Nevertheless, the costs required to develop new technologies and the speed at which new knowledge is developed make sustainable long-term growth even more dependent on the continual and full leverage of a company's technology basis. Therefore, firms are contemporarily using multiple channels for converting their technologies into incomes, among which external exploitation paths (such as patent sale or licensing out, new venture spin-off or contract research) are used more and more (Mohr et al., 2005; Haour, 2004);
- *The entrepreneurial nature of R&D.* Traditionally, R&D was considered part of the firm's overhead costs (Ortt and Smits, 2006) and conceived as a technology-led unit where all innovation opportunities were generated and developed until ready to be released to manufacturing and marketing. Nowadays, internal R&D becomes the repository of the firm's core technological competencies but, at the same time, it is the *engine* of the innovation process and performs critical *brokering* functions, such as the scouting of the external environment for the

identification of valuable sources of knowledge and the integration of internally generated with externally acquired technologies (Ortt and Smits, 2006);

- *Birth and growth of markets for technology.* The search for multiple channels for commercializing the output of firms' innovative efforts, the specialization in knowledge production and the related division of labour within innovative activities have brought the birth of so-called *markets for technology* (Arora et al., 2001). The capability to interact with these markets for technology has become a further critical determinant of most successful firms' innovative behaviour (MacPherson, 1997a, 1997b; Mueller and Zenker, 2001; Jones et al., 2000);
- *Management of R&D and innovation on an international scale.* Finally, the management of technological innovation has assumed a prominent international dimension. In fact, studies of the internationalization of innovation processes indisputably show that foreign R&D is becoming a significant component of many countries' R&D base (Jones and Teegen, 2002; United Nations, 2005).

5.3.2   Emerging paradigms in the management of technological innovation

Chesbrough (2003) and Haour (2004) have carefully studied these high-profile changes in the management of technology and have systematized them into two similar and insightful models of the technological innovation process, the *open innovation* paradigm and the *distributed innovation* system. Chesbrough (2003) compares the *closed innovation* paradigm, typically adopted by firms in past decades, with the *open innovation* one, used by modern and highly competitive enterprises (including Procter & Gamble, IBM and Intel). Closed innovation holds that 'companies must generate their own ideas, and then develop them, build them, market them, distribute them, service them, finance them, and support them on their own' (p. xx). According to Chesbrough, this logic is no longer sustainable in those contexts where some *erosion factors* are in place (for example, the growing mobility of highly experienced and skilled people, the increasing presence of private venture capital, and the existence of a market for technology). Here a new approach is emerging, that assumes that firms 'can and should use external ideas as well as internal ones, and internal and external paths to market' (p. xxiv) as they look to advance their technology. Similarly, Haour (2004) believes that technology firms must learn to leverage a wide range of alternative channels for realizing the value of their technology base: they ought to 'set up licensing activities, as IBM has done, co-develop, but also sell certain innovation projects, spin out ventures and become involved in innovation mining' (p. 87).

5.4   The organization for innovation

These emerging paradigms in the management of technological innovation have a very general nature and do not account for those organizational and practical issues that innovative firms have to deal with. Indisputably, one of the major problems for modern companies that want to revolutionize their attitude towards technological innovation is to design an organization that adequately supports and nurtures its innovative efforts (Tirpak et al., 2006). We call this *organization for innovation*, which is defined as the set of organizational dimensions that influence a firm's capability to manage technological innovation efficiently and effectively.

Several research contributions have been written so far that deeply investigate the problem of designing a specific dimension of this organization; the main variables that have been studied can be classified as follows:

- *Organizational structure variables*:
  - *Macro-level variables*:
    - *The organization for external innovation*: this is concerned with the choice of the innovation activities to be internally undertaken and with the selection of the organizational forms according to which the innovative firm should interact with external organizations (Lichtenthaler, 2004; Chiesa and Manzini, 1998; Croisier, 1998; Brockhoff, 1992);
    - *The coexistence of innovating and operating organizations within the firm's overall structure*: this entails the decision as to whether to dedicate a separate organization for pursuing radical innovation opportunities (O'Reilly and Tushman, 2004; Govindarajan and Trimble, 2005; Galbraith, 1984);
    - *The organizational decentralization of innovative activities*: this deals with the hierarchical level of the firm's organization at which R&D activities are located (Chiesa, 2001; Rieck and Dickson, 1993; Eto, 1992);
    - *The international organization of innovative activities*: this is concerned with the geographical localization of R&D and innovation processes (von Zedtwitz and Gassmann, 2002; Chiesa, 1996a, 1996b);
    - *The organizational separation between research and development*: this involves the decision whether to locate research and development activities in separate organizational units (Chiesa, 2001);
    - *The resource allocation mechanisms in the organization for innovation*: this is concerned with the choice of the mechanisms through which financial resources are allocated to the units that comprise the

organization for innovation (Argyres and Silverman, 2004; West, 2000; Birkinshaw and Fey, 2000);

- *Micro-level variables*:

  - *The organization of R&D units*: this is concerned with the organization of researchers, engineers and scientists working in the same R&D unit (Chiesa, 2001; Allen, 2001; Eto, 1992; Kay, 1988);
  - *The organization of new-product development teams* (Clark and Fuji-moto, 1991);
  - *The cross-functional integration in the new-product development process*: this deals with the choice of the organizational mechanisms through which the coordination of the functions relevant to the NPD process can be achieved (Griffin and Hauser, 1996; Vasconcellos, 1994; Wood and Brown, 1998; Song et al., 1996; Nihtilä, 1999);

- *Informal organization variables*:

  - *Informal organizational roles and knowledge management systems*: these are necessary for nurturing innovation and spurring creativity in the organization (Tushman and Nadler, 1986; Narduzzo, 1999; Brown and Duguid, 2001);

- *Human resource management variables*:

  - *Reward systems and career paths* for scientists and technical professionals (Risher, 2000; Katz and Allen, 1997; Thompson et al., 1988);
  - *Control mechanisms and managerial styles* to be applied to the different units of the organization for innovation (Abernethy and Brownell, 1997; Holt, 1978).

5.5   Research objectives and methodology

This paper aims at answering the following basic research question: how can a firm design an organization for innovation that fits with its external environment and with the approaches it employs for managing technological innovation? We will concentrate here on the structural dimensions of the organization for innovation; in particular, we will focus on the *macro-level variables* listed in the previous section.

This research problem is fundamentally addressed from the standpoint of contingency theory (Galbraith, 1973). According to this approach, there is not a best way of organizing a firm; the most appropriate solutions to the major organizational design problems depend on a set of contingency variables such as the characteristics of the external environment in which the firm competes, its strategic positioning, and the technology it is actually leveraging (Birkinshaw et al., 2002). The theoretical framework we adopt in the paper is set out in Figure 5.2, which replicates the general model depicted in Figure 5.1.

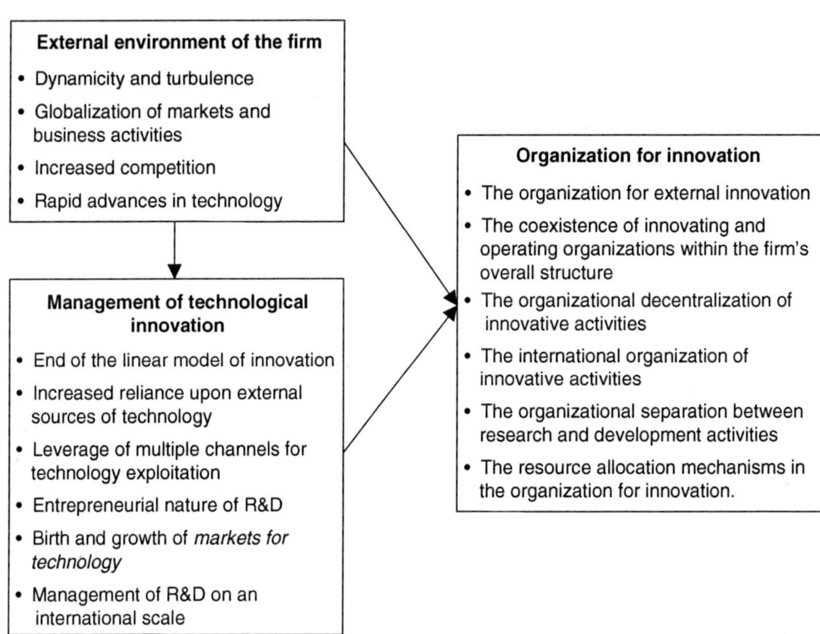

Figure 5.2   The chapter's theoretical framework

This framework advances the argument that two major interrelated contingency variables influence the way in which the macro-level structural dimensions of the organization for innovation should be designed: the characteristics of the external environment in which the firm is competing and the strategies and approaches it employs for managing technological innovation (in Figure 5.2 we list some of the major characteristics that these two variables have assumed in the last decades). For instance, the fragmentation and globalization of markets, and rapid changes in clients' requirements and their heterogeneity, bring firms to geographically dispersed development labs in order to get as close as possible to the final market and easily exploit local opportunities (this is an example of influence exerted by the external environment on the characteristics of the organization for innovation). Similarly, a strong reliance upon technology developed by external organizations causes firms to put in place appropriate organizational mechanisms for accessing these sources of specialized knowledge, such as corporate venturing initiatives or licensing in committees (this is an example of influence exerted by the way in which the innovation process is managed in the organization for innovation). The two aforementioned contextual variables are nevertheless strictly interrelated; specifically, the way in which the innovation process is managed often reflects some characteristics of the external environment of the firm. For instance, a strong reliance upon external sources of technology is mainly the result of the increase in the costs required to develop new technologies, their complexity and degree of specialization, as well as the acceleration in the speed at which knowledge is developed.

From a methodological point of view, we will undertake analytical theory-building (or relationship-building) research (Handfield and Melnyk, 1998); more specifically, we will use an analytical conceptual approach, whose purpose is 'to add new insights into traditional problems through logical relationship building' (Wacker, 1998, p. 373). Basically, we will apply the contingency theory standpoint (as synthesized in the framework in Figure 5.2) for interpreting the best available theories on the organization for innovation; in this way, we will deduce new relationships between our three fundamental research concepts (external environment of the firm, management of technological innovation, and organization for innovation), that will allow us to answer this chapter's basic research question. Our conceptualizations will be illustrated through some empirical observations, as is usual with analytical conceptual research (Wacker, 1998).

In the remainder of the paper, the results will be presented assuming the perspective of the manager or the decision-maker who is actually called upon to design the organization for innovation for his/her company. For each structural dimension, therefore, we will: 1) define the variable and its role in the organization for innovation; 2) examine the major alternatives available to the decision-maker; and 3) analyse the advantages and disadvantages of the different solutions and their distinctive fields of application. Moreover, empirical cases describing the experience of innovative and successful firms will be provided in order to enrich the discussion. In this way, we will advance a systematization of the problem of the design of the organization for innovation, an issue that has been only fragmentarily addressed in the literature so far, and we will throw light upon the great complexity of this challenge, a project that entails the coordination of several interconnected variables.

5.6　Designing the organization for innovation: discussion and empirical cases

5.6.1　The organization for external innovation

The first challenge firms should confront when designing the structure of their organization for innovation is the identification of the most adequate *degree of openness* towards the external environment; this requires identifying those stages of the innovation process that are going to be internally undertaken and those for which the innovative firm is going to rely on external organizations; it calls for specific solutions both during the generation of a technological innovation and throughout its exploitation and commercialization.

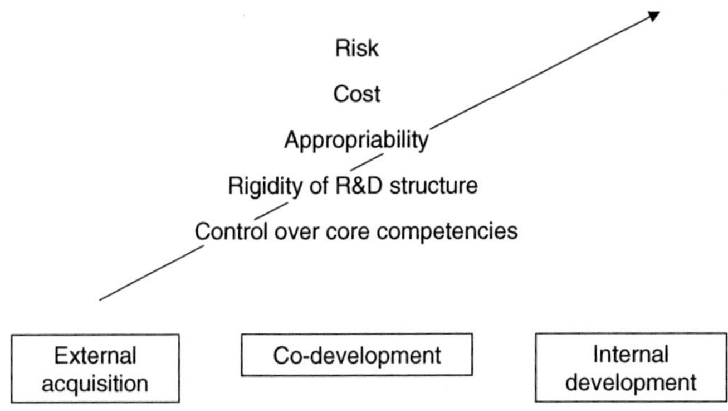

Figure 5.3   Advantages and disadvantages of alternative organizational modes for the generation of technological innovation (adapted from Chiesa, 2001)

Balancing the internal and external generation of innovation

Firms are increasingly exploiting external sources of technology in order to complement their technical expertise (Chatterji, 1996; Roberts, 2001); this calls for the recognition of the R&D activities that will nurture the firm's core competencies and that therefore should be kept internal, and the choice of an adequate balance between internal development, external acquisition and the co-development of other technical competencies. Each of these three alternatives has a different impact over the major critical dimensions of the process of technology generation, as it is shown in Figure 5.3. In particular, the risks and the costs inherent in the development of a specific technology, as well as the rigidity of the firm's R&D structure, are higher when internal development is preferred to the co-development and external acquisition modes. Nevertheless, internal development allows for a higher appropriability of the developed technology and ensures closer control over the firm's core competencies.

In the generation of a definite technology, external acquisition becomes more appropriate than internal development under the following conditions:

- The higher the complexity and the degree of specialisation of the technology (Hagedoorn, 1993);
- The higher the costs and the technical risks that its development process entails (Cooper and Kleinschmidt, 1987);
- The higher the pace of advancement in the specific technological discipline (Sen and Rubinstein, 1990);
- The higher the availability of external sources of technical knowledge (Chesbrough, 2003);
- The higher the appropriability of the technology (Tidd et al., 2005).

These conditions are met, for instance, in the pharmaceutical industry, where firms have been relying intensively on external sources of technology for a long time (Arora and Gambardella, 1990).

The capability of a company to profitably exploit external sources of technology requires that it proactively screens the external environment in order to identify which potential sources to rely on. In regard to this, firms should monitor private technical and scientific service companies, search for collaborative R&D in the innovation ecosystem and monitor possible relationships with entrepreneurial universities. Moreover, the organizational mode to be adopted for accessing this pool of external resources should be carefully selected; the most diffused alternatives in this respect are: acquisitions, licensing-in agreements, minority-equity investments, joint ventures, joint R&D agreements, funding of research at universities or governmental labs, alliances and partnerships, R&D consortia, networking and R&D outsourcing (Roberts and Berry, 1985; Brockhoff, 1991; Chatterji, 1996; Chiesa, 2001).

Boxes 5.1 and 5.2 describe the organizational approaches adopted by two leading and highly innovative firms, Cisco and Procter & Gamble, for leveraging available external sources of technology. Cisco has intensively applied an external acquisition strategy for complementing its competence basis; this strategy has entailed the financing of R&D activities of small entrepreneurial start-ups, under the agreement that the network equipment manufacturer retains the possibility of acquiring these firms in case their research results in something that can be commercially exploited. This approach is remarkable since it allows Cisco to lower the risks and the costs inherent in the development of radical technological capabilities, while maintaining a strong appropriability over the outcome of the R&D activities it subsidizes and a close control over its core competencies.

Procter & Gamble is an example of a firm that has purposefully and systematically decided to rely on the knowledge available in its external environment in order to sustain its innovation processes; in order to enable this strategy, it has established a set of proprietary and open networks through which it scans its knowledge-rich external environment. This is an organizational solution that allows Procter & Gamble to reach and scan an enormous pool of potential knowledge contributors, although the appropriability of the knowledge that it makes possible is rather weak.

Balancing the internal and external exploitation of technology

Firms should not look outside their boundaries only to access external organizations capable of providing valuable technical inputs to their innovation process. They have understood that opening up to the external environment can be a viable alternative for creating and capturing value from their technological innovations. The process through which firms transfer technological

---

**Box 5.1 Cisco's *spin-in* strategy for accessing external
sources of technology**

Cisco, the leading networking equipment manufacturer, has since 1994
adopted a particular strategy, called *spin-in*, for leveraging the technological knowledge retained by external organizations. When the company
needs a technology that is not part of its core competency base, it proactively scans the external environment searching for a small start-up that
is currently working in the field. Cisco commits itself to finance the start-
up's research expenses, under the agreement that Cisco will have the
possibility to acquire the start-up in case its research activities produce
something suitable for commercially exploitation. Since 1995, Cisco has
acquired 87 small firms, most of them located in the San Francisco area;
49 were working on service-provider technologies. An interesting version of the *spin-in* strategy is called *spin-out, spin-in*; this is generally
adopted when there are no small firms currently working on the specific
technology essential for Cisco. In this case it encourages some valuable
researchers to leave the company through a *spin-out* process and finances
the research activities of the newly founded firm. As well, it maintains the
possibility of acquiring the *spin-out* in case it produces relevant research
results. This strategy was adopted in 1999 with Andiamo, a *spin-out*
firm operating in the field of big-disk hardware and software for web-
server applications; it was reincorporated into Cisco in 2003. According
to Cisco, the *spin-in* strategy allowed it to increase the speed of activating
new research projects, to maintain flexibility in corporate research labs
and to ensure an entrepreneurial and stimulating environment where
new technological opportunities are far more likely to flourish.

(adapted from Conti, 2006)

---

knowledge, not yet developed into a final product or service, to an external
organization in exchange for compensation, either monetary or in terms of
knowledge transfer, is called *external exploitation of technological innovation*
(Lichtenthaler, 2004). The problem, again, is to find the most adequate balance between internal and external exploitation of technology; the major
advantages and disadvantages of choosing an external exploitation path are
listed in Table 5.1.

The external exploitation of a technological innovation should be pursued
under the following conditions (Mohr et al., 2005):

- The technology does not fit with the firm's corporate mission or business
  model (Chesbrough, 2003);

Box 5.2   Procter & Gamble's *Connect & Develop* innovation model

Procter & Gamble has always generated technological opportunities and innovations capable of sustaining its impressive growth within the boundaries of its global research facilities, which employed the most talented scientists and researchers. By 2000, however, P&G's top management realised that this *invent-it-ourselves* approach was no longer sustainable, because of the dramatic changes in the innovation environment of the firm. This impression was confirmed by the collapse of P&G's R&D productivity and innovation success rate. A. G. Lafley, the company's CEO, realized that relevant innovation was being undertaken by a dispersed system of actors surrounding P&G research facilities; these included small entrepreneurial companies, individuals, and government and university labs. He estimated that for each of the 7,500 P&G researchers there were elsewhere in the world about 200 scientists or technicians who were equally talented. Lafley decided to reinvent the company's innovation model, and stipulated that almost 50 per cent of P&G's innovations should be acquired from external sources; this approach was called *Connect & Develop* and it was aimed at systematically finding good ideas from outside the firm and bringing them within the company's boundaries, in order to capitalize on and exploit them through the use of internal R&D capabilities. In order to sustain the *Connect & Develop* model, an appropriate organization ought to be put in place: P&G leverages several networks that represent the platform for the *Connect & Develop* strategy. It is possible to distinguish between:

- *Proprietary networks*, specifically developed by P&G in order to support the new innovation model. The most important two are the *technology entrepreneurs* network and the *suppliers network*. The first comprises 70 technology entrepreneurs and P&G senior employees who systematically: 1) examine scientific literature, patent databases and other data sources; 2) build connections, organizing meetings with universities and industry researchers; 3) analyse products and visit marketplaces; and 4) promote the gathered ideas and connections to managers of P&G's business units. They are based around the world and organised in six *Connect & Develop* hubs, in China, India, Japan, Western Europe, Latin America and the United States. Each hub focuses on technological opportunities and innovation that are typical of its region. So far, technology entrepreneurs have identified almost 10,000 product ideas and technologies that have undergone a structured evaluation process. The suppliers' network connects the 50,000 researchers of the 15 major P&G suppliers. A secure IT infrastructure has been implemented so that P&G can share with its suppliers new technological opportunities and ask for assistance when it faces a specific problem. This platform is reinforced by personal meetings between P&G and suppliers' technology leaders that help the reciprocal understanding of core capabilities and favour the flow of ideas.

* *Open networks*, sponsored or simply joined by P&G in order to sustain its *Connect & Develop* activities. P&G participated in the creation of *NineSigma*, a brokering company that connects firms that have technology and innovation problems with consultants, government and private labs, universities and firms that can find appropriate solutions. Moreover, it was heavily influenced by *InnoCentive*, an Eli Lilly initiative similar to *NineSigma*, although one more focused on technical problems. In 2000, P&G invested, together with other *Fortune 100* companies, in Yet2.com, an online marketplace for intellectual property exchange and technology transfer. Finally, in 2003 it sponsored a business called YourEncore, a network connecting about 800 distinguished retired scientists and engineers from 150 companies.

(adapted from Huston and Sakkab, 2006)

Table 5.1 Advantages and disadvantages of external exploitation of technology (adapted from Mohr et al., 2005; Lichtenthaler, 2004; Chesbrough, 2003)

EXTERNAL EXPLOITATION OF TECHNOLOGY

Advantages	Disadvantages
Maximize the return on technology and innovation investments	Risk of losing control over proprietary technologies
Find a way to market to innovations that do not fit the company's business model	Inefficiency of technology markets and high transaction costs
Share costs and risks of the commercialization process	Share the revenues of the commercialization process with third parties
Acquire lacking complementary assets (such as distribution channels)	'Not-sold-here' syndrome
Leverage the entrepreneurial spirit of researchers and technical professionals working outside the boundaries of a large corporation	

- The innovative firm misses some critical complementary assets (for example, production capacity or distribution channels) or has insufficient financial resources to internally exploit the innovation (Teece, 1986);
- The window of opportunity is tight and the firm cannot move quickly enough;
- The market potential for the innovation is smaller than foreseen;
- The destination market is characterized by demand-side increasing returns and offering the technology to competitors may encourage the standardization of the firm's innovation (Schilling, 2003);
- The high costs required to develop the technology and the rapid advances in knowledge generation force the innovative firm to leverage multiple channels for maximizing the return on its innovation investments;
- The appropriability of the innovation is high and therefore the risk of losing control over proprietary knowledge and technologies is low.

In order to best profit from external exploitation of technology, firms should learn to scout and choose the potential acquirers of their proprietary technical expertise, build formal and informal bridges across their boundaries through the establishment, for example, of ad hoc gatekeeping functions, and to select the most appropriate organizational mode for pursuing an external commercialization effort. As far as this last issue is concerned, a firm can organize the external exploitation of a technological innovation in several ways (Lichtenthaler, 2004; Haour, 2004; Chesbrough, 2003); through the sale of the rights of use of the novel technology, the spin-out of a new venture that ends the development process and brings the technology into the market, the establishment of joint ventures or partnerships aimed at the innovation's commercial exploitation, or the sale of the whole innovation project to a third party.

Box 5.3 describes the case of Generics, a successful technology-intensive company whose business model encompasses a particular combination of organizational modes for the external exploitation of its innovative capabilities. The example of Generics shows how a firm can commercially make the most of its knowledge basis while at the same time using various channels for external technology exploitation (for example, the sale of technical services, a new venture spin-out, and seed capital financing) and how the sustainability of this business model is ensured by the capability to create mutual reinforcing mechanisms between these different channels.

5.6.2 The coexistence of innovating and operating organizations within the firm's overall structure

Galbraith (1984) states that one of the most important reasons behind the difficulties that firms encounter in managing incremental and radical

> ## Box 5.3 Exploiting technological innovation through multiple channels: the case of Generics
>
> **Generics** is a technology-intensive firm whose core business is centred on the generation and commercial exploitation of scientific and technological knowledge. It was founded in 1986 in Cambridge, Great Britain; as of 2004 it employed almost 230 people, of whom 150 were technical professionals and scientists with advanced degrees, and owned state-of-the-art laboratory facilities. It went public in 2000 and is listed on the London Stock Exchange. Generics delivers value from its huge scientific and technological competence base through three major interrelated channels:
>
> - *Sale of technical services.* Generics helps its clients improve their competitiveness by developing for them new products, processes or solving technical problems. These projects are performed by Generics under a contractual agreement signed with the client that clearly defines the intellectual property rights it will be granted, both in terms of scope and of geographical extension. This contract R&D activity is a source of innovation for Generics that retains the possibility to exploit it outside the scope defined by the contract.
> - *New venture spin-out.* Generics encourages small groups of employees with commercially valuable ideas to prepare a business case and a spin-out proposal and to submit it to the *Innovation Exploitation Board*. This board is made up of five to seven Generics employees with relevant and heterogeneous technical competencies that meets every week to evaluate spinning-out candidates. When the board approves a proposal, the technical professionals (two or three) who have sponsored it can leave the laboratories and create a spin-out firm. The team moves to another building. Generics therefore acts like an incubator for these new ventures. All intellectual property rights are transferred to the start-up, whose main shareholder is Generics itself; the minority equity is owned by the founding team. When the venture has developed, Generics helps the management to find a suitable buyer for the firm; most of the sales revenues of course go to the major shareholder, that is Generics, and help finance the firm's seed capital activity. Each year, several start-ups are generated.
> - *Seed capital.* Generics manages several funds that invest in its own intellectual property, in new spin-out ventures and external start-ups operating in technologies and business areas familiar to Generics. Each fund has its own management team searching for new

> opportunities and managing the portfolio. When Generics puts seed capital into external ventures, it acts as a venture capitalist; this is possible because of the firm's scientific and technical competencies that allow for effective due-diligence processes.

(adapted from Haour, 2004)

innovations at the same time is that they require two significantly different organizations:

- The *Operating Organization* (OO), which is the set of structures, processes, values, managerial practices and organizational roles that are necessary to manage everyday business activities and generate incremental improvements to existing products and processes;
- The *Innovating Organization* (IO), which is indeed essential to foster the generation, deployment and commercialization of radical and disruptive technological breakthroughs.

At a macro-organizational level, the way in which these two different organizations coexist within the innovating firm is a crucial determinant of the company's ability to manage both incremental and radical innovations. In respect of this basic design challenge, two major alternatives exist:

An organizational fusion of the innovating and operating organizations

In this first case, it is not possible to distinguish between the two different types of organizations. In other words, functional units such as R&D, marketing, finance, manufacturing and business development are responsible at the same time for: 1) managing everyday business activities, where efficiency and the capability to respect established procedures and rules is a critical success factor; 2) developing and implementing incremental improvements to existing products or services, that typically require proactively gathering market information and timely and efficient reaction to business opportunities that come to light; 3) generating, deploying and actually bringing to market radical innovations, which indeed call for an extremely specialized knowledge in certain technological domains and a huge amount of creativity in order to generate breakthrough technological opportunities and find fruitful business applications for them.

   As the innovating and operating organisations coincide, a further design choice comes into play between:

- a function-oriented organisation, where all R&D activities are aggregated within the same organizational unit, alongside the other functions

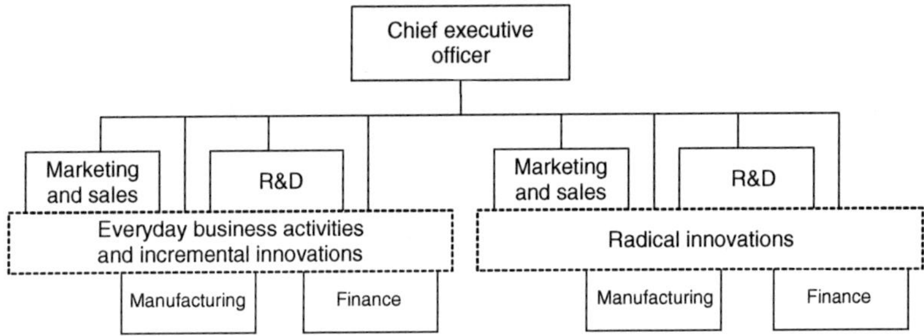

Figure 5.4   The ambidextrous organization

inherent in the technological innovation process – marketing, finance, manufacturing, for example;

- a product-oriented organization, which is typical of medium and large firms with several product lines and implies that major functions, including R&D, are aggregated according to products.

The choice between a function- or product-oriented architecture basically depends on the company's overall structure. When a multi-divisional or M-form organization (Chandler, 1962) is in place, R&D activities are typically organized according to a product-oriented model, whereas the adoption of a unitary-form (U-form) organization is more likely to result in a function-oriented solution.

Organizational separation of the innovating and operating organizations

In this second case, the firm establishes a separate organization that incorporates all the functions (R&D, marketing, and manufacturing) that are part of the process of the identification, development and commercialization of radical innovations (Figure 5.4). The innovating organisation, in this case, relies on procedures, managerial principles and shared values that are totally different from those adopted in the operating organisation and specifically designed to foster radical innovation. The resulting structure is called *innovation-oriented, dual-purpose* or *ambidextrous* (Holt, 1978; Tushman and O'Reilly, 1996; Govindarajan and Trimble, 2005).

The organizational fusion and separation of the innovating and operating organizations show advantages and disadvantages that are necessary to understand in order to choose the most appropriate balance between the two. For instance, an ambidextrous organization allows for a simple coordination of the units taking part in the generation and exploitation of radical technological opportunities, provides an environment that stimulates creativity and innovative thinking, and simplifies the allocation of financial and human resources between incremental and radical innovation projects. On the other hand, it is characterized by high complexity and low efficiency,

Table 5.2 Advantages and disadvantages of the separation between the innovating and operating organizations (adapted from Tushman and O'Reilly, 1996; Davila et al., 2006)

ORGANIZATIONAL SEPARATION BETWEEN INNOVATING AND OPERATING ORGANIZATIONS

Advantages	Disadvantages
Simple integration and communication among the functional units participating in generation, development and exploitation of radical innovations	Organizational complexity
High flexibility and a possibility of quickly reallocating resources in order to respond to new conditions and opportunities	Low efficiency
Stimulus to innovative activities because of a concentrated, loosely organized unit and a positive climate	Duplication of resources
Possibility of creating interesting positions with status and salary of such a nature that could attract talented professionals	Weakening of the contact with other departments and decrease in the power of the line organization
Breaking down of departmental barriers and reduction of frictions and conflicts	Danger of isolation of the innovation unit that may prevent the rest of the company from a creative thinking
Simple allocation of resources between incremental and radical innovation projects	Necessity to establish appropriate integration mechanisms with the rest of the company

due to an unavoidable duplication of resources, and entails the danger of isolating the unit dedicated to radical innovation projects from the rest of the organization. These and other pros and cons of the separation between the innovating and the operating organizations that an ambidextrous solution brings about are summarized in Table 5.2.

The capability to pursue radical and discontinuous innovations is perhaps the most critical challenge for sustaining the competitive advantage in today's hypercompetitive business arena (Lynn et al., 1996; Tushman and O'Reilly, 1996); nevertheless incumbents often suffer from a sort of *success syndrome* or *organizational inertia* (Hannan and Freeman, 1984), that is both *structural* and *cultural* (Tushman and O'Reilly, 1996; Stringer, 2000) and prevents them from continuously generating and profiting from radical (or disruptive) technological breakthroughs. An ambidextrous organization has the major advantage of fostering the capability of incumbent companies to at the same time pursue evolutionary and revolutionary change (Macher and Richman, 2004), as shown by the case of Ciba Vision (see Box 5.4), which

---

Box 5.4 Pursuing radical innovation through an ambidextrous organisation: the case of Ciba Vision

Ciba Vision, created in the early 1980s as a business unit of Ciba-Geigy (now Novartis), develops and sells contact lenses and eye-care products to optometrists. Although the firm had launched some successful products, in the second half of the 1980s it was suffering dramatically from competition from the market leader Johnson & Johnson. Ciba Vision's president, Glenn Bradley, understood that without radically innovative products his company risked steady decline and even failure. He decided that the firm should continue making money in the mature business of traditional contact lenses and to invest that money in pursuing breakthrough products. Therefore, in 1991, Bradley launched six R&D projects, each focusing on a radical innovation (daily-disposable and extended-wear lenses, for example); moreover, he decided that these projects would absorb the whole corporate R&D budget and that traditional units would continue pursuing only incremental innovations by themselves. Bradley faced the problem of deciding how to manage and organize these new projects; he decided not to integrate them within the company's traditional organization, fearing that conflicts in resource allocation and conventional procedures and conservative cultural principles could have hampered the creativity and the focus each project needed to succeed. He therefore chose to create an independent unit for each project, with its own R&D, finance and marketing functions, and to locate it in dedicated facility. Each unit hired its own staff, established its own reward systems, designed its business processes and, ultimately, came out with a unique organizational structure and climate. Anyway, Bradley knew that each unit needed to share competencies and resources with the traditional businesses and the other newly founded units. He therefore decided that the leaders of the breakthrough projects should report to a single senior executive, in this case Adrian Hunter, vice president for R&D; he had close relationships with executives throughout Ciba Vision and worked with Bradley resolving conflicts between old businesses and the breakthrough units. Project leaders were also invited to participate in Bradley's executive team meetings. Furthermore, Ciba Vision's incentive system was enhanced so that managers were rewarded on the basis of the overall company performance, rather than on their own business unit's. Finally, a new vision statement for the whole company was elaborated (*Healthy Eyes for Life*); this served the purpose of making clear the relationships and complementarities between new and traditional business units and helped provide a common working cause that prevented organizational fragmentation. The new organizational

> structure worked very well; Ciba Vision launched several successful innovative products from 1991 to 1996, overtook Johnson & Johnson in some market segments and revitalized its sales figures; moreover, the well-established traditional contact-lens business continued to generate cash to be invested in new breakthrough projects.
>
> (adapted from O'Reilly and Tushman, 2004)

was created in the early 1980s as a business unit of Ciba-Geigy. The case of Ciba Vision provides an interesting example of the improvements in innovative performance that an ambidextrous organization is able to achieve, and it suggests different ways by which a firm can prevent the risk that the unit devoted to radical innovation projects becomes too isolated from the rest of the company (for example, coordination at the senior management level, change in the reward systems, development of shared values). This type of organizational structure has also been successfully adopted by USA Today for launching its online news service, USAToday.com, by IBM to spur innovation into its new consulting business and by DaimlerChrysler, BMW, Matsushita and Microsoft, all of which have hived off and relocated their innovating organizations to Silicon Valley to enhance their creative and innovative thinking (Davila et al., 2006). Obviously, opening up the organization for innovation, as discussed in the previous paragraph, is another organizational solution that helps foster the firm's capability to generate and exploit radical innovations; other effective approaches include engagement in corporate venturing initiatives or the establishment of corporate venture-capital funds (Stringer, 2000). Well-known examples of corporate venture capital funds are J&J Development Corporation, the Johnson & Johnson fund that has been investing since 1973 (Stringer, 2000), and Intel Capital, Intel's corporate VC program that has helped the company explore new technological opportunities and business areas by funding and monitoring research projects undertaken by the Silicon Valley start-up community (Chesbrough, 2003).

Nevertheless, an ambidextrous organization should not be considered as the best solution for each company, independent from the context in which the company operates and the competitive strategy it adopts. Generally speaking, an ambidextrous organization is suitable for those firms that compete in fast-moving, dynamic and technology-intensive markets, and which pursue a technological leadership strategy. Missing the opportunity to master a new paradigm shift can be really detrimental for a firm's performance; the speed at which new technologies supersede the older ones is so high that it is almost impossible to recover from a loss of technological edge. Under these conditions, therefore, the firm had better tolerate and absorb the incremental costs and complexity the ambidextrous organization entails, in order to enhance its capability to identify, develop and commercially exploit radical technological innovations. On the other hand, for firms operating in mature and low-tech markets, especially when pursuing a cost-leadership advantage, the need to keep abreast of the latest technological developments is not so pivotal and the rewards brought by the ambidextrous organization do not outweigh its shortcomings. In this context, an ambidextrous structure is best set up on an ad hoc basis when the firm sets out to enter a new or emerging business with a breakthrough technological innovation.

5.6.3 The organizational decentralization of innovative activities

A further structural dimension of the organization for innovation deals with the choice of the hierarchical level at which R&D activities take place. In recent decades companies have increasingly decentralized their R&D tasks as a response to the increased dynamicity and turbulence of markets, the heterogeneity of clients' needs and the necessity of scouting a large number of scientific/technical domains and market segments. Focusing on the hierarchical distribution of R&D activities within large multinational companies, where this organizational design problem is far more challenging than in case of small and simple firms, two basic alternatives can be identified (Chiesa, 2001):

1. *Totally centralized.* In this case the whole R&D activity is undertaken at corporate level, with a single top manager in charge of the firm's R&D, reporting to an executive such as the CEO or president. This structure was predominant among large American corporations in the first decades of the 20th century (such as Du Pont), in big multinational pharmaceutical companies (such as Bayer) until the second half of the 20th century and in many large corporations established in Far Eastern countries more recently;
2. *Totally decentralized.* This structure implies that all R&D is concentrated at divisional level; all R&D activities are conducted within business units, with R&D directors reporting directly to divisional managers. A paradigmatic example is Intel, whose R&D is undertaken almost exclusively at a business-unit level, with a corporate technology planning function which is responsible for technology strategy development and implementation.

A strong decentralization of R&D gives the opportunity to easily identify market opportunities and threats and to efficiently adapt new products and processes to the requirements of the various businesses in which the firm operates; moreover it simplifies the transfer of the outcomes of R&D activities to manufacturing and marketing and allows for a closer control over milestones, budgets and quality targets. Nevertheless, in case of a strong

Table 5.3   Advantages and disadvantages of a strong decentralization of R&D activities (adapted from Chiesa, 2001; Rieck and Dickson, 1993; Lewis and Linden, 1990; Argyres and Silverman, 2004)

STRONG DECENTRALIZATION OF R&D ACTIVITIES

Advantages	Disadvantages
Possibility of scouting and identifying market needs, opportunities and threats	Risk of under-investment in developing core technological competencies and bounded innovation
Possibility of adapting new products and processes to specific business requirements	Risk of losing the capability to synthesize and integrate knowledge from different sources and technical domains
Simple transfer from R to D	Risk of delaying investments into promising technologies not yet exploited or exploitable at the business level
Simple transfer from R&D to manufacturing and marketing	Problems in supporting radical innovation programs with uncertain and delayed outputs
Possibility of measuring R&D performance more simply	Problems in building a long-term vision in technology strategy
Great emphasis on development time, costs and quality	Difficulties in leveraging a common technology basis across different businesses

decentralization of R&D, a firm risks losing its long-term vision in technology strategy; this may result in the delay of investment into promising technologies not yet exploitable at a commercial level, in underinvestment in developing core competencies and bounded innovation, and in the lack of support for radical innovation projects with uncertain and delayed outputs. These and other advantages and disadvantages of a strong decentralization of R&D activities are summarized in Table 5.3.

Although a trend towards the decentralization of R&D activities is discernible, firms tend to avoid the major disadvantages of totally decentralized structures and prefer intermediate solutions called 'hybrid architectures', where R&D is done both at corporate and divisional level (Roberts, 1995a, 1995b). Box 5.5 describes the R&D organization put in place by GlaxoSmithKline (GSK) in 2000 after its birth; this represents a noteworthy example of a hybrid architecture. In this case, the first activities of the drug discovery and development process (that is, pre-discovery research) as well as its final stages (that is, development and launch) were centralized and operated at a corporate level. The central part of the process (that is, discovery research), was highly decentralized and organized around six centres of excellence, each working in a specific therapeutical area. The strategic reasons leading GSK to adopt this form of organization are discussed in Box 5.5.

Box 5.5   GSK's drug development organization

GlaxoSmithKline (GSK) is a leading pharmaceutical firm that resulted from the merger of Glaxo Wellcome and SmithKline Beecham that took place on 17 January 2000. In 2000, the pharmaceutical industry was severely challenged: although expectations about the demand for health-care products and services were extremely favourable and dominant large pharmaceutical firms were raising their R&D investments, the industry suffered from a pronounced *productivity crisis*. The time and costs needed to bring a new drug into the market were dramatically rising (see Figure A below for a representation of the drug development process), whereas the number of approved drugs did not proportionally grow.

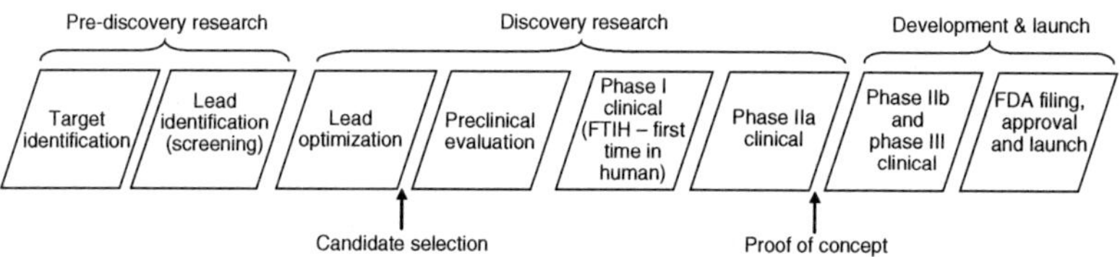

Figure A   The process of drug discovery and development

These competitive pressures exacerbated the managerial and organizational differences between the various stages of the drug development process. The need to lower development costs brought pharmaceutical companies to leverage new and extremely expensive technologies (such as combinatorial chemistry, high-throughput screening and rational drug design) at the front end of the development process, that is, in the pre-discovery research phase. Scale became more and more important in this activity as a consequence of its increased capital intensity. Scale also turned out to be a critical competitive weapon in later stages of drug development, where large clinical trials are run and the FDA approval process needs to be efficiently managed. Conversely, the need to enhance the success rate of the process severely challenged pharmaceutical firms, especially in the middle phase of drug development – lead optimisation, preclinical tests and Phase I clinical trials. These activities are highly labour-intensive, since their effectiveness basically depends on researchers' ability to improve the lead's activity against the target, its ease of entry into the bloodstream or the duration of its activity. Converting promising compounds into products is therefore a highly innovative task that requires flexibility and responsiveness typical of small biotech firms.

In 2000, GSK's CEO, Jean-Pierre Garnier, appointed Tadataka Yamada as chairman of R&D; he was assigned the responsibility of restructuring the R&D function of the company in order to respond to the above-mentioned competitive challenges. The solution he designed is a relevant example of how the decentralization of R&D activities, their organizational separation and geographical dispersion can be effectively combined. Actually, GSK's R&D organization is divided into three sub-organizations (see Figure B):

1. The first comprised two research organizations, Genetics Research and Discovery Research, that focused on the pre-discovery phase. Genetics Research had the purpose of identifying molecular targets and Discovery Research engaged in lead identification (screening) activities. They used capital-intensive methods (high-throughput screening machines and combinatorial chemistry facilities) in order to *automate* the target and lead identification stages so that more drugs were generated in a faster and cheaper way; three major automation facilities were located in Tres Cantos, Spain (high-throughput screening), Harlow, UK (chemistry) and Upper Providence, USA (chemistry and high-throughput screening). This part of the organization was totally centralized, that is, it operated at corporate level undertaking target and lead identification activities for all the therapeutical area where GSK operated;

2. The second part of GSK's R&D organization focused on the central stage of the drug development process, which starts with the lead identification phase and ends with Phase IIa of clinical trials. The need to foster the flexibility, responsiveness and innovativeness of the researchers involved in these labour-intensive tasks brought Yamada to totally decentralize this part of the organization. He created six Centres of Excellence for Drug Discovery (CEDDs), each focusing on a small set of therapeutical areas. These areas were: 1) neurology; 2) psychiatry; 3) antibacterials and host defence; 4) respiratory, inflammation and respiratory pathogens; 5) cardiovascular, cancer and urogenital; 6) metabolic, bone and antivirals. Each CEDD was led by a senior vice-president selected by Yamada and contained no more that 350 scientists, in order to avoid bureaucracy and barriers to day-to-day communication. The R&D Executive Committee, chaired by Yamada, set the overall budget for the six CEDDs and the leader of each CEDD was free to decide how the respective budget was allocated to specific projects. Moreover, each CEDD identified diseases of interest and suggestions were relayed to the Genetics and the Discovery Research groups to identify target and leads for that disease. The centralized research groups maintained the authority to allocate their resources where they wanted and the CEDD was not charged for their

services nor was it obliged to accept any compound that resulted from its suggestions. Moreover, a CEDD could license-in compounds from other firms. When it received a lead from Discovery Research, the CEDD started its activities and the compound progressed along the stages of the drug development process according to the decisions of the CEDD's members, without the review by corporate research executives. Each CEDD, therefore, was a semi-autonomous business with an entrepreneurial culture more typical of a small biotechnology firm than a pharmaceutical multinational.

3. When a compound passed Phase IIa, it was presented to the Development Investment Board (DIB) that evaluated if the CEDD achieved proof of concept (PoC) for the compound. In that case, the latter was transferred to a centralized organization, the Worldwide Development Group, that was responsible for the capital-intensive Phase IIb and Phase III of clinical trials and eventually for the FDA approval process and regulatory affairs.

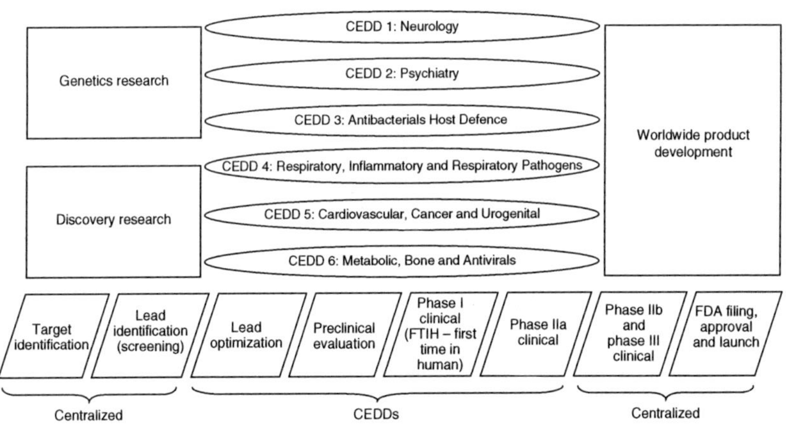

Figure B   Organizational structure for GSK R&D

The international organization of GSK's R&D function was also interesting as Yamada decided to adopt a typical *centres of excellence* solution for the CEDD structure. Each CEDD, located in a specific geographical area that allowed it to leverage on a diffused knowledge base in the respective scientific domain, had the global responsibility for the lead optimization and preclinical trials of those compounds effective in a definite therapeutical area. Because of the interdisciplinary nature of pharmaceutical research, which requires competencies crossing the boundaries of a single therapeutical domain, each CEDD participated (acting like a hub) in a network of satellites and small research sites that provided it with the required transversal competencies (see Table A). The choice to concentrate GSK's worldwide lead optimisation activities for a definite therapeutical area in a single facility was due to the necessity of achieving a huge knowledge specialization in narrow scientific disciplines, to protect proprietary competencies and to monitor critical scientific evolutionary trends.

Table A   Geographical distribution of CEDDs

NEUROLOGY	PSYCHIATRY	ANTIBACTERIALS AND HOST DEFENCE
<u>CEDD</u>: Harlow (UK)	<u>CEDD</u>: Verona (Italy)	<u>CEDD</u>: Upper Providence, PA (USA)
<u>SATELLITE</u>: Stevenage (UK)	<u>SATELLITE</u>: Harlow (UK)	<u>SATELLITES</u>: Verona (Italy), Harlow (UK), Upper Merion, PA (USA)
<u>SMALL SITE</u>: Milan (Italy) RESPIRATORY, INFLAMMATION AND RESPIRATORY PATHOGENS	CARDIOVASCULAR, CANCER AND UROGENITAL	METABOLIC, BONE AND ANTIVIRALS
<u>CEDD</u>: Stevenage (UK)	<u>CEDD</u>: Upper Merion, PA (USA)	<u>CEDD</u>: Research Triangle Park, NC (USA)
<u>SATELLITES</u>: Upper Merion, PA (USA), Upper Providence, PA (USA)	<u>SATELLITES</u>: Harlow (UK), Research Triangle Park, NC (USA), Stevenage (UK) <u>SMALL SITES</u>: Rennes (France) Les Ulis (France), Tsukuba (Japan)	<u>SATELLITES</u>: Stevenage (UK), Upper Providence, PA (USA), Upper Merion, PA (USA), Harlow (UK)

Although the success of this new organizational structure has still to be proven, some interesting evidence emerges: whereas only 10 new chemical entities entered clinical development in the four years ahead of the GSK merger, in the following five years there were about 34.

(adapted from Huckman and Strick, 2005; Jack, 2005)

Among the available hybrid architectures, two major alternatives can be identified (Chiesa, 2001):

1. *Centrally led hybrid structure*: corporate R&D plays a key role, while divisional innovative activities deal typically (but not necessarily) with the final stages of the innovation process, that is, adaptation and commercial launch. This is the case, among the others, with ABB, Toshiba and Matsushita;

2. *Centrally supported hybrid structure*: most R&D is done at divisional level, while corporate innovative activities have mainly a support role, covering a limited part of the innovation process. For example, corporate R&D focuses on basic or applied research, scanning or technology-forecasting activities, or offers technical services, such as rapid or virtual prototyping, useful for all divisional R&D units. This is the solution adopted, for example, by NEC, Xerox and Alcatel.

The innovating firm should therefore search for the most appropriate balance between a heavy centralization and a heavy decentralization, identifying the fundamental requirements of the market in which it operates and the competitive strategy it is actually pursuing (Argyres and Silverman, 2004; Chiesa, 2001). For instance, companies working with several product lines that nevertheless share the same technological basis are better off moving toward a higher concentration of R&D in order to exploit efficiency and critical-mass advantages. This is true also for those firms operating in extremely technology-intensive sectors (aerospace, pharmaceuticals, advanced chemistry) where R&D requires a heavy specialization in knowledge production and the capability to exploit the synergies across traditionally separate scientific disciplines. On the contrary, firms that serve very heterogeneous client segments or run completely distinct business units could tolerate the poor efficiency of heavily decentralized organizations in order to enhance their capability for timely reactions to local opportunities and changing client needs. Moreover, the locus of R&D activities is likely to influence the type of technological innovations the firm is capable of achieving (Argyres and Silverman, 2004). Centralized R&D typically generates innovations that have a larger impact on future technological developments within and outside the industry; moreover, since it facilitates *capability-broadening* research, it is likely to produce innovations that leverage previous developments undertaken by a wide array of organizations into different technological domains. By contrast, divisional R&D directs its efforts mainly to a specific product or market, and typically produces innovations that have less overall impact and affect a narrower range of technological domains. For this reason, a decentralized structure is perhaps more suitable when the innovating firm aims primarily at developing incremental innovations or product extensions, while a more centralized organization is better suited to radical breakthrough projects; a hybrid structure is then the most appropriate solution when mastering both evolutionary and revolutionary change is a competitive imperative.

5.6.4 The international organization of innovative activities

Firms enhance the geographical dispersions of their innovative activities under the influence of several factors, which can be classified as follows

Table 5.4 Main drivers of R&D internationalization (adapted from Gassmann and von Zedtwitz, 1998)

INPUT-ORIENTED	OUTPUT-ORIENTED	EXTERNAL
Access local informal networks and scientific communities	Get closer to final markets and lead users	Rationalize innovation processes after mergers and acquisitions
Employ qualified personnel not available in the home country	Improve reputation in the foreign market	Increase the presence in historically important foreign markets
Exploit local infrastructures supporting innovation and R&D activities	Adapt R&D activities to local production processes	Optimize tax and administrative processes

EFFICIENCY-ORIENTED	POLITICAL/SOCIOCULTURAL
Balance R&D risks	Take advantage of favourable patenting laws
Reduce transaction costs with local production, marketing and distribution units	Access local subsidies for R&D and innovation activities
Reduce R&D personnel costs	Overcome protectionist barriers
Improve the flexibility of the overall R&D organization	Exploit favourable social and labour conditions
Lower the time-to-market of new products making use of many time zones	

(see Table 5.4): 1) input-related drivers, which refer to the need to access human, technological and information resources that are located in different geographical areas; 2) output-related drivers, which refer to the desire to improve the effectiveness and the value of the outcome of R&D activities (that is, new products and processes) through, for example, customers' proximity and a better local image; 3) external drivers, that is, exogenous forces that push firms to geographically disperse their R&D; 4) efficiency-oriented drivers, which refer to the need to reduce the cost and, more generally, to improve the efficiency of R&D activities; 5) political and sociocultural drivers, which bring firms to internationalize their innovative activities for exploiting favourable institutional and governmental conditions.

However, the internationalization of R&D is not unchallenged; reasons against it and in favour of a stronger centralization of innovative tasks are plenty. They can be divided into (see Table 5.5): 1) reasons for centralized R&D, such as the capability to exploit economies of scale and

Table 5.5 Main determinants of R&D centralization (adapted from Gassmann and von Zedtwitz, 1998)

REASON FOR CENTRALIZATION OF R&D	REASONS AGAINST INTERNATIONALIZATION OF R&D
Economies of scale and synergy effects	Risk of losing control over specific know-how
Achievement of a critical mass in R&D	Complexity inherent in parallel development
Avoidance of 'not-invented-here' syndrome	Coordination and communication costs
Uniformity of R&D and innovation culture	Language and cultural problems
Improvement of control and coordination	Staffing difficulties

synergetic effects, easy career planning for R&D personnel, and a straightforward allocation of technological competencies to business units; 2) reasons against internationalized R&D, including difficulties in achieving critical mass, language and coordination problems, and the risk of losing proprietary know-how.

As a consequence, an initial problem should be faced, that is, the choice of an appropriate degree of internationalization of the company's innovation processes that is capable of balancing the main advantages and disadvantages of either going totally global or staying completely local (Chiesa, 2001; Gassmann and von Zedtwitz, 1998; Jones and Teegen, 2002). A strong internationalization of R&D ensures market and customer proximity, adaptation of innovations to local business processes, closeness to lead users, and closeness to production, marketing and distribution facilities; moreover, it provides the opportunity to tap into local pockets of specialized technological competencies, to exploit economic and natural advantages and to improve the firm's local image. Nevertheless, it also has serious drawbacks, such as difficulties in exploiting economies of scale and achieving critical mass, serious communication and integration difficulties and high coordination costs, the risk of incurring in the not-invented-here syndrome and of losing control over and compromising confidentiality of R&D results.

Designing the internationalization of innovative activities does not mean only identifying the most adequate degree of geographical dispersion. It also requires selecting an appropriate approach for the organization of foreign R&D units' activities. The most diffused alternatives in this sense are (Bartlett and Ghoshal, 2002; Archibugi and Mitchie, 1995; Chiesa, 2001):

- *The global approach.* Innovative tasks are concentrated within the company's headquarters, where the generation of new knowledge, the identification of technical and business opportunities and their translation into innovative products and processes take place. Innovations are then transferred to the foreign markets where the company operates, thus allowing for their worldwide exploitation. This approach is appropriate when products are quite undifferentiated and/or customers' needs are relatively homogeneous and/or when the firm basically pursues a cost-leadership strategy. Many Japanese firms (for example, Honda, Toyota, Matsushita) employed this model until the 1980s;

- *The international approach.* New knowledge is generated and translated into innovative products and processes centrally, that is, within the firm's headquarters. The new or improved products or processes, however, are adapted to the needs of local markets by geographically decentralized R&D units that, therefore, focus mainly on the final stages of the innovation process. This model is appropriate when the innovative firm owns a foundation of technological competencies that are critical for its competitive edge, that should be carefully protected against imitation and that can be leveraged across the set of related businesses which the firm operates. Many corporations in the USA (for example, General Electric, Procter & Gamble, Kraft) have adopted this philosophy;

- *The multinational approach.* Innovative activities are highly decentralized in the foreign countries where the company operates. Decentralized R&D units are engaged in research projects and in transforming the results of these efforts into new or improved products and processes that fit the requirements of the local market. Therefore, innovations are generated and exploited on a local scale. This multinational approach is appropriate when the firm's competitive strategy is focused on a high degree of local responsiveness and customer service and when the differences among the countries in which the company operates (in terms of habits, culture and customer needs) are marked. Nestlé, Philips and Unilever are examples of firms employing this approach;

- *The transnational approach.* Foreign R&D units are highly dispersed, independent and specialized. They add to the global activities of the company with differentiated contributions; therefore, knowledge is generated jointly and shared on a global scale. This approach is useful when the number, complexity and degree of sophistication of technologies incorporated into new products and services are high. Furthermore, it is appropriate for those firms that manage their technological innovation process while pursuing contrasting strategic objectives (developing cost-competitive and high-quality products and rapidly adapting them to the changing requirements of a very fragmented and heterogeneous customer audience). Firms that have successfully adopted this approach include Ford and IBM;

- *The centres of excellence approach.* A significant geographical dispersion of R&D activities is achieved. Each decentralized R&D unit is responsible for the entire development of a product line to be globally diffused in the various local markets where the company operates, or for the development of knowledge in a specific scientific or technological domain. This approach is appropriate for undifferentiated products that require a low degree of personalization or when the innovating firm needs to access and leverage pockets of knowledge that are geographically dispersed. This last aspect clearly emerges in the case of GlaxoSmithKline discussed in Box 5.5. The discovery research of GSK was in fact organized around six Centres of Excellence for Drug Discovery (CEDDs), each operating in a specific therapeutical field and located in a geographical area that allowed the firm to access specialized bodies of scientific knowledge. Moreover, each CEDD was assigned the worldwide responsibility for the lead optimization activities and the pre-clinical trials of compounds effective in a defined therapeutical area.

The choice of the most adequate organizational solution requires that the advantages and the disadvantages of each are understood. Table 5.6 highlights the most important ones.

5.6.5 The organizational separation between research and development activities

Literature and managerial practice have largely acknowledged the existence of radically different activities within the R&D process. Many dichotomous distinctions have been proposed that contrast, for example, experimentation to exploitation programmes (Hedlund, 1986), exploratory to development tasks (Kodama, 1995), and investment-mode to harvesting-mode R&D (Coombs, 1996). These taxonomies basically reflect the traditional separation between research and (experimental) development (OECD, 2002) and demonstrate evidence that these two activities require significantly different skills, organizational mechanisms and managerial approaches. The major differences in the managerial principles required to successfully master research and development are listed in Table 5.7.

Notwithstanding the different characteristics of research and development, traditionally these two activities have been kept organizationally united. It was only during the second half of the 20th century that, in technology-intensive sectors such as pharmaceuticals and advanced chemistry, firms started to dedicate separate organizational units to research and development tasks, and this trend is still in place. In some sense, this phenomenon derives from the diffusion that hybrid R&D organizational models have been experiencing since then: according to these structures, research-like tasks are typically concentrated at corporate level and developmental ones, on the contrary, are decentralized within business units. Moreover, there is clear evidence that, even when research and development are undertaken at the same hierarchical level, they are increasingly kept separate, from an

Table 5.6 Advantages and disadvantages of the models for the internationalization of innovative activities (adapted from Chiesa, 2001; Bartlett and Ghoshal, 2002)

GLOBAL		INTERNATIONAL		MULTINATIONAL		TRANSNATIONAL		CENTRES OF EXCELLENCE	
Advantages	Disadvantages	Advantages	Disadvantages	Advantages	Disadvantages	Advantages	Disadvantages	Advantages	Disadvantages
Economies of scale and specialization	Difficulties in catching and exploiting local opportunities	Leveraging of the company's core competencies	Lower efficiency than global model	Strong responsiveness to local needs	Fragmentation of innovative activities	Exploitation of dispersed capabilities	High complexity	Economies of scale and specialization	Weak responsiveness to local needs
Protection of core technical competencies	Low sensitivity to foreign market needs	Favoured generation of new knowledge	Lower sensitivity to local needs than multinational model	Flexibility in adapting to changing local requirements	Risk of differentiation without real necessity	Leveraging local excellences	High coordination costs	Protection of core technical competencies	Transfer of innovations to other subsidiaries (NIH syndrome)
Simple control over key technology trajectories				Close and positive relationships with local governments	Risk of duplication of innovative activities	Strong local responsiveness	Necessity to establish appropriate integration mechanisms	Control over key technology trajectories	
Integration with other business functions						Flexibility in adapting to changing local requirements			
Short development times									

Table 5.7   Main differences between research and development organizations (adapted from Chiesa, 2001)

Research organizations	Development organizations
Culture	*Culture*
– Researchers are given freedom to express their own ideas – Opportunities from outside the organization are well accepted – Mistakes are not penalized but conceived as a means of learning – Direct and informal communication is stimulated	– Clear goals are established and engineers are required to strictly stick to them – Engineers' main concern is to identify and solve areas of weakness – Time-to-market and respect for budgets are of paramount importance – Formal communication channels are predominant
Organization	*Organization*
– Small number of hierarchical levels – Establishment of highly specialized teams – Intellectual property and patent strategies – Tight relationships with external centres of excellence – Long-term commitment – Internal and external information sharing	– High number of hierarchical levels – Use of formal and structured planning systems – Pressure on deadlines and temporal milestones – Use of multifunctional teams that integrate different specialists – Cross-functional integration with marketing and manufacturing – Coordination of many outside engineers and technical service providers

organizational point of view. The major reasons behind this organizational separation are:

- The evolution of the competitive environment has exacerbated the need to separate research from development. The most relevant aspect is the importance that time has acquired as a competitive weapon. In other words, firms are pushed to bring their innovations to market as quickly and cost-effectively as possible, in order to avoid missing the window of opportunity that is getting narrower and narrower as a consequence of the soaring market dynamicity and global competition. This raises the importance of timeliness and efficiency as critical performance dimensions in new product development and calls for the implementation of ad hoc managerial practices (for example, cross-functional integration, performance measurement systems, concurrent engineering approaches). On the other hand, technologies are increasingly complex and costly, breakthrough innovations often arise from the fusion of traditionally separated technological domains and therefore firms specialize in a few core competencies where they are more likely to excel; these are complemented through accessing external sources of technology. This increases the importance of typical research managerial principles, such as the creation of highly specialized core teams, the exchange of information among different fields of research, and the commitment towards the identification of external centres of excellence with which to cooperate;

- As discussed in the previous paragraph, both research and development activities are being increasingly geographically dispersed, as a response to the globalization of markets, science and technology. Nevertheless, the motivations upon which research facilities are internationally placed are quite different from development localization criteria. Research is internationalized mainly with the purpose of accessing pockets of technical and scientific knowledge, while development is similarly dispersed in order to increase proximity to important customers, monitor local market opportunities and effectively react to them in a timely manner. In order to fully exploit the advantages that the internationalization of innovation activities is capable of providing, it is advisable to keep the two organizationally separate.

From the point of view of the manager who is called in to design the organization for innovation for his/her company, an important factor to consider is the degree of organizational separation between research and development. The major advantages of a strong separation between the two are (Chiesa, 2001):

- The possibility of adopting different management approaches that are the most appropriate for each stage of the R&D process. The organizational separation between research and development is a prerequisite for pursuing a specialization in applied managerial principles that is likely to enhance the effectiveness of each stage of the R&D process;
- The institutionalization of a decisional break at the point when a new product or process has to be evaluated for possible future developments. The organizational separation between research and development helps establish a moment in which the output of the first stages of the R&D process is formally evaluated and the best point at which to proceed with developmental activities is assessed through structured techniques.

However, a strong separation has also a major disadvantage; in particular, it entails a higher organizational complexity and requires that appropriate mechanisms are put in place in order to ensure the ultimate integration between research and development functions. Examples of these mechanisms are:

- The establishment of committees, involving people from research, development and possibly other business functions, that have the purpose of coordinating the various activities along the stages of the R&D process;

- The design of a physical layout that favours communication and ideas exchange between scientists and engineers working in the research and development organisations.

Therefore, the organizational separation between research and development activities should be pursued under the following conditions:

- When the innovating firm faces intense competition in its industry and adopts a competitive strategy that requires it to maintain an extreme specialization and updating of its competence basis and, at the same time, to bring to market new products and services as quickly and as efficiently as possible;
- When the firm has a highly geographically dispersed R&D organization through which it pursues radically different objectives, such as accessing external sources of technical knowledge and developing products or services that fit the heterogeneous needs of local clients;
- When the innovating firm operates in an industry where development activities require a huge amount of resources and are very capital-intensive; under these conditions, the firm cannot tolerate the risk that new products enter the development stage without a well-assessed market potential and a controlled probability of successful technical completion. For this reason, the decisional break that the separation between research and development entails becomes a fundamental organizational mechanism.

A business arena where these conditions are generally met is the pharmaceutical industry; Box 5.5, which discusses the structure of GSK's drug-discovery process, provides an interesting example of organizational separation between the different phases of the innovation process. Specifically, it shows how pre-discovery research, discovery research, and development and launch activities were kept organizationally separate and located at different hierarchical levels by GSK's top management.

5.6.6   The resource allocation mechanisms in the organization for innovation

The resource allocation problem within the R&D organization can be approached according to two different mechanisms that are at the extremes of a continuum of solutions (Birkinshaw and Fey, 2000; Argyres and Silverman, 2004):

- *Internal tax;*
- *Internal market.*

When a *pure* internal tax approach is adopted, it is as if R&D activities were funded by the company's divisions through the payment of a predefined *tax*. In other words, top management establishes the amount of money to be allocated to R&D activities in a certain time period (often a single year); this amount is calculated on the basis of alternative criteria, such as a fixed percentage of the firm's overall turnover or as an established percentage increase over the previous R&D budget. Company divisions are called on to contribute to the achievement of the overall figure with an amount that generally depends on the percentage of the firm's turnover (or net operating profit, or other types of economic results) that they are responsible for. As a consequence, the assignment of responsibilities over specific R&D activities to each organizational unit is made directly by top management, on the basis of a top-down hierarchical control approach.

In the second case, innovative activities are funded by company divisions on the basis of an internal market system, regulated by a set of transfer prices. In particular, each business unit that needs technical support in one or more phases of the R&D process it is engaged in is free to purchase it from one of the firm's R&D units capable of offering the required service (whether belonging to the same business unit or not), and to pay a fixed *price* as a counterpart. This implies that top management establishes, on the basis of alternative mechanisms, such as market-based or cost-based approaches, adequate transfer prices that should guide internal transactions. It is also possible to bring this resource funding system towards a more market-like paradigm; in this case transfer prices are not centrally defined, but all R&D units capable of offering a specific technical service are free to fix their own price, thus entering into competition one against the other (an *autonomous transfer price system*). Each business unit will choose the best alternative from its own perspective, thus creating the possibility of turning to external sources of technology if internal proposals are not satisfactory. The internal market approach implies that the specific activities an R&D unit is engaged in are not previously planned by top management; they depend on the technical needs perceived by those divisions choosing to acquire its service. In practice, each approach that is actually applied by large divisionalized companies includes a mix of internal tax hierarchical control and market-like transactions (Hennart, 1993). Firms generally recognize the disadvantages and the potential dangers in the two *pure* models and then develop *mixed* systems to alleviate the greatest weaknesses of the two solutions. This is clear in the cases reported in Box 5.6, where the resource allocation approaches used in the R&D organizations of ABB, Ericsson, HP and Xerox are briefly described. The model used in ABB, for instance, is mainly an internal-market one, but the firm adopts specific corporate funding mechanisms for high-impact projects in order to avoid the risk of becoming too focused on the short-term.

The most important contingency variable that should be considered for selecting between an internal tax or an internal market allocation mechanism

> ### Box 5.6 The use of *mixed* resource allocation systems: the cases of ABB, ERICSSON, HP and XEROX
>
> **ABB.** Research in ABB is split, with some taking place in the ten corporate research centres and the rest taking place in specific business units. Moreover, funding for corporate research centres comes primarily from the business units, the results being a system in which research expenditure is essentially the decision of the business units. The influence of commercial managers in R&D decisions is, accordingly, very high. However, to ensure that the resource allocation system does not become too focused on the short term, there are a number of corporate funding vehicles for high-impact and high-risk projects.
>
> **ERICSSON.** Ericsson has no corporate research because all its R&D activities are carried out at the business-unit level. There is, however, a vice-president responsible for corporate research, and his job is to integrate the research activities of the three business units to ensure that technology is shared and new projects are coordinated. In terms of funding mechanisms, R&D budgets are defined at a business unit level. A contracting system exists, however, because the individual development centres (more than 40) are operated as profit centres. Thus, Ericsson ends up with a mixed funding system, less contract-based than ABB's, but more so than HP's. Finally, the lack of corporate research, and indeed the absence of any *pure* research per se, means that commercial input to R&D decision-making is strong.
>
> **HP.** HP operates a pure model in which research is done in four corporate labs and funded entirely through a corporate *tax* that is paid by the business units. Business units in turn are responsible for doing all development work. There is a risk with this model that research becomes divorced from the needs of the business units, but this is not felt to be a problem by HP because of the relationships between individuals in corporate labs and business units were typically very strong.
>
> **XEROX.** Xerox operates a mixed system. Research is conducted primarily (but not exclusively) at a corporate level, and is funded through a combination of: a) straight *tax* on business units based on their revenues; b) negotiated tax on business units; and c) specific contracts with business units. This system is intended to generate business-unit commitment to research projects at early stages while not making the system too focused on the short term. As a result, Xerox ends up placed between ABB and HP in the extent to which it uses market-like systems.
>
> (adapted from Birkinshaw and Fey, 2000)

is concerned with the characteristics of the activities undertaken within the controlled R&D units. According to the information-processing contingency theory (Galbraith, 1973; Tushman and Nadler, 1978; Egelhoff, 1982; Daft and Lengel, 1986), the higher the variability, the uncertainty and the complexity of the tasks that are undertaken (West, 2000; Gupta et al., 1994), the more the information needed to coordinate and control them, that would be a prerequisite for an internal market system to be effectively implemented, are difficult to codify and exchange without misunderstanding and high costs. Research is typically far more complex, dynamic and uncertain than the development stages of the innovation process; therefore, firms should adopt resource-allocation systems overbalanced towards a hierarchical internal-tax model in order to control research activities, whereas units mainly involved in development projects ought to be subject to resource allocation approaches that are far more market-oriented.

5.7   Paradigmatic configurations of the organization for innovation

So far we have discussed the structural dimensions of the organization for innovation separately; in practice, however, the effectiveness of the innovating firm's design choices depends also on its capability to coherently match variables and form some sort of regime. Theoretical development and empirical observations made so far have revealed the following relationships between the various dimensions of the organisation for innovation that have been studied:

- *The organizational separation between research and development and the international organization of innovative activities.* The drivers of the internationalization of innovative activities generally vary along the stages of the innovation process; for instance, for basic and applied research the most important aspect is closeness and access to external sources of highly specialized technologies, whereas for new product development the critical point is proximity to geographically dispersed customers and the possibility of effectively exploiting local market opportunities (Chiesa, 1996a, 1996b). In order to locate and organize both research and development in the optimum way, their organizational separation becomes a fundamental prerequisite. This was evident, for instance, in the case of GSK, discussed in Box 5.5;
- *Organizational decentralization* and *the international organization of innovative activities.* In divisionalized firms, different business units may rely on very diverse bodies of technological knowledge. In the case that a relevant internationalization of innovative activities is in place, a strongly decentralized organization for innovation would be necessary because it allows the R&D activities of each business unit to be internationally organized on the basis of specific criteria (Leiponen and Helfat, 2006). In the

case of GSK (Box 5.5), for instance, discovery research was totally decentralized in the various therapeutical fields where the company operates; this allowed the R&D activities of each field to be located in the most favourable geographical areas;

- *The organization for external innovation* and *the international organization of innovative activities*. The globalization of markets has brought a worldwide dissemination of highly specialized knowledge; as a result, opportunities for technological collaborations and for the exploitation of the firm's knowledge basis (for example, in the form of a licensing-out agreement) can flourish everywhere. For this reason, firms that want to get the most from external innovation approaches, both in the phase of generation and of exploitation of their technologies, internationalize innovation activities to an extent that allows them to leverage the knowledge-abundant worldwide landscape. Most of the companies that have mastered open innovation in recent years have a very geographically disseminated organization for innovation; this is the case with both Cisco Systems and Procter & Gamble, whose organization for external innovation was briefly discussed in boxes 5.1 and 5.2;
- *The organizational decentralization of innovative activities* and *the resource allocation mechanisms in the organization for innovation*. The use of internal markets as a resource-allocation mechanism is more functional when at least part of the firm's R&D is undertaken at the business-unit level. This decentralization is necessary for creating some sort of internal competition between the R&D functions of the various business units; this is likely to result in improved R&D effectiveness and efficiency and is one of the most important advantages of the internal market resource-allocation approach. The example of Ericsson discussed in Box 5.6 is paradigmatic in this sense;
- *The organization for external innovation* and *the resource allocation mechanisms in the organization for innovation*. Firms that wish to encourage the openness of their innovation process, especially in the phase of technology generation, should prefer an internal market resource-allocation mechanism. In particular, they should give each business unit the opportunity to acquire the needed technical knowledge from internal units as well as external organizations. This would create positive competition between internal R&D units and would foster the idea that both internal and external sources of technology are equally valued by senior management.

5.8 Conclusions

In this section the coverage of this chapter and its contribution to the overall volume's purposes will be provided.

First of all, we have tried to highlight the critical evolutionary trends that have been reshaping the external environment of the firm in the last decades. These changes have had a deep impact on the way in which firms gain and try to maintain a competitive advantage over time and, consequently, and on the approaches they pursue to cope with technological innovation. A new paradigm in the management of technology has emerged; this stresses the importance of innovative firms systematically accessing external sources of technical knowledge in order to complement their competence base, and proactively leveraging multiple channels (or innovation-to-cash paths) in order to get the most from their innovative efforts. These models have been labelled an 'open-innovation paradigm' (Chesbrough, 2003) or a 'distributed innovation system' (Haour, 2004) and share, as a common feature, the openness of the innovating firm towards the external environment.

This chapter then introduced the concept of organization for innovation, defined as the set of organizational dimensions that influence the capability of a firm to manage technological innovation efficiently and effectively. Moreover, in line with the theoretical approach suggested by the contingency theory, we showed that the most effective organization for innovation is influenced by the external environment in which it competes as well as by the strategies and the approaches it uses for managing technological innovation.

The chapter then focused on the design of the following structural dimensions of the organisation for innovation: 1) the organization for external innovation; 2) the coexistence of innovating and operating organizations within the firm's overall structure; 3) the organizational decentralization of innovative activities; 4) the international organization of innovation processes; 5) the organizational separation between research and development; and 6) the resource-allocation mechanisms. For each critical dimension, we discussed advantages and disadvantages, outlined distinctive fields of application of the major design alternatives and provided evidence as to how the most innovative firms structure their organization for innovation in order to face the challenges posed by the external environment and to leverage the opportunities it offers.

With respect to the conceptual model adopted in this book, this chapter has contributed an examination of the elements highlighted in Figure 5.5.

Fundamentally, we identified the fundamental aspects of the *internal organization of the firm* that are more likely to influence its overall innovativeness (we called this set of variables 'organization for innovation'); together, we attempted to disclose the basic characteristics of the *external environment of the firm* that are capable of influencing the organization for innovation. The central section of the chapter helped investigate the relationship between these two basic elements: we discussed how the structural dimensions of the organization for innovation should be designed in order to allow the company to respond to the challenges posed by the external environment and to leverage the opportunities it offers, through an effective and efficient management of

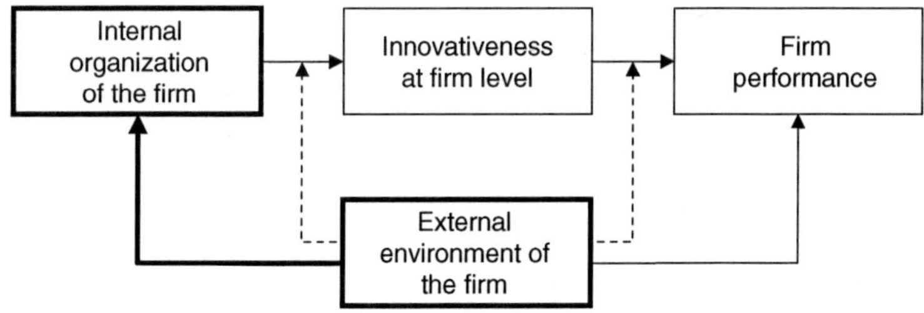

Figure 5.5 A schematic representation of this chapter's coverage of the innovation model

technology. Thus we provided a basis for deepening the investigation of the relationships included in the model; this paves the way for understanding if and how the alignment of the organization for innovation with the external environment of the firm can positively affect the company's overall innovativeness and, in turn, its overall performance; we also clarified the moderating role of the external environment.

5.9   Future research

In this section, some possibilities for future research in the domain of the organization for innovation and its relationship with the external environment of the firm are outlined.

First of all, it would be interesting to extend the analysis of the emerging paradigmatic configurations in the organization for innovation, searching for confirmatory empirical evidence and studying the conditions (such as the characteristics of the external environment or of the firm) under which each configuration is more effective, that is, likely to positively impact the company's innovativeness level and, in turn, its overall performance.

Second, scholars would be interested in extending the analysis of the organization for innovation that has been put forward in this paper, so that further organizational variables are included. Here attention has been above all been paid to the design of the structural dimensions of the organization for innovation; besides this, other critical variables could be:

- *Informal organizational aspects* (such as critical roles for the innovation process, knowledge management through communities of practice);
- *Coordination and control mechanisms* (such as bureaucratic versus personal control styles).

Several studies have shown that, at the roots of the success of most innovative firms, there are individuals performing functions not formally recognized within the firm's organizational structure, although they are critical to the effectiveness of innovation processes (Tushman and Nadler, 1986). A set of informal organizational roles has been therefore identified that represents a critical ingredient of the organization for innovation: 1) idea generator; 2) gatekeeper; 3) champion or internal entrepreneur; and 4) sponsor. It would be interesting to investigate if and how new organizational roles are actually emerging in the most innovative firms as a response to the evolution in the technological innovation paradigm and the external environment.

Another critical informal organizational dimension involves those approaches through which knowledge is generated and transferred within the organization for innovation; communities of practice represent an effective means in this respect. In light of the openness towards the external environment in the current innovation paradigm, it would be interesting to investigate how knowledge generated within communities of practice belonging to separate companies can be effectively exchanged across firms' boundaries.

As far as control mechanisms are concerned, this variable deals with the choice of the best approaches to be applied so that, within the organization for innovation, researchers, scientists and engineers work towards common objectives and their activities are coordinated and monitored. In this respect two basic alternatives emerge: bureaucratic or personal and group control (Holt, 1978). Broadly speaking, when a bureaucratic approach is adopted, the coordination and control of R&D activities is achieved through mechanisms such as task specialization, budgets, reporting and reward systems, standard procedures, and rules and programmes. In the case of personal and group control, by contrast, organizational principles such as feedback to subordinates from supervisors, horizontal and vertical channels of communication for idea exchange, exercise of autonomy and sharing of common values and principles are to the fore. It would be interesting to investigate which of these approaches is most suited to supporting the critical functions required by the technological innovation paradigm that is actually being pursued within most innovative organizations.

References

Abernethy, M. A. and P. Brownell (1997) 'Management Control Systems in Research and Development Organisations: the Role of Accounting, Behaviour and Personnel Controls', *Accounting, Organizations and Society*, 22: 3/4, pp. 233–48.

Allen, T. J. (2001) *Organizing for Product Development.* Working Paper No. 4229-01, MIT Sloan School of Management.

Archibugi, D. and J. Michie (1995) 'The Globalisation of Technology: a New Taxonomy', *Cambridge Journal of Economics*, 19: 1, pp. 121–40.

Argyres, N. S. and B. S. Silverman (2004) 'R&D, Organization Structure, and the Development of Corporate Technological Knowledge', *Strategic Management Journal*, 25: 8/9, pp. 929–58.

Arora, A. and A. Gambardella (1990) 'Complementarity and External Linkages: the Strategies of the Large Firms in Biotechnology', *The Journal of Industrial Economics*, 38: 4, pp. 361–79.

Arora, A., A. Fosfuri and A. Gambardella (2001) *Markets for Technology* (Cambridge, MA: MIT Press).

Bartlett, C. A. and S. Ghoshal (2002) *Managing across Borders. The Transnational Solution* (Boston: Harvard Business School Press).

Bayus, B. L. (1994) 'Are Product Life Cycles Really Getting Shorter?', *Journal of Product Innovation Management*, 11: 4, pp. 300–08.

Bayus, B. L. (1998) 'An Analysis of Product Lifetimes in a Technologically Dynamic Industry', *Management Science*, 44: 6, pp. 763–75.

Birkinshaw, J. and C. F. Fey (2000) *Organizing for Innovation in Large Firms*, SSE/EFI Working Paper Series in Business Administration, No. 2000:5.

Birkinshaw, J., R. Nobel and J. Ridderstråle (2002) 'Knowledge as a Contingency Variable: do the Characteristics of Knowledge Predict Organization Structure?', *Organization Science*, 13: 3, pp. 274–89.

Brockhoff. K. (1991) 'Research and Development Cooperation between Firms. A Classification of Structural Variables' *International Journal of Technology Management*, 6: 3/4, pp. 361–73.

Brockhoff, K. (1992) 'R&D Cooperation between Firms – A Perceived Transaction Cost Perspective', *Management Science*, 38: 4, pp. 514–24.

Brown, J. S. and P. Duguid (2001) 'Knowledge and Organization: a Social-practice Perspective', *Organization Science*, 12: 2, pp. 198–213.

Chandler, A. (1962) *Strategy and Structure* (New York: Doubleday & Company Inc).

Chatterji, D. (1996) 'Accessing External Sources of Technology', *Research-Technology Management*, 39: 2, pp. 49–56.

Chatterji, D. and T. A. Manuel (1993) 'Benefiting from External Sources of Technology', *Research-Technology Management*, 36: 6, pp. 21–6.

Chesbrough, H. (2003) *Open Innovation: the New Imperative for Creating and Profiting from Technology* (Boston: Harvard Business School Press).

Chiesa, V. (1996a) 'Strategies for Global R&D', *Research-Technology Management*, 39: 5, pp. 19–25.

Chiesa V. (1996b) 'Managing the Internationalization of R&D Activities', *IEEE Transactions on Engineering Management*, 43: 1, pp. 7–23.

Chiesa, V. (2001) *R&D Strategy and Organisation* (London: Imperial College Press).

Chiesa, V. and R. Manzini (1998) 'Organizing for Technological Collaboration: a Managerial Perspective', *R&D Management*, 28: 3, pp. 199–212.

Clark, K. B. and T. Fujimoto (1991) *Product Development Performance: Strategy, Organization and Management in the World Auto Industry* (Boston: Harvard Business School Press).

Conti, P. (2006) 'Crescere con i laboratori delle start-up più inventive', *Nova-IlSole24Ore*, June 8, p. 9.

Coombs, R. (1996) 'Core Competencies and the Strategic Management of R&D', *R&D Management*, 26: 4, pp. 345–55.

Cooper, R. G. and E. J. Kleinschmidt (1987) 'What Makes a New Product a Winner?: Success Factor at the Project Level', *R&D Management*, 17: 3, pp. 175–89.

Croisier, B. (1998) 'The Governance of External Research: Empirical Test of Some Transaction-cost-related Factors', *R&D Management*, 28: 4, pp. 289–98.

Daft, R. L. and R. H. Lengel (1986) 'Organizational Information Requirements, Media Richness and Structural Design', *Organization Design*, 32: 5, pp. 554–71.

Davila, T., M. Epstein and R. Shelton (2006) *Making Innovation Work: How to Manage it, Measure It and Profit from It* (Upper Saddle River: Wharton School Publishing).

Egelhoff, W. G. (1982) 'Strategy and Structure in Multinational Corporations: an Information Processing Approach', *Administrative Science Quarterly*, 27: 3, pp. 435–58.

Eto, H. (1992) 'Classification of R&D Organisational Structures in Relation to Strategies', *IEEE Transactions on Engineering Management*, 38: 2, pp. 145–56.

Galbraith, J. R. (1973) *Designing Complex Organisations* (Reading, MA: Addison-Wesley).

Galbraith, J. R. (1984) 'Human Resource Policy for Innovating Organisations', in N. Tichy, C. Fombrum and M. A. Devanna (eds), *Strategic Human Resource Management* (New York: John Wiley & Sons).

Gassmann, O. and M. von Zedtwitz (1998) 'Organization of R&D on a Global Scale', *R&D Management*, 28: 3, pp. 147–61.

Govindarajan, V. and C. Trimble (2005) 'Organizational DNA for Strategic Innovation', *California Management Review*, 47: 3, pp. 46–76.

Griffin, A. and J. H. Hauser (1996) 'Integrating R&D and Marketing: a Review and Analysis of the Literature', *Journal of Product Innovation Management*, 13: 3, pp. 191–215.

Gupta, P. P., M. W. Dirsmith and T. J. Fogarty (1994) 'Coordination and Control in a Government Agency: Contingency and Institutional Theory Perspectives on GAO Audits', *Administrative Science Quarterly*, 39: 2, pp. 264–84.

Gupta, A. K. and D. Wilemon (1996) 'Changing Patterns in Industrial R&D Management', *Journal of Product Innovation Management*, 13: 6, pp. 497–511.

Hagedoorn, J. (1993) 'Understanding the Rationale of Strategic Technology Partnering: Interorganizational Modes of Cooperation and Sectoral Differences,' *Strategic Management Journal*, 14: 5, pp. 371–85.

Handfield, R. B and S. A. Melnyk (1998) 'The Scientific Theory-building Process: a Primer Using the Case of TQM', *Journal of Operations Management*, 16: 4, pp. 321–39.

Hannan, M. T. and J. H. Freeman (1984) 'Structural Inertia and Organizational Change', *American Sociological Review*, 49: 2, pp. 149–64.

Haour, G. (2004) *Resolving the Innovation Paradox. Enhancing Growth in Technology Companies* (Basingstoke: Palgrave).

Hedlund, G. (1986) 'The Hypermodern MNC – A Heterarchy?', *Human Resource Management*, 25: 1, pp. 9–35.

Hennart, J. F. (1993) 'Explaining the Swollen Middle: Why Most Transactions are a Mix of "Market" and "Hierarchy"', *Organization Science*, 4: 4, pp. 529–47.

Holt, K. (1978) *Organization for Product Innovation* (Trondheim: Norwegian Institute of Technology – Division of Industrial Management).

Howells, J. (1999) 'Research and Technology Outsourcing', *Technology Analysis & Strategic Management*, 11: 1, pp. 17–29.

Huckman, R. S. and E. P. Strick (2005) *GlaxoSmithKline: Reorganizing Drug Discovery*, Harvard Business School Case, No 9-605-074.

Huston, L. and N. Sakkab (2006) 'Connect and Develop. Inside Procter & Gamble's New Model for Innovation', *Harvard Business Review*, 85, pp. 58–66.

Jack, A. (2005) 'Glaxo's Catalyst for Creativity', *Financial Times*, 18 March.

Jones, G., A. Lanctot and H. Teegen (2000) 'Determinants and Performance Impacts of External Technology Acquisition', *Journal of Business Venturing*, 16: 3, pp. 255–83.

Jones, G. and H. Teegen (2002) 'Factors Affecting Foreign R&D Location Decisions: Management and Host Policy Implications', *International Journal of Technology Management*, 25: 8, pp. 791–813.

Katz, R. and T. J. Allen (1997) 'Managing Dual-ladder Systems in RD&E Settings', in R. Katz (ed.) *The Human Side of Managing Technological Innovation* (Oxford, New York: Oxford University Press).

Kay, N. (1988) The R&D Function: Corporate Strategy and Structure, in G. Dosi et al., (eds), *Technical Change and Economic Theory* (London: Pinter Publishers).

Kodama, F. (1995) *Emerging Patterns of Innovation* (Boston: Harvard Business School Press).

Leiponen, A. and C. E. Helfat (2006) 'When Does Distributed Innovation Activity Make Sense? Location, Decentralization and Innovation Success', discussion paper No 1063, The Research Institute of the Finnish Economy (available at: http://www.etla.fi/files/1680_Dp1063.pdf).

Lewis, W. and L. H. Linden (1990) 'A New Mission for Corporate Technology', *Sloan Management Review*, 31: 4, pp. 57–67.

Lichtenthaler, E. (2004) 'Organising the External Technology Exploitation Process: Current Practices and Future Challenges', *International Journal of Technology Management*, 27: 2/3, pp. 254–71.

Lynn, G. S., J. G. Morone and A. S. Paulson (1996) 'Marketing Discontinuous Innovation: the Probe and Learn Process', *California Management Review*, 38: 3, pp. 7–37.

Macher, J. T. and B. D. Richman (2004) 'Organisational Responses to Discontinuous Innovation: a Case Study Approach', *International Journal of Innovation Management*, 8: 1, pp. 87–114.

MacPherson, A. (1997a) 'The Contribution of External Services Inputs to the Product Development Efforts of Small Manufacturing Firms', *R&D Management*, 27: 2, pp. 127–44.

MacPherson, A. (1997b) 'The Role of External Technical Support in the Innovation Performance of Scientific Instruments Firms: Empirical Evidence from New York State', *Technovation*, 17: 3, pp. 141–51.

Mohr, J., S. Sengupta and S. Slater (2005) *Marketing of High-technology Products and Innovations* (Upper Saddle River: Pearson Education).

Mueller, E. and A. Zenker (2001) 'Business Services as Actors of Knowledge Transformation: the Role of KIBS in Regional and National Innovation Systems', *Research Policy*, 30: 9, pp. 1501–16.

Narduzzo, A. (1999) 'Staffing e risorse umane', in M. Sobrero (ed.), *La gestione dell'innovazione. Strategia, organizzazione e tecniche operative* (Rome: Carocci).

Nelson, R. (1993) *National Innovation Systems* (New York: Oxford University Press).

Nevens, T. M., G. L. Summe and B. Uttal (1990) 'Commercializing Technology: What the Best Companies Do', *Harvard Business Review*, 68: 4, pp. 154–63.

Nihtilä, J. (1999) 'R&D – Production Integration in the Early Phases of New-Product Development Projects', *Journal of Engineering and Technology Management*, 16: 1, pp. 55–81.

OECD (2002). *Frascati Manual. Proposed Standard Practice for Surveys on Research and Experimental Development* (available at: www1.oecd.org/publications/e-book/9202081e.pdf).

Ortt, J. R. and R. Smits (2006) 'Innovation Management: Different Approaches to Cope with the Same Trend', *International Journal of Technology Management*, 34: 3/4, pp. 296–318.

O'Reilly, C. A. and M. L. Tushman (2004) 'The Ambidextrous Organization', *Harvard Business Review*, 82: 4, pp. 74–84.

Rieck, R. M. and K. E. Dickson (1993) 'A Model of Technology Strategy', *Technology Analysis and Strategic Management*, 5: 4, pp. 397–412.

Risher, H. (2000) 'Compensating Today's Technical Professionals', *Research-Technology Management*, 43: 1, pp. 50–6.

Roberts, E. B. (1995a) 'Benchmarking the Strategic Management of Technology – I', *Research-Technology Management*, 38: 1, pp. 44–56.

Roberts, E. B. (1995b) 'Benchmarking the Strategic Management of Technology – II', *Research-Technology Management*, 38: 2, pp. 18–26.

Roberts, E. B. (2001) 'Benchmarking Global Strategic Management of Technology', *Research-Technology Management*, 44: 2, pp. 25–36.

Roberts, E. B. and C. A. Berry (1985) 'Entering New Businesses: Selecting Strategies for Success', *Sloan Management Review*, 26: 3, pp. 3–17.

Rothwell, R. (1994) 'Towards the Fifth-generation Innovation Process', *International Marketing Review*, 11: 1, pp. 7–31.

Rothwell, R. and W. Zegveld (1985) *Reindustrialisation and Technology* (Harlow: Longman).

Schilling, M. (2003) 'Technological Leapfrogging: Lessons from the US Video Game Console Industry', *California Management Review*, 45: 3, pp. 5–32.

Sen, F. and A. H. Rubenstein (1990) 'An Exploration of Factors Affecting the Integration of In-house R&D with External Technology Acquisition Strategies of a Firm', *IEEE Transactions on Engineering Management*, 37: 4, pp. 246–58.

Song, X. M., S. M. Neeley and Y. Zhao (1996) 'Managing R&D – Marketing Integration in the New-Product Development Process', *Industrial Marketing Management*, 25: 6, pp. 545–53.

Stringer, R. (2000) 'How to Manage Radical Innovation', *California Management Review*, 42: 4, pp. 69–88.

Teece, D. (1986) 'Profiting from Technological Innovation. Implications for Integration, Collaboration, Licensing and Public Policy', *Research Policy*, 15: 6, pp. 285–305.

Thompson, P. H., R. Zenger Baker and N. Smallwood (1988) 'Improving Professional Development by Applying the Four-stage Career Model', in R. Katz (ed.) *Managing Professionals in Innovative Organizations* (Cambridge, MA: Ballinger Publishing Company).

Tidd, J., J. Bessant and K. Pavitt (2005) *Managing Innovation – Integrating Technological, Market and Organisational Change*, 3rd edition (New York: John Wiley & Sons).

Tirpak, T. M., R. Miller., L. Schwartz and D. Kashdan (2006) 'R&D Structure in a Changing World', *Research-Technology Management*, 49: 5, pp. 19–26.

M. Tushman and D. Nadler (1978) 'Information Processing as an Integrated Concept in Organization Design', *Academy of Management Review*, 3, 3, pp. 613–624.

Tushman, M. and D. Nadler (1986) 'Organizing for Innovation', *California Management Review*, 8: 3, pp. 79–92.

Tushman, M. L. and C. A. O'Reilly (1996) 'Ambidextrous Organizations: Managing Evolutionary and Revolutionary Change', *California Management Review*, 38: 4, pp. 7–30.

United Nations (2005) *UNCTAD Survey on the Internationalisation of R&D. Current Patterns and Prospects on the Internationalisation of R&D* (available at: www.unctad.org/wir).

Vansoncellos, E. (1994) 'Improving the R&D–Production Interface in Industrial Companies', *IEEE Transactions on Engineering Management*, 42: 3, pp. 315–21.

von Zedtwitz, M. and O. Gassmann (2002) 'Market versus Technology Drive in R&D Internationalization: Four Different Patterns of Managing Research and Development', *Research Policy*, 31: 4, pp. 569–88.

Wacker, J. G. (1998) 'A Definition of Theory: Research Guidelines for Different Theory-building Research Methods in Operations Management', *Journal of Operations Management*, 16: 4, pp. 361–85.

West, J. (2000) 'Institutions, Information Processing and Organization Structure in Research and Development: Evidence From the Semiconductor Industry', *Research Policy*, 29: 3, pp. 349–73.

Wind, J. and V. Mahajan (1997) 'Issues and Opportunities in New-Product Development: an Introduction to the Special Issue', *Journal of Marketing Research*, 34: 1, pp. 1–12.

Wolf, M. (2006) 'The World Must Get to Grips with Seismic Economic Shifts', *Financial Express*, 7 February (available at: www.financialexpress - bd.com).

Wood, S. C. and G. S. Brown (1998) 'Commercializing Nascent Technology: the Case of Laser Diodes at Sony', *Journal of Product Innovation Management*, 15: 2, pp. 167–83.

6
Exploring Knowledge Flows and Losses in the 'Open Innovation' Age

Paul Trott

6.1   Introduction

The management of innovation has a large and diverse body of literature. It recognizes that while there is much complexity and uncertainty in managing innovation and new-product development, much is known. There is considerable agreement on many of the factors that contribute to success and the activities and processes that need to be undertaken if innovation is to occur and a firm's performance is to improve (Table 6.1 captures some of the key studies that have influenced our understanding from the past 50 years; see References, pp. 144–50).

The studies in Table 6.1 have contributed to the accepted view that a firm's ability to successfully develop innovative new products is not only the result of public and private investments in tangibles and intangibles by individual elements in the economy, but that it is also strongly influenced by the character and intensity of the *interactions* between the elements of the system (see Figure 1.1, Chapter 1 above, 'Innovation systems and firm performance: a model'). This position is strongly advocated in the literature on National Innovation Systems (Freeman, 1982; Lundvall, 1992; Nelson, 1993). In this view, innovation and technological development in particular depend increasingly on the ability to utilize new knowledge produced elsewhere and to combine this with knowledge already available in the economy and with its actors. The capacity to absorb new knowledge, to transfer and diffuse knowledge and the ability to learn through interaction are crucial success factors in innovation (see Cohen and Levinthal, 1989; Chesbrough, 2003). New and commercially useful knowledge is not only the result of the conscious action of creative individuals; it is also the outcome of the interaction and learning processes among various actors in innovation systems – producers, users, suppliers, public authorities and scientific institutions – which David and Foray (1995) have labelled the 'knowledge distribution power' of the innovation system. The need for connectivity and the complexity of the interactions this entails therefore emerges as a major factor influencing the

Table 6.1 Key studies of innovation management

Study	Date		Focus
1	Carter & Williams	1959	Industry & technical progress
2	Project Hindsight – TRACES (Isenson)	1968	Historical reviews of US-government-funded defence industry
3	Wealth from knowledge (Langrish et al.)	1972	Queen's Awards for technical innovation
4	Project Sappho (Rothwell et al.)	1974	Success and failure factors in chemical industry
5	Stanford study (Maidique and Zirger)	1984	Success factors in US electronics industry
6	Minnesota studies (van de Ven)	1989	14 case studies of innovations
7	Rothwell	1992	25-year review of studies
8	Sources of innovation (Wheelwright and Clark)	1992	Different levels of user involvement
9	MIT studies (Utterback)	1994	Five major industry-level cases
10	Project NEWPROD (Cooper)	1999	Longitudinal survey of success and failure in new products
11	Radical innovation (Leifer et al.)	2000	Review of mature businesses
12	TU Delft study (van der Panne et al.)	2003	A major literature review of success and failure factors
13	Chesbrough	2003	Open innovation systems along the supply chain

Sources: van der Panne et al. (2003); Trott (2005)

management of innovation. The development of network theory and network models of innovation has helped to illustrate further the prominence now given to internal and external interactions (networks) within the innovation process (Dhanaraj and Parkhe, 2006; Parkhe et al., 2006). All these knowledge flows contribute to the wealth of knowledge held by the organization (Woolgar et al., 1998; Rothwell, 1992; Major and Cordey-Hayes, 2002).

More recently, Chesbrough (2003), adopting a business strategy perspective, presents a persuasive argument that the process of innovation has shifted from one of closed systems, internal to the firm, to a new mode of open systems involving a range of players distributed up and down the supply chain. Critics may argue that network models of innovation that emphasize external linkages have been around for many years (Taguchi and Nonaka, 1995; Trott, 1995, 2005). Significantly, however, it is Chesbrough's emphasis on the new knowledge-based economy that informs the concept of 'open innovation'. In particular it is the use of cheap and instant information flows which places even more emphasis on the linkages and relationships of firms. It is from these linkages and the supply chain in particular that firms have to ensure that they have the capability to fully capture and utilize ideas. Furthermore, the product innovation literature, in applying the open-innovation paradigm, has recently been debating the strengths and limitations of so called 'user toolkits' which seem to ratchet up further this drive to externalize the firm's capabilities to capture innovation opportunities (von Hippel, 2001).

Recently authors such as Thomke (2003), Schrange (2000) and Dodgson et al. (2005) have emphasized the importance of learning through experimentation. This is similar to Nonaka's work in the early 1990s which emphasized the importance of learning by doing in the 'knowledge creating company'. However, Dodgson et al. argue that there are significant changes occurring at all levels of the innovation process, forcing us to reconceptualize the process with emphasis placed on the three areas that have experienced most significant change through the introduction and use of new technologies. These are: technologies that facilitate creativity; technologies that facilitate communication; and technologies that facilitate manufacturing. For example, they argue that information and communication technologies have changed the way individuals, groups and communities interact. Cell phones, email and websites are obvious examples of how people interact and how information flows in a huge osmosis process through the boundaries of the firm. When this is coupled with changes in manufacturing and operations technologies enabling rapid prototyping and flexible manufacturing at low costs, the process of innovation seems to be undergoing considerable change (Dodgson et al.; 2003; Chesbrough, 2003; Schrange, 2000). Models of innovation need to take account of these new technologies which allow immediate and extensive interaction with many collaborators throughout the process from conception to commercialization. The innovation systems and firm performance model presented in Chapter 2 emphasize how these considerable external environment changes impact on the innovativeness of the firm and hence firm performance.

Yet, at the same time senior managers of firms are also witnessing increased threats of counterfeiting, risks of product imitation and information leakage. The value of counterfeit products marketed annually in the world is estimated to be over US$1 trillion. Nowhere is this more evident than in China (Hung, 2003). The extent of product counterfeiting operations in China is astounding; estimates range from 10 per cent to 20 per cent of all consumer goods manufactured in the country. Rising incomes have created an enthusiasm for foreign goods and brands, but Chinese consumers have become so accustomed to cheap, pirated goods that they are unwilling to pay full prices for the real thing. Many argue that authentic manufacturers have contributed to the problem of counterfeiting due to their unyielding self-interest of pursuing lowest possible manufacturing cost (McDonald and Roberts, 1994; Tom et al., 1998). Even in the face of increased counterfeiting these firms continue to seek strategic alliances in developing countries. It may be that given the short-term gains of lower production costs, firms may be either lacking in risk management or even willing to risk the loss of intellectual property, with its potential long-term damage of loss of competitive advantage, for the sake of short-term gains.

How then do firms on the one hand become more open and on the other hand protect their valuable intellectual property and skills? In this chapter, I explore what has changed and whether successful firms are employing a new range of management skills or whether there is an acceptance that knowledge is being lost but at a price worth paying. In order to address this apparent new paradigm we need to look at what has gone before. The following section presents the background to how our understanding of innovation management has changed.

6.2   Knowledge flows within innovation

It was US economists after the Second World War who championed the linear model of science and innovation. Since then, largely because of its simplicity, this model has taken a firm grip on people's views on how innovation occurs. Indeed, it dominated science and industrial policy for 40 years. It was only in the 1980s that management schools around the world seriously began to challenge the sequential linear process. The recognition that innovation occurs through the interaction of the science base (dominated by universities and industry), technological development (dominated by industry) and the needs of the market was a significant step forward. The explanation of the interaction of these activities forms the basis of models of innovation today.

As far back as 1934 Schumpeter (1934) argued that modern firms equipped with R&D laboratories had become the central innovative actors in the 20th century. It was this capacity to gather and apply knowledge to industrial ends that was recognized. Since his work others have contributed to the debate (Chandler, 1962, 1977; Nelson and Winter, 1982; Cohen and Levinthal, 1990; Hamel and Prahalad, 1990; Pavitt, 1990; Barney, 1991; Patel and Pavitt, 2000). This emerging Schumpeterian or evolutionary theory of dynamic firm capabilities is having a significant impact on our understanding of how firms compete today. Success in the future, as in the past, it is argued, lies in the ability to acquire and utilize knowledge and apply this to the development of new products. Uncovering how to do these remains one of today's most pressing management challenges.

The issue of an organization's capacity to acquire knowledge was addressed by Nelson and Winter (1982) who emphasize the importance of 'innovative routines'. They argue that the practised routines that are built into the organization define a set of competencies that the organization is capable of doing confidently. These routines are referred to as an organization's core capabilities. Teece (1986) distinguishes between 'static routines', which refer to the capability to replicate previously performed tasks, and 'dynamic routines', which enable a firm to develop new competencies. Indeed, dynamic organizational routines are very often those activities that are not easily identifiable and may be dominated by tacit knowledge. Furthermore, over long periods organizations build up a body of knowledge and skills through experience and learning-by-doing. In addition to these internal organizational processes, Kay (1993) suggests that the *external linkages* that a company has developed over time and the investment in this network of relationships (generated from its past activities) form a distinctive competitive capability. Indeed, Kay argues that firms should outsource activities if carrying them out internally would require excessive investment to attain the lowest unit cost. Moreover, this can be transformed into competitive advantage when added to additional distinctive capabilities such as technological ability and marketing knowledge (Casper and Whitley, 2003).

Increasingly economists are using the notion that firms possess discrete sets of capabilities or competencies as a way of explaining why firms are different and how firms change over time. To summarize they argue that competitive advantage resides not in a firm's products but in their competencies. These are defined as knowledge, skills, management processes and routines acquired over time that are difficult to replicate – this is most likely because firms are constantly changing and updating them. However, knowledge or technology in itself does not mean success; firms must be able to convert intellect, knowledge and technology into offerings that customers want. This ability is referred to as a firm's competencies: *the ability to use its assets to perform value-creating activities*. This frequently means integrating several assets such as: product technology and distribution; product technology and marketing effort; and distribution and marketing. Indeed, it is the investment in intangible assets that seems to be a determinant of core competencies (Onyeiwu, 2003).

According to Hamel and Prahalad (1990) a firm's ability to generate profits from its technology assets depends on the level of protection it has over these assets and the extent to which firms are able to imitate these competencies. For example, are competencies at the periphery or the centre of a firm's long-term success? If they are at the centre and difficult for other firms to imitate then long-term profits are assured; for example, over the past 50 years few firms have been able to imitate Honda's success in developing performance engines.

From an innovation and long-term competitiveness perspective, the traditional cost and efficiency concerns are far less important than the question of how to identify and to retain a company's competitive core and not to lose its future ability to compete in fast-moving and unpredictable markets. The strategic management literature is divided on this issue. There are tools like Hamel and Prahalad's (1994) three tests for critical business processes, namely 'customer value', 'competitor differentiation' and 'extendibility', that can be used to identify core competencies and authors like Quinn (1999) are optimistic that they can be identified but warn companies never to outsource their core (defined as 'best in world') competencies. Other writers such as McIvor (2000, p. 48) are much less confident that these competencies can be accurately predicted: 'A current competency may cease to be a source of competitive advantage if there is a change in customer requirements or competitors develop innovative technologies'. Nevertheless, there appears to be a general consensus in the strategic management literature that at least complementary skills or organizational competencies can be handled and developed by alliances and opened up to collaboration and that goods and services of little strategic value can be purchased on the open market (Brandes et al., 1997). A number of researchers, however, believe that the core competencies and most special skills related to competitive advantage need to be protected and kept in-house (Reve, 1990; Quinn, 1999). Hamel (1991) maintains that core skills can be learnt from the other party and absorbed into one's own company just as much as one's own skills can be absorbed by a partner and one's unique competitive advantage lost in the process. Bower et al. (1997) observed the behaviour of technology leaders in the close-knit North Sea upstream offshore oil and gas industry and found that participating in networks sharing leading-edge technology was exposing firms to the risk of their competitive edge being lost to competitors. This dilemma, of the need to share and exchange information yet at the same time protect oneself from knowledge appropriation, has been discussed with respect to collaboration agreements in the aerospace sector (Jordan and Lowe, 2004).

The inability to retain a company's competitive core will not only endanger its future competitiveness but can also create a serious risk of dependency on outside providers. A crucial question is whether the desired access to 'best in industry' capabilities is sufficient to sustain competitive advantage, in particular where the provider serves many masters and its particular expertise ceases to be unique and becomes best-practice industry standard. While there is no shortage of advice in the literature on how to manage the risk of dependency from outside providers and suppliers in general (see, for instance, Currie and Willcocks, 1998, who suggest multi-vendor approaches and shorter-term contracts for handling large-scale long-term total outsourcing contracts with IT/IS providers). The specific problem that access to world-leading expertise via outsourcing may well be compromised by the 'levelling-out' of unique advantages when leading service providers spread their world-leading expertise to several clients has received only limited attention.

6.2.1 The capability to access and exchange knowledge

Central to this debate about access to information and knowledge via networks is the concept of absorptive capacity (Cohen and Levinthal, 1990;

Zahra and George, 2002). This is the firm's ability to absorb and put new knowledge to novel uses. It means recognizing the values of external information, assimilating it within the firm and applying it to commercial ends. The above discussions have illustrated the importance placed on interaction (both formal and informal) within the innovation process. Indeed, innovation has been described as an information-creation process that arises out of social interaction (Trott et al., 1995). In effect, the firm provides a structure within which the creative process is located (Nonaka and Kenny, 1991; Nonaka, Sasaki and Ahmed, 2002). These interactions provide the opportunity for thoughts, potential ideas and views to be shared and exchanged. However, we are often unable to explain what we normally do; we can be competent without being able to offer a theoretical account of our actions (Polanyi, 1966). This has been referred to as 'tacit knowledge' (Sternberg et al., 2000). A great deal of technical skill is 'know-how' and much industrial innovation occurs through on-the-spot experiments, a kind of action-oriented research with ad hoc modifications during step-by-step processes, through which existing repertoires are extended. Such knowledge can only be learned through practice and experience. This view has found significant support from a study of Japanese firms (Nonaka, 1991), where the creation of new knowledge within an organization depends on tapping the tacit and often highly subjective insights, intuitions and hunches of individual employees and making those insights available for testing and use by the organization as a whole. Hence, this implies that certain knowledge and skills, embodied in the term 'know-how', are not easily understood; moreover, they are less able to be communicated. This would suggest that to gain access to such knowledge one may have to be practising in this or related areas of knowledge. Cohen and Levinthal (1990) refer to this condition as 'lockout' suggesting that failure to invest in research and technology will limit an organization's ability to capture technological opportunities. 'Once off the technological escalator it's difficult to get back on' (p. 128).

In addition to informal interactions, the importance of formal interactions is also highlighted. There is a substantial amount of research stressing the need for a 'shared language' within organizations to facilitate internal communication (Allen, 1977, Tushman, 1978; Woolgar et al., 1998; Rothwell, 1992). The arguments are presented along the following lines: if all actors in the organization share the same specialized language, they will be effective in their communication. Hence, there needs to be an overlap of knowledge in order for communication to occur. Such arguments have led to developments in cross-function interfaces, for example between R&D, design, manufacturing and marketing (see Souder, 1988; Nonaka and Takeuchi, 1995). 'Concurrent engineering' is an extension of this; in this particular case a small team consisting of a member from each of the various functional departments manages the design, development, manufacture and marketing of a product.

Such thinking is captured in network models of innovation, which stress the importance of interaction and communication within and between functions and with the external environment. This networking structure allows lateral communication, helping managers and their staff to unleash creativity. These models emphasize the importance of informal and formal networking, across all functions within the firm and with other firms external to the firm. For example, Powell et al. (1996) argue that the locus of explorative innovations is to be found in networks of inter-organizational relationships and that a firm's success crucially depends on its 'centrality-position' in such networks and the experience gained in managing its networks. They argue that internal capability and external collaboration, rather than being substitutes, are complementary:

> Internal capability is indispensable in evaluating research done outside, while external collaboration provides access to news and resources that cannot be generated internally ... A network serves as a locus of innovation because it provides timely access to knowledge and resources that are otherwise unavailable, while also testing internal expertise and learning capabilities.

This, however, introduces a tension between the need for diversity, on the one hand, in order to generate novel linkages and associations, and the need for commonalty on the other, to facilitate effective internal communication. Clearly there will be an organizational trade-off between diversity and commonality of knowledge across individuals (Beveridge, 1957; Martindale, 1995; McCrae, 1987; Shadish, 1989). A key question that emerges here is whether the open-innovation paradigm and the utilization of ICT can facilitate this part of the innovation process.

6.2.2 Flows of market knowledge

Marketing can provide the necessary information and knowledge required by the firm to ensure the successful development of innovative new products and the successful acceptance and diffusion of new products. In both cases it is usually the insights with respect to understanding potential customers that marketing supplies. Uncovering and understanding these insights is where effective marketing is extremely valuable. The deep insights necessary for truly innovative products requires great skill as much of the information gained from customers for such products needs to be ignored (Veryzer, 2003). Research within marketing has shown for many years that gaining valuable insight from consumers about innovative new market offerings, especially discontinuous new products, is extremely difficult and can sometimes lead to misleading information (Veryzer, 2003; King, 1985; Tauber, 1974; Martin, 1995; Hamel and Prahalad, 1994). Indeed, frequent responses from consumers are along the lines of 'I want the same product only cheaper and better'. Von Hippel has suggested that consumers have difficulty in understanding and articulating their needs and has described this phenomenon as 'sticky information', that is, information which is difficult to transfer (similar to the notion of tacit knowledge). Recently 'user toolkits' have been shown to facilitate the transfer of so called 'sticky information' and have enabled firms to better understand the precise needs and desires of customers (Franke and Piller, 2004). The greater uncertainties involved with discontinuous innovations demands both insight and foresight from firms. Advanced technology presents significant technical and market uncertainty, especially when the technology is emerging and industry standards have yet to be established. Appreciating and understanding the potential new technology and uncovering what the market will and will not embrace is a key challenge for marketing. Indeed, bridging uncertainty over technology and market need is critical for a commercially viable new product.

Highly innovative or discontinuous new products are particularly demanding in terms of early timely information if they are to avoid being harshly judged later by the market. Whether this information and knowledge is provided by marketing personnel or by R&D scientists and engineers does not matter but its input to the new-product development process is essential. The product development team needs to determine the answers to the following questions: what are the potential applications of a technology as a product and which application(s) should be pursued first?; what benefits can the proposed product offer to potential customers?; and what is the potential market size and is this sufficient? (Leifer et al., 2000, p. 81).

There has been much written in the NPD literature about the need to involve customers at an early stage in the process and to integrate them into the process in order to fully capture ideas (Cooper, 1999; von Hippel, 1986; Brown and Eisenhardt, 1995, 1998; Thomke, 2003). Despite this customer involvement NPD has been limited and largely passive in most industries (Weyland and Cole, 1997). There are many reasons for this limited utilization of consumers in NPD and some I have touched on above, but perhaps the most limiting factor is the disconnection between customers and producers. Nowadays, technology enables an innovative way of involving and integrating customers into the product development process. In this context, it is here that new technologies, most notably in the form of 'toolkits', offer considerable scope for improving connection between consumers and producers. Franke and Piller's (2004) study analysed the value created by so-called 'toolkits for user innovation and design'. This was a method of integrating customers into new-product development and design. The so-called toolkits allow customers to create their own product, which in turn is produced by the manufacturer. An example of a toolkit in its simplest form is the development of personalized products through uploading digital family photographs via the internet and having these printed on to products such as clothing or cups, thereby allowing consumers to create personalized individual

Table 6.2   Customer roles in NPD (adapted from Nambisan, 2002, p. 395)

Customer role	NPD phase	Key issues/managerial challenges
Customer as resource	Ideation	Appropriateness of customer as a source of innovation Selection of customer innovator Need for varied customer incentives Infrastructure for capturing customer knowledge Differential role of existing (current) and potential (future) customers
Customer as co-creator	Design and development	Involvement in a wide range of design and development tasks Nature of the NPD context: industrial/consumer products Tighter coupling with internal NPD teams Managing the attendant project uncertainty Enhancing customers' product/technology knowledge
Customer as user	Product testing	Time-bound activity Ensuring customer diversity
	Product support	Ongoing activity Infrastructure to support customer-customer interactions

products for themselves. User toolkits for innovation are specific to given product or service type and to a specified production system. Within those general constraints, they give users real freedom to innovate, allowing them to develop their custom product via iterative trial and error (von Hippel, 2001; Franke and Piller, 2004). Nambisan (2002) offers a theoretical lens through which to view these 'virtual customer environments'. He considers the underlying knowledge-creation issues and the nature of the customer interactions and identifies three roles: customer as resource; customer as co-creator and customer as user. These three distinct but related roles provide a useful classification with which to examine the process of NPD. This classification recognizes the considerably different management challenges for the firm if it is to integrate the customer into the NPD process (see Table 6.2).

6.2.3   A look at the evidence for 'open innovation'

While Chesbrough (2003a; 2006) acknowledges the rich source of antecedents to the 'open-innovation paradigm' there may be many scholars of R&D management and innovation management who would argue that this so called paradigm represents little more than the repackaging and representation of concepts and findings presented over the past 30 years. Within

Table 6.3 Information leakage risks with open and closed systems of innovation (adapted from Hoecht, 2004)

Strategic orientation	Strategy	Level of info leakage risk	Key control means	Degree of control	Main source of risk
Closed	**Internal 'to make'**	Low	Bureaucratic control	High	Own employees
	Acquisitive 'to buy'	Low	Bureaucratic and legal control	Medium-high	Employees
	Cooperative (joint ventures)	Medium	Legal control, trust	Medium	Employees and links of partner
	Cooperative (strategic alliance)	Medium-high	Legal control, trust	Medium-low	Employees and links of partner
Open	**External 'to outsource'**	Principally high (but depends on core competencies and nature of industry)	Social control: reputation concerns, professional ethics and trust	Low	Service provider staff and consultants

the field of R&D management it is the pioneering work of Alan Pearson and Derek Ball more than 30 years ago that has done so much to develop thinking in this area (cf. Hutcheson, Pearson and Ball, 1996; Pearson and Ball, 1993; Epton, Pearson, and Payne, 1984; Griffiths and Pearson, 1973). In particular the network model of innovation advocated by Rothwell and Zigveld (1985) emphasized the need for external linkages within the innovation process. As far back as 1959 Carter and Williams discovered that a key characteristic of technically progressive firms was their high quality of incoming information. Thomas Allen's (1977) work on gatekeepers in the 1960s also showed the importance of good external linkages to acquire information and knowledge from outside the organization. SPRU's Project SAPPHO (1974) also confirmed the need for high-quality external linkages in successful innovation. Furthermore, previous research has shown that industrial companies who conduct their own R&D are better able to access externally available information (for example, Tilton, 1971; Allen, 1977, Mowery, 1983; Cohen and Levinthal, 1989). R&D departments therefore have long recognized the importance of information and knowledge beyond their own organizations. And, moreover, substantial amounts of effort have been expended to improve the ability of firms to acquire external knowledge, addressing issues of the 'not-invented-here' syndrome (NIH), investing in scanning and networking and absorptive capacity. Furthermore, 15 years ago Rothwell (1992) presented the case for a fifth-generation model of R&D management emphasizing the need for increased external focus utilizing information technologies; hence the need for firms to adopt a more outward-looking focus to their R&D, technology management and NPD has been repeatedly stressed by many. What has not been addressed are the risks of increased leakage of information as a result of a more open approach. This is the focus of the next section and Table 6.4 attempts to review some of the recent studies on open innovation and assess the extent to which there is an increased risk of information leakage.

6.3   Information leakage and knowledge losses

The information-sharing-knowledge-loss dilemma has received substantial attention in the innovation and knowledge management literature in recent years. Firms in knowledge-intensive industries in particular need to engage in collaborative R&D to sustain their competitive advantage and need to 'open up' to knowledge sharing with their partner organizations if they wish to reap the benefits of such collaboration. Inkpen and Dinar (1998), for example, highlighted the importance of alliance partners as a particularly important source of new external knowledge, and Lincoln et al. (1998) emphasized the need for open communication and rich knowledge sharing as a key success factor for knowledge acquisition. While there is little doubt in the literature on the merits of open communication for successful learning, there is also an increasing awareness that the information sharing required to facilitate such learning can lead to the leakage of commercially sensitive knowledge (Norman, 2004). Organizations participating in R&D alliances in particular face the challenge of attempting to maintain a sufficiently 'open' knowledge-exchange regime for meeting their collaborative R&D objectives while sufficiently controlling knowledge flows to minimize unintended leakage of sensitive knowledge and technologies (Oxley and Sampson, 2004). The principal ways in which this trade-off can be addressed is either by careful design of suitable relationship governance structures and relationship management instruments or by attempting to limit the scope of alliance activities in terms of the degree of knowledge sharing (Oxley and Sampson, 2004).

In this context, Hoecht and Trott (1999) have developed a conceptual framework that links organizations' collaborative research and technology development strategies with their associated risk of knowledge loss and information leakage and the most suitable combinations of trust and control instruments to manage this risk. This conceptual framework identifies the most important sources of information leakage for different strategies (graded from highly closed to open) and lists the principal control instruments and the likely effectiveness for each strategy.

Table 6.4 Overview of studies of open innovation and information leakage risks

Open innovation study	Level of analysis: industry sector; firm	Key feature of open innovation system	Risks of information leakage
Chesbrough & Crowther (2006)	Mature asset-intensive industries: Chemicals; Consumer packaged goods; Inks & coatings.	Increased openness amongst in-bound supply activities	Increase in risk from other firms' research staff and management
Chesbrough (2003a)	Xerox, IBM, Lucent, Intel, Merck and Millennium Computers.	Increased openness over supply chain; increased licensing in and out.	Increase in risk from other firms' research staff and management
Christensen et al. (2005)	Digital stereophonic amplifiers	Small technology entrepreneurs seeking cooperation with larger firms	Increase in risk from other firms' research staff and management
Prugl and Scheier (2006)	Computer games sector	Customer involvement in NPD	Limited due to information asymmetry
Lettl, Herstatt and Gemuenden (2006)	Four case studies from medical equipment producers	Lead users in NPD	Limited due to non-competitive nature of relationship
Hienerth (2006)	16 cases from rodeo and kayak industry	Commercialisation process	No increased risk due to stage of NPD process
Lefebvre and Lefebvre (2007)	Case study of automotive industry supplier	NPD amongst supply chain	Increase in risk from other firms' research staff and management
West and Gallagher (2006)	Open source software	No contractual relationships or trust relationships	Increased risks due to complete lack of control and governance
Dodgson, Gann and Salter (2006)	Single study of P&G	Strategic planning and increased use of licensing	Limited increase in risk but breach of secrecy; changing employer always a risk

Research networks in the biotechnology industry illustrate particularly well the complex relationship between academic demands for free information exchange, commercial concerns about intellectual property rights and the social control of individuals participating in research networks. Academic credibility relies on openness and publication of research findings, as only published findings can be scrutinized, peer-reviewed and credited to the research team which made the discovery. The credibility of researchers, the scientific community's trust in the validity of their research and, closely linked, their personal integrity or trustworthiness, tends to be directly related to their accumulated social capital in the research community – accumulated direct interpersonal experiences with other researchers (process-based trust), reputation (intermediated trust), academic peer-review, and recognition by research organizations (institutional trust). Liebeskind and Oliver (1998) show that as a result of the intrusion of commercial interests into academic research institutions, the collaborative and interpersonal trust relationships between academic scientists tend to weaken as a consequence of a move 'from handshake to contract'.

Commercial interests increase the opportunity costs of trusting other scientists as their potential betrayal can become very costly and intellectual property contracts and confidentiality agreements legally restrict access to information. However, while the commercialization of academic research can lead to network ossification as networks become more exclusionary, Liebeskind and Oliver (1998) also observed the building of new trust relationships between university and biotechnology firm scientists during the course of commercial-academic research projects. They emphasize the importance of 'trust brokers' or 'boundary spanners', highly respected scientists employed or associated with biotechnology firms, for forging these new linkages. These individuals can only fulfil their role if they enjoy a high level of academic credibility and maintain the goodwill and trust bestowed on them by their commercial clients or employers. Despite the obvious reliance on reputational concerns and social control within research networks one should not be surprised to find that most collaborative links in the biotechnology industry are not of an inter-firm nature but take place between commercial firms and academic research institutions (Zucker et al., 1996). In the commercial-academic research collaboration, the academic institution's and participating academic scientist's long-term interest in securing commercial funding increases the commercial firm's sanctioning power against its collaborators. Furthermore, the research partners are more complementary in the sense that academic institutions are less interested in the progression from scientific discovery to commercial exploitation than are rival firms. Not only legal and social control mechanisms, but also the perceived interests and incentive structure, influence the decision to trust research collaborators. Hoecht (2004) showed the types of information leakage risks and the strategies that can be used to control these risks in more detail. It will become clear that 'social control', including trust and reputational concerns, are much more important for handling outsourcing strategy risks than the traditional control instruments (bureaucratic control and legal contracts) that are used for managing information leakage risks within companies and in other inter-organizational ventures such as acquisitions and joint ventures.

Given that most of the information required for innovation is gathered rather than created – no matter how strong the firm's R&D – and that most of this is to be found outside the firm (Macdonald, 1998), the risks of information leakage would seem to be even greater in the age of open innovation. In the next section I explore the threat of information leakage and risks posed by product imitation and counterfeiting to the open innovation paradigm.

6.4   Imitation, counterfeiting and innovation

In the dominant legal perspective, counterfeiters and imitators are seen as 'parasites' that siphon knowledge and intellect from healthy companies that have invested scarce resources in developing products and services with a competitive advantage. Counterfeit products, then, are those products that have been shown (usually via some legal body) to infringe an owner's intellectual property rights (IPR), typically a trademark or a patent. Discussions of counterfeit products have become polarized with brand owners arguing that almost every imitative competitive product is a counterfeit – usually rarely the case and even more difficult to demonstrate – and imitators arguing that strict intellectual property laws frustrate the development of knowledge. Conventional perspectives on the economics of innovation would argue, in support of the patent and copyright holders, that it is necessary to offer some incentive and reward for investment in designs, ideas and inventions; this is usually achieved through intellectual property protection, which can be used to establish a monopoly for a period of time. However, there is an acknowledgment that it may be possible that this incentive can become too attractive, leading to ineffective markets and a lack of competition (Thurow, 1997; Sachs, 1999). It is not surprising then that some industries seek more protection than others; it is well known that intellectual property enforcement is more effective in some industries than others (Bale, 1998).

To characterize imitation it is necessary to consider the concept of reverse engineering (RE). This is generally understood to mean the process of taking something (a device, an electrical component, a software program, etc.) apart and analysing it in detail, usually with the intention of constructing a new, similar but different or improved device or program that performs the same function without actually infringing any intellectual property from the original. For example, in the world of software engineering, end-user license agreements (EULA) form an essential part of the knowledge-building process. These EULAs determine what can be copied and what cannot. Software engineers use EULAs to develop software that can integrate with products and systems to build innovative new applications. The objective is to analyse an application to see how it works, how it connects to other programs and processes, and how the other programs and processes connect to it. No code penetration is involved, and no decompiling. And, usually, the goal isn't to copy an application but to integrate with it or look for potential problems within it. For example, prior to Microsoft developing a grammar checker for its word processing application 'Word', other software providers developed similar software that Word users could buy and use. Not surprisingly, restrictions on how software can be developed are viewed by many in the industry as hindering innovation. It is this association with intellectual property infringement which contributes to a pejorative view of imitation and reverse engineering. Consequently, the value of imitation and reverse engineering and the inherent skills involved are all too often not fully recognized – they are overlooked aspects of the innovation process. Furthermore, popular models of innovation assume a close tie between basic discovery (scientific research) and industrial supremacy, which does not always exist (Bessant and Francis, 1999; van der Panne et al., 2003). The picture created within the traditional linear model is that of R&D expenditure at one end and successful new products at the other. This model has been invoked in nearly all the arguments for the support of science from government right up to the present time. Policy-makers routinely refer to science as the 'seed corn' on which technology draws.

The linear metaphor, often portrayed as a pipeline, is a useful approximation for radical innovations, in which new scientific discoveries lead to developments in unprecedented technological capabilities. But such breakthroughs are rare exceptions, even in technology-intensive sectors (Pavitt, 1991; Rothwell, 1992; Freeman, 1995). Much of what we recognize as innovation originates not from formal R&D, but from informal learning by doing, by using, by trial and error and by interacting. Examples such as Pfizer's Viagra or even the cell phone could be listed here. Reverse engineering skills, product know-how and understanding customers' requirements are the major sources of incremental innovations and product modifications (Bessant and Francis, 1999). Hence, this linear model places too much emphasis on breakthroughs and mistakenly identifies exceptional cases of how product innovations are initiated as typical. This view devalues the necessary skills of reverse engineering and imitation.

Freeman's (1987) study of the Japanese innovation system revealed recognition of the widespread use of reverse engineering in the 1950s and 1960s. In particular, Freeman identified the Japanese integrated approach to product and process design as one of the major sources of the competitive success of Japan. While there were few radical technological breakthroughs, there were significant developments in product design and process design leading to spectacular improvements in quality and design. More recently, Hobday et al. (2004) emphasized the importance of imitation skills and copy-and-develop technological learning strategies in helping Korea grow into a technological leader (see also Kim, 1993). Studies of industrial history show that the United States also reverse engineered technologies imported from Britain; this then evolved into a position of conducting substantial original scientific research (Church, 1999; Nelson and Winter, 1982; Nelson, 1993). Similarly, it is reverse engineering activities such as imitating, copying or improving foreign products that currently underpin China's strategy of acquiring foreign technologies.

It is the integrated nature of the reverse engineering process that seems to underpin its effectiveness. While the necessary and more widely recognized skills of analysing how the product, device or program was put together are crucial, it is the often overlooked learning process that deserves closer examination. The process is characterized by the following:

- the integration of a small project group from production engineering, design, marketing and R&D;
- emphasis on trial and error and on iteration and feedback amongst the group;
- emphasis on collective technological learning;
- sensing potential market needs;
- the purposeful search for relevant information from existing sources within the firm and with external suppliers, customers and research centres;
- a very close relationship with an emphasis of learning together between suppliers of components and sub-assemblies;
- the merging of existing process knowledge with newly acquired information.

6.4.1 Unauthorized imitation/reverse engineering: non-consensual acquisition of technical knowledge

It seems that many multinational corporations (MNCs) claim counterfeit activities when in effect what is occurring is imitation and reverse engineering, where indigenous firms set out to manufacture a product similar to one already available on the world market, but without direct foreign investment or transfer of blueprints for product and process design. Yet reverse engineering is the main method of learning from competitors' product technologies. In addition, equipment suppliers and informal exchanges among production engineers are channels for learning about process technologies. Genuine reverse engineering and imitation, albeit unauthorized, are necessary activities to ensure competition and innovation – and key attributes of a free market system (Freeman, 1982, 1995; Pavitt, 1991; Rothwell, 1992).

In terms of a first step to achieve greater conceptual clarity in the counterfeiting debate, I suggest that it may be useful to use the term 'non-consensual acquisition of technology' to allow for the potentially positive aspects of such behaviour in a technology-learning and new-product-development context to be more easily recognized. 'Non-consensual acquisition of technology' covers only one element of counterfeiting, and helps our analysis by excluding other counterfeiting dimensions such as counterfeiting currency. Where companies use the technology property of others to develop their own technology capability without the consent of the other party, we believe that this should not be condemned outright without due consideration of the learning, new-product development and innovation context.

6.5   Discussion and future research

Against a backcloth of the 'open-innovation' paradigm this paper has explored knowledge flows within the innovation process from several standpoints. It has revealed and confirmed that accessing and utilizing these flows of knowledge is a fundamental part of the innovation process. Indeed the development of models of innovation confirms that knowledge flows are a cornerstone. Hence, it is not unreasonable to consider that any suggestion that these flows are now under transformation (Chesbrough, 2003; Thomke, 2003; Schrange, 2000 and Dodgson et al., 2005) warrants serious consideration.

We have seen in the above discussions that information and knowledge flows have always been recognized as critical to innovation (Allen, 1977). Arguably it is no different now except that ICT makes it easier and quicker, but this also implies it is easier and quicker for competitors to access and use it. It seems that the new paradigm may also facilitate copying and product imitation. Indeed, this raises the first research question: *Is the current intellectual property legislation relevant to the open innovation environment?* This is especially so given the speed at which knowledge can be transformed into products and pushed onto world markets. R&D laboratories and personnel offices may argue that all is secured in their 'watertight ship' and that employment contracts prevent personnel from leaking information and knowledge, but this paper has illustrated that innovation no longer occurs in laboratories but within networks over the internet.

This chapter also discussed the challenge of information leakage and non-consensual acquisition of knowledge. It illustrated the difficulties faced by firms when dealing with collaborators and outsourcing partners in particular. The risks of information leakage are ever more real when one considers that innovating firms openly acknowledge that they are heavily dependent on external information for their innovation (Macdonald and Lefang, 2003). Given that this is well understood as a key issue for senior managers, how are they reacting to the open innovation age, where even more of a firm's information can be transferred and traded over the internet and mobile communication highways? Indeed, this is the second research question: *How can senior managers best protect their firm's valuable information in general and information that may put in peril its core competencies in particular?* Firms need to ask themselves what level of the firm's knowledge is being traded at present. In answering this question they will also have to address the dilemma highlighted in this chapter, that of the need to share knowledge in order to access knowledge yet try to set up protections against knowledge leakage. This leads us to our final research question: *As more and more knowledge is shared across industries what are the risks of a levelling out of expertise?*

The argument that the innovation process is being reshaped by ICT, modern flexible manufacturing systems and new creative technologies (including 'user toolkits') seems reasonable and persuasive. The innovation systems and firm performance model presented in part 6.1 emphasizes how these considerable external environment changes impact on the innovativeness of the firm and hence firm performance. But whether this represents a paradigm shift is unclear. Traditionalists may argue that the introduction and mass utilization of ICT and the like is merely the use of modern tools to facilitate the innovation process, which itself remains largely unchanged. Modernizers may argue that these new technologies are changing the way individuals, groups and communities interact and operate to such an extent that the actual process of innovation is now different. Time will tell, but either way a new batch of research questions now needs to be addressed. The answers to these will help deliver the evidence on what has changed and how firms should respond.

References

Abernathy, W. J. and J. M. Utterback (1978) 'Patterns of Industrial Innovation', *Technology Review*, 80, pp. 40–7.

Allen, T. J. (1977) *Managing the Flow of Technology* (Cambridge, MA: MIT Press).

Bale, H. (1998) 'The Conflict between Parallel Trade and Product Access and Innovation: the Case of Pharmaceuticals', *Journal of International Economic Law*, 1, pp. 637–53.

Barney, J. (1991) 'Firm Resources and Sustained Competitive Advantage', *Journal of Management Studies*, 17: 1, pp. 99–120.

Bessant, J. (2002) 'Challenges in Innovation Management', in L. Shavinina (ed) *International Handbook on Innovation* (Mahwah: Lawrence Erlbaum Associates).

Bessant, J. and D. Francis (1999) 'Developing Strategic Continuous Improvement Capability,' *International Journal of Operations and Production Management*, 19, pp. 1106–19.

Beveridge, W. I. B. (1957) *The Art of Scientific Investigation*, 3rd edition (New York: Vintage).

Bower, D. J. and W. Keogh (1997) 'Conflict and Cooperation in Technology-based Alliances', *International Journal of Innovation Management*, 1: 4, pp. 387–409.

Brandes, H., J. Lilliecreutz and S. Brege (1997) 'Outsourcing – Success or Failure? Findings from Five Case Studies', *European Journal of Purchasing & Supply Management*, 3: 2, pp. 63–75.

Brown, S. L. and K. M. Eisenhardt (1995) 'Product Development: Past Research, Present Findings and Future Directions', *Academy of Management Review*, 20: 2, pp. 343–78.

Carter, C. F. and B. R. Williams (1959) 'The Characteristics of Technically Progressive Firms', *Journal of Industrial Economics*, March, pp. 87–104.

Casper, S. and R. Whitley (2003) 'Managing Competencies in Entrepreneurial Technology Firms: a Comparative Institutional Analysis of Germany, Sweden and the UK', *Research Policy, 33*, pp. 89–106.

Chandler, A. D. (1977) *The Visible Hand: The Managerial Revolution in American Business* (Cambridge, MA: The Belknap Press).

Chandler, A. D. (1962) *Strategy and Structure: Chapters in the History of American Industrial Enterprise* (Cambridge, MA: MIT Press).

Chesbrough, H. (2003a) *Open Innovation: The New Imperative for Creating and Profiting from Technology* (Boston: Harvard Business School Press).

Chesbrough, H. (2003b) 'The Era of Open Innovation', *Sloan Management Review*, 44: 3 (Spring): pp. 35–41.

Chesbrough, H. (2003c) 'Open Innovation: How Companies Actually Do It', *Harvard Business Review*, 81: 7 (July): pp. 12–14.

Chesbrough, H. (2006) 'Open Innovation: A New Paradigm for Understanding Industrial Innovation', in H. Chesbrough, W. Vanhaverbeke and J. West (eds), *Open Innovation: Researching a New Paradigm* (Oxford: Oxford University Press), pp. 1–12.

Chesbrough, H. and A. Kardon Crowther (2006) 'Beyond High Tech: Early Adopters of Open Innovation in Other Industries', *R&D Management*, 36: 3 (June), pp. 229–36.

Christensen, C. M. (1997) *The Innovator's Dilemma: When New Technologies Cause Great Firms to Fail* (Cambridge, MA: HBS Press).

Christensen, J. F., M. H. Olesen and J. S. Kjær (2005) 'The Industrial Dynamics of Open Innovation – Evidence from the Transformation of Consumer Electronics', *Research Policy*, 34: 10, pp. 1533–49.

Church, R. (1999) 'New Perspectives on the History of Products, Firms, Marketing and Consumers in Britain and the United States since the Mid-nineteenth Century', *Economic History Review*, LII, pp. 405–35.

Clark, R. B. (1985) 'The Interaction of Design Hierarchies and Marketing Concepts in Technological Evolution', *Research Policy*, 14, pp. 235–51.

Cohen, W. M. and D. A. Levinthal (1990) 'A New Perspective on Learning and Innovation', *Administrative Science Quarterly*, 35: 1, pp. 128–52.

Cohen, W. M and D. A. Levinthal (1994) 'Fortune Favours the Prepared Firm', *Management Science*, 40: 3, pp. 227–51.

Cohen, W. and D. Levinthal (1989) 'Innovation and Learning: the Two Faces of R&D', *The Economic Journal*, 99, pp. 569–96.

Cooper, R. G. (1990) 'New Products: What Distinguishes the Winners', *Research and Technology Management*, (Nov-Dec), pp. 27–31.

Cooper, R. G. (1999) 'The Invisible Success Factors in Product Innovation,' *Journal of Product Innovation Management*, 16: 2, pp. 115–33.

Cooper, R. G. 'New Product Leadership: Building in the Success Factors', *New-Product Development & Innovation Management*, 1: 2, pp. 125–40.

Currie, W. L. and L. P. Willcocks (1998) 'Analysing Four Types of IT Sourcing Decisions in the Context of Scale, Client/Supplier Interdependency and Risk Mitigation', *Information Systems Journal*, 8: 2, pp. 119–43.

David, P. A. and D. Foray (1995) 'Accessing and Expanding the Science and Technology Knowledge Base', *STI-Review*, 16, pp. 3–68.

Dhanaraj, C. and A. Parkhe (2006) 'Orchestrating Innovation Networks', *Academy of Management Review*, 31: 3, pp. 659–69.

Dodgson, M., D. Gann and A. Salter (2005) *Think, Play, Do* (Oxford: Oxford University Press).

Dodgson, M., D. Gann and A. Salter (2006) 'The Role of Technology in the Shift Towards Open Innovation: the Case of Procter & Gamble', *R&D Management*, 36: 3, pp. 333–46.

Epton, S. R., R. Payne and A. W. Pearson, 'The Management of Cross-Disciplinary Research', *R&D Management*, 14: 2, pp. 69–79

Franke, N. and F. Piller (2004) 'Value Creation by Toolkits for User Innovation and Design: The Case of the Watch Market', *Journal of Product Innovation Management*, 21: 6, pp. 401–16.

Freeman, C. (1982) *The Economics of Industrial Innovation*, 2nd edition (London: Frances Pinter).

Freeman, C. (1987) *Technology Policy and Economic Performance; Lessons from Japan* (London: Pinter Publishers).

Freeman, C. (1991) 'Networks of Innovators: A Synthesis of Research Issues'. *Research Policy*, 20: 5, pp. 499–514.

Freeman, C. (1995) 'The National Systems of Innovation in Historical Perspective', *Cambridge Journal of Economics*, 19, (February), pp. 5–24.

Galbraith, J. R. (1982) 'Designing the Innovative Organisation', *Organisational Dynamics*, Winter, pp. 3–24.

Gallouj, F. (2002) 'Interactional Innovation: a Neo-Schumpeterian Model', in J. Sundbo and L. Fuglsang (eds) *Innovation as Strategic Reflexivity* (London: Routledge).

Grant, R. M. (1997) *Contemporary Strategic Analysis: Concepts, Techniques, Applications* (Oxford: Blackwell).

Griffiths, D. and A. W. Pearson (1973) 'The Organization of Applied R&D with Particular Reference to the Customer–Contractor Situation', *R&D Management* 3: 3, pp. 121–4.

Hamel, G. (1991) 'Competition for Competence and Interpartner Learning Within International Strategic Alliances', *Strategic Management Journal*, 12, pp. 83–104.

G. Hamel and C. K. Prahalad (1990) 'The Core Competence of the Corporation', *Harvard Business Review*, May/June, pp. 79–91.

Hamel, G. and C. K. Prahalad (1994) 'Competing for the Future', *Harvard Business Review*, 72: 4, pp. 122–8.

Hienerth, C. (2006) 'The Commercialization of User Innovations: the Development of the Rodeo Kayak Industry', *R&D Management*, 36: 3, pp. 273–94.

Hobday, M., H. Rush and J. Bessant (2004) 'Approaching the Innovation Frontier in Korea: the Transition Phase to Leadership', *Research Policy*, 33: 10, pp. 1433–57.

Hoecht, A. (2004) 'Control in Collaborative Research and Technology Development. A Case Study in the Chemical Industry', *Journal of Managerial Psychology*, 19: 3, pp. 218–34.

Hoecht, A. and P. Trott (1999) 'Trust, Risk and Control in the Management of Collaborative Technology Development', *International Journal of Innovation Management*, 3: 1, pp. 257–70.

Hung, C. L. (2003) 'The Business of Product Counterfeiting in China and the Post-WTO Membership Environment', *Asia Pacific Business Review*, 10: 1, pp. 58–77.

Hutcheson, P., A. W. Pearson and D. F. Ball (1996) 'Sources of Technical Innovation in the Network of Companies Providing Chemical Process Plant and Equipment', *Research Policy*, 25: 1, pp. 25–41.

Isenson, R. (1968) *Technology in Retrospect and Critical Events in Science (Project Traces)* (Chicago: Illinois Institute of Technology/National Science Foundation).

Jordan, J. and J. Lowe (2004) 'Protecting Strategic Knowledge: Insights from Collaborative Agreements in the Aerospace Sector', *Technology Analysis and Strategic Management,* 16: 2. pp. 241–59.

Kardes, F. R. (1999) *Consumer Behaviour: Managerial Decision Making* (New York: Addison-Wesley).

Katz, R. (2002) 'Managing Technological Innovation in Business Organizations', in: L. Shavinina (ed.) *International Handbook on Innovation* (Mahwah: Lawrence Erlbaum Associates).

Kay, J. (1993) *Foundations of Corporate Success* (Oxford: Oxford University Press).

Kelly, P. and M. Kranzberg (1978) *Technological Innovation: A Critical Review of Current Knowledge* (San Francisco: San Francisco Press).

Kim, L. (1993) 'National System of Industrial Innovation: Dynamics of Capability Building in Korea', in: R. Nelson (ed.) *National Innovation Systems; A Comparative Analysis* (New York: Oxford University Press).

King, S. (1985) 'Has Marketing Failed or Was It Never Really Tried?', *Journal of Marketing Management,* 1: 1, pp. 1–19.

Langrish, J., M. Gibbons, W. G. Evans and F. R. Jevons (1972) *Wealth from Knowledge* (London: Macmillan).

Lefebvre, E. and L. A. Lefebvre (2008) *E-collaboration in the Automotive Supply Chain: Determinants and Impacts on Performance,* this volume, Chapter 8.

Leifer, R., G. Colarelli O'Connor, L. S. Peters, M. Rice, R. W. Veryzer and C. M. McDermott (2000) *Radical Innovation* (Boston: Harvard Business School Press).

Lettl, C., C. Herstatt and H. G. Gemuenden (2006) 'Users' Contributions to Radical Innovation: Evidence from Four Cases in the Field of Medical Equipment Technology', *R&D Management,* 36: 3: pp. 251–72.

Liebeskind, J. and A. Oliver (1998) 'From Handshake to Contract: Intellectual Property, Trust and the Social Structure of Academic Research', in C. Lane and R. Bachman (eds) *Trust Within and between Organizations. Conceptual Issues and Empirical Applications* (Oxford: Oxford University Press), pp. 118–45.

Lundvall, B. A. (1992) 'Introduction to National Systems of Innovation', in B. A. Lundvall (ed.) *National Systems of Innovation* (London: Pinter), pp. 1–22.

Macdonald, S. (1998) *Information for Innovation: Managing Change from an Information Perspective* (Oxford: Oxford University Press).

Macdonald, S. and B. Lefang (2003) 'Worlds Apart: Patent Information and Innovation in SMEs', in R. Blackburn (ed.) *Intellectual Property and Innovation Management* (Routledge, London), pp. 123–43.

Maidique, M. and B. Zirger (1984) 'A Study of Success and Failure in Product Innovation. The Case of the US Electronics Industry,' *IEEE Transactions on Engineering Management,* 31: 4, pp. 192–203.

Major, E. and M. Cordey-Hayes (2003) 'Encouraging Innovation in Small Firms through Externally Generated Knowledge', in L. Shavinina (ed.) *International Handbook on Innovation* (Oxford: Elsevier).

Martin, J. (1995) 'Ignore Your Customer', *Fortune,* 8 (1 May), pp. 121–5.

Martindale, C. (1995) 'Creativity and Connectionism', in S. M. Smith, T. B. Ward, and R. A. Finke (eds) *The Creative Cognition Approach* (Cambridge, MA: MIT Press), pp. 249–68.

McCrae, R. R. (1987) 'Creativity, Divergent Thinking, and Openness to Experience', *Journal of Personality and Social Psychology,* 52, pp. 1258–65.

McDonald, G. M. and C. Roberts (1994) 'Product Piracy: The Problem Will Not Go Away', *Journal of Product & Brand Management*, 3: 4, pp. 55–65.

McIvor, R. (2000) 'Strategic Outsourcing: Lessons from a Systems Integrator', *Business Strategy Review*, 11: 3, pp. 41–50.

Miyata, Y. (2002) 'An Analysis of Research and Innovative Activities of US Universities', in L. Shavinina (ed.) *International Handbook on Innovation* (Mahwah: Lawrence Erlbaum Associates).

Mowery, D. C. (1983) 'Economic Theory and Government Technology Policy', *Policy Sciences*, 16: 1, pp. 27–43

Nambisan, S. (2002) 'Designing Virtual Customer Environments for New-Product Development: Toward a Theory, *Academy of Management Review*, 27: 3, pp. 392–413.

Nelson, R. R. and S. G. Winter (1982) *An Evolutionary Theory of Economic Change* (Cambridge, MA: The Belknap Press of Harvard University).

Nelson R. R. (ed.) (1993) *National Systems of Innovation: A Comparative Study* (Oxford: Oxford University Press).

Nonaka, I. (1991) 'The Knowledge Creating Company', *Harvard Business Review*, 69, Nov–Dec, pp. 96–104.

Nonaka, I. and M. Kenney (1991) 'Towards a New Theory of Innovation Management: A Case Study Comparing Canon, Inc. and Apple Computer, Inc.', *Journal of Engineering and Technology Management*, 8, pp. 67–83.

Nonaka, I., K. Sasaki and M. Ahmed (2002) 'Continuous Innovation: The Power of Tacit Knowledge', in L. Shavinina (ed.) *International Handbook on Innovation* (Mahwah: Lawrence Erlbaum Associates).

Nonaka, I. and H. Takeuchi (1995) *The Knowledge-creating Company* (New York: Oxford University Press).

Onyeiwu, S. (2003) 'Some Determinants of Core Competencies: Evidence from a Binary-Logit Analysis', *Technology Analysis and Strategic Management*, 15; 1, pp. 43–63.

Ortt, R. J. and P.L. Schoormans (1993) 'Consumer Research in the Development Process of a Major Innovation', *Journal of the Market Research Society*, 35: 4, pp. 375–89.

Oxley, J. and R. Sampson (2004) 'The Scope and Governance of International R&D Alliances', *Strategic Management Journal*, 25: 9, pp. 723–49.

Parkhe, A., S. Wasserman and D. Ralstan (2006) 'New Frontiers in Network Theory Development', *Academy of Management Review*, 31: 3, pp. 560–68.

Patel, P. and K. Pavitt (2000) 'How Technological Competencies Help Define the Core (Not the Boundaries) of the Firm', in G. Dosi, R. Nelson and S. G. Winter (eds) *The Nature and Dynamics of Organisational Capabilities* (Oxford: Oxford University Press).

Pavitt, K. (1990) 'What We Know About the Strategic Management of Technology', *California Management Review*, 32 (3), pp. 17–26.

Pavitt, K. (1991) 'Key Characteristics of the Large Innovating Firm', *British Journal of Management*, 2, pp. 41–50

Pearson, A. W. and D. Ball (1993) 'A Framework for Managing Communication at the R&D-Marketing Interface', *Technovation*, 13: 7, pp. 439–47.

Polanyi, M. (1966) *The Tacit Dimension* (London: Routledge and Kegan Paul).

Powell, W., K. Koput and L. Smith-Doerr (1996) 'Interorganizational Collaboration and the Locus of Innovation: Networks of Learning in Biotechnology', *Administrative Science Quarterly*, 41: 1, pp. 116–46.

Prügl, R. and M. Schreier (2006) 'Learning from Leading-edge Customers at The Sims: Opening up the Innovation Process using Toolkits', *R&D Management*, 36: 3, pp. 237–50.

Quinn, J. B. (1999) 'Strategic Outsourcing: Leveraging Knowledge Capabilities', *Sloan Management Review*, Summer, pp. 9–21.

Reve, T. (1990) 'The Firm as a Nexus of Internal and External Contracts, in M. Aoki (ed.) *The Firm as a Nexus of Treaties* (London: Sage).

Rothwell, R. and W. Zigweld (1985) *Reindustrialisation and Technology* (London: Longman).

Rothwell R. (1992) 'Successful Industrial Innovation: Critical Factors for the 1990s', *R & D Management*, 22: 3, pp. 64–84.

Rothwell, R. (ed.) (1994) *The Handbook of Industrial Innovation* (Brookfield: Edward Edgar Publishing).

Rothwell, R. and W. Zegvelt (1982) *Innovation and the Small and Medium-sized Firm* (London: Frances Pinter).

Rothwell, R., C. Freeman, A. Horlsey, V. T. P. Jervis, A. B. Robertson and J. Townsend (1974) 'SAPPHO updated: Project SAPPHO phase II', *Research Policy*, 3, pp. 258–91.

Sachs, J. (1999) 'Helping the World's Poorest', *The Economist*, 14 August, pp. 16–22.

Schrange, M. (2000) *Serious Play – How the World's Best Companies Stimulate to Innovate* (Boston, Harvard Business School Press).

Schumpeter, J. A. (1934) *The Theory of Economic Development* (Boston: Harvard University Press).

Shadish Jr., W. R. (1989) 'The Perception and Evaluation of Quality in Science', in B. Gholson, W. R. Shadish Jr., R. A. Neimeyer and A. C. Houts (eds) *The Psychology of Science: Contributions to Metascience* (Cambridge: Cambridge University Press), pp. 383–426.

Souder, W. E. (1988) 'Managing Relations between R&D and Marketing in New Product Development Projects', *Journal of Product Innovation*, 5: 1, pp. 6–19.

Sternberg, R. J., G. B. Forsythe, J. Hedlund, J. A. Horvath., R. K. Wagner, W. M. Williams and E. L. Grigorenko (2000) *Practical Intelligence in Everyday Life* (Cambridge: Cambridge University Press).

Sundbo, J. (2002) 'Innovation as Strategic Process', in J. Sundbo and L. Fuglsang (eds) *Innovation as Strategic Reflexivity* (London: Routledge).

Takeuchi, H. and I. Nonaka (1995) *The Knowledge Creating Company* (Oxford. Oxford University Press).

Tauber, E. M. (1974) 'Predictive Validity in Consumer Research', *Journal of Advertising Research*, 15: 5, pp. 59–64.

Teece, D. (1986) 'Profiting from Technological Innovation: Implications for Integration, Collaboration, Licensing and Public Policy', *Research Policy*, 15, pp. 285–305.

Teece, D. and G. Pisano (1994) 'The Dynamic Capabilities of Firms: an Introduction', *Industrial and Corporate Change*, 3: 3, pp. 537–55.

Thomke, S. H. (2003) *Experimentation Matters: Unlocking the Potential of New Technologies for Innovation* (Boston: Harvard Business School Press)

Thurow, L. C. (1997) 'Needed: a New System of Intellectual Property Rights', *Harvard Business Review*, 75 (Sept–Oct.), pp. 95–103.

Tom, G., B. Garibaldi, Y. Zeng and J. Pilcher (1998) 'Consumer Demand for Counterfeit Goods', *Psychology and Marketing*, 15: 5, pp. 405–21.

Trott, P., M. Cordey-Hayes and R. A. F. Seaton (1995) 'Inward Technology Transfer as an Interactive Process: A Case Study of ICI', *Technovation*, 15:1, pp. 25–43.

Trott, P. (2005) *Managing Innovation and New-Product Development*, 3rd edition (London: Prentice Hall).

Tushman, M. L. (1978) 'Task Characteristics and Technical Communication in Research and Development', *Academy of Management Review Journal*, 20: 2, pp. 75–86.

Utterback, J. M. (1979) 'The Dynamics of Product and Process Innovation in Industry', in C. T. Hill and J. M. Utterback (eds) *Technological Innovation for a Dynamic Economy* (New York: Pergamon Press).

Utterback, J. (1994) *Mastering the Dynamics of Innovation* (Boston: Harvard Business School Press).

van der Panne, G., C. van Beers and A. Kleinknecht (2003) 'Success and Failure of Innovation: A Literature Review', *International Journal of Innovation Management*, 7: 3, pp. 309–38.

van de Ven, A. H. (1989) 'Central Problems in the Management of Innovation', in L. Tushman and W. L. Moore (eds), *Readings in the Management of Innovation*, 2nd edition, (New York: Harper Business), pp. 103–22.

Veryzer, R. W. (2002) 'Marketing and the Development of Innovative Products', in: L. Shavinina (ed.) *International Handbook on Innovation* (Mahwah: Lawrence Erlbaum Associates).

Veryzer, R. (2003) 'Marketing and the Development of Innovative Products', in L. Shavinina (ed.) *International Handbook on Innovation* (Pergamon Press, Canada), pp. 6–17.

von Hippel, E. (1986) 'Lead Users: A Source of Novel Product Concepts', *Management Science*, July, 32: 7, pp. 791–805.

von Hippel, E. and S. Thomke (1999) 'Creating Breakthroughs at 3M', *Harvard Business Review*, Sept–Oct, 77: 5, pp. 47–57.

von Hippel, E. (2001) 'Perspective: User Toolkits for Innovation', *Journal of Product Innovation Management*, 18: 4, pp. 247–57.

von Hippel, E. (1978) 'Cooperation between Rivals: Information Know-how Trading', *Research Policy*, 16, pp. 291–302.

Wayland, R. and P. Cole (1997) *Customer Connections* (Boston: Harvard Business School Press).

West, J. and S. Gallagher (2006) 'Challenges of Open Innovation: the Paradox of Firm Investment in Open-source Software', *R&D Management*, 36: 3, pp. 319–31.

Wheelwright, S. and K. Clark (1992) *Revolutionising Product Development* (New York: Free Press).

Woolgar, S., J. Vaux, P. Gomes, J-N. Ezingeard and R. Grieve (1998) 'Knowledge and the Speed of Transfer and Imitation of Organisational Capabilities: An Empirical Test', *Organisation Science*, 6: 1, pp. 76–92.

Zahra, S. and G. George (2002) 'Absorptive Capacity: a Review, Reconceptualisation, and Extension', *Academy of Management Review*, 27: 2, pp. 185–203.

Zucker, L., M. Darby and P. Yusheng (1996) 'Collaboration Structures and Information Dilemmas in Biotechnology: Organizational Boundaries of Trust Production, in R. Kramer and T. Tyler (eds) *Trust in Organizations: Frontiers of Theory and Research* (London: Sage), pp. 90–113.

7
The Role of Knowledge Clusters in R&D Acquisition and Innovation Success

Torsten Brodt and Sebastian Knoll

7.1 Introduction

The information and telecommunication (ICT) industry as well as the media industry are fertile parents to a plethora of electronic ('e') and mobile ('m') products and applications (Sorenson et al., 2002, Brodt and Heitmann 2004). A common denominator of these industries is that they are based on fast-paced and converging technology development. Winners in the market are in most cases also technology leaders or capable of turning a base technology into a superior product meeting customer needs. While access to technology and market know-how becomes increasingly important to succeed in the competition, size, history and equity become less and less critical requirements. On the one hand this allows e- and m-start-ups to realize tremendous growth rates and on the other hand it spurs the quest for external knowledge sourcing both at established players and start-ups.

Hence, it is not surprising that the telecommunications industry is heavily relying on external R&D-collaboration or buy-in of know-how within the product development process (Arundel and Bordoy 2002, Anderson and Jönsson, 2006). However, time pressure in innovation as well as the need to internalize key technologies make the ICT and media industries also very active players in mergers and acquisitions (M&As) (Deogun and Scannel, 2001; Warner, 2003). Scholarly research has identified the need to speed up the sourcing of technology and know-how as a key motivation for the increase in M&As (Capron et al., 1998, Bresman et al., 1999). In particular for the ICT and media industry, acquisitions are an increasing popular choice for expansion of the firm's technology and knowledge base (Chaudhury and Tabrizi, 1999; Hagedoorn and Duysters, 2002).

A company's knowledge base can generally consist of diverse kinds of knowledge, such as that required in manufacturing, operational efficiency or knowledge related to new-product development, customer needs and brand experience. In our paper we focus on acquisitions where the prime goal is to acquire the research and development capabilities (that is, knowledge related to new products) of a target company to achieve synergies with existing operations.[1,2] We term this transaction an 'R&D acquisition'. These acquisitions are quite frequent (Wysocki, 1997) and can be a major source of value (Ahuja and Katila, 2001). A successful R&D acquisition that leads to synergies requires an integration of the acquired company or business unit (Haspeslagh and Jemison, 1991). However, the integration process is difficult and often the integration fails (Jemison and Sitkin, 1986), and the acquiring company destroys value. For example, Bert et al. (2003) report a failure rate of around 50 per cent. Clearly, a seamless integration of the relevant information systems (IS) is an integral and complex task within the M&A environment (Sumi and Michio, 2002).

Academic research has not yet addressed this problem adequately. A multitude of studies have been conducted on M&As; however, as King et al. (2004) report, there is a discordance about the significance of success factors in acquisitions. More specifically, little research has focused on acquisitions, where managing the systematic growth of a firm's knowledge base (Ahuja and Katila, 2001; Heo and Yoo, 2002) and the impact of different types of integration mechanisms (Napier, 1989) are at the centre of interest.

We aim to address this research gap by developing a knowledge-focused, testable model of R&D acquisition success. By considering the characteristics of the key asset – the R&D knowledge – a most relevant variable for post-acquisition merger activities, we derive distinct early-integration strategies. These strategies set the stage for integration momentum and effective enhancement of the innovation capabilities. Keeping the introductory description of the ICT industry in mind, we propose a model that might generate useful insights for various ICT practitioners in the field of M&A, such as internal M&A departments, investment bankers and consultants. The approach can also help to schedule and focus the integration of information systems in relation to business integration. The illustration of our findings with an actual mobile media case study will help to clarify the applicability of the model for young as well as established companies.

7.2 Theory and background: knowledge transfer as the key to synergies and acquisition success

Generally, acquisitions involve two major components, each of which influences their success: 1) strategic and financial analysis before making the deal (Hitt et al., 2001); and 2) firm integration after the deal is closed (Haspeslagh and Jemison, 1991). In this paper we focus on the second component, the integration of the firm and its pre-acquisition assessment. We assume that the acquisition makes sense from a strategic and financial perspective. An R&D acquisition is successful if the buyer can integrate the acquired company in a way that it increases performance through the realization of knowledge synergies. Knowledge synergies are achieved, for example, when the parent and the acquired unit increase revenues or reduce costs through jointly developed new products and the use of previously unknown process know-how. All these activities presume knowledge transfer[3] from the acquired company to the parent and vice versa. Therefore, we start with a review of the literature on knowledge transfer related to the acquisition of R&D intensive firms. From the review emerges a considerable gap concerning the mode and timing of integration mechanisms in R&D acquisitions. Consequently, we focus on that aspect and develop a testable model that links different integration mechanisms in the early stage of an R&D acquisition to integration success based on the knowledge characteristics of the target. We then illustrate the model with a practice case and conclude the paper with a discussion of the findings.

7.3 Knowledge transfer in the context of R&D acquisitions

Knowledge transfer occurs at various levels of the organization – between individuals, groups of individuals, organizational functions, business units and organizations themselves. We focus on knowledge transfer at the functional (R&D unit) and business-unit level, which leads to two relevant literature streams: 1) knowledge transfer within the firm (intra-company knowledge sharing); and 2) knowledge transfer in acquisitions including the literature on post-merger integration. Appendix 7.1 (p. 163 below) gives an overview of the reviewed studies.

7.4 Knowledge transfer within the firm

Research on knowledge transfer within the firm emerges from studies on the choice of international knowledge transfer modes (see Bresman et al., 1999 for a review). By now, a large body of research has investigated the factors that influence intra-firm knowledge. The factors that influence intra-company knowledge transfer can be separated in two broad categories: 1) factors related to the characteristics of the transferred knowledge; and 2) organizational factors. The predominant factors related to knowledge characteristics are the degree of codification, observability, complexity (Zander and Kogut, 1995), the degree of embeddedness, and knowledge distance (Cummings and Teng, 2003). The degree of codification expresses the extent to which knowledge can be articulated in documents and software (Zander and Kogut, 1995). This factor is identical to what Bresnan et al. and Cummings and Teng refer to as the 'articulability of knowledge' (Bresman et al. 1999; Cummings and Teng 2003). The degree of embeddedness expresses 'how many knowledge elements and related sub-networks will need to be transferred, absorbed, adapted and adopted by the recipient, and/or how many other recipients will be required to do so to allow the knowledge to be applied to the recipient' (Cummings and Teng, 2003). Knowledge distance is the 'degree to which the source and the recipient possess similar knowledge' (Cummings and Teng, 2003).

Organizational factors influencing knowledge transfer are: organizational structure in terms of formal hierarchical structure and informal lateral relations (Tsai, 2002), length of network paths (Hansen, 2002), intensity of communication (Tsai, 2002, Cummings and Teng, 2003), norm distance (Cummings and Teng, 2003), tie strength (Hansen, 1999, 2002) and absorptive capacity of the recipient (Szulanski, 1996, 2000). Norm distance is the degree to which knowledge transfer parties share the same organizational culture and value systems (Cummings and Teng, 2003). Absorptive capacity of the recipient is the ability of the recipient to exploit outside sources of knowledge (Szulanski, 1996).

7.5   Knowledge transfer in acquisitions

The literature on knowledge transfer and extension in acquisitions is still immature, although knowledge access is a major driver for acquisition activities (Ahuja and Katila, 2001). A branch of research on mergers and acquisitions which focuses on post-acquisition integration touches on the topic (for example, Haspeslagh and Jemison, 1991). However, the central concern of this research stream is not on factors facilitating knowledge transfer but on the issue of how knowledge transfer may lead to overall value creation (Capron et al., 1998; Bresman et al., 1999). Another line of research which is slowly evolving explicitly studies the knowledge-transfer process after an acquisition. Bresman et al.'s study of 42 international acquisitions identified articulability of knowledge, degree of communication and level of use of integrating mechanisms as the key factors influencing knowledge transfer after acquisitions. Finkelstein and Halebian (2002) add similarity of industrial environments in acquirers and targets as an important factor. Their argument is that an acquirer from a similar industry is likely to have similar standard processes, shared experiences and internal arrangements which ease communication and knowledge transfer.

The review shows that factors that facilitate knowledge transfer after acquisitions are similar to factors that facilitate knowledge transfer within the firm.

7.6   Determinants of knowledge transfer

Based on the literature review, Figure 7.1 summarizes the factors that influence knowledge transfer. The 'plus' or 'minus' after the variable indicates the influence of the factor on knowledge transfer. A 'neutral' (0) was assigned when the relationship between the factor and knowledge transfer was moderated by additional variables (which are not presented in the model). In order to pre-assess an R&D acquisition the decision-maker needs to understand the

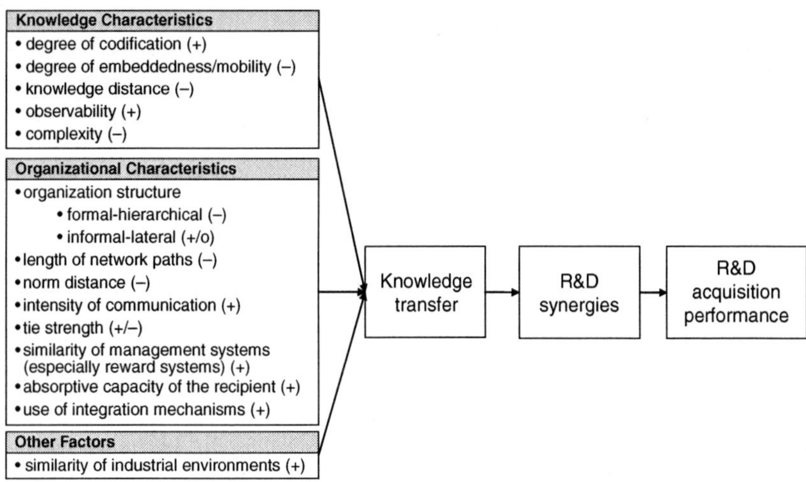

Figure 7.1   Factors influencing knowledge transfer

organizational and management requirements that are necessary to facilitate knowledge transfer after the acquisition. The overview in Figure 7.1 helps the acquisition manager in various ways. It allows an assessment in advance of: 1) whether the potential knowledge she plans to acquire is likely to lead to knowledge synergies based on the knowledge characteristics; 2) whether a successful integration is feasible based on the organizational characteristics (of parent and target company); and 3) roughly what organizational changes would be required for the achievement of 'optimal' knowledge synergy.

The overview can give an initial hint to general answers to these questions but is yet too undifferentiated to provide specific answers. It is beyond the scope of this paper to develop more thorough case-specific integration models. However, an interesting point emerges from our review of the knowledge-transfer literature: the positive impact of the intensive use of integration mechanisms such as joint R&D meetings, joint R&D personnel, and training programs on post-merger integration performance is unquestioned (Jemison and Sitkin, 1986; Haspeslagh and Jemison 1991; Bresman et al., 1999; Birkinshaw et al., 2000). Similarly, the criticality of IS-integration is a prevalent topic in academia (for example, Heo and Yoo, 2002) and practice (for example, Picard and McConville, 2000). One of the most prominent success stories based on a superior performance in post-merger R&D integration coupled with IS-integration can be seen in the case of Cisco Systems (Kraemer and Dedrick, 2002). However, the research of later incidences neither considers the timing of the application of different integration mechanisms nor does it relate specific integration mechanisms to the knowledge characteristics of the target firm. This is a significant shortcoming; especially as recent research (for example, Bert et al., 2003) suggests that the window of opportunity to realize merger synergies in R&D acquisitions has a very limited time span.[4] This in turn implies that wrong timing and/or application of integration mechanisms early in the process can be fatal for acquisition success. We therefore enhance the approach to link knowledge-base characteristics to the selection and timing of post-merger integration mechanisms.

7.7   A knowledge-based model for the selection and timing of post-merger integration mechanisms

7.7.1   Principal structure – linking knowledge-asset specification to acquisition success

Our model follows this general logic: the knowledge-asset characteristics and the organizational characteristics of the R&D unit as two interdependent components are the starting points (Birkinshaw, 2002). They suggest a specific early-integration mode (see Figure 7.2). In line with Bert et al. (2003), 'early integration' covers a time period of up to one year after the acquisition. We argue that the choice of the early integration mode is critical for acquisitions success. Two factors are suggested as moderating elements of the model. The organizational structure and the knowledge characteristics of the acquiring firm (see Ahuja and Katila, 2001) and the nature of the external environment (see Bhattachrya et al., 1998) are the key moderating factors found in the literature. However, for reasons of simplicity, these are omitted from the succeeding discussion.

To establish the link between knowledge-asset characteristics of the target firm and its organizational structure we draw on research by Birkinshaw (2002). He empirically proved a correlation between R&D knowledge characteristics and the structure of R&D centres.[5] Birkinshaw consolidated knowledge characteristics from Zander and Kogut (1995) into the two constructs – 'observability' and 'mobility'. Observability is 'the extent to

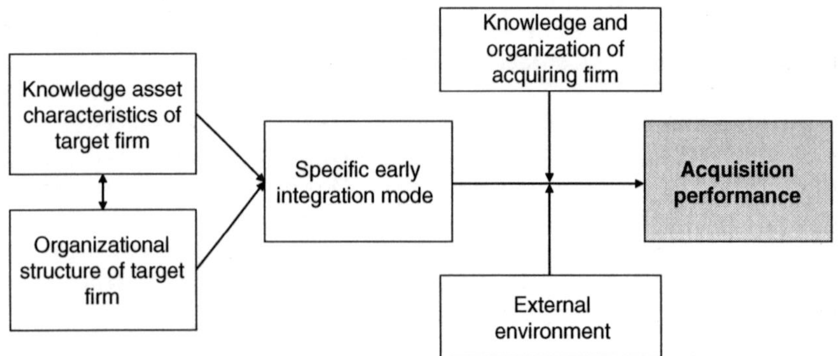

Figure 7.2   The general logic of the model

which the knowledge-base can be understood through observation' (Birkinshaw, 2002), and mobility is 'the extent to which the knowledge base of the R&D centre can be separated from its physical setting' (Birkinshaw, 2002). The observability construct is related to the degree of codification and complexity. Mobility can be paraphrased as the opposite of embeddedness (Birkinshaw, 2002). Birkinshaw measured the two constructs by conducting a multi-item scale questionnaire survey. (A similar questionnaire is included below in Appendix 7.2). Based on the two dimensions, Birkinshaw identifies three archetypes of R&D centres which differ in structure through the level of autonomy, defined as 'resource and decision power' and the level of network integration, defined as 'the integration with other R&D units' (Birkinshaw, 2002). We refer to these three archetypes as cases 1, 2 and 3. Key relationships are illustrated in Figure 7.3.

Examples of R&D centres with high autonomy and low network integration (Case 1) are historically grown R&D centres with a focused task profile and often deep roots in a particular region. Due to the focused task profile there is little integration with other R&D centres in the R&D network required. Case 2 R&D centres are to be found in young R&D teams in the software or telecommunications industry. These teams are typically staffed with young and fairly mobile engineers or software experts. Moreover, these teams can often perform their tasks without proprietary R&D systems. In order to keep this fluctuating knowledge in an R&D network, low levels of autonomy and a strong integration with adjacent R&D centres are effective means of organization. Case 3 is illustrated by the automotive industry where mid to large-scale R&D centres are often organized as regional clusters with strong organizational integration and high levels of autonomy.

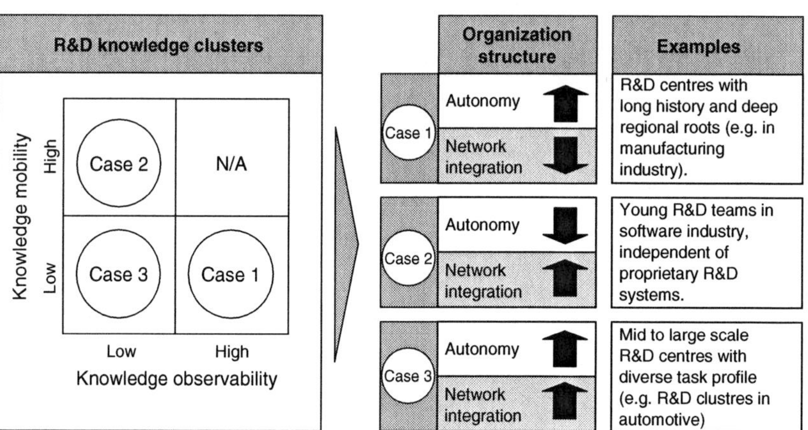

Figure 7.3 The relationship between R&D knowledge clusters and R&D centre structure (adapted from Birkinshaw, 2002)

Based on the organization structure of the different types of R&D centres we derive a specific set of integration mechanisms for the early stage of the integration for each case. We therefore link knowledge characteristics of R&D centres to specific post-merger integration mechanisms. We distinguish 'task integration' and 'human integration' as two major sets of post-R&D-merger integration activities (Birkinshaw et al., 2000). 'Task integration' focuses on resource sharing and transfer mechanisms, such as joint R&D meetings or the use of a knowledge-management system, whereas 'human integration' emphasizes the 'creation of positive attitudes towards the integration among employees on both sides' (Birkinshaw et al., 2000).

The two integration modes are not completely independent but generate useful conceptual pathways and indicators for early integration foci for achieving acquisition success.

Counter-intuitive effects of collaboration systems and tools occurring during M&A activities emphasize the necessity of the two pathway concepts. To achieve relevant degrees of task integration, companies employ a variety of tools and systems. In the realms of R&D management, companies build on instruments such as knowledge repositories for data sharing and integration approaches such as Quality Function Deployment. Interestingly, it was found that the usage of these instruments enhances the quality of collaboration within the group of involved employees, but hinders company-wide integration (Griffin and Hauser, 1993; Calabrese, 1997). This effect is even amplified in M&A situations, where a cross-company collaboration becomes important (Heo and Yoo, 2002). To plan successful post-merger integration, this effect must be considered and might be countered only with human integration.

7.8   Model-based propositions

In the following we develop a testable model in the form of propositions for the relationship between the choice of early-stage integration mechanisms and R&D acquisition success based on (that is, moderated by) the knowledge characteristics 'mobility' and 'observability' (see Figure 7.4).

Case 1: Mobility low and observability high

R&D centres based on knowledge which is rather immobile but highly observable usually portray a high degree of organizational autonomy due to a successful research history and are rather focused on a specific research task. These centres are more vertically integrated into the organization, have fewer horizontal links to other R&D centres and are deeply rooted in the local economy (Birkinshaw 2002). Hence, the acquirer needs to establish a clear definition of the exchange relationship between the newly acquired R&D centre and the vertical organization of the parent company. Interface design

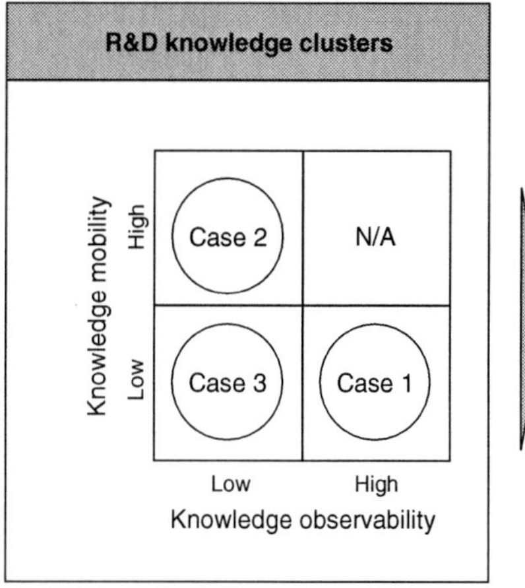

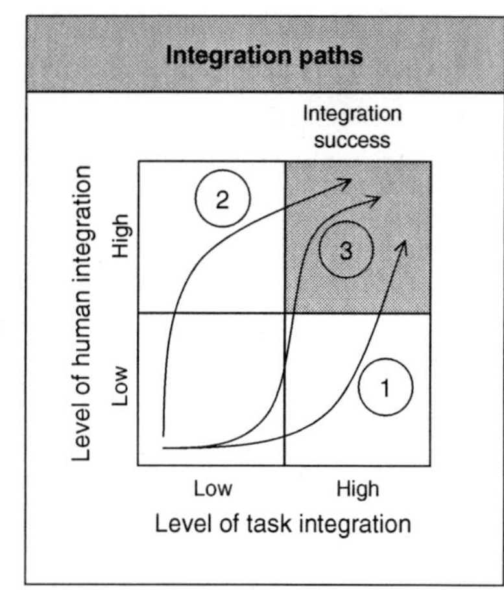

Figure 7.4   The relationship between knowledge clusters and successful integration paths (adapted from Birkinshaw, 2000, 2002)

and task integration should therefore be the prime foci. Due to the high level of autonomy, human integration is rather a peripheral concern in the early stages of the integration process. Therefore:

Proposition 1: *Integration success of R&D acquisitions involving a low level of knowledge mobility and a high level of knowledge observability is positively associated with high levels of task integration and low levels of human integration during the early integration period.*

Case 2: Mobility high and observability low

The 'Case 2 R&D centres' are typically small R&D units with proprietary knowledge residing in a team of a few researchers. These R&D centres usually display high mobility and low observability of knowledge. Orchestrating and controlling the R&D effort requires limited autonomy and a strong integration into the R&D network (Birkinshaw, 2002). The key success factor in the acquisition most likely is team integration to: 1) reduce the risk of know-how loss through employee fluctuation; and to 2) create a sense of belonging to the parent company to increase the willingness to share knowledge. Therefore human integration should be the focus in the early phase of the integration:

Proposition 2: *Integration success of R&D acquisitions involving a high level of knowledge mobility and a low level of knowledge observability is positively associated with low levels of task integration and high levels of human integration during the early integration period.*

Case 3: Mobility low and observability low

Low observability and low mobility frequently result from significant R&D unit size, old age and the considerable reach of the research conducted. These factors generate high complexity for post-merger integration activities.[6] R&D centres of this type serve a wide range of products, have deep local roots and their own way of doing things which is hard to change from the outside. These R&D units should be granted a high level of autonomy to allow self-organization. Furthermore, they should be tightly integrated into the R&D network of the overall organization to achieve knowledge synergies (Birkinshaw, 2002). In order to achieve integration success a threefold process should be pursued: in a first step task integration should target the overall regulation of resource sharing to define the areas of synergy. The second step needs to address human integration in order to build a positive employee attitude as a basis for the third step, renewed task integration to achieve the full potential for synergy. The integration mode in Case 3 is clearly long-term and must ensure the self-organization capability of the acquired unit. Therefore:

Proposition 3: *Integration success of R&D acquisitions involving a low level of knowledge mobility and a low level of knowledge observability is positively associated with high levels of task integration and low levels of human integration during the early integration period. However, a strong ramp-up of human integration is inevitable after quick win realization.*

Stressing the importance of taking the appropriate integration path in the early integration phase, our model provides a decision-maker with the means of identifying the most appropriate integration mode dependent on an acquisition target's knowledge assets. He then must assess whether his own corporation has the resources to manage the integration process to set up a best-fit R&D organization structure in the required time.

7.9 Model enhancement

To operationalize the constructs it is suggested to use measures which have already been established in prior studies. For mobility and observability measures from Zander and Kogut (1995) and Birkinshaw (2002) can be applied. For the constructs of human integration and task integration measures from Birkinshaw et al.'s (2000) study are appropriate. All items are measured on seven-point Likert scales. In order to capture acquisition performance, we suggest multiple measures:

1. A subjective measure asking executives to rate the integration success on a seven-point Likert scale. This is necessary because some of the smaller

    transactions may not be significantly reflected in accounting data and stock prices;
2. Accounting measures of profitability established in numerous M&A studies, such as ROA, ROE and ROS;
3. Monitoring the stock price performance. It is suggested that accounting measures and stock prices are monitored up to three years after the acquisition.

We assume that all synergies from the transaction should be realized by then, that is, the acquisition should be fully integrated. A longer time period would make it difficult to logically link performance variance to a single acquisition due to possible strategy changes (Harrison et al., 1991). Data on completed acquisitions is derived from standard financial databases (such as the Genios M&A database). The case example is R&D acquisition in the mobile communication technology market.

For the illustration of the model designed above we have chosen a technology company, Bamboo Mediacasting Inc, which is active in the market for mobile telecommunication technology. We interviewed two executives of the company.[7] (See Appendix 7.2 for the questionnaire.) The company is a venture-financed start-up company founded in the year 2000 in Israel. Its major business activity is in the development of mobile multicasting technology (14 of the 21 employees are R&D engineers). Based on its R&D the company achieved innovation leadership. However, its resource position might not allow a full set-up of marketing and sales operations in the relevant markets in Europe, the US and Asia. As the incumbent technology providers lack the multicasting expertise but posses the market access, an acquisition of the entire company might be a likely scenario.

Bamboo fits into Case 2 of R&D units. The technology consists of proprietary software and hardware, which has to be integrated into a mobile telecommunication network to enable multicasting functionality. The knowledge resides with a few highly skilled engineers with partly international educational backgrounds. Additionally, technical documentation is not very advanced because resources are scarce and occupied with operational start-up activities. The knowledge thus has low observability and high mobility, which in turn requires a potential buyer to strongly integrate the R&D activities with a reasonably low level of autonomy into its own R&D network.

The speed and intensity of integration will be major success factors. Today the engineers are strongly tied to the start-up company by stock-option plans and emotional binding. After an acquisition these mechanisms need to be replaced to a certain degree by monetary incentives but also by the creation of a consistent feeling of belonging to the new company. Speed plays a critical role not only due to rapid market development but also because the existence of a small number of engineers can impact the R&D performance and provide competitors with access to technical know-how.

Therefore, a potential buyer must focus on human integration first and generate a strong level of leadership, strong bilateral communication, provide retention plans and improve individual personal situations.

7.10 Conclusion and implications

This paper contributes to the discussion about the factors affecting the success of the integration of acquisitions where the main goal is to acquire the R&D capabilities of the target firm. The ICT and media industries are significantly permeated with this type of M&A. A glance at historic performance, however, shows that this strategy so far is a risky game with mediocre outcomes. Furthermore, research is immature and to a large part discordant as to the reasons for the suboptimal outcomes. We argue that the choice of early-stage integration mechanisms, that is, integration mechanisms which are applied within the first year of the acquisitions, have a significant influence on the acquisition success. We propose that:

1. R&D acquisitions involving a low level of knowledge mobility and a high level of knowledge observability should focus on task integration;
2. Acquisitions involving a high level of knowledge mobility and a low level of knowledge observability should focus on high levels of human integration; and
3. Acquisitions involving a low level of both observability and mobility should focus on high levels of task integration at the early stage of the integration process.

Relating to the overall innovation system conceptualized for this book, this paper contributes to the understanding of aspects of internal organization and the innovation success of a firm.

For practitioners the insights of this research will help to better understand the role of early-stage integration mechanisms in successful R&D acquisitions. This will aid managers in: 1) assessing potential R&D acquisitions depending on their firm's integration capability; 2) deciding which kinds of integration mechanism to focus on in the early phases of R&D integrations; and 3) timing their R&D acquisitions depending the resource availability for the required integration mechanism. Focused actions can also be derived for the IS-based knowledge-management systems, which need to be integrated post merger in order to effectively leverage the merged R&D-knowledge base. Eventually, our research might help to lift the returns on the extremely high levels of R&D investment in the ICT industry to a sustainable level.

Appendices

Appendix 7.1

Table 7.A1 Review of knowledge transfer literature

Author	Study	Findings
Knowledge transfer within the firm		
Cummings & Teng (2003)	Study of 69 firms in 15 industries to identify the key factors affecting knowledge transfer success	• Transfer success increases with *decreased* 1) knowledge embeddedness; 2) knowledge distance; 3) norm distance between source and recipient – and with *increased* articulability of knowledge
Hansen (1999)	Study of 120 new-product development projects in 41 business units in a large electronics company to examine the task of developing new products in the least amount of time	• Weak links help a project team to quickly search for useful knowledge in other sub-units • Weak inter-unit ties are suitable for knowledge transfer (high transfer speed) if knowledge is not complex. If complex knowledge is transferred, strong inter-unit ties are required.
Hansen (2002)	Study of 120 new-product development projects in 41 business units of a large multi-unit company to explain effective knowledge sharing	• Project teams with short inter-unit network paths to units that possess related knowledge obtain more existing knowledge from other units and complete their projects faster • While established direct relations mitigate problems of transferring non-codified knowledge, they were harmful when the knowledge to be transferred was codified, because they were less needed but still involved maintenance costs
Szulanski (1996)	Study consisting of 271 observations of 122 best-practice transfers in eight companies to analyse the internal stickiness of knowledge transfer. Stickiness refers to the difficulty in transferring knowledge.	• The three most important origins of stickiness are: 1) the lack of absorptive capacity of the recipient; 2) causal ambiguity; and 3) an difficult relationship between the source and the recipient.
Szulanski (2000)	Cross-sectional analysis of primary data collected through a two-step survey of 122 best-practice transfers in eight companies.	• A process model of knowledge transfer is derived from his 1996 study. The model identifies stages of transfer and factors that are expected to correlate with transfer difficulties at different stages of the transfer.

(Continued)

Table 7.A1 (Continued)

Author	Study	Findings
Tsai (2002)	In-depth case study of a large, multi-unit petrochemical company to assess how a multi-unit organization can coordinate its units and encourage them to share knowledge with their competitors inside the organization	• A formal hierarchical structure, in the form of centralization, has a significant negative effect on knowledge sharing • Informal lateral relations, in the form of social interactions, have a significant positive effect on knowledge sharing among units that compete with each other for market share, but not among units that compete with each other for internal resources
Zander and Kogut (1995)	Study of 44 major innovations of Swedish companies to examine the central proposition that the transfer speed and imitation of capabilities are related to the dimensions of the underlying knowledge	• The degree of codification, the observability and the complexity of knowledge and how easily capabilities are taught has a significant influence on the speed of transfer

Knowledge transfer in acquisitions

Author	Study	Findings
Bresman et al. (1999)	Study of 42 international acquisitions involving knowledge transfer to identify factors that facilitate knowledge transfer as well as patterns of knowledge transfer	• Tacit knowledge is best transferred through intensive communication, with many visits and meetings, and when the acquisition is fully integrated • Articulated knowledge (such as patents) can be made available to the other party with little personal interaction • Over time, transfer of articulable knowledge decreases and transfer of tacit knowledge increases • Intensive use of integrating mechanisms such as joint R&D meetings, mixed project teams and cultural training sessions eases implementation and helps retention of personnel
Finkelstein and Haleblian (2002)	Study of 96 organizations to examine positive and negative transfer effects in acquisitions	• Acquisitions performance is positively associated with the similarity of industrial environments in acquirers and targets

Appendix 7.2: Questionnaire

In order to match your R&D activities with the knowledge terminology of Birkinshaw (2002) please answer the following questions:

1. Observability: To what extent do you agree with the following questions about your R&D unit? (where 1 = disagree completely to 7 = agree completely)

A competitor can easily learn how to develop our product by studying our employees at work	☐1 ☐2 ☐3 ☐4 ☐5 ☐6 ☐7
A competitor can easily learn how to develop our product by taking a tour of the plant	☐1 ☐2 ☐3 ☐4 ☐5 ☐6 ☐7
A competitor can easily learn how to develop our product by examining our machines	☐1 ☐2 ☐3 ☐4 ☐5 ☐6 ☐7
New R&D personnel can easily learn their job by studying a complete set of blueprints	☐1 ☐2 ☐3 ☐4 ☐5 ☐6 ☐7
New R&D personnel can easily learn their job by talking to experienced R&D personnel	☐1 ☐2 ☐3 ☐4 ☐5 ☐6 ☐7
Educating and training new R&D personnel is a quick and easy job	☐1 ☐2 ☐3 ☐4 ☐5 ☐6 ☐7

2. Mobility: To what extent do you agree with the following questions about your R&D unit? (where 7 = disagree completely to 1 = agree completely)

For our most important product, knowledge about many different technologies needs to be combined	☐1 ☐2 ☐3 ☐4 ☐5 ☐6 ☐7
The tasks of R&D units can not be divided between units since all equipment must be kept in one location	☐1 ☐2 ☐3 ☐4 ☐5 ☐6 ☐7
The tasks of R&D units can not be divided between units since the tasks demand daily face-to-face communication between personnel	☐1 ☐2 ☐3 ☐4 ☐5 ☐6 ☐7
We can achieve satisfactory quality only because of our firm's long experience with the technology	☐1 ☐2 ☐3 ☐4 ☐5 ☐6 ☐7
To achieve high product quality it is important that our R&D personnel have long experience in the specific R&D unit in which they are working	☐1 ☐2 ☐3 ☐4 ☐5 ☐6 ☐7
Workers in important parts of the manufacturing process have to be in constant contact with engineers or product quality will go down	☐1 ☐2 ☐3 ☐4 ☐5 ☐6 ☐7

3. If you had to decide on an exit option for your company, especially one including a close/exclusive cooperation in R&D with an established player, which of the below mentioned options would you prefer?

- Acquisition (typically least autonomy and strongest integration)
- Merger
- Licensing
- Minority equity
- Joint venture
- Joint R&D
- R&D contract
- Research funding
- Consortium
- Networking
- Outsourcing (typically strong autonomy and least integration)

4. Please provide a brief description on your three most important decision criteria for answer 3.

Criteria 1:
Criteria 2:
Criteria 3:

5. If not included in 3) what role do the characteristics of your company's R&D knowledge play in the area of cooperation?

6. Independent of any equity and governance-related issues, if you had to link your R&D operations to those of a global telecommunication equipment provider, what would be the most successful type of cooperation?

Notes

1. Obviously there are valuable acquisitions where the realization of synergies with existing R&D operations is not the prime concern (for example when the parent company pursues a pure portfolio management approach); however such acquisitions are not the focus of this paper.
2. Other modes of access to external knowledge are excluded from our investigation. These would comprise the spectrum of R&D collaboration from transactions to contracting and licensing. For an overview see Chiesa and Manzini (1998).
3. In this paper knowledge includes all forms of technology. Therefore if we talk about transferring knowledge, technology transfer is included.
4. Best-practice mergers realize a minimum of 70 per cent of total synergies within the first year after acquisition. After year two the synergy potential is close to zero.
5. We assume that the form and structure of the target in the R&D acquisition is comparable to what Birkinshaw (2000) refers to as an 'R&D Center'.
6. Typically these types of acquisition are not driven by mere R&D access but other strategic acquisition objectives (such as customer base, sales channels, scale). One practical example was the acquisition of Volvo by Ford in 1999.

7. Information on the company was generated through interviews with the company's CEO and COO (Appendix 7.2), discussion during a joint research project and internet research (www.bamboomc.com).

References

Ahuja, G. and R. Katila (2001) 'Technological Acquisition and the Innovation Performance of Acquiring Firms: a Longitudinal Study', *Strategic Management Journal*, 22, pp. 197–220.

Anderson, J. and M. Jönsson (2006) 'Mobile Transitions', *Business Strategy Review*, Spring, pp. 20–5.

Arundel, A. and C. Bordoy (2002) 'In-House vs. Ex-House: The Sourcing of Knowledge for Innovation', in J. de la Mothe and A. Link (eds) *Networks, Alliances and Partnerships in the Innovation Process*, Vol. 28 (Dordrecht: Kluwer Academic Publishers) pp. 67–90.

Bert, A., T. MacDonald and T. Herd (2003) 'Two Merger Integration Imperatives: Urgency and Execution', *Strategy & Leadership*, 31, pp. 42–49.

Bhattachrya, S., V. Krishnan and V. Mahajan (1998) 'Managing Product Definition in Highly Dynamic Environments', *Management Science*, 44, pp. 50–64.

Birkinshaw, J. (2002) 'Managing Internal R&D Networks in Global Firms: What Sort of Knowledge is Involved?' *Long Range Planning*, 35, pp. 245–67.

Birkinshaw, J., H. Bresman and L. Hakanson (2000) 'Managing the Post-Acquisition Integration Process: How the Human Integration and Task Integration Processes Interact to Foster Value Generation', *Journal of Management Studies*, 37, pp. 395–425.

Bresman, H., J. Birkinshaw and R. Nobel (1999) 'Knowledge Transfer in International Acquisitions', *Journal of International Business Studies*, 30, pp. 439–62.

Brodt, T. and M. Heitmann (2004) 'Customer-centric Development of Radically New Products', European Case Proceedings of the Tenth Americas Conference on Information Systems, New York.

Calabrese, G. (1997) 'Communication and Cooperation in Product Development', *R&D Management*, 27, pp. 239–52.

Capron, L., P. Dussage and W. Mitchell (1998) 'Resource Redeployment Following Horizontal Acquisitions in Europe and North America, 1988–1992', *Strategic Management Journal*, 19, pp. 631–61.

Chaudhury, S. and B. Tabrizi (1999) 'Capturing the Real Value in High-Tech Acquisitions', *Harvard Business Review*, 77, pp. 123–30.

Cummings, J. and B. Teng (2003) 'Transferring R&D Knowledge: The Key Factors Affecting Knowledge Transfer Success', *Journal of Engineering and Technology Management*, 20, pp. 39–68.

Deogun, N. and K. Scannel (2001) 'Year End Review of Markets and Finance 2000 – Market Swoon Stifles M&A's Red-Hot, But Old Economy Supplies a Surprise Bounty', *Wall Street Journal*, p. R4.

Finkelstein, S. and J. Haleblian (2002) 'Understanding Acquisition Performance: The Role of Transfer Effects', *Organization Science*, 13, pp. 36–47.

Griffin, A. and J. R. Hauser (1993) 'The Voice of the Customer', *Marketing Science*, 12, pp. 1–17.

Hagedoorn, J. and G. Duysters (2002) 'External Sources of Innovative Capabilities: The Preferences for Strategic Alliances or Mergers and Acquisitions', *Journal of Management Studies*, 39, pp. 167–88.

Hansen, M. T. (1999) 'The Search-transfer Problem: The Role of Weak Ties in Sharing Knowledge across Organizational Sub-units', *Administrative Science*, 44, pp. 82–112.

Hansen, M. T. (2002) 'Knowledge Networks: Explaining Effective Knowledge Sharing in Multiunit Companies', *Organization Science*, 13, pp. 232–48.

Harrison, J. S., M. A. Hitt and R. D. Ireland (1991) 'Synergies and Post-Acquisition Performance: Differences versus Similarities in Resource Allocations', *Journal of Management*, 17, pp. 173–90.

Haspeslagh, P. C. and D. B. Jemison (1991) *Managing Acquisitions: Creating Value through Corporate Renewal* (New York: The Free Press).

Heo, D. and Y. Yoo (2002) 'Knowledge Sharing in Post Merger Integration', *Sprouts, Working Papers on Information Environments, Systems and Organizations*, 2: 4 Article 12.

Hitt, M. A., J. S. Harrison and R. D. Ireland (2001) *Mergers & Acquisitions: A Guide to Creating Value for Shareholders* (New York: Oxford University Press).

Jemison, D. B. and S. Sitkin (1986) 'Acquisitions: The Process Can Be a Problem', *Harvard Business Review*. 64: 2, pp. 87–95

King, D., D. Dalton and C. Daily (2004) 'Meta-Analysis of Post-Acquisition Performance: Indications of Unidentified Moderators', *Strategic Management Journal*, 25, pp. 187–200.

Kraemer, K. L. and J. Dedrick (2002) 'Strategic Use of the Internet and E-Commerce: Cisco Systems', *Strategic Information Systems*, 11, pp. 5–29.

Napier, N. (1989) 'Merger and Acquisitions, Human Resource Issues and Outcomes: A Review and Suggested Typology', *Journal of Management Studies*, 26, pp. 271–89.

Picard, D. and J. McConville (2000) *Post-Merger Integration in the Age of Technology*, PricewaterhouseCoopers.

Sorenson, C., L. Mathiassen and M. Kakihara (2002) *Mobile Services: Functional Diversity and Overload*, Working Paper Series, London School of Economics and Political Science.

Sumi, T. and T. Michio (2002) 'Ramp New Enterprise Information Systems in a Merger and Acquisition Environment: A Case Study', *Journal of Engineering and Technology Management*, 19, pp. 93–104.

Szulanski, G. (1996) 'Exploring Internal Stickiness: Impediments to the Transfer of Best Practice within the Firm', *Strategic Management Journal*, 17, pp. 27–43.

Szulanski, G. (2000) 'The Process of Knowledge Transfer: A Diachronic Analysis of Stickiness', *Organization Behavior and Human Decision Processes*, 82, pp. 9–27.

Tsai, W. (2002) 'Social Structure of Coopetition Within a Multiunit Organization: Coordination, Competition, and Intraorganizational Knowledge Sharing', *Organization Science*, 13, pp. 179–90.

Warner, A. (2003) 'Buying Versus Building Competence: Acquisition Patterns in the Information and Telecommunications Industry 1995–2000', *International Journal of Innovation Management*, 7, pp. 395–415.

Wysocki, B. (1997) 'Many Mergers Driven by Search for Fresh Talent', *Chicago Tribune*, 28 December, p. 67.

Zander, U. and B. Kogut (1995) 'Knowledge and the Speed of the Transfer and Imitation of Organizational Capabilities: An Empirical Test', *Organization Science*, 6, pp. 76–92.

8
E-collaboration in the Automotive Supply Chain: Determinants and Impacts on Performance

Elisabeth Lefebvre, Louis A. Lefebvre, Amal Amarouch,
Luc Cassivi and Gaël le Hen

8.1 Introduction

This chapter explores one specific aspect of the 'open-innovation' paradigm (Chesbrough, 2003) by analysing collaborative new-product development (NPD) among business partners involved in one supply chain. By definition, 'open innovation assumes that useful knowledge is widely distributed, and that even the most capable R&D organization must identify, connect to, and leverage external knowledge sources as a core process in innovation' (Chesbrough, 2006, p. 2). Implicitly, the open-innovation paradigm therefore implies that interorganizational networks or supply chains play a salient role in the innovation process. However, our common understanding of open-innovation practices remains limited (West et al., 2006, p. 294).

More specifically, this chapter attempts to assess the relative importance of determinants of cross-border electronically mediated collaboration (e-collaboration) and examine the performance improvements derived from such collaboration. The focus here is not at the firm level but rather at the supply-chain level in the context of new-product development in the automotive sector. This line of inquiry seems relevant for the following reasons:

1. In the case of complex products such as aeroplanes, network systems, power plants or cars, firms reorganize themselves into supply chains defined here as 'the integration of key business processes from end-user through original suppliers that provides products, services and information that add value for customers and other stakeholders' (Lambert and Cooper, 2000). As a consequence, the locus of competition has moved from individual organizations to supply chains (Christopher, 1992; Cassivi et al., 2004); Furthermore, these supply chains are not only 'reshaping the global business architecture' but are also becoming, as some authors believe, 'the dominant organizational paradigm' (Parkhe et al., 2006, p. 560).

2. New-product development represents one key business process in a supply-chain context which is considered as knowledge-intensive, high value-added and strategic. New-product development is increasingly conducted among geographically dispersed teams from different organizations. Past research in the specific context of new-product development remains scarce (for a few exceptions, see Wierba et al., 2002; McDonough et al., 2001);

3. The emergence of efficient e-collaboration tools such as internet-based virtual project rooms or 3D viewing and modelling technologies creates the electronically mediated (or virtual) environment for effective cross-border and interorganizational collaborative product development work (Lu et al., 2005);

4. The automotive sector, considered as a 'medium-high tech manufacturing' sector (Leydesdorff et al., 2006; OECD, 2001) faces fierce competition from developing countries. Since the automotive sector is part of the techno-economic backbone of many industrialized countries, the struggle to maintain value-added and knowledge-intensive activities such as new-product development is ongoing while manufacturing facilities have long been established in some developing countries in Asia or South America. The competition will become even fiercer as countries such as China enter this sector.

This chapter is organized as follows: we will first briefly discuss conceptual and theoretical issues related to global virtual teams, e-collaboration tools, determinants of the use of these tools and alleged performance improvements derived from such use (Section 8.2). We next present the methodology used (Section 8.3). Finally, we discuss the study results (Section 8.4) ending with some concluding remarks and research implications.

8.2   Conceptual and theoretical issues

8.2.1   Defining global virtual teams (GVTs)

As a relatively recent concept, virtual teams (VTs) suffer from the lack of a unified definition among researchers even though a virtual team constitutes a critical pillar for any successful organization that is willing to respond to ever-increasing global challenges and thereby survive in the competitive world market. In a comprehensive review of prior research on VTs, Martins et al. (2004) indicated that there is a considerable overlap in the core definition, with small variations in the specifics. Most of the studies (Bell and Kozlowski, 2002; Lipnack and Stamps, 1999; Lurey and Raisinghani, 2001) define VTs as a group of people working together through computer-aided technologies on a common project while crossing different boundaries (location, time, organization). Other authors define VTs according to the degree of face-to-face contact (Fiol and O'Connor, 2005) but most agree that virtualness should be defined according to the extent of technology used in the place of face-to-face contact (Griffith and Neale, 2001; Kirkman et al., 2004; Zigurs, 2003; Bell and Kozlowski, 2002; Chudoba et al., 2005). More and more studies focus on hybrid teams since a purely face-to-face team that does not use electronic communication technology is rather rare in organizations today (Griffith and Neale, 2001).

When VTs are dispersed around the world, they are referred to as global virtual teams (Montoya-Weiss et al., 2001). Due to the globalization of business and the advancements in information-technologies, global virtual teams (GVTs) are becoming increasingly present in organizations, leading to growing interest and research on this subject (Jarvenpaa and Leidner, 1999; Maznevski and Chudoba, 2000; McDonough et al., 2001). Unfortunately, most of the studies were conducted with students in academic environments which do not necessarily reflect the reality of industrial environments (Powell et al., 2004). In this chapter, we retain Martins et al.'s (2004, p. 808) definition of VTs as 'teams whose members use technology to varying degrees in working across locational, temporal, and relational boundaries to accomplish an interdependent task' and focus on these teams in the context of new-product development projects carried out simultaneously in different countries around the world.

8.2.2   GVTs in the context of new-product development (NPD)

In order to be more effective in their NPD activities, multinational firms rely increasingly on global virtual teams. To launch a new product, these firms have to overcome competitive pressures from foreign rivals while dealing with the ever-growing risks and uncertainties related to NPD processes.

Previous research did not determine clearly whether GVTs are more effective than traditional teams in managing the NPD process (Schmidt et al., 2001). Moreover, previous findings on the decisions made by GVTs are not consistent. Comparison between GVTs and face-to-face teams suggested that the former makes more effective decisions than the latter (Schmidt et al., 2001) but not necessarily better decisions (Powell et al., 2004). These studies point to the poor co-ordination within GVTs which leads to substantial loss of time and also delays in reaching effective decisions (Schmidt et al., 2001). Electronic collaboration certainly fosters the dissemination of information quickly among the global team members despite their geographic dispersion and thus allows better communication. Global e-collaboration, therefore, may be defined as 'the use of e-collaboration technologies for supporting collaboration among organizational members in two or more countries' (Munkvold, 2005, p. 78).

8.2.3   The emergence of e-collaboration in supply chains

Information among supply-chain members was historically exchanged through paper-based documents such as faxes or catalogues. This type of information-sharing caused delays, the inefficient manual re-entry of data into the information systems of each supply-chain member, multiple errors, and miscommunications among and business partners. The internet and World Wide Web nowadays provide a common network platform that allows unparalleled levels of information openness (Markus and Christiannse, 2003) and enables supply-chain members to collaborate electronically in real time and in a leveraged manner. Moreover, e-collaboration represents 'more than a technological substitution for traditional face-to-face collaboration (Rutkowski et al., 2002) as it enables the coordination of various decisional activities beyond transactions among supply-chain partners (Johnson and Whang, 2002).

The selection of specific e-collaboration tools depends on many issues including the IT infrastructure, the organizational culture and the communication environment. Two issues need to be considered when attempting to better understand the effectiveness of e-collaboration tools – the type of communication technologies being used, and how to use those technologies. Daft and Lengel (1984) developed the concept of media richness, which refers to the extent that the media transmits a higher volume and variety of information (including non-verbal cues, which serve to reduce uncertainty of meaning that can be found in face-to-face meeting interactions). Videoconferencing is considered to be high in media richness. A high degree of media richness has been linked positively to team effectiveness, efficiency, the amount of communication, the relationships among team members and team commitment (Martins et al., 2004).

8.2.4 E-collaboration tools for new-product development

Numerous firms reported how successfully they use the e-collaborative tools in evaluating new products at different stages. These tools reduce the design time because firms evaluate and modify their new designs faster and can make changes more rapidly and earlier in the NPD process without changing the product design repeatedly. The electronic collaboration in GVTs helps firms bring together information located in various parts of the world. On the other hand, it can remove the socialization aspects of human communication. To compensate, some studies recommend that GVTs meet face-to-face at the early stages of the NPD project so they can build better relationships, develop trust and establish common understanding which will later improve their performance (Maznevski and Chudoba, 2000; Robey et al., 2000).

Different types of technologies support e-collaboration among the GVT members. Examples of e-collaboration technologies are websites, instant messaging, groupware including e-mail, databases, discussion arenas, bulletin boards and calendars, videoconferencing, weblogs and Wikis. It is accepted that there is a large selection of e-collaboration tools which require that the team members are proficient in a new kind of literacy – relating to document formats such as forms, graphs, charts and maps and also visual representations such as images, graphics, and video and audio presentation of information (Gillam and Oppenheim, 2006).

In the context of new-product development, several functional teams are involved and a vast number of technologies ensure efficient interactions between them. With the advent of Web-based tools, collaborative engineering encompasses technical and social aspects of product development (Lu et al., 2005). Technologies such as CAD systems or other systems that facilitate communication and coordination are critical to the integration of partners in the product-development process (Ragatz et al., 1997; Baba and Nobeoka, 1998). Collaborative engineering encourages design teams involved in a relationship to create and maintain joint processes (Baba and Nobeoka, 1998) but also to develop decision-making models that focus on knowledge transfer and management (Troussier, 2000). These challenges have pushed firms to adopt different e-collaboration tools for communication (forums, whiteboards, chat rooms) but also for dedicated tasks such as document-sharing, project management and technical communication (Delinchant et al., 2002).

8.2.5   Determinants of the use of e-collaboration tools

While a significant body of research on the benefits of e-collaboration tools is steadily increasing, one of the areas that demands more research attention is the understanding of the determinants of use of e-collaboration tools. Maznevski and Chudoba (2000) examined team effectiveness in terms of the relationship between technology use, primary choice of communication medium and group conclusions. They also looked at how structural characteristics such as tasks, organizational culture and team characteristics interacted with technology. Their findings suggest that a global team's most effective use of technology will be shaped by the dimensions of the team's task and its context. In previous work, DeSanctis and Jackson (1994) showed that the benefits of using a more complex medium increased as the tasks became more complex. Other research on GVTs has mostly focused on the role of cultural diversity and its influence on teams' communication patterns (Maznevski and Chudoba, 2000; Shachaf, 2005; Robey et al., 2000; Sarker and Sahay, 2004). Other characteristics such as differences in language, tradition and cultural values may make effective communication more difficult (Bell and Kozlowski, 2002). Training is another issue that has been suggested as supporting the performance of GVTs, most notably in communication using electronic media (Hertel et al., 2005).

8.2.6   Performance improvements derived from e-collaboration tools

E-collaboration tools bring people together to work on interdependent tasks without taking into account the geographic, temporal or organizational barriers. The teams' members are assigned according to their knowledge, skills and abilities (Martins et al., 2004). This certainly allows an organization to enrich the pool of its resources at a more effective cost (Kerber and Buono, 2004). Furthermore, since the pool of knowledge is more diversified, interactions between team members with different professional and cultural backgrounds foster creativity, since creativity mainly happens as a direct result of inter-action (Leenders et al., 2003). Because of the global distributed nature of business today and the technical advancements of e-collaboration tools, orga-nizations with global teams can react in a more responsive way all over the world. While e-collaboration tools offer all these benefits, a good understand-ing of these tools is necessary for the management to ensure effectiveness. A team's extent of virtualness (its use of e-collaboration tools) depends on the nature of the task, the technological resources and members' skills and capa-bilities (Griffith and Neale, 2001; Bell and Kozlowski, 2002). Because global VTs live and work in different countries, cultural diversity, language differ-ences and varying IT sophistication become important variables to consider while studying the use of e-collaboration tools.

In the context of complex product development, there is a significant level of product and engineering data, process uncertainty and frequent engineer-ing changes. Firms are actively seeking more sophisticated e-collaboration tools to effectively manage product engineering, thus enabling them to con-trol design and engineering and measure progress during the development process. Product lifecycle management (PLM) seems to be a powerful tool sup-porting this endeavour. PLM is an approach that supports both engineering data (drawings, project plans and part files) and the product-development process during the total product life-cycle (Rouibah and Ould-Ali, 2006). Product data is accessible to different GVT members, allowing them to effec-tively collaborate, which leads eventually to a shorter development cycle and reductions in time and cost for organizations. Although some authors (see for instance, Cassivi et al., 2004) attempted to measure the impact of e-collaboration on the performance of individual firms acting along the different modes of a supply chain, the measurement of supply-chain perfor-mance is plagued with difficulties and our common understanding of such measures remains incomplete.

8.3 Methodology

8.3.1 Industrial context

The focal firm is a large multinational responsible for the development of components, parts and systems that will be integrated into the next gen-eration of cars. These include advanced navigation systems, ESC (electronic stability control), improved ABS (antilock braking systems) or hybrid systems, and are considered as complex products combining precision mechan-ics, software, electronics and hydraulics. The automotive sector is highly

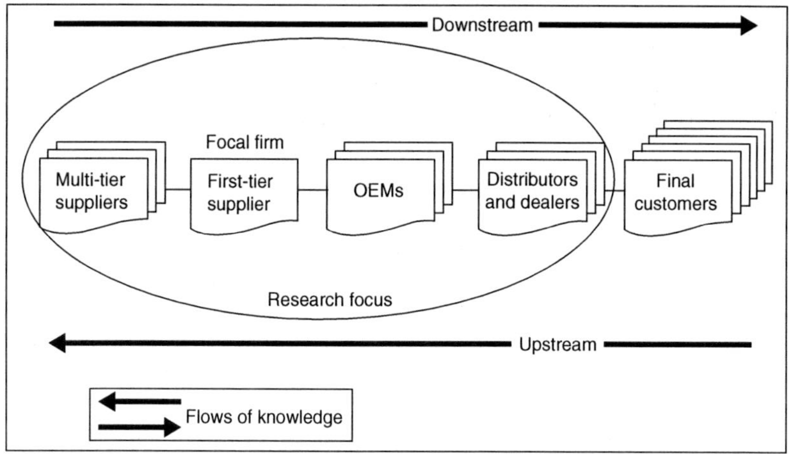

Figure 8.1   The automotive supply chain under investigation

globalized. For instance, global outsourcing has been going on for a few decades and is increasingly integrated from multi-tier suppliers to dealers. Mass customization is also a powerful trend that promotes the integration of dealers because most of the automotive customer data resides in their management systems. In such a context, the new-product development process has been extended to lower tiers of suppliers (upstream) and to car manufacturers and dealers (downstream).

Figure 8.1 indicates the scope of this research initiative. The supply chain under investigation entails four layers: multi-tier suppliers, one first-tier supplier (considered here as the focal firm), OEMs (original equipment manufacturers – or car makers) and dealers. Final customers have to be excluded as the supply chain is not yet extended to them. The large multinational acts as the key sponsor of the diffusion of e-collaboration tools within its business units and among its business partners. This large multinational also acts as the focal point in an increasingly integrated supply chain where key partners invest more and more resources in the development of new products. For instance, first-tier suppliers not only design, manufacture and deliver parts and components to the multinational but they: 1) perform R&D activities for the development of products (to reduce costs and increase security); 2) provide technical services (such as the calibration of a component) to the multinational firm; and 3) analyse installation and maintenance issues for the multinational's customers. As a result, the product-development process is extended upstream and downstream along the supply chain, and the use of e-collaboration tools is deployed among key partners.

8.3.2   Research design

The empirical evidence was gathered in two main consecutive but complementary phases.

Phase I: A field study carried out in one large multinational firm allowed us to gain a better understanding of the ongoing collaboration between new-product development teams. In particular, the deployment of e-collaboration tools was mapped and the new functionalities of these tools were analysed. Empirical results from this first phase are briefly discussed in section 8.4.1.

Phase II: A questionnaire that had been pre-tested and validated with project and R&D managers was sent to all members of the three new-product development teams (N = 110). Members of these teams were geographically dispersed over three continents and were involved in product-development activities either in the business units of the large multinational, or in different firms that are key partners of the multinational (selected suppliers and customers). The three new development teams can therefore be characterized as a global virtual team. A total of 61 respondents participated in the survey, which corresponds to a 55.5 per cent response rate. They included downstream specialists (manufacturing, sales, and marketing) – 24 per cent; upstream specialists (engineering, product design) – 45 per cent; and product managers – 31 per cent.

The questionnaire provided two sets of data: 1) factual data on respondents; and 2) their assessment of several critical issues such as characteristics of the team, cultural factors, characteristics of e-collaboration tools and the performance improvements derived from the use of e-collaboration tools (Table 8.1). For the perceptual variables, previously tested multi-scale constructs were used (Appendix 8.1). Construct reliability proved to be

Table 8.1   Construct reliability – Cronbach alpha coefficients

1. Team context		**Performance improvements** **derived from the use** **of e-collaboration tools**	
Level of involvement in the team	0.62	Communication improvements	0.76
Accessibility of team members	0.71	Time reductions	0.82
Training for e-collaboration teams	0.71	Creativity enhancement	0.84
		Manufacturing improvements	0.95
		Product improvements	0.81
		Cost reductions	0.78
Cultural factors		**Characteristics of** **e-collaboration tools**	
Language differences	N/A	Usefulness	0.81
Professional background differences	0.69	Ease of use	0.76
Behavioural differences	0.69		

satisfactory since the Cronbach alpha coefficients are within the guidelines set by van de Ven and Ferry (1980), ranging 0.62 to 0.95 (Table 8.1).

In this chapter, the main focus is on the results from the e-survey (sections 8.4.2 and 8.4.3).

8.4   Results and discussion

8.4.1   Deployment of e-collaboration tools

The e-collaboration tools rely on a product life-cycle management (PLM) application called e-Vis for saving data files, exchanging data, controlling data exchanges, exporting data files and viewing 3D models. The four e-collaboration tools are briefly described in Table 8.2. The way team members use these tools is also outlined in Table 8.2.

The above e-collaboration tools support the so-called 'seamless 3D model pipeline', which includes the integration of 3D CAD systems with CAE-CAM (computer-aided engineering and computer-aided manufacturing). The 3D models can also be used upstream in the supply chain by manufacturing equipment such as CNC (computer numerical control) machines to directly manufacture parts or components or to create tools or moulds. PDM (product data management) systems need also to be implemented in order to store and maintain information on the product, including technical documentation, product specifications, bills of material, part classification, and so on. PDM systems can also handle 3D CAD models, 2D drawings or CNC programs. As a consequence, each member of the GVT from any of the four layers of the supply chain (Figure 8.1) can access real-time product information, be involved in the new-product development process and participate to decision-making. Access to and participation in the process is, however, made secure by several mechanisms and procedures (including electronic signatures).

As indicated in Figure 8.1 the deployment of the four collaboration tools does not yet directly reach the final customers since customer data resides in the dealers' management systems. The next challenge to be addressed is to allow direct customer input into the design, a process by which supply-chain organizations can co-create added value.

8.4.2   Determinants of the level of use of e-collaboration tools

Which factors best explain the level of use of the four e-collaboration tools? Table 8.3 provides some answers by displaying the results from the multiple regression analysis where the level of use of the e-collaboration tools is the dependent variable and the team context, cultural factors and the characteristics of these tools are the independent variables. Together the eight factors displayed in the table explain 21.8 per cent of the variance. The following pertinent comments can be made based on the data in Table 8.3.

Table 8.2   Description of e-collaboration tools

3D model visualization:
1. A dedicated 3D model viewer is used by team members. Functions of the viewer (Digital Mock-up (DMU) format) include product structure, rotation and zoom, measurement (exact geometry), mark-up or redlining (to write comments), etc.
2. The 3D models (in DMU format) are saved on e-Vis, which allows team members to improve product design and have a better understanding of the product (how the parts fit together, the main dimensions, the weight, how the geometry looks, holes, width, etc.).

3D models (CAD) publication:
1. In order to have CAD design engineers export data from their CAD/ADM into e-Vis, native 3D CAD models are converted into a DMU (Digital Mock-up) format through an 'export menu'.
2. A first-tier supplier programmes the the 'export menu', which allowed 3D CAD data to first be extracted from the EDM (electronic data management) system, and then converted into a DMU format, and finally saved in e-Vis (according to a document structure specified by the engineer).

3D models conferencing:
1. From a PC or laptop, a conference can be initiated by team members to discuss technical issues using a 'shared' 3D model in a DMU format. Any action (measurement, rotation, etc.) made by one team member is seen by online colleagues. Other (secondary) users can also be involved in the conference.
2. A command-sharing principle dictates the 3D conferencing (the content of a screen is not necessarily transmitted from one PC to another). This type of conferencing is therefore suitable for 'graphic-intensive' applications such as 3D models visualization, and enables quasi-real-time interactions between the participants of the 3D conference.

3D models application sharing:
1. A variant of 3D conferencing, application sharing, allows 3D conferencing between more than two viewer applications (which is the limit for 3D conferencing).
2. Application sharing also enables different applications (e.g. Microsoft Word) to be shared or even the sharing of an entire desktop between different PCs. The conference participants can also view and control one participant's application if required. Enabled by high bandwidth, it sends the content of a screen to another PC. Consequently, application-sharing (via such applications as NetMeeting from Microsoft and Centra) is suitable for applications such as Microsoft Word or Excel, but it is not suitable for sharing a viewer application.

Training emerges as a significant variable that explains the level of use of e-collaboration tools. The so-called '3D pipeline' requires the integration of 3D CAD systems with CAE/CAM systems; this is plagued by a number of difficulties including incompatibilities between different systems and the coexistence of 3D and 2D models. Appropriate training is required and appears to be a strong and significant determinant of the level of use of

Table 8.3   Determinants of the level of use of e-collaboration tools

Team context		Characteristics of e-collaboration tools	
Level of involvement in the team	0.038	Usefulness	0.131
Accessibility of team members	0.021	Ease of use	0.120
Training for e-collaboration teams	0.390 ***		
Cultural factors			
Language differences	0.520 ****	Adjusted R^2	21.8% ****
Professional background differences	−0.106		
Behavioural differences	−0.038		

$*p < 0.10;$ $**p < 0.05;$ $***p < 0.01;$ $****p < 0.001$

e-collaboration tools. It should be noted that the multinational, as the key sponsor of the e-collaboration tools, provided training to all members of the new-product development teams.

Cultural differences hamper e-collaboration. This seems to be the case for professional backgrounds and behavioural differences ($\beta = -0.106$ and $\beta = -0.038$ respectively), although it is not that significant. Surprisingly, language differences are significantly and positively related to the level of use of e-collaboration tools ($\beta = 0.520$, $p = 0.0000$). English is the common language of communication among team members whose mother tongue for the vast majority of respondents is not English. The type of e-collaboration tools here offer visual representations, on which are based technical specifications, the assessment of impacts for the proposed design changes, and the like. Team members in the field study believed it is much easier to point to a particular problem or point of discussion on a visual representation than to try to 'explain it in words'. Furthermore, in the context of new-product development, engineers are known to have a strong 'visual culture' (Henderson, 1999), which is also found to be present in team members from manufacturing, sales, marketing and product managers, who usually rely on 2D models and physical prototypes.

The characteristics of the e-collaboration tools, namely their usefulness and ease of use, are positive but not significant determinants of the level of use of these tools. E-Vis, as described in Table 8.2, was considered by team members as 'just another wave of change' which brings its own burden of adjustments but does not seem to drastically increase the complexity of the day-to-day work.

8.4.3   Performance improvements derived from e-collaboration tools and the role of communication improvement as an intervening variable

Structural-equation modelling represents a powerful tool for testing propositions involving a set of interrelated dependence relationships such as the

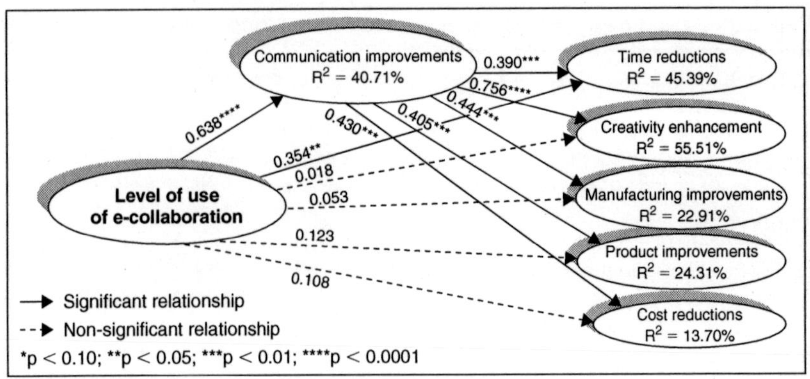

Figure 8.2   Performance improvements derived from the use of e-collaboration tools: results from the LISREL analysis

Table 8.4   Overall fit statistics for the proposed structural equation model

Chi-square $= 0.268$	Standardized RMR $= 0.020$
Degrees of freedom $= 4$	RMSEA $= 0.0000$
Chi-square/degrees of freedom $= 0.067$	GFI $= 0.996$
P $= 0.99179$	AGFI $= 0.970$

ones displayed in Figure 8.2. The structural-equation model is estimated using the LISREL program. Table 8.4 presents the criteria for assessing the fit of the proposed model. The assessment of fit is good when based on the following observations:

- The level of the chi-square test is not significant for the proposed model ($p = 0.99179$). A significant chi-square value would indicate that the model is not appropriate (Bagozzi et al., 1998; Gefen et al., 2000).
- The root mean square residual (RMR), which represents the measure of the average unexplained variances and co-variances, should be close to zero if the empirical data is to fit the proposed model (Hair et al., 1998, Gefen et al., 2000). With an RMR of 0.020 and an RMSEA of 0.0000, this second criterion is met. A goodness of fit (GFI) above 0.90 is usually recognized as an indication of good fit. The adjusted goodness of fit (AGFI) proposed by Joreskog and Sorbom (1979) also meets the desired threshold of 0.90 and is viewed as being more conservative than the GFI. With both the GFI and the AGFI well above 0.90 (0.996 and 0.970 respectively), the fit is excellent.

The use of the path diagram to display the LISREL parameters facilitates the interpretation of the results (Figure 8.2). The most striking result is that the improved communication plays the role of an intervening variable between the level of use of e-collaborative tools and the other performance improvements derived from the use of these tools.

The level of use of e-collaboration tools has a significant impact on communication improvements (0.638****) which in turn has a significant impact on time reductions (0.390***), creativity enhancement (0.765****), manufacturing improvements (0.444***), product improvements (0.405***) and cost reductions (0.430***). However, the level of e-collaboration tools fails to show direct significant relationships with four independent variables (although all relationships are positive), with the exception of time reductions (0.354***).

Results suggest that communication among members from global virtual teams is the cornerstone on which rest tangible monetary benefits (reductions in cost and time), competitive-based benefits (product and manufacturing improvements) and intangible benefits (creativity enhancement). Non-monetary benefits, especially creativity enhancement, which displayed by far the strongest relationship (0.756****), are important as they ensure sustainable competitive positioning in the longer term.

8.5 Conclusion

The prevalence of e-collaboration tools as a dominant way to conduct new-product-development activities seems to be an irreversible trend. The results from empirical evidence gathered from three global virtual teams allow us to partially respond to two fundamental questions: How can organizations promote more effectively the use of e-collaboration tools?; and, Are these tools worthwhile?

The answer to the first question may be divided into two main issues:

1. Some determinants of the level of use of e-collaboration tools cannot (or should not) be changed in the short term. This is obviously so in the case of cultural differences: bridging across different cultures requires much more time than the typical lifespan of a new-product-development project. However, strong awareness of these differences appears advisable and, in the case of collaborative engineering, could even be capitalized upon. Language differences are the strongest determinants (Beta = 0.520, p = 0.0000) of the level of use of e-collaboration tools: language barriers are removed to a large extent as members of virtual teams can better express their ideas through visual representations such as 3D models and prototypes. The visual culture of these teams can be emphasized in order to remove some other cultural factors such as behavioural differences in multi-country, multi-firm and multidisciplinary teams.
2. Other determinants can be directly acted upon. Multinationals make large investments to improve the IT infrastructure but training remains the key to the effective use of new IT functionalities and systems. Training may prove to be a difficult task when spread among different firms. In this

study, however, the multinational firm went to a great deal of effort to offer training to all team members (whether or not they were its employees) in order to ensure deployment of e-collaboration tools, making them easier to use and more efficient.

In response to the second question – Are e-collaboration tools worthwhile? – the answer from the members of the global virtual teams (and not the IT consultants) seemed to be positive; the results indicate that communication improvements are significantly enhanced through the use of e-collaboration tools, which allow for synchronous and more effective communication. They also reduce the information asymmetry between team members, and improves the quality of their decisions. In particular, better communication reduces the frequency of changes late in the product-development stage, which are for the most part counterproductive. Results also point to communication improvements as a strong intervening variable between the level of use of e-collaboration tools and performance improvements derived from these tools. In other words, communication, which is positively and significantly related to the use of e-collaboration tools, is revealed as one of the core functions of e-collaboration tools. These findings confirm previous work exploring the importance of the selection of e-collaboration tools that found that communication is the core of any GVT process. As Hulnick put it (cited in Powell et al., 2000): 'if technology is the foundation of the virtual business relationship, communication is the cement'.

The empirical results provided in this chapter seem also to support the 'open-innovation' paradigm, at least to some extent. The innovation process is indeed open among selected business partners operating in one supply chain, but appears to be closed to any other organizations. This raises a number of public policy issues: How can innovative activities that span across organizations and countries be tracked?; and, To what extent does open innovation occur across global supply chains? Is it possible to isolate specific national patterns of innovative activities when departing from the closed innovation model? Under what frame conditions, especially regarding intellectual property law and market structure, would open innovation be most effective?

Besides the practical implications raised above, this research certainly has theoretical implications. First, it may be considered as a point of departure from previous studies on how different factors (contextual and cultural, as well as the characteristics of e-collaboration tools themselves) determine the use of e-collaboration tools. These issues are relevant to forging a better understanding of the functioning of GVTs. Future research efforts should therefore be directed towards the use of advanced e-collaborative tools such 3D collaborative technologies. While technical research on these tools is prolific, future studies would benefit from a better understanding of the interaction between the use of these technologies and the supply-chain performance. In particular, with improved communication among GVTs, the generation and transfer of knowledge for new-product development activities would occur faster within the supply chain. This may constitute one of the most critical competitive advantages in the so-called knowledge-based economy.

Second, this exploratory research also departs from previous work by moving the level of analysis from individual firms to supply chains. This obviously entails some difficulties in the research design as it demands a deeper understanding of the complex interactions between firms. However, the research design closely reflects the reality of the chosen sector and is in line with the grounded theory approach (Strauss and Corbin, 1990). Such an approach may be worthwhile to pursue in the future.

Acknowledgments

This research was part-funded by SSHRC and FQRSC. The authors are grateful to the editors and the external reviewer for their insightful comments.

Appendix 8.1   Constructs and their measures

Table 8.A1   Constructs and their measures

Team context:
– Level of involvement in team:
You were involved at the very early stages of the project;
You spend a large part of your working time on this project.

– Accessibility of team members:
The people in the development team are geographically dispersed;
The people in the development team are difficult to reach.

– Training for e-collaboration teams:
The training you received showed the basic features of the cooperation tools;
The training you received showed what job-related tasks the cooperation tools were
  good for solving.

Cultural factors:
– Language differences: (N/A)
– Professional background differences:
Differences exist among team members concerning technical terms used (jargon);
Differences exist among team members concerning professional background
  (for example, engineering vs. marketing).

– Behavioural differences:
Differences exist among team members concerning time orientation (for example,
  short-term vs. long-term);
Differences exist among team members concerning tolerance of ambiguity and
  uncertainty;
Differences exist among team members concerning how decisions are made.

(Continued)

Table 8.A1   (Continued)

Impacts of e-collaboration tools:
– Communication improvements:
The quality of the decisions and technical discussions with colleagues were better
  (for example, more transparency);
The information asymmetry in the team was reduced.

– Time reductions:
Less travel was required;
The number of changes was reduced;
The time required to perform task(s) was reduced;
You were able to begin task(s) earlier and resolve issues earlier
  (e.g. manufacturability).

– Creativity enhancement:
You were able to explore more issues;
You were able to generate more alternatives;
The alternatives were more creative.

– Manufacturing improvements:
The production time was reduced;
The manufacturability was improved.

– Product improvements:
The technical performance of the part/component was better (functional
  performance);
The life-cycle performance of the part/component was better (maintainability).

– Cost reductions:
The investments in manufacturing and assembly equipment were reduced;
The product and production costs were lower.

Characteristics of e-collaboration tools

– Usefulness:
The functionalities provided by the e-collaboration tools are useful;
The information provided in the 3D models is useful.

– Ease of use:
The software is easy to use ('user-friendly');
It is easy to get help to learn a new feature of the e-collaboration tools.

References

Baba, Y. and K. Nobeoka (1998) 'Towards Knowledge-based Product Development: the 3-D CAD Model of Knowledge Creation', *Research Policy*, 26: 6, pp. 643–59.

Bagozzi, R., Y. Yi and L. W. Phillips (1991) 'Assessing Construct Validity in Organizational Research', *Administrative Science Quarterly*, 36: 3, pp. 421–58.

Bell, B. S. and S. W. J. Kozlowski (2002) 'A Typology of Virtual Teams', *Group & Organization Management*, 27: 1, pp. 14–49.

Cassivi, L., E. Lefebvre, L. A. Lefebvre and P. M. Léger (2004) 'The Impact of E-collaboration Tools on Performance', *International Journal of Logistics Management*, 15: 1, pp. 91–110.

Chesbrough, H. (2003) *Open Innovation: The New Imperative for Creating and Profiting from Technology* (Boston: Harvard Business School Press).

Chesbrough, H. (2006) 'Open Innovation: A New Paradigm for Understanding Industrial Innovation', in H. Chesbrough, W. Vanhaverbeke and J. West (eds) *Open Innovation* (Oxford. Oxford University Press).

Christopher, M. (1992) *Logistics and Supply Chain Management* (London: Pitman).

Chudoba, K. M., E. Wynn, M. Lu and M. B. Watson-Manheim (2005) 'How Virtual Are We? Measuring Virtuality and Understanding its Impact in a Global Organization', *Information Systems Journal*, 15: 4, pp. 279–306.

Daft, R. L. and R. H. Lengel (1984) 'Information Richness: A New Approach to Managerial Behavior and Organization Design', *Research in Organizational Behavior*, 6, pp. 191–233.

Delinchant, B., V. Riboulet, L. Gerbaud, P. Marin, F. Noell and F. Wurtz (2002) 'E-cooperative Design among Mechanical and Electrical Engineers: Implications for Communication between Professional Cultures', Professional Communication, *IEEE Transactions*, 45: 4, pp. 231–49.

DeSanctis, G. and B. M. Jackson (1994) 'Coordination of Information Technology Management: Team-based Structures and Computer-based Communication Systems', *Journal of Management Information Systems*, 10: 4, pp. 85–110.

Fiol, C. M. and E. J. O'Connor (2005) 'Identification in Face-to-face, Hybrid, and Pure Virtual Teams: Untangling the Contradictions', *Organization Science*, 16: 1, pp. 19–32.

Gefen, D., D. Straub and M. Boudreau (2000) 'Structural Equation Modeling and Regression Guidelines for Research Practice', *Communications of the AIS*, 4: 7, pp. 41–79.

Gillam, C. and C. Oppenheim (2006) 'Reviewing the Impact of Virtual Teams in the Information Age', *Journal of Information Science*, 32: 2, pp. 160–75.

Griffith, T. L. and M. A. Neale (2001) 'Information Processing in Traditional, Hybrid, and Virtual teams: From Nascent Knowledge to Transactive Memory', *Research in Organizational Behaviour*, 23, pp. 379–421.

Hair, J. F., R. E. Anderson, R. L. Tatham and W. C. Black (1998) *Multivariate Data Analysis*, 5th edition (New Jersey: Prentice Hall).

Henderson, K. (1999) *On Line and On Paper: Visual Representations, Visual Culture and Computer Graphics in Design Engineering* (Cambridge, MA: MIT Press).

Hertel, G., S. Geister and U. Konradt (2005) 'Managing Virtual teams: A Review of Current Empirical Research', *Human Resource Management Review*, 15, pp. 69–95.

Hulnick, G. (2000) 'Doing Business Virtually', *Communication World*, 17: 3, pp. 33–6.

Jarvenpaa, S. L. and D. E. Leidner (1999) 'Communication and Trust in Global Virtual Teams', *Organization Science*, 10: 6, pp. 791–815.

Johnson, E. and S. Whang (2002) 'E-business and Supply Chain Management: An Overview and Framework', *Production and Operations Management*, 11: 4, pp. 413–23.

Joreskog, K. C. and D. Sorbom (1979) *Advances in Factor Analysis and Structural Equations Models* (Cambridge: Abt Books).

Kerber, K. W. and A. F. C. Buono (2004) 'Leadership Challenges in Global Virtual Teams: Lessons from the Field', *S.A.M. Advanced Management Journal*, 69: 4, pp. 4–10.

Kirkman, B. L., B. Rosen, P. P. Tesluk and C. B. Gibson (2004) 'The Impact of Team Empowerment on Virtual Team Performance: The Moderating Role of Face to Face Interaction', *Academy of Management Journal*, 47: 2, pp. 175–92.

Lambert, D. M. and M. Cooper (2000) 'Issues in Supply Chain Management', *Industrial Marketing Management*, 29: 1, pp. 65–83.

Leenders, R., J. M. L. van Engelen and J. Kratzer (2003) 'Virtuality, Communication and New Product Team Creativity: A Social Network Perspective', *Journal of Engineering and Technology Management*, 20: 1–2, pp. 69–92.

Leydesdorff, L., W. Dolfsma and G. van der Panne (2006) 'Measuring the Knowledge Base of an Economy in Terms of Triple-helix relations among Technology, Organization, and Territory' *Research Policy*, 35: 2, pp. 181–99.

Lipnack, J. and J. Stamps (1999) 'Virtual Teams: The New Way to Work', *Strategy & Leadership*, 27: 1, pp. 14–18.

Lu, SC-Y, J. Zhang, C. Wang and F. Grobler (2005) 'Modelling Design Processes and Stakeholder Perspectives to Support Collaborative Engineering Negotiation: a Case Study of Designing Individualised Prostheses over the Internet', *International Journal of Computer Applications in Technology*, 2: 1, pp. 2–17.

Lurey, J. S. and M. S. Raisinghani (2001) 'An Empirical Study of Best Practices in Virtual Teams', *Information & Management*, 38: 8, pp. 523–44.

Markus, M. Y. and E. Christiannse (2003) 'Adoption and Impact of Collaboration Electronic Marketplace', *Information Systems and e-Business Management*, 1: 2, pp. 139–55.

Martins, L. L., L. L. Gilson and M. T. Maynard (2004) 'Virtual Teams: What Do We Know and Where Do We Go From Here?', *Journal of Management*, 30: 6, pp. 805–35.

Maznevski, M. L. and K. M. Chudoba (2000) 'Bridging Space over Time: Global Virtual Team Dynamics and Effectiveness', *Organization Science*, 11: 5, pp. 473–92.

McDonough, E. F., K. B. Kahn and G. Barczak (2001) 'An Investigation of Global, Virtual, and Collocated New-Product Development Teams', *The Journal of Product Innovation Management*, 18: 2, pp. 110–20.

Montoya-Weiss, M., M. Massey and M. Song, (2001) 'Getting it Together: Temporal Coordination and Conflict Management in Global Virtual Teams', *Academy of Management Journal*, 44: 6, pp. 1251–62.

Munkvold, B. E. (2005) 'Experiences from Global e-collaboration: Contextual Influences on Technology Adoption and Us', *IEEE Transactions on Professional Communication*, 48: 1, pp. 1–9.

OECD (2001) *Science and Industry Scoreboard: Towards a Knowledge-based Economy* (Paris: OECD).

Parkhe, A., S. Wasserman and D. Ralston (2006) 'New Frontiers in Network Theory Development', *Academy of Management Review*, 31: 3, pp. 560–68.

Powell, A., G. Piccoli and B. Ives (2004) 'Virtual Teams: A Review of Current Literature and Directions for Future Research,' *The DataBase for Advances in Information Systems*, 35: 1, pp. 6–36.

Ragatz, G. L., R. B. Handfield and T. V. Scannell (1997) 'Success Factors for Integrating Suppliers into New-Product Development', *Journal of Product Innovation Management*, 14: 3, pp. 190–202.

Robey, D., H. Khoo and C. Powers (2000) 'Situated Learning in Cross-functional Virtual Teams', *IEEE Transactions on Professional Communication*, 43: 1, pp. 51–66.

Rouibah, K., S. Ould-Ali (2006) 'Dynamic Data Sharing and Security in a Collaborative Product Definition Management System', *Robotics and Computer-Integrated Manufacturing*, pp. 1–17.

Rutkowski, A. F., D. R. Vogel, M. M. van Genuchten, T. M. A. Belmans and M. Favier (2002) 'E-collaboration: The Reality of Virtuality', *IEEE Transactions on Professional Communication*, 45: 4, pp. 219–42.

Sarker, S. and S. Sahay (2004) 'Implications of Space and Time for Distributed Work: an Interpretive Study of US-Norwegian Systems Development Teams', *European Journal of Information Systems*, 13: 1, pp. 3–20.

Schmidt, J. B., M. M. Montoya-Weiss and A. Massey (2001) 'New-Product Development Decision-making Effectiveness: Comparing Individuals, Face-to-face Teams, and Virtual Teams', *Decision Sciences*, 32: 4, pp. 575–600.

Shachaf, P. (2005) 'Bridging Cultural Diversity through E-mail', *Journal of Global Information Technology Management*, 8: 2, pp. 46–7.

Strauss, A. and J. Corbin (1990) *Basics of Qualitative Research: Grounded Theory Procedures and Techniques* (Newbury Park: Sage).

Troussier, N. (2000) 'A Way to Identify and Manage the Knowledge Provided by Mechanical Simulations in Engineering Design', *Computing and Information Systems*, 7: 3, pp. 79–84.

van de Ven, A., and D. Ferry (1980) *Measuring and Assessing Organizations* (New York: Wiley Interscience).

West, J., W. Vanhaverbeke and H. Chesbrough (2006) 'Open Innovation: A Research Agenda', in H. Chesbrough, W. Vanhaverbeke and J. West (eds) *Open Innovation* (Oxford: Oxford University Press).

Wierba, E. E., T. A. Finholt and M. P. Steves (2002) 'Challenges to Collaborative Tool Adoption in a Manufacturing Engineering Setting: A Case Study', Proceedings of the 36th HICSS, *IEEE Computer Society Press*, pp. 3594–603.

Zigurs, I. (2003) 'Leadership in Virtual Teams: Oxymoron or Opportunity?', *Organizational Dynamics*, 31: 4, pp. 339–51.

9
Innovation and Labour Productivity in the Swiss Manufacturing Sector: An Analysis Based on Firm Panel Data

Spyros Arvanitis

9.1 Introduction

This chapter investigates: 1) the determinants of innovation performance: and b) the impact of innovation performance on labour productivity of Swiss manufacturing firms in the period 1994–2002. The study is in the spirit of the paper by Crépon, Duguet and Mairesse, published in *Economics of Innovation and New Technology* (Crépon et al., 1998).

Our model of the innovative behaviour of Swiss manufacturing firms builds on the wide agreement in the economic literature that demand prospects, type and intensity of competition, market structure, factors governing the production of knowledge (appropriability, technological opportunities), resource endowment, and firm size (as a variable controlling for further unobserved influences) are the main determinants of a firm's innovative activity. Labour productivity depends on physical and human capital as well as on new knowledge and innovation. Economies that develop more and more in the direction of a 'knowledge-based economy' rely increasingly on technological innovation. Hence, it is important to have some insights with respect to the (quantitative) relationship between innovation and economic performance.

The data used in this study come from the KOF panel database and were collected in 1996, 1999 and 2002 respectively, based on a questionnaire quite similar to that used in the CIS. Most of the qualitative data refer to three-year periods (1994–1996; 1997–1999; 2000–2002). The database contains, among other things, firm data on several innovation indicators, on various innovation determinants (demand perspectives, conditions of market competition, appropriability conditions and technological opportunities), on firm performance (value added per employee) and other firm characteristics. We use an (unbalanced) panel of a total of 1691 manufacturing firms.

As a first step, we specify an *innovation equation* containing, as independent variables: measures of demand expectations; measures of the intensity of price and non-price competition; the number of competitors in the most important market segment a firm is operating in; measures of technological opportunities (sources of external knowledge, technological potential); measures of the effectiveness of imitation protection; and measures for skill shortage and shortage of internal financing. Further, it contains controls for industry affiliation and firm size. Firm size is inserted in the form of a polynomial (linear and quadratic term) with respect to the number of employees. This allows testing for scale effects. We use five dichotomous innovation measures (product innovations, yes/no; process innovations, yes/no; R&D activities, yes/no; at least one patent application, yes/no; products new to the market, yes/no) and three metric measures (R&D expenditure as a percentage of sales; sales share of new products; sales share of considerably modified (already existing) products). The use of a wide spectrum of indicators helps to test the robustness of the specification of the innovation equation. The equations of the five dichotomous variables are estimated: a) by a simple probit for the pooled data using year dummies; or b) by a probit with random effects in order to take into consideration heterogeneity due to the panel character of the data. The equations of the three metric variables are estimated: a) by a simple tobit (for the pooled data using year dummies) in order to take account of the truncation of the variables (a lot of zero values as downward limit); or b) by a tobit with random effects.

In a second step, we specify a *labour productivity equation* (value added per employee) containing a variable for human capital (share of employees with tertiary-level education), a variable for physical capital (value added share of non-labour firm income), a measure of R&D personnel shortage and an instrumented innovation variable. Further, it contains controls for industry affiliation and firm size. As instruments we use the independent variables of the innovation equation specified in the first step. We investigate also in this second equation all eight innovation variables already introduced in the first step. Hence, we estimate eight different models, each one with two methods: 1) two-stage least squares with pooled data and year dummies; and 2) generalized two-stage least squares with random effects.

We refrain here from separately specifying equations for innovation input and innovation output to postulate a knowledge production function because, with the exception of innovation input determining innovation output per definition, all other determinants are identical in both equations. We prefer to investigate directly the (presumably) different impact of innovation input and innovation output on economic performance without the transmitting role of a knowledge production function, for whose identification our mostly qualitative data would be too crude.

The new elements that this paper adds to empirical literature are: 1) the use of a broad spectrum of variables covering most factors proposed and discussed in the literature as possible determinants of innovative activity; and 2) the consideration of several innovation indicators, thus allowing testing of the robustness of the relationship between innovation and economic performance; and 3) the use of panel data for the period 1994–2002, since only few studies until now could dispose of panel data.

Section 9.2 gives a short summary of related empirical literature. In Section 9.3 we present the framework of analysis and the specification of the innovation and the productivity equation respectively. Section 9.4 deals with the data used in the study. In Section 9.5 we discuss the empirical results. Section 9.6 contains a summary and some conclusions.

9.2   Summary of the empirical literature

We concentrate here on empirical studies that: a) develop a multi-equation model for innovation and productivity at the firm level: and b) use CIS-like micro-data.[1]

Crépon et al. (1998) studied the links between productivity, innovation and research based on a structural model that explained productivity by innovation output, and innovation output by research investment based on a cross-section of French firm data. They found that the probability of engaging in R&D increases with the firm's size, its market share and diversification, and with demand-pull and technology-push indicators. R&D capital intensity increases with the same variables, except for size (linear effect only). Innovation output, as measured by patent numbers or innovative sales, rises with R&D capital intensity, and demand-pull and technology-push indicators. Finally, firm productivity correlates positively with a higher innovation output, after controlling for labour skill and physical capital intensity. In a further study using French data, Duguet (2006) distinguished two types of innovation, namely incremental innovation and radical innovation. He found for a cross-section of French firm data that radical innovations are the only significant contributors to TFP growth.

Lööf et al. (2001), Janz et al. (2003) and Griffith et al. (2006) conducted comparative studies for many countries using the framework of analysis developed by Crépon et al. (1998). The first study covers three Nordic countries (Finland, Norway and Sweden); the second compares German firms with Swedish firms, and the third deals with four European countries – France, Germany, Spain and the UK. All three studies are cross-section investigations based on CIS data. Lööf et al. found that the estimated elasticity of productivity with respect to innovation output is higher in Norway than in the other two countries. Rather surprisingly, no significant relationship was found between innovation and productivity in Finland. The authors were reluctant to draw definite conclusions from these findings because of data errors, differences in model specification or unobserved country-specific effects. Janz et al. analysed the relationship between productivity, innovation output and R&D expenditure for a pooled sample of German and Swedish firms. The analysis showed that the two main parameter estimates, the elasticity of labour productivity with respect to innovation output and the elasticity of innovation output with respect to innovation input, are not significantly different between the two countries. Finally, the authors of the third study found, using different innovation output measures, that the innovation output is significantly determined by the innovation effort in all four countries. In contrast to that, productivity effects of innovation showed up only for France, Spain and UK, but not for Germany.

In a study based on Irish panel data Love and Proper (2005) estimated a recursive system of equations comprising an innovation production function which related knowledge inputs to innovation success and equations which related innovation to productivity. Results indicated that external sources of knowledge are important determinants of innovation success. Product innovation has a strong positive effect on growth and has a negative contemporaneous effect, but a positive lagged effect on productivity. Process innovation has a positive effect on productivity with no lagged effect.

Finally, Lööf and Heshmati (2006) and van Leeuwen and Klomp (2006) discuss and apply alternative econometric approaches and model specifications. The former study uses Swedish cross-section firm data to examine the sensitivity of the estimated relationship between innovation and firm performance by carrying out comparisons in a number of ways (assuming different error structure for the same data source, estimating the same model with different data bases, using different classifications of firms' performance and/or innovation, etc.). In the latter study, which is based on Dutch firm data, the value-added production-function framework is replaced by a revenue-function approach. A positive impact on productivity is found only for revenue per employee but not for value added per employee.

On the whole, the comparability of existing studies is rather limited due not only to data problems but also to differences with respect to model specification and applied econometric methodology.

9.3 Framework of the analysis

9.3.1 Specification of the innovation equation

Dependent variables. In view of the complexity of the innovation process, characterized by several stages, ranging from basic research to the penetration of the market with new products, an approach relying on a single measure of innovation may leave out important relationships and produce results which are not robust (see, for example, Kleinknecht et al., 2002). In this study we use a set of innovation measures covering several stages of the innovation process, namely five binary indicators (product innovations, yes/no; process innovations, yes/no; R&D activities, yes/no; patent applications, yes/no; products new for the (world) market, yes/no) and three metric indicators (R&D expenditure/sales; sales share of new products; sales share of considerably modified (existing) products) (see Table 9.1).

Table 9.1 Definition and measurement of model variables

Variable	Definition
Dependent variables	
INNOPD	Introduction of product innovations, yes/no
INNOPC	Introduction of process innovations, yes/no
R&D	R&D activities, yes/no
PAT	Patent applications, yes/no
WN	Introduction of products new to the market (innovative new products)
LRDS	Log of R&D expenditures divided by sales
LNEWS	Log of sales share of new products
LIMPS	Log of sales share of (already existing) considerably modified products
LQL	Log of value added per employee
Independent variables	
Innovation model	
D	Expectations with respect to demand development in the next three years; transformation of a five-level ordinal variable (level 1: 'strong decrease'; level 5 'strong increase') to a binary variable (value 1: levels 4 and 5 of the original five-level variable; value 0: levels 1, 2 and 3 of the original variable)
IPC	Intensity of price competition; transformation of a five-level ordinal variable (level 1: 'very weak'; level 5 'very strong') to a binary variable (value 1: levels 4 and 5 of the original five-level variable; value 0: levels 1, 2 and 3 of the original variable)
INPC	Intensity of non-price competition; original and transformed binary variable as IPC
Market environment	
16–50 competitors; six to 15 competitors; up to five competitors	Three dummies for the market types: 16 to 50 main competitors on the (worldwide) product market; six to 15 main competitors; up to five competitors (reference group: more than 50 competitors)
APPR	Overall effectiveness of formal and informal mechanisms of appropriation of innovation returns; transformation of a five-level ordinal variable (level 1: 'not effective'; level 5 'very effective') to a binary variable (value 1: levels 4 and 5 of the original five-level variable; value 0: levels 1, 2 and 3 of the original variable)
TPOT	Technological potential, i.e. scientific and technological knowledge relevant to the firm's innovative activity; transformation of a five-level ordinal variable (level 1: 'very low'; level 5 'very high') to a binary variable (value

(Continued)

Table 9.1   (Continued)

Variable	Definition
	1: levels 4 and 5 of the original five level variable; value 0: levels 1, 2 and 3 of the original variable)
External knowledge sources	
Users; suppliers; competitors; affiliated firms; universities; patent disclosures; fairs, exhibitions	Importance of seven different innovation-related external sources of information; transformation of a five-level ordinal variable (level 1: 'not important'; level 5 'very important') to a binary variable (value 1: levels 4 and 5 of the original five level variable; value 0: levels 1, 2 and 3 of the original variable)
FIN_IMPED	Importance of the shortage of internal financing resources as an impediment to innovative activity; original and transformed binary variable, as for the variables for the knowledge sources
SKILL_IMPED	Importance of the shortage of skilled labour as an impediment of innovative activity; original and transformed binary variable as FIN_IMPED
L; L^2	Number of employees (in full-time equivalents); square of the number of employees
NEW_IND	Average sales of new products in a firm's 2-digit industry of principal activity
IMP_IND	Average sales of (already existing) considerably modified products in a firm's 2-digit industry of principal activity
Productivity model	
LHK	Logarithm of the share of employees with tertiary-level education
RDSKILL_IMPED	Importance of the shortage of R&D personnel as an impediment to innovative activity; original and transformed binary variable as for the variables for the knowledge sources
LC	Logarithm of capital income per employee (capital income = value added minus labour costs)
FOREIGN	foreign firm, yes/no
Year 1999; year 2002	Time dummies for 1999 and 2002 (reference year: 1996)
High-tech manufacturing	Chemicals; plastics; electrical and non-electrical machinery; electronics, scientific instruments (reference group: low-tech manufacturing: food; beverage and tobacco; textiles; clothing and leather; wood processing; paper, printing; glass, stone and clay; metal; metal-working; watches; other manufacturing; energy.

The ordinal variables refer to the three-year periods 1994–1996, 1997–1999 and 2000–2002 respectively; the quantitative variables refer to the years 1995, 1998 and 2001 respectively.

Independent variables. For specifying the innovation equation we apply an eclectic approach by taking into account a series of important factors that are considered to be relevant for innovation at firm level in economic literature. There is a wide agreement that demand growth potential (the 'demand-pull' hypothesis; see Schmookler, 1966), type and intensity of competition, market structure and firm size, as well as factors governing the generation of knowledge (appropriability of the returns of innovations, technological opportunities in the relevant fields of activities; the 'technology-push' hypothesis; see Phillips, 1966; Rosenberg, 1976) are the main determinants of the innovation activity at firm level. In accordance to this tradition, the empirical model used in this study comprises variables for the most important determinants of innovative activity as noted in the literature (see, for example, Dasgupta, 1986; Dosi, 1988; Cohen and Levin, 1989; and Cohen, 1995 for reviews of this literature).

We distinguish four groups of explanatory variables (see Table 9.1 for the definition and the measurement of the model variables). First, we include an indicator for demand conditions: variable D measures the expected development of demand on the relevant product markets in the medium-term (the next three years).

A second category of explanatory variables is related to the (product) market conditions under which the firms operate, particularly the competitive pressures they are exposed to. Mostly, market concentration, a structural variable, is taken to reflect competitive pressures. Standard industrial organization models of product differentiation and monopolistic competition typically predict that more intense product market competition, measured by an increase in the substitutability between differentiated products, reduces post-entry rents, and therefore increases market concentration (see, for example, Kamien and Schwartz, 1970; Dixit and Stiglitz, 1977; see also the discussion in Aghion et al., 2005). In the game-theoretic literature the impact of market structure upon the schedule of innovation is shown to depend critically on the difference between profit rates preceding and following the innovation (see, for example, Reinganum, 1981). This dependence being quite complicated, most studies do not reach theoretically unambiguous results with respect to the effects of market concentration on innovation (see Reinganum, 1989 for a review of such studies). Recently, Aghion et al. (2005) developed a model that predicts an inverted-U relationship between product-market competition and innovation. The authors found strong evidence for this model using UK panel data. In sum, the issue of whether or not positive effects in the tradition of Schumpeter are stronger than negative free competition effects' as some empirical studies find (see, for example, Geroski, 1995; Blundell et al., 1999) has to be resolved at the empirical level.

We use three variables to capture the influence of the market environment; 1) a measure of the intensity of price competition on a firm's specific market (variable IPC); 2) a measure of the intensity of non-price competition; and

3) a measure of the market structure as reflected by the number of main competitors on a firm's most important (worldwide) product market. We expect a positive effect of the intensity of non-price competition on innovation. This is in accordance with models of product differentiation, in which product quality is the main dimension of competition among firms and which are interpreted as models of incremental innovation (see, for example, Stoneman, 1983; Levin and Reiss, 1988). We do not have an *a priori* expectation with respect to the effect of price competition. A positive effect would confirm the 'free-competition effect', a negative one the Schumpeterian effect. We do not dispose of a quantitative measure of market concentration of the innovation-relevant market (such as the. share of patents of the four largest firms), so we cannot test the hypothesis of a U-inverted relationship. Our variable is defined only for some intervals with respect to the number of main competitors on a firm's most important (worldwide) product market – up to five competitors, six to 15 competitors, 16 to 50 competitors, 50 and more competitors. What we can test with these data is the relationship between a certain market environment and innovation. To this end, we include in our model three dummies for the three market types (up to five competitors, five to 15 competitors, 16 to 50 competitors). Also in this case we do not have *a priori* sign expectations.

A third category of exploratory variables refers to the factors governing the production of knowledge (appropriability, technological opportunities). The theoretical literature focuses primarily on the effect of imperfect appropriability of results of innovation activities on the incentives to innovate (see, for example, Spence, 1984; Levin and Reiss, 1984). There is a twofold incentive problem. On the one hand, the existence of imperfect appropriability (above a critical level of the underlying knowledge spillovers) decreases the incentives to innovate because of external losses of innovation rents caused by imperfect appropriability ('outgoing spillovers'). On the other hand, imperfect appropriability also increases the incentives to utilize spillovers coming from outside the firm ('incoming spillovers'). The extent of incoming spillovers depends also on the amount of external knowledge that is available or can be anticipated as being available (technological opportunities).

We use a measure of appropriability based on the firms' assessment of the overall effectiveness of formal and informal mechanisms of protection of innovation returns (variable APPR; see Levin et al., 1987). We expect a positive effect of this variable.

Technological opportunities representing the supply conditions of innovation-generating activities are proxied by two (sets of) variables. The first variable reflects the general technological potential characterizing the fields of activity that are relevant for the firm (variable TPOT). TPOT tries to capture the extent of overall accumulation of 'basic knowledge', an important part of which comes from science-oriented basic research. We expect a positive effect for this variable. The second (group) of technological opportunity variable(s) measures the importance of several sources of external knowledge for a firm's innovative activities (see Klevorick et al., 1995). We use information for seven different sources of information, namely users, suppliers (of equipment, components and the like), competitors, affiliated firms, universities, patent disclosures and fairs and exhibitions. In accordance with theoretical reasoning (see, for example, Cohen and Levinthal, 1989, 1990) we expect a joint positive effect for the entire set of these variables but not necessarily for each of them.

Fourth, measures for financial and human resources assigned to the generation of new products and new processes are taken into account. Thus, in the innovation equation are also included a measure of shortage of internal financial resources for innovation (variable FIN_IMPED) and a measure of shortage of skilled labour (variable SKILL_IMPED). We expect negative effects for both variables.

Furthermore, firm size, an explanatory variable used in most innovation studies (see, for example, Cohen 1995), is also included in the present study. Firm size, which is expected to be positively related to innovation, plays a special role: it may prove to be an independent (additional) determinant of adoption, in which case it stands for firm-specific effects not explicitly modelled (such the as scope of activities and the level of management capabilities) and/or it may function as a proxy for other variables in the model, if it is strongly correlated with them (size-dependence of the model variables; see Arvanitis, 1997); we concentrate here on the effects as an additional determinant. We use the number of employees in full-time equivalents as a measure of firm size. We include a linear and a quadratic term with respect to the number of employees (variables L, L2) in the innovation equation in order to capture possible non-linearities. We expect that innovation increases with firm size but at a decreasing rate.

Finally, we control for the manufacturing sub-sectors (dummy for high-tech manufacturing) and the time (two time dummies for 1999 and 2002 for the estimates with pooled data). We expect time dummies to reflect the effects of macroeconomic conditions on innovation not already captured by the demand variable D. In the equations for the sales share of new products and the sales share of considerably modified (existing) products) we control also for the length of the product life-cycle by inserting the average of these variables at industry level as an additional independent variable (variables NEW_IND and IMP_IND respectively). We expect positive signs for both control variables.

9.3.2 Specification of the productivity equation

The productivity equation (dependent variable: logarithm of value added per employee) contains proxies of the intensity of human capital (variable LHK; logarithm of the share of employees with tertiary-level education), a variable for shortage of R&D personnel (variable RDSKILL_IMPED; R&D personnel shortage is a specific problem of the Swiss economy, especially in boom periods), physical capital (variable LC; logarithm of capital income per employee) and knowledge capital approximated alternatively by the five binary and the three metric innovation indicators that already served as dependent variables of the innovation equations (see Table 9.1). Further, we control for firms being a foreign ones or not (dummy variable FOREIGN; foreign firm, yes/no), for firm size, industry affiliation and time (if necessary). We expect positive effects for the resource endowment variables LC and LHK and a negative one for RDSKILL_IMPED. Our main hypothesis with respect to the binary innovation indicators is that innovation activities would contribute, as an additional production factor, to an improvement of labour productivity in firms compared to firms that are not involved in such activities (see Griliches, 1979, 1995). The use of several binary variables for different kinds of innovation activities allows the testing of the robustness of the innovation effect on economic performance. Positive effects are expected also for the three metric variables that measure the intensity of innovative activity. The signs for the variable FOREIGN as well as for the firm size dummies are not *a priori* clear.

Finally, we take into account the endogenous character of innovative activities by estimating a productivity equation, in which the innovation indicators are instrumented. As instruments we use the independent variables of the innovation equation as specified above.

9.4 Data

The data used in this study were collected in the course of three surveys among Swiss enterprises in the years 1996, 1999 and 2002 using a questionnaire which included, along with questions on some basic firm characteristics (sales, exports, employment, investment and employees' vocational education), several innovation indicators quite similar to those in the Innovation Surveys of the European Community (CIS).[2] The survey was based on a (with respect to firm size) disproportionately stratified random sample of firms with at least five employees covering all relevant industries of the manufacturing sector, the construction sector and selected service industries as well as firm size classes (on the whole 28 industries and within each industry three industry-specific firm size classes with full coverage of the upper class of large firms). We used in this study data for manufacturing firms in 18 industries. Answers were received from 33.5 per cent (1996), 33.7 per cent (1999) and 44.6 per cent (2002) respectively of the manufacturing firms in the underlying sample. The response rates did not vary much across industries and size classes, with a few exceptions (over-representation of machinery, underrepresentation of clothing/leather and wood processing). The final data set includes 1691 enterprises from all fields of activity and size classes and may be considered as representative of Swiss manufacturing (see Table 9.A1 in

Appendix 9.1 for the structure of the data set used by industry, firm size class and year respectively).

9.5 Results

9.5.1 The innovation equation

For each binary innovation variable we estimated: a) a probit model with the pooled data for all three cross-sections and two time dummies; and b) a probit model with random effects.[3] In both cases heteroscedasticity-robust standard errors according to the White procedure were computed. All estimations were conducted with STATA, Version 8. Table 9.2 shows the estimates for the five binary variables. The rather high share of variance due to heterogeneity ($\tau = 0.41$–0.61) in Table 9.2 shows that the consideration of random effect is the appropriate methodology.

We use the estimates for the binary variables INNOPD and INNOPC as a reference in order to describe the main pattern of the determinants of innovation activities, which we then compare: a) with the pattern for the other three binary indicators; and b) with that for the three metric variables.

Demand expectations: Positive medium-term demand expectations (variable D) in one period have a positive effect on the likelihood of introducing a product and/or a process innovation in the next period. This result is in accordance to theory and also to many other empirical studies based on micro-data.

Competition: As expected, there is a positive correlation between the intensity of non-price competition (variable INPC) and the propensity to introduce product and/or process innovations. We also find a positive effect of the intensity of price competition (variable IPC) but only for process innovation. In this case the 'free-competition effect' seems to be more important than the Schumpeterian effect. Intuitively, it is quite reasonable to assume that high price competition for (obviously) highly substitutable products would be a strong incentive for reducing production costs through process innovation (see, for example, Levin and Reiss, 1988).[4]

All three dummies for the market structure have positive and statistically significant coefficients in the estimates for product innovation but not in the estimates for process innovation. This means that all three concentration thresholds define market environments for which the likelihood of product innovations is significantly larger than in the polypolistic market with more than 50 competitors. In the random-effect estimates for product innovations the differences between the coefficients of the three dummies are statistically significant but the coefficient for the threshold (six to 15 competitors) is significantly smaller than the respective coefficients for the other two thresholds (16 to 50 competitors) and (up to five competitors). In the simple probit model with time dummies two thresholds have the same coefficient. Thus, there is no monotonic positive relationship between concentration (as

Table 9.2   Innovation equation: determinants of innovation; several dichotomous innovation indicators

Explanatory variables	INNOPD		INNOPC		R&D		PAT		WN	
	(Probit pooled data)	(Probit random effects)	(Probit pooled data)	(Probit random effects)	(Probit pooled data)	(Probit random effects)	(Probit pooled data)	(Probit random effects)	(Probit pooled data)	(Probit random effects)
D	0.341***	0.352**	0.487***	0.437***	0.453***	0.575***	0.188**	0.281**	0.426***	0.496***
IPC	(0.094)	(0.140)	(0.084)	(0.107)	(0.094)	(0.147)	(0.078)	(0.115)	(0.075)	(0.105)
	0.100	0.128	0.173**	0.224**	0.097	0.122	0.237***	0.331***	0.076	0.099
INPC	(0.086)	(0.130)	(0.079)	(0.100)	(0.084)	(0.130)	(0.080)	(0.122)	(0.078)	(0109)
	0.279***	0.443***	0.228***	0.271***	0.208***	0.329***	0.005	0.092	0.009	0.018
	(0.074)	(0.120)	(0.070)	(0.090)	(0.073)	(0.116)	(0.069)	(0.102)	(0.068)	(0.094)
Market environment:										
16 to 50 competitors	0.312**	0.559***	0.131	0.205	0.202*	0.325	0.167	0.310	0.025	0.043
	(0.127)	(0.212)	(0.128)	(0.165)	(0.124)	(0.203)	(0.136)	(0.204)	(0.134)	(0.187)
6 to 15 competitors	0.312***	0.439***	0.175*	0.177	0.373***	0.515***	0.299***	0.502***	0.094	0.140
	(0.103)	(0.170)	(0.101)	(0.133)	(0.102)	(0.170)	(0.110)	(0.175)	(0.108)	(0.154)
up to 5 competitors	0.386***	0.611***	0.147	0.167	0.443***	0.674***	0.352***	0.586***	0.293**	0.431***
	(0.116)	(0.195)	(0.113)	(0.148)	(0.115)	(0.196)	(0.120)	(0.191)	(0.116)	(0.168)
APPR	0.060	0.181***	−0.008	0.103**	0.027	0.073	0.215***	0.278***	0.066*	0.097**
	(0.038)	(0.059)	(0.033)	(0.043)	(0.038)	(0.056)	(0.036)	(0,054)	(0.035)	(0.048)
TPOT	0.314***	0.443***	0.373***	0.455***	0.382***	0.566***	0.158**	0.239**	0.299***	0.418***
	(0.084)	(0.129)	(0.077)	(0.101)	(0.082)	(0.134)	(0.072)	(0.107)	(0.070)	(0.100)
External sources of information:										
Users	0.253***	0.363***	0.097	0.140	0.172**	0.262**	0.063	0.093	0.168**	0.222**
	(0.075)	(0.120)	(0.072)	(0.091)	(0.075)	(0.119)	(0.071)	(0.105)	(0.069)	(0.097)
Suppliers	−0.118	−0.119	−0.081	−0.128	−0.126	−0.161	−0.348***	−0.426***	−0.039	−0.052
	(0.087)	(0.135)	(0.129)	(0.168)	(0.085)	(0.135)	(0.085)	(0.125)	(0.080)	(0.112)
Competitors	−0.245***	−0.389***	−0.103	−0.139	−0.202**	−0.335***	−0.098	−0.151	−0.322***	−0.408***
	(0.080)	(0.131)	(0.075)	(0.096)	(0.079)	(0.129)	(0.075)	(0.111)	(0.074)	(0.106)

(*Continued*)

Table 9.2 (Continued)

Explanatory variables	INNOPD		INNOPC		R&D		PAT		WN	
	(Probit pooled data)	(Probit random effects)	(Probit pooled data)	(Probit random effects)	(Probit pooled data)	(Probit random effects)	(Probit pooled data)	(Probit random effects)	(Probit pooled data)	(Probit random effects)
Affiliated firms	0.062	0.137	0.085	0.095	0.069	0.175	0.056	0.081	−0.038	−0.036
	(0.092)	(0.149)	(0.122)	(0.160)	(0.071)	(0.150)	(0.080)	(0.120)	(0.077)	(0.111)
Universities	−0.013	−0.073	−0.001	−0.065	0.117	0.148	0.157**	0.299**	0.108	0.091
	(0.094)	(0,145)	(0.085)	(0.109)	(0.093)	(0.148)	(0.080)	(0.122)	(0.078)	(0.110)
Patent disclosures	0.352***	0.520**	0.260**	0.350**	0.315**	0.435**	0.755***	1.043***	0.231**	0.278**
	(0.129)	(0.208)	(0.107)	(0.141)	(0.131)	(0.203)	(0.098)	(0.153)	(0.092)	(0.129)
Fairs, exhibitions	0.165**	0.281**	0.101	0.173*	0.218***	0.340***	0.040	0.041	0.064	0.104
	(0.077)	(0.122)	(0.072)	(0.093)	(0.074)	(0.123)	(0.072)	(0,106)	(0.069)	(0.098)
F1N_IMPED	−0.294***	−0.433***	−0.153*	−0.150	−0.109	−0.115	−0.030	−0.104	−0.087	−0.096
	(0.084)	(0.133)	(0.083)	(0.106)	(0.084)	(0.133)	(0.080)	(0.126)	(0.080)	(0.116)
SKILL_IMPED	−0.182**	−0.253*	−0.024	0.004	−0.129	−0.224*	−0.135*	−0.158	−0.041	−0.031
	(0.083)	(0.130)	(0.079)	(0.102)	(0.082)	(0.132)	(0.082)	(0.120)	(0.078)	(0.111)
L	1.4E+03***	2.2E−03***	7.7E−04***	9.3E−04***	1.9E−03***	2.9E−03***	1.2E−03***	1.8E−03***	6.7E−04***	9.2E−04***
	(3.5E+04)	(4.7E+04)	(2.0E−04)	(2.2E−04)	(3.8E−04)	(5.2E−04)	(1.9E−04)	(2.6E−04)	(1.2E−04)	(1.8E−04)
L^2	−6.8E−08***	−1.0E−07***	−3.7E−08***	−4.3E−08***	−9.0E−08***	−1.4E−07***	−5.9E−08***	−8.6E−08***	−3.9E−08***	5.2 E−08***
	(1.7E−08)	(3.2E−08)	(9.9E−09)	(1.5E−08)	(1.9E−08)	(3.3E−08)	(9.4E−09)	(1.7E−08)	(8.6E−09)	(1.9E−09)
High-tech manufacturing	0.349***	0.563***	0.035	0.026	0.437***	0.726***	0.386***	0.614***	0.380***	0.580***
	(0.076)	(0.140)	(0.071)	(0.096)	(0.075)	(0.147)	(0.070)	(0.123)	(0.069)	(0.113)
Year 1999	−0.248***		−0.625***		−0.096		0.140*		−0.087	
	(0.082)		(−0.080)		(0.082)		(0.080)		(0.078)	
Year 2002	0.197*		−0.377***		0.147		0.330***		0.195**	
	(0.106)		(0.099)		(0.103)		(0.089)		(0.087)	
Const.	−0.412**	−0.912***	0.016	−0.620***	−0.638***	−1.027***	−2.137***	−3.032***	−1.432***	−2.055***
	(0.162)	(0.243)	(0.154)	(0.190)	−0.163	(0.245)	(0.170)	(0.314)	(0.159)	(0.247)
N	1691	1691	1691	1691	1691	1691	1691	1691	1691	1691
Pseudo R^2	0.179		0.113		0.195		0.231		0.142	
LR (χ^2)	255***	90***	187***	87***	293***	97***	405***	161***	300***	142***
T		0.605		0.406		0.610		0.572		0.509
LR (χ^2); $\tau = 0$		41***		20***		42***		62***		54***

measured by the number of competitors) and the propensity to innovate. How can we interpret economically the effects of the concentration thresholds in the case of product innovations? They seem to reflect the ability of innovative SMEs to operate in market 'niches' (with fewer than 50 competitors) based on product differentiation due to incremental product innovation rather than the market power in the narrow sense of 'high-concentration markets' with permanently high entry barriers.

Appropriability: As expected, a high appropriability of innovation returns, as measured by a high effectiveness of formal and informal protection mechanisms (variable APPR), is important for both kinds of innovation.

Technological opportunities: The variable TPOT measuring the overall effect of externally available knowledge that is relevant for a firm's innovative activity shows a statistically significant positive effect in all four estimates for INNOPD and INNOPC. A joint test for the seven single external sources of information showed that the overall effect is positive. Three single sources, namely users, patent disclosures and fairs and exhibitions, have a significant positive effect on the propensity to introduce product innovations. Patent disclosures and fairs and exhibitions are also a relevant information source for process innovations. The variable for knowledge from competitors has a negative sign in the estimates for product innovations. Spillovers from competitors are obviously not a means to encourage innovative activities in a firm. The coefficients of the variables for suppliers, universities and affiliate firms are statistically insignificant. On the whole, incoming spillovers are transmitted only through a few channels.

Shortages of resources: Lacking enough (internal) financial resources for innovation is a serious obstacle to innovative activities, especially product innovations, as the negative sign of this variable shows. Since we control for a firm's specific demand development as well as for macroeconomic conditions (time dummies), this kind of impediment seems to be of a structural nature, and thus is a possible matter of concern for policy-makers. Skill shortages are relevant only for product innovations. Also in this case we identify a structural obstacle to innovative activity that could also reveal a policy problem.

Firm size: In the panel framework used here we find the same pattern as in the single cross-sections in earlier studies, namely a significantly positive coefficient for the linear term L and a significantly negative coefficient for the quadratic term (L^2) (see, for example, Arvanitis, 1997). This non-linear relationship shows that the likelihood to innovate increases with firm size but at a diminishing rate.

Control variables: There is a positive effect for firms in high-tech manufacturing presumably reflecting further advantages of firms in this sub-sector that are not captured by the other model variables. This effect is found only for product innovations. Obviously the differences between high-tech and low-tech manufacturing are not primarily related to differences in the efficiency of production techniques. The signs and the magnitudes of the coefficients of the time dummies in the pooled data probit estimates for product innovations show that the general economic conditions were quite unfavourable for innovative activities in the period 1997–1998 (year 1999) compared to the reference period 1994–1996 and improved in the period 2000–2002 (year 2002). For process innovations the general conditions were in both periods worse than in the reference period (significant negative signs of both time dummies). This result is contrary to the theoretical expectation that firms increase their activities with respect to cost-saving process innovations under adverse economic conditions (see, for example, Utterback and Abernathy, 1975).

In sum, all four groups of hypothesized variables and also firm size are statistically relevant. This general finding is in accordance to previous cross-section studies with Swiss firm data (see, for example, Arvanitis and Hollenstein, 1996, for a similar analysis using data from 1993).

Other binary innovation indicators: For the dichotomous variable R&D we obtain almost the same pattern as for INNOPD with the exception of the variable APPR (positive but statistically insignificant coefficient) and the variable FIN_IMPED (negative but statistically insignificant coefficient). A further difference occurs in the results with respect to the variable for market concentration: in the case of the variable R&D (random effects estimates) the coefficients of the dummies become larger with increasing concentration. This result can be interpreted as (weak) evidence for the Schumpeterian competition effect. The coefficients of the time dummies are statistically insignificant. This means that the general economic conditions did not influence the likelihood of conducting R&D but only the R&D intensity (see below).

For the variables PAT and WN we obtain similarities to the reference pattern for product innovations with respect to demand expectations (D), appropriability (APPR), technological potential (TPOT), patent disclosures as an important external information source and firm size. There are also some differences as to the relevance of market conditions: non-price competition is not relevant for PAT and WN, price competition only for WN; for the likelihood to file patent applications (PAT) we observe, similar to R&D, a (rather weak) tendency to increase with rising market concentration (Schumpeterian effect). This is not the case for WN. University knowledge seems to be important only for patenting. Finally the variables for resource shortages show the expected negative sign but are statistically insignificant in the estimates for PAT and WN. For both indicators general economic conditions became more favourable in the last period 2000–2002.

On the whole, for the four binary indicators referring mainly to product innovations we find a series of robust results across all estimates that are in accordance with theoretical expectations and are worth mentioning once more: positive effects for demand expectations, technological potential, patent disclosures as an important external knowledge source and firm size; also stronger positive effects for firms operating on a market niche with up to five competitors than for firms operating in markets with more than five competitors (with the exception of process innovation); also partly positive influence of intensity of non-price competition, appropriability conditions and users as a relevant knowledge source. Finally, belonging to high-tech manufacturing contributes to a higher innovation performance, even after controlling for all other determinants.

Metric innovation variables: We estimated: a) a tobit model with pooled data and time dummies; and b) a tobit model with random effects for each of the three metric innovation indicators, namely the logarithm of R&D intensity (LRDS; R&D expenditure divided by sales), the logarithm of the sales share of new products (LNEWS) and the logarithm of the sales share of significantly modified (already existing) products (LIMPS).[5] In these estimations all firms in the sample, both innovating and non-innovating ones, were taken into consideration. We could do this because data for the independent variables were also available for non-innovating firms. In this way, the usual problems of selectivity bias due to considering only innovating firms could be avoided. All estimations were conducted with STATA, Version 8. Table 9.3 shows the estimates for the three metric variables. We also find a considerable amount of heterogeneity in these estimates ($\tau = 0.36$–0.64 in Table 9.3).

Demand conditions: We find also for these indicators significant positive effects of demand expectations on innovation performance.

Competition: The intensity of non-price competition is important for input-oriented as well as output-oriented indicators; the intensity of price competition is relevant for the variable IMPS that measures the sales share of considerably modified existing products, which are more price-sensitive than thoroughly new products (variable LNEWS). Market niches with up to five competitors as well as markets with six to 15 competitors are, as a market environment, significantly more favourable for innovation than markets with 16 to 50 competitors or those with more than 50 competitors; this result is valid for all three metric variables. But there is no monotonic positive relationship between concentration (as measured by the number of competitors) and innovation intensity. In both estimates for LRDS we find a tendency for R&D intensity to increase with increasing concentration.

Appropriability: We find positive effects for the variables LRDS and LNEWS; appropriability is not relevant for modified products with a lower degree of innovativeness than completely new products.

Technological opportunities: The (anticipated) technological potential is also quite relevant with respect to these innovation measures variables. Users as

Table 9.3 Innovation equation: determinants of innovation; metric innovation indicators

Explanatory variables	LRDS		LNEWS		LIMPS	
	(Tobit pooled data)	(Tobit random effects)	(Tobit pooled data)	(Tobit random effects)	(Tobit pooled data)	(Tobit random effects)
D	1.402***	1.269***	0.638***	0.519***	0.470***	0.357***
	(0.269)	(0.245)	(0.110)	(0.105)	(0.123)	(0.120)
IPC	0.515*	0.386	0.070	0.088	0.416***	0.412***
	(0.276)	(0.261)	(0.111)	(0.109)	(0.126)	(0.124)
INPC	0.644***	0.697***	0.203**	0.177**	0.273***	0.266**
	(0.239)	(0.222)	(0.098)	(0.094)	(0.110)	(0.107)
Market environment:						
16 to 50	0.710	0.591	0.480**	0.415**	0.234	0.160
competitors	(0.466)	(0.439)	(0.190)	(0.186)	(0.213)	(0.210)
6 to 15	1.783***	1.589***	0.523***	0.455***	0.450***	0.411**
competitors	(0.374)	(0.369)	(0.155)	(0.156)	(0.173)	(0.175)
up to 5	2.092***	2.112***	0.485***	0.444***	0.441**	0.443**
competitors	(0.409)	(0.405)	(0.168)	(0.170)	(0.188)	(0.191)
APPR	0.275**	0.279**	0.082*	0.089*	0.003	0.019
	(0.122)	(0.111)	(0.050)	(0.047)	(0.056)	(0.053)
TPOT	1.488***	1.198***	0.294***	0.196**	0.370***	0.333***
	(0.250)	(0.235)	(0.103)	(0.100)	(0.116)	(0.114)
External sources of information:						
Users	0.324	0.220	0.266***	0.265***	0.221**	0.204*
	(0.242)	(0.227)	(0.099)	(0.097)	(0.112)	(0.111)
Suppliers	−0.849***	−0.636**	0.029	0.066	−0.095	−0.057
	(0.286)	(0.267)	(0.116)	(0.113)	(0.131)	(0.129)
Competitors	−0.531**	−0.542**	−0.239**	−0.217**	−0.352***	−0.385***
	(0.255)	(0.237)	(0.104)	(0.101)	(0.117)	(0.116)
Affiliated firms	0.168	0.259	0.040	0.065	0.299**	0.238*
	(0.275)	(0.272)	(0.112)	(0.112)	(0.125)	(0.126)
Universities	0.759***	0.666**	−0.005	−0.009	0.206	0.216*
	(0.275)	(0.261)	(0.113)	(0.112)	(0.127)	(0.127)
Patent	1.064***	0.818***	0.094	0.091	0.151	0.172
disclosures	(0.333)	(0.314)	(0.134)	(0.131)	(0.150)	(0.149)
Fairs,	0.404*	0.332	0.336***	0.311***	0.253**	0.296***
exhibitions	(0.244)	(0.230)	(0.100)	(0.098)	(0.112)	(0.111)
FIN_IMPED	−0.448	−0.301	−0.256**	−0.235**	−0.239*	−0.198
	(0.283)	(0.275)	(0.116)	(0.116)	(0.130)	(0.132)
SKILL_IMPED	−0.391	−0.342	−0.154	−0.152	−0.139	−0.121
	(0.279)	(0.263)	(0.112)	(0.111)	(0.126)	(0.126)
NEW_IND			1.020***	1.074***		
			(0.105)	(0.112)		
IMP_IMD					1.014***	1.035***
					(0.135)	(0.143)
L	7.5E−04***	1.0E−03***	3.5E−04***	3.8E−04***	4.9E−04***	5.7E−04***
	(2.5E−04)	(2.9E−04)	(1.3E−04)	(1.5E−04)	(1.4E−04)	(1.6E−04)

(Continued)

Table 9.3 (Continued)

Explanatory variables	LRDS		LNEWS		LIMPS	
	(Tobit pooled data)	(Tobit random effects)	(Tobit pooled data)	(Tobit random effects)	(Tobit pooled data)	(Tobit random effects)
L^2	−4.3E−08***	−5.5E−08**	−2.1E−08*	−2.2E−08*	−3.7E−08***	−4.1E−08)***
	(1.7E−08)	(1.9E−08)	(1.2E−08)	(1.3E−08)	(1.3E−08)	(1.4E−08)
High-tech manufacturing	2.169***	2.345***				
	(0.249)	(0.277)				
Year 1999	0.641**		−0.222**		−0.133	
	(0.273)		(0.112)		(0.126)	
Year 2002	1.287***		−0.040		−0.038	
	(0.307)		(0.124)		(0.140)	
Const.	−1.903***	−1.298**	−1.414***	−1.539***	1.551***	−1.667***
	(0.562)	(0.525)	(0.272)	(0.267)	(0.319)	(0.317)
N	1691	1691	1691	1691	1691	1691
N(left-censored)	471	471	518	518	576	576
Pseudo R^2	0.072		0.056		0.044	
LR(χ^2)	504***	383***	339***	275***	267***	233***
τ (χ^2)		0.637***		0.442***		0.360***

Note: see Table 9.1 for the variable definitions; ***, **, * denote statistical significance at the 1%, 5% and 10% test level respectively; heteroscedasticity-robust standard errors (White procedure); τ: share of variance that can be traced back to heterogeneity.

a knowledge source show positive effects for both categories of innovative products but not for R&D intensity. In the estimates for LRDS we also obtain positive effects for university knowledge. Thus, the acquisition and utilization of science-based knowledge seems to correlate positively with R&D intensity. On the other hand, the likelihood of becoming involved in R&D activities (variable R&D) is not dependent on such specialized knowledge.

Firm size: We obtain the standard pattern as for the binary variables (positive linear term, negative quadratic term).

Shortages of resources: The coefficients for the variables for shortages in finance and high-skilled personnel are throughout negative but only in the case of estimates for LNEWS are they statistically significant.

Control variables: For the variable LRDS the affiliation to high-tech manufacturing is positively related to a higher innovation performance. In the estimates for LNEWS and LIMPS the control variables for the length of product life-cycle NEW_IND and IMP_IND respectively show, as expected, a positive and statistically significant effect. In the estimates for these two variables the dummy variable for high-tech manufacturing had to be dropped because of high multi-collinearity with NEW_IND and IMP_IND respectively.

The general economic conditions as reflected by the time dummies are relevant only for LRDS.

9.5.2 The productivity equation

We estimated eight different models, five with the instrumented binary innovation variables and three with the instrumented three metric indicators, each one of them using two methods: a) two-stage least squares with pooled data and year dummies and; b) generalized two-stage least squares with random effects. The independent variables of the innovation equation in Tables 9.2 and 9.3 were used as instruments. All estimations were conducted with STATA, Version 8. The high share of variance due to heterogeneity ($\tau = 0.53$–0.73 in tables 9.4 and 9.5) shows that introducing random effects is the appropriate methodology for our panel data. Table 9.4 shows the estimates of the productivity equation with five alternative binary measures of innovation. Table 9.5 shows the respective estimates with the three metric innovation indicators.

As expected, the coefficients of the variables for resource endowment (LHK; LC) are positive and highly statistically significant across all estimates. The elasticity of capital income per employee varies between 0.046 and 0.073 in Table 9.4, meaning that an increase of 1 per cent of this variable is correlated with an increase of 0.046 per cent to 0.073 per cent of labour productivity; the elasticity of the share of employees with tertiary-level education is lower (0.023–0.030) but much more stable across the model versions presented in this table. The coefficient of the variable FOREIGN is also positive and highly significant; this can be interpreted as a hint that foreign firms are, after controlling for all other factors, more productive than domestic ones. Further, the coefficient of the shortage variable RDSKILL_IMPED is negative and statistically significant in all estimates, with the exception of the estimates with INNOPD. Thus, this kind of resource shortage should be a matter of particular policy concern.

Now we turn to the binary innovation variables. The coefficients of all five instrumented innovation indicators are positive and statistically significant.[6] They vary between 0.23 (variable WN) and 0.58 (variable R&D). An economic interpretation of these coefficients is that, for example, on average a switch from a firm without product innovations to a firm that has introduced product innovations is correlated to an increase of 41 per cent to 44 per cent of labour productivity.[7] The smallest impact is found for WN (21 per cent) and the largest for PAT (46 per cent).

We also find throughout a significant positive impact for all three metric indicators. A change of 1 per cent of the R&D intensity (R&D expenditure divided by sales) causes an increase of 0.052 per cent to 0.056 per cent of productivity, all other things being equal.[8] As a comparison, the respective effects for human capital and physical capital are 0.046 per cent and 0.027 per cent respectively. The corresponding effects for the sales share of new products

Table 9.4 Productivity equation; dependent variable: value added per employee LQL; dichotomous innovation indicators

Explanatory variables	2SLS pooled data (INNOPD instrumented)	G2SLS random effects (INNOPD instrumented)	2SLS pooled data INNOPC instrumented	G2SLS random effects INNOPC instrumented)	2SLS pooled data (R&D instrumented)	G2SLS random effects (R&D instrumented)	2SLS pooled data (PAT instrumented)	G2SLS random effects (PAT instrumented)	2SLS pooled data (WN instrumented)	G2SLS random effects (WN instrumented)
LHK	0.073***	0.050***	0.074***	0.067***	0.051***	0.046***	0.056***	0.048***	0.063***	0.055***
	(0.014)	(0.014)	(0.014)	(0.013)	(0.014)	(0.014)	(0.013)	(0.013)	(0.013)	(0.013)
RDSKILL_IMPED	−0.005	−0.030	−0.048**	−0.049**	−0.041*	−0.040*	−0.063***	−0.057***	−0.054**	−0.052**
	(0.026)	(0.023)	(0.023)	(0.022)	(0.023)	(0.023)	(0.022)	(0.021)	(0.021)	(0.021)
LC	0.026***	0.024***	0.030***	0.023***	0.028***	0.026***	0.027***	0.026***	0.027***	0.025***
	(0.007)	(0.004)	(0.008)	(0.004)	(0.007)	(0.004)	(0.008)	(0.004)	(0.007)	(0.004)
INNOPD	0.500***	0.552***								
	(0.112)	(0.125)								
INNOPC			0.454***	0.411***						
			(0.100)	(0.105)						
R&D					0.502***	0.582***				
					(0.101)	(0.120)				
PAT							0.371***	0.393***		
							(0.080)	(0.094)		
WN									0.231***	0.294***
									(0.083)	(0.105)
FOREIGN	0.114***	0.087***	0.137***	0.085***	0.130***	0.109***	0.131***	0.093***	0.105***	0.072***
	(0.033)	(0.032)	(0.036)	(0.033)	(0.033)	(0.032)	(0.032)	(0.030)	(0.031)	(0.030)
Year 1999	0.086***		0.130***		0.061**		0.042*		0.054**	
	(0.026)		(0.032)		(0.024)		(0.023)		(0.022)	
Year 2002	0.093***		0.159***		0.092***		0.066**		0.103***	
	(0.027)		(0.032)		(0.027)		(0.029)		(0.026)	

(Continued)

Table 9.4 (Continued)

Explanatory variables	2SLS pooled data (INNOPD instrumented)	G2SLS random effects (INNOPD instrumented)	2SLS pooled data INNOPC instrumented	G2SLS random effects INNOPC instrumented)	2SLS pooled data (R&D instrumented)	G2SLS random effects (R&D instrumented)	2SLS pooled data (PAT instrumented)	G2SLS random effects (PAT instrumented)	2SLS pooled data (WN instrumented)	G2SLS random effects (WN instrumented)
Const.	11.664***	11.687***	11.714***	11.819***	11.666***	11.657***	11.999***	12.020***	11.990***	12.026***
	(0.105)	(0.098)	(0.103)	(0.087)	(0.098)	(0.098)	(0.067)	(0.057)	(0.064)	(0.056)
Industry dummies	yes (17)	yes (17)	Yes (17)	yes (17)	yes (17)	yes (17)	yes (17)	yes (17)	yes (17)	
Firm size dummies	yes (6)	yes (6)	Yes (6)	yes (6)	yes (6)	yes (6)	yes (6)	yes (6)	yes (6)	yes (6)
N	1691	1691	1691	1691	1691	1691	1691	1691	1691	1691
R^2	0.015		0.043		0.034		0.129		0.181	
F	12***		13***		12***		13***		14***	
SER	0.395		0.395		0.391		0.371		0.361	
R^2 overall		0.096		0.120		0.104		0.150		0.155
Wald (χ^2)		235***		220***		243***		263***		265***
τ		0.590		0.725		0.574		0.623		0.597

Notes: see Table 9.1 for the variable definitions; ***, **, * denote statistical significance at the 1%, 5% and 10% test level respectively; heteroscedasticity-robust standard errors (White procedure); τ: share of variance that can be traced back to heterogeneity.

Table 9.5   Productivity equation; dependent variable; value added per employee LQL; metric innovation indicators.

Explanatory variables	2SLS pooled data (LRDS instrumented)	G2SLS random effects (LRDS instrumented)	2SLS pooled data (LNEWS instrumented)	G2SLS random effects (LNEWS instrumented)	2SLS pooled data (LIMPS instrumented)	G2SLS random effects (IMPS instrumented)
LHK	0.048***	0.043***	0.059***	0.053***	0.057***	0.055***
	(0.015)	(0.015)	(0.014)	(0.014)	(0.014)	(0.014)
RDSKILL_IMPED	−0.056**	−0.059**	−0.052**	−0.048**	−0.055**	−0.046*
	(0.023)	(0.023)	(0.023)	(0.023)	(0.024)	(0.023)
LC	0.027***	0.026***	0.025***	0.023***	0.027***	0.023***
	(0.007)	(0.004)	(0.007)	(0.004)	(0.007)	(0.004)
LRDS	0.052***	0.056***				
	(0.011)	(0.011)				
LNEWS			0.100***	0.113***		
			(0.030)	(0.036)		
LIMPS					0.135***	0.141***
					(0.031)	(0.038)
FOREIGN	0.119***	0.101***	0.111***	0.089***	0.124***	0.107***
	(0.034)	(0.032)	(0.032)	(0.031)	(0.033)	(0.033)
Year 1999	0.013		0.053**		0.056**	
	(0.025)		(0.024)		(0.025)	
Year 2002	0.051*		0.114***		0.109***	
	(0.031)		(0.026)		(0.028)	
Const.	11.784***	11.788***	11.827***	11.853***	11.840***	11.874***
	(0.087)	(0.074)	(0.087)	(0.081)	(0.082)	(0.075)
Industry dummies	yes (17)	yes (17)	yes (17)	yes (17)	yes (17)	yes (17)
Firm size dummies	yes (6)	yes (6)	yes (6)	yes (6)	yes (6)	yes (6)
N	1691	1691	1691	1691	1691	1691
R^2	0.126		0.141		0.045	
F	11***		13***		12***	
SER	0.371		0.372		0.392	
R^2 overall		0.148		0.141		0.116
Wald (χ^2)		241***		259***		227***
T		0.549		0.525		0.621

Notes: see Table 9.1 for the variable definitions; ***, **, * denote statistical significance at the 1%, 5% and 10% test level respectively; heteroscedasticity-robust standard errors (White procedure); τ: share of variance that can be traced back to heterogeneity.

and the sales share of highly improved (already) existing) products are larger, namely 0.100 per cent to 0.113 per cent and 0.135 per cent to 0.141 per cent respectively. Thus, the output-oriented variables LNEWS and LIMPS show a considerably larger effect on economic performance than the input-oriented measure LRDS.

9.6   Summary and conclusions

The results for the innovation equations can be summarized as follows: favourable demand conditions are an important precondition for innovative activities to be undertaken by private enterprises (introduction of product and/or process innovations, R&D activities, patenting). They also enhance innovation performance as measured by R&D intensity (LRSD) or the sales shares of innovative products (LNEWS, LIMPS). This result is quite in accordance with theoretical expectations.

Competition pressures are more important for affecting the intensity of innovation activities than they are for influencing the basic decisions to engage in innovation activities as measured by the binary indicators. The most robust result across all estimates with respect to market environment is that a market niche with up to five competitors is considerably more favourable for a firm than most other market constellations. The finding is complementary and not contradictory to the finding with respect to the intensity of price and non-price competition. A monotonic relationship between innovation and market concentration could be found only for single indicators. These results are more in accordance with the 'free competition' effect than with the traditional Schumpeterian effect.

Further, appropriability conditions are significantly positively related to most innovation indicators. This is also quite compatible with theoretical prediction (see, for example, Spence, 1984). On the whole, the variables measuring the influence of technological opportunities have a positive effect on innovation, as expected from theory (see Levin and Reiss, 1988; Levin and Levinthal, 1989). In particular, the intense use of patent disclosures and users as knowledge sources is shown to be positively correlated with innovation in most estimates. University knowledge seems to be relevant mainly to R&D intensity, but not to the basic decision to engage in R&D. Moreover, firms with a high patenting propensity show a tendency to use university knowledge.

Shortages of resources are relevant primarily for the basic decision to get involved in innovation activities. Engaging in high-tech manufacturing is throughout a characteristic of above-average innovative firms.

For all eight indicators used in this study we found that innovation increases at a diminishing rate as firm size increases. This effect seems to be quite robust across all estimates. It can be interpreted as a hint that large firms do not have advantage vis-à-vis small firms with respect to innovation. Thus, our evidence contradicts the so-called neo-Schumpeterian hypothesis with respect to the influence of firm size on innovation performance.

Rather unexpectedly, the shares of the innovative products are not dependent on general economic conditions; instead they depend on the development of the specific demand for such products as measured by the variable D. On the other hand, R&D intensity varies with general economic conditions;

for both the periods 1997–1999 and 2000–2002 it was on average higher than for the reference period 1994–1996. On the whole, evidence with respect to the effect of macroeconomic conditions on innovation is not conclusive.

According to our findings, neither of the two 'extreme' hypotheses ('demand-pull' or 'technology-push') seems to be predominant. Both effects are found to be important to a firm's innovation performance.

The results for the productivity equations can be summarized as follows: we find significantly positive coefficients for all eight instrumented innovation variables. The magnitude of the impact effect on productivity of the five dichotomous variables varies between 21 per cent and 46 per cent. This means that, depending on the concrete innovation indicator, the shift from a firm without innovation activities to the one with such activities correlates with a productivity increase of 21 per cent to 46 per cent. Further, a 1 per cent change of the R&D intensity (R&D expenditure divided by sales) flows through into an increase of 0.054 per cent in productivity, all other things being equal. The respective effects for the sales share of new products and the sales share of highly improved (already existing) products are larger, namely 0.106 per cent and 0.138 per cent respectively.

Finally, the persistence of the negative effects of the shortage of internal finance for innovation and qualified personnel (in some of the estimates of the innovation equations) as well as for R&D personnel (in most estimates of the productivity equation) points to possible structural problems that should be a matter of concern to economic policy-makers.

Appendices

Appendix 9.1

Table 9.A1 Composition of the dataset

Industry	N	Percentage of firms
Food, beverage, tobacco	125	7.4
Textiles	54	3.2
Clothing, leather	27	1.6
Wood processing	79	4.7
Paper	41	2.4
Printing	107	6.3
Chemicals	98	5.8
Plastics, rubber	86	5.1
Glass, stone, clay	79	4.7
Metal	39	2.3
Metalworking	252	14.9
Machinery	260	15.4

(Continued)

Table 9.A1 (Continued)

Industry	N	Percentage of firms
Electrical machinery	73	4.3
Electronics, instruments	162	9.6
Watches	59	3.5
Vehicles	32	1.9
Other manufacturing	78	4.6
Energy	39	2.3
Firm size		
5 to 19 employees	399	23.6
20–49 employees	370	21.9
50–99 employees	296	17.5
100–199 employees	298	17.6
200–499 employees	213	12.6
500–999 employees	71	4.2
1000 employees and more	44	2.6
Year 1996	512	30.3
Year 1999	512	30.3
Year 2002	666	39.4
Total	1691	100

Table 9.A2 Descriptive statistics

Variable	Mean	Standard deviation	Min.	Max.
INNOPD	0.773	0.419	0	1
INNOPC	0.648	0.478	0	1
RD	0.675	0.468	0	1
PAT	0.393	0.489	0	1
WN	0.346	0.476	0	1
LRDS	4.890	3.598	0	12.024
LNEWS	1.935	1.484	0	4.605
LIMPS	1.951	1.544	0	4.605
LQL	11.806	0.407	10.821	13.789
D	0.258	0.437	0	1
IPC	0.756	0.430	0	1
INPC	0.519	0.500	0	1
16–50 competitors	0.130	0.337	0	1
6–15 competitors	0.480	0.500	0	1
up to 5 competitors	0.263	0.441	0	1
APPR	0.598	0.211	0	1
TPOT	0.379	0.485	0	1

(*Continued*)

Table 9.A2   (Continued)

Variable	Mean	Standard deviation	Min.	Max.
Users	0.561	0.496	0	1
Suppliers	0.226	0.418	0	1
Competitors	0.333	0.471	0	1
Affiliated firms	0.248	0.432	0	1
Universities	0.265	0.441	0	1
Patent disclosures	0.169	0.375	0	1
Fairs, exhibitions	0.481	0.500	0	1
FIN_IMPED	0.223	0.416	0	1
SKILL_IMPED	0.235	0.424	0	1
L	241.7	758.5	5	20.180
NEW_IND	1.690	0.495	0.166	2.515
IMP_IND	1.725	0.437	0.083	2.225
High-tech manufacturing	0.498	0.500	0	1
LHK	−1.956	0.965	0	1.260
SKILL_IMPED	0.213	0.409	0	1
LC	−1.154	2.621	0	0.946
FOREIGN	0.142	0.350	0	1

Table 9.A3   Correlation between the innovation indicators

	INNOPD	INNOPC	R&D	PAT	WN	LRDS	LNEWS
INNOPC	0.476						
R&D	0.717	0.520					
PAT	0.375	0.243	0.409				
WN	0.389	0.269	0.396	0.427			
LRDS	0.698	0.490	0.924	0.502	0.482		
LNEWS		0.683	0.479	0.617	0.352	0.471	0.649
LIMPS	0.639	0.491	0.587	0.325	0.327	0.602	0.528

Acknowledgements

This study was financially supported by the Swiss Science Foundation (SNF). The author acknowledges gratefully the fruitful comments and suggestions by two editors and the participants of the Workshop 'Innovation Systems and Firm Performance', Kasteel Oud-Poelgeest, Oegstgeest, The Netherlands, 4–6 October 2006.

Notes

1. The volume by Kleinknecht (1996) contains studies on the determinants of innovation for France, Germany, the Netherlands and Switzerland in the mid-nineties; Raymond et al. (2004) give a survey of recent studies of the determinants of innovation. See also the papers in the Special Issue of *Economics of Innovation and New Technology*, June/July 2006. Wieser (2005) provides a survey of empirical work on the relationship between research and development and productivity at the firm level.
2. Versions of the questionnaire in German and French are available at www.kof.ethz.ch.
3. We refrain here from presenting marginal effects instead of coefficients because most of the model variables are dummy variables and the economic interpretation of marginal effects is in this case rather problematic.
4. An alternative strategy would be of course product innovation.
5. In order to be able to calculate the logarithms of R&D intensity for firms without R&D expenditures, we put these firms at the minimum value of R&D intensity of the firms with R&D expenditure which was 0.00001. We then calculated the logarithms of RDS and subtracted in $(0.00001) = -11.513$ to get 0 values for the firms without R&D expenditures. The minimum value for the sales share of new products was 0.4, thus minimum $LNEWS = -0.916$, for the sales share of considerably modified (already existing) products 0.6, thus the minimum $LIMPRS = -0.511$; also in this case we performed a linear transformation of the data in order to get zero values for the firms without sales of considerably modified products.
6. This result is much less clear without instrumented variables.
7. We calculated the relative increase of labour productivity by the formulas: $100^*\ln (1 + 0.072) = 6.9$ and $100^*\ln (1 + 0.076) = 7.3$ respectively; see Halvorsen and Palmquist (1980), p. 475.
8. We found an elasticity of R&D capital of 0.043 in an earlier study based on cross-section data for 1990 (see Arvanitis and Hollenstein, 2002).

References

Aghion, P., N. Bloom, R. Blundell, R. Griffith and P. Howitt (2005) 'Competition and Innovation: An Inverted-U Relationship', *Quarterly Journal of Economics*, 115, pp. 701–28.

Arvanitis, S. (1997) 'The Impact of Firm Size on Innovative Activity: An Empirical Analysis Based on Swiss Firm Data', *Small Business Economics*, 9, pp. 473–90.

Arvanitis, S. and H. Hollenstein (1996) 'Industrial Innovation in Switzerland: A Model-based Analysis with Survey Data', in A. Kleinknecht (ed.), *Determinants of Innovation and Diffusion. The Message from New Indicators* (London: Macmillan Press).

Arvanitis, S. and H. Hollenstein (2002) 'The Impact of Technological Spillovers and Knowledge Heterogeneity on Firm Performance: Evidence from Swiss Manufacturing', in A. Kleinknecht and P. Mohnen (eds) *Innovation and Firm Performance* (London: Palgrave).

Blundell, R., R. Griffith and J. van Reenen (1999) 'Market Share, Market Value and Innovation in a Panel of British Manufacturing Firms', *Review of Economic Studies*, 66, pp. 529–54.

Cohen, W. M. (1995) 'Empirical Studies of Innovative Activity', in P. Stoneman (ed.) *Handbook of Innovation and Technological Change* (Oxford: Blackwell).

Cohen, W. M. and R. C. Levin (1989) 'Empirical Studies of Innovation and Market Structure', in R. Schmalensee and R. D. Willig (eds) *Handbook of Industrial Organization* (London: North-Holland).

Cohen, W. M. and D. A. Levinthal (1989) 'Innovation and Learning: The Two Faces of R&D', *Economic Journal*, 99, pp. 569–96.

Cohen, W. M. and D. A. Levinthal (1990) 'Absorptive Capacity: A New Perspective on Learning and Innovation', *Administrative Science Quarterly*, 35, pp. 128–52.

Crépon, B., E. Duguet and J. Mairesse (1998) 'Research, Innovation and Productivity: An Econometric Analysis at the Firm Level', *Economics of Innovation and New Technology*, 7, pp. 115–58.

Dasgupta, P. (1986) 'The Theory of Technological Competition', in J. E. Stiglitz and G. F. Mathewson (eds) *New Developments in the Analysis of Market Structure* (Cambridge, MA: MIT Press).

Dixit, A. and J. Stiglitz (1977) 'Monopolistic Competition and Optimum Product Diversity', *American Economic Review*, 68, pp. 297–308.

Dosi, G. (1988) 'Sources, Procedures, and Microeconomic Effects of Innovation', *Journal of Economic Literature*, 26, pp. 1120–71.

Duguet, E. (2006) 'Innovation Height, Spillovers and TFP Growth at the Firm Level: Evidence from French Manufacturing', *Economics of Innovation and New Technology*, 15: 4/5, pp. 415–42.

Geroski, P. (1995) *Market Structure, Corporate Performance and Innovative Activity* (Oxford: Oxford University Press).

Griffith, R., E. Huergo, J. Mairesse and B. Peters (2006) 'Innovation and Productivity across Four European Countries', *NBER Working Papers Series No. 12722*, Cambridge, MA.

Griliches, Z. (1979) 'Issues in Assessing the Contribution of Research and Development to Productivity Growth', *Bell Journal of Economics*, 10, pp. 92–116.

Griliches, Z. (1995) 'R&D and Productivity: Econometric Results and Measurement Issues', in P. Stoneman (ed.) *Handbook of the Economics of Innovation and Technological Change* (Oxford: Blackwell).

Halvorsen, R. and R. Palmquist (1980) 'The Interpretation of Dummy Variables in Semilogarithmic Equations', *American Economic Review*, 70: 3, pp. 474–5.

Janz, N., H. Lööf and B. Peters (2003) 'Firm Level Innovation and Productivity – Is There a Common Story Across Countries?', *ZEW Discussion Paper No. 03/26*, Mannheim.

Kamien, M. and N. Schwartz (1970) 'Market Structure, Elasticity of Demand and Incentive to Invent', *Journal of Law and Economics*, 13: 1, pp. 241–52.

Kleinknecht, A. (ed.) (1996) *Determinants of Innovation and Diffusion. The Message from New Indicators* (London: Macmillan Press).

Kleinknecht, A., K. van Montfort and E. Brouwer (2002) 'The Non-trivial Choice between Innovation Indicators', *Economic of Innovation and New Technology*, 11: 2, pp. 109–21.

Klevorick, A. K., R. C. Levin, R. R. Nelson and S. G. Winter (1995) 'On the Sources and Significance of Interindustry Differences in Technological Opportunities', *Research Policy*, 24, pp. 185–205.

Levin, R. C., A. K. Klevorick, R. R. Nelson and S. G. Winter (1987) 'Appropriating the Returns from Industrial Research and Development', *Brookings Papers on Economic Activity*, 3, pp. 783–831.

Levin, R. C. and P.C. Reiss (1984) 'Tests of a Schumpeterian Model of R&D and Market Structure', in Z. Griliches (ed.) *R&D, Patents and Productivity* (Chicago: University of Chicago Press).

Levin, R. C. and P. C. Reiss (1988) 'Cost-reducing and Demand-creating R&D with Spillovers', *Rand Journal of Economics*, 19, pp. 538–56.

Lööf, H. and A. Heshmati (2006) 'On the Relationship between Innovation and Performance: A Sensitivity Analysis', *Economics of Innovation and New Technology*, 15: 4/5, pp. 317–44.

Lööf, H., A. Heshmati, R. Asplund and S.-O. Naas (2001) 'Innovation and Performance in Manufacturing Industries: A Comparison of the Nordic Countries', *SSE/EFI Working Paper Series in Economics and Finance*, No. 457, Stockholm.

Love, J. H. and S. Proper (2005) 'Innovation, Productivity and Growth: An Analysis of Irish Panel Data', Paper presented at the 32nd Conference of the European Association for Research in Industrial Economics (EARIE), Porto, 1–4 September.

Phillips, A. (1966) 'Patents, Competition, and Technical Progress', *American Economic Review*, 56, pp. 301–10.

Raymond, W., P. Mohnen, F. Palm and S. S. van der Loeff (2004) 'An Empirically-based Taxonomy of Dutch Manufacturing: Innovation Policy Implications', *MERIT-Infonomics Research Memorandum Series No. 2004-011*, Maastricht.

Reinganum, J. F. (1981) 'Market Structure and the Diffusion of New Technology', *Bell Journal of Economics*, 12, pp. 618–24.

Reinganum, J. F. (1989) 'The Timing of Innovation: Research, Development and Diffusion', in R. Schmalensee and R. Willig (eds) *Handbook of Industrial Organization*, Vol. 1 (New York: Elsevier Science Publishers), pp. 849–908.

Rosenberg, N. (1976) *Perspectives on Technology* (Cambridge: Cambridge University Press).

Schmookler, J. (1966) *Invention and Growth. Schumpeterian Perspectives* (Cambridge, MA: MIT Press)

Spence, M. (1984) 'Cost Reduction, Competition and Industry Performance', *Econometrica*, 25, pp. 101–21.

Stoneman, P. (1983) *The Economic Analysis of Technological Change* (Oxford: Oxford University Press).

Utterback, J. M. and W. J. Abernathy (1975) 'A Dynamic Model of Process and Product Innovation', *OMEGA*, 3, pp. 639–56.

van Leeuwen, G. and L. Klomp (2006) 'On the Contribution of Innovation to Multi-factor Productivity Growth', *Economics of Innovation and New Technology* 15: 4/5, pp. 367–90.

Wieser, R. (2005) 'Research and Development, Productivity and Spillovers: Empirical Evidence at the Firm Level', *Journal of Economic Surveys*, 19: 4, pp. 587–621.

10
Financial Constraint and R&D Investment: Evidence from CIS

Amaresh K Tiwari, Pierre Mohnen, Franz C. Palm,
and Sybrand Schim van der Loeff

10.1 Introduction

The connection between finance and investment starts with any violation of the Modigliani-Miller theorem (Modigliani and Miller, 1958), usually modelled formally via imperfect information. According to Ross, Westerfield and Jordan (1993) about 80 per cent of all financing is done with internally generated funds. Explanations for this behaviour usually highlight the role of information asymmetries (Myers and Majluf, 1984) and agency issues (Jensen and Meckling, 1976) in raising the costs of external funds.

The notion of financial constraint that is employed in this paper is that of credit rationing which arises due to informational asymmetry between the borrower/firm and the lender about the quality of project that a firm wishes to undertake and also due to the risk of bankruptcy in the event of the failure of the project. Gale and Hellwig (1985) compare optimal contracts with the first best situation. First best situations are those that arise when borrowers and lenders share the same information about the nature and the outcome of the project, that is, there are situations where there is no informational asymmetry. An optimal contract is incentive-compatible, which allows borrowers to truthfully reveal (since the firm has more information about the project than the lender) the outcome of the project and also takes into consideration that borrowers in their optimization program account for the possibility of bankruptcy and the costs associated with it. Gale and Hellwig (1985) also show that standard debt contracts that require a fixed repayment when the firm is solvent and that require the firm to be declared bankrupt if this fixed payment cannot be met and the creditor is allowed to recoup as much of the debt as possible from the firm's assets, are also optimal. In equilibrium, a standard debt contract, which is also optimal, will usually involve credit-rationing in the sense that the optimal loan is smaller and the interest rate is higher than it would have been under the first best outcome.

Empirically, the existence of financial constraints for innovative firms is most frequently investigated by examining the sensitivity of R&D investment to financial factors (see Himmelberg and Petersen, 1994; Harhoff, 1998; Mulkay, 2001. It is estimated by using the same models as for physical investment (see Mulkay et al., 1999), that is to say, by using the reduced form of accelerator models of investment (see Fazzari, Hubbard and Peterson, 1988; Bond et al., 1997), or by using the structural framework of Euler equations as in Bond and Meghir (1994). Himmelberg and Petersen (1994) find a large and significant relationship between R&D and internal finance for US small firms in high-tech industries. Similar results are obtained by Mulkay, Hall and Mairesse (2001) with French and United States firms. In addition, they find that cash flow has a much larger impact on R&D investment for US firms than for the French ones. Harhoff's results about German firms are less conclusive. He finds a weak but significant cash flow effect on R&D by using an investment accelerator model, while Euler-equation estimates appear to be non-informative. However, Kaplan and Zingales (1997, 2000) and Cleary (1999) provide evidence that cash flow sensitivity need not identify liquidity constrained firms, that is, sensitivity is not monotonic in the degree of constraints. Cash flow provides information about future investment opportunities, hence, investment cash flow sensitivity may equally occur because firms are sensitive to demand signals. On the theoretical side, Gomes (2001) and Aydogan (2003) simulate dynamic investment models, demonstrating that significant cash flow coefficients are not necessarily generated by financing frictions. Conversely, Gomes (2001) shows that financing frictions are not sufficient to generate significant coefficients on cash flow.

Among the many ways to study the effect of financing frictions on physical/R&D investment is to construct an index of financial constraints based on a standard intertemporal investment model augmented to account for financial frictions. External finance constraints affect the intertemporal substitution of investment today for investment tomorrow, via the shadow value of scarce external funds. Recently Gomes, Yaron and Zhang (2006) showed that one can rewrite a constrained problem as an unconstrained one with embedded multipliers that give a characterization of the shadow value, as a measure of the premium on external finance. This shadow value, in turn, depends on observable financial variables and proxies that signal the worthiness of firms – as debt, equity, liquidity, cash flow and bond ratings to name a few. A generalized method of moments estimation of the model provides an estimate of the shadow value that is then used as an index of financial constraint. Many papers in the literature on financing frictions use this approach to study the effect of financing premium on the behaviour of such variables as investment (Whited, 1992; Bond and Meghir, 1994), stock return (Gomes, Yaron and Zhang, 2006; Whited and Wu, 2006), and the term structure of interest rates (Dow, Gorton and Krishnamurthy, 2004).

However, in our data set, which we have obtained from the Community Innovation Survey (CIS), we do not have information on balance sheets of the firms/enterprises,[1] which would allow us to assess the effect of internal/external finance on the behaviour of R&D investment. But, from a question asked of the firms we know whether and to what degree a firm was hampered in its pursuit of R&D activities by the presence of financial constraints. This avoids the task of constructing an index of financial constraint to study the behaviour of R&D investment in the presence of capital market frictions. That is, we have an index of financial constraint that is a function of the financial position of the firm and its willingness to undertake R&D activities.

The above statement needs some further explanation. A constructed index of financial constraint is only a function of the financial state variable and this index is purged of the effects of future expected profitability. However, this is not the case for firms reporting whether they are financially constrained or not in our data set. In other words, the firms reporting that they are financially constrained are also the ones that express a willingness to invest in R&D activities but whose financial position is not sound enough for them to take up R&D activities. That is, if two firms are equal in every other respect but one firm is in a better financial position than the other, then the firm in a better financial position is less likely to hit its debt limit than the firm whose financial position is not as sound. *Ceteris paribus*, the worse the financial position of the firm, the greater is the loan demanded, which implies a higher repayment obligation to the lending agency and hence a greater risk of bankruptcy. This risk is the prime factor for under-investment. That is, firms might get *some* external finance to finance their projects, but not to the extent that they desire or require.

There are many situations when a firm may report that financial factors are constraining innovation. The prerequisite is that the firm is attempting to undertake innovative activity. The firm must then consider that its attempt to pursue that activity has been hampered by the lack of finance and/or the cost of that finance. It need not be that all firms that are financially constrained would report that they are financially constrained; for example, they may not be innovation-active in the period, or they may face other kinds of constraints that inhibit their R&D activities, which imply that the financial constraint is not binding.

The aim of this chapter is twofold. The first is to study the effect of financial constraint, as reported by firms among other variables, on innovation activity, here measured by R&D investment; the second is to establish the determinants of financial constraint.

There are many problems to be faced when estimating the impact of financial and other variables on innovation; the selection and endogeneity of the explanatory variables are chief among them. Problems of sample selection arise since it is only firms that choose to indulge in R&D activities that report R&D expenditure. Savignac (2005) examines the impact of financial constraints on innovation for established firms in France. An indicator based on the firm's assessment of financial constraints is found to significantly reduce the probability that a firm undertakes innovation activities. However, in her paper she only accounts for the endogeneity of the indicator when indicating whether a firm is financially constrained or not. But, the endogeneity of other control variables could also lead to inconsistent estimates. To overcome the potential endogeneity of the regressors we use Lewbel's (2006) approach to handling such problems. For studying the determinants of R&D investment we use Lewbel's semiparametric estimator that handles both the problem of selection and of endogeneity. For the binary response model, with which we study the determinants of financial constraint, we employ Lewbel's (2000, 2004) semiparametric binary choice model that accounts for endogeneity of the regressors.

Our results generally support the view that financial constraints affect R&D investment and that the financial constraints are less binding in the presence of other constraints on innovation, such as market or economic uncertainty or regulation and organizational rigidities. Other significant determinants of R&D investment that we have found are the age of firms, market share, cooperation in R&D activities and firms' share of innovative sales.

Ideally, we would have liked to assess the impact of the financial position of the firms after controlling for investment opportunities or for future expected profitability. However, the Community Innovation Surveys do not provide us with the balance-sheet information for the firms. Instead of this financial information we include age and a dummy for group membership of the firm. Our results suggest that age and belonging to a group are significant determinants of financial constraint. We believe that these variables reveal the effect of the financial health of the firm. Our results also suggest that the presence of other constraints on innovation, such as market uncertainty, regulation and organizational rigidities, also reduces the probability of a firm being financially constrained, though their influence is not so significant. Expected future profitability, as proxied by the share of innovative sales in the total sales of the firm, increases the probability of financial constraint after controlling for information costs that are implied by the financial position of the firm, which is proxied by age, market share and a dummy for belonging to a group.

The rest of the paper is organized as follows. Section 10.2 describes the data. Section 10.3 presents the theoretical model of R&D investment in the presence of financial constraints and Section 10.4 the empirical model. Section 10.5 discusses the results and Section 10.6 concludes.

10.2   Data

The data used for our analysis are collected by Statistics Netherlands (CBS). The Dutch Innovation Surveys are conducted every two years. To implement our model we used the fourth Dutch Innovation Survey, CIS 3.5, which pertains to the years 2000–2. The Innovation Survey data are collected at the enterprise level. A combination of a census and a stratified random sampling is used. A census is used for the population of large (250 or more employees) enterprises, and stratified random sampling is used for small and medium-sized enterprises. The size of an enterprise is measured by the number of employees, and the stratum variables are the economic activity and the size of an enterprise, where the economic activity is given by the Dutch standard industrial classification.

Since in our model we want to control for the endogeneity of the regressors, we use as instruments lagged values of some of our potential endogenous regressors. Hence we merged CIS 3.5 with CIS 3, which contains information for the years 1998–2000. This leaves us, after cleaning the data, with a total of 3958 enterprises for our analysis, out of which 1531 report to be innovating.

Appendix 10.3 at the end of this chapter shows a table directly borrowed from the CIS 3.5 questionnaire. Section 8a of the table asks an innovating firm if it is hampered in its pursuit of innovating activities. Section 8b of the questionnaire asks the non-innovating firms if it is important for them to take up innovating activity and whether they are hampered in some way or another. The number of non-innovating firms that answered in the affirmative to question 8b is 95. These 95 firms could be thought of as potentially innovating firms. Thus the total number of innovating and potentially innovating firms is 1626. If either type of firm, innovating as well as potentially innovating, replies in the affirmative to the general hampering question then it is asked to fill out Section 9, in which it is asked to specify the hampering factor(s) and to what extent they affect its innovation projects. We construct a binary variable *DFIN* that takes value 1 if the firm answers that, because of financial problems, some of its projects are: a) seriously delayed; b) prematurely terminated; or c) did not start. Out of 1626 innovating as well as potentially innovating firms, 583 firms reported that they were hampered in some way or another in their innovation activities. Of these, 178 firms reported that they were hampered due to financial reasons.

10.3 The theoretical model

In this section we present a model of financial constraint and then study the decision of the firm to innovate and its decision on how much to invest in R&D in the presence of financial constraint[2]. Please refer to Appendix 10.1 for a more detailed discussion of the model, which builds upon and expands what follows.

If firms wish to undertake risky ventures but lack the necessary resources, they can turn to investors (banks or other deposit-taking financial institutions) for external finance. Venture capital and other types of non-deposit private equity are not considered in our analysis. The firm is assumed to be risk-neutral; it maximizes the expected value of its 'wealth'. The returns to the risky venture are described by a revenue function f: an investment of R units produces a revenue of $f(s, R)$ units in state s (s being the state of nature). The revenue function is also assumed to exhibit decreasing returns to scale. Assume that $f(s, R) = s\phi(R; .)$; '.' represents other parameters characterizing the firm. A crucial assumption is that agents have asymmetric information. The firm observes the state of nature free of charge, but the lender can only observe this state by paying some observational cost. Gale and Hellwig (1985) have shown that the optimal contract between the firm and the lender is a standard debt contract that involves a fixed repayment obligation and a declaration of bankruptcy if and only if the repayment obligation cannot be met, and a confiscation of whatever wealth remains in the event of bankruptcy.

Under an optimal contract the firm maximizes its wealth taking into account the possible risk of bankruptcy and subject to the constraint that the zero profit condition of the lender is satisfied. The zero profit condition states that the expected return from lending to the firm should at least be equal to the amount that the lender can earn from lending this amount at the risk-free rate of interest ir. Let R_{op} be the amount of R&D capital demanded by the firm under an optimal contract.

To invoke the notion of financial constraint, let us now see what happens under the assumption that both the lender and the firm can directly observe the state of nature. In such a situation, which is termed first best (since the firm and the lender share the same information about the nature of the project and the lender can costlessly observe the states of nature), the problem is the same for both the firm and the lender.

Let R_{fb} be the solution to the firm's problem under the first best situation. Gale and Hellwig (1985) have shown that $R_{fb} \geq R_{op}$, that is to say, the amount of R&D capital demanded in the first best situation, is at least as great as the amount lent under an optimal contract. R_{fb} is strictly greater than R_{op} if there is a positive probability of bankruptcy and if the cost borne by the lender for investigation in the event of bankruptcy is positive.

However, it should be noted that R_{op} is a function of the distribution of the states of nature over which it bases its expectations and which we seek to capture through the expected future profitability $E(\pi)$, firm characteristics FC, the organizational and the institutional constraints that the firm faces and which deter a firm from taking up R&D activities CON, the liquid wealth W_0 that the firm has at its disposal, and the risk-free rate of interest ir.

$$R_{op} = R_{op}(E(\pi), FC, CON, ir) \tag{1}$$

Gale and Hellwig (1985, 1986) and Gomes, Yaron and Zhang (2006) show that $R'_{op_{ir}} < 0$, $R'_{op_W} > 0$. It can be shown that $R'_{op_E} > 0$ and $R'_{op_{CON}} < 0$. In words this means that as the risk-free rate of interest rises the demand for R&D capital decreases, as the liquid wealth of the firm increases the demand for R&D capital increases and as the future expected profitability, $E(\pi)$, increases the demand for R&D capital increases. Also since the fixed payment to the lender when the firm is solvent increases with the amount lent, the effects of ir, W_0, $E(\pi)$, and CON on the fixed payment to the lender are qualitatively the same as those on R_{op}.

Let r be the equilibrium rate of interest that the firm pays so that the lender's zero profit constraint is satisfied. This rate of interest is the interest rate actually paid by the firm when it is not bankrupt. This implies that $r = r(R_{op})$.

Since the fixed repayment obligation by the firm to the lender increases with the amount of loan it can be shown that the rate of interest is non-decreasing in the amount of R&D demanded under an optimal contract. Equation (1) implies that:

$$r = r(E(\pi), FC, CON, ir). \tag{2}$$

Since the demand for R&D capital increases in expectation of future profitability it can be shown that $r'_E > 0$ and since the demand decreases due to presence of institutional factors that hamper R&D activities, $r'_{CON} < 0$. Also, since the demand for external sources of funding decreases with the increase in the internal wealth of the firm, this implies that $r'_{W_0} < 0$.

Define the function fin^3 as

$$fin = fin\{(E(\pi), FC, CON, ir), \varepsilon\}, \tag{3}$$

where, ε is an idiosyncratic disturbance term. The inequalities discussed above imply that $fin'_E \geq 0$, $fin'_{CON} \leq 0$ and $fin'_{W_0} \leq 0$. We say that a firm is financially constrained if,

$$fin \geq F, \tag{4}$$

where F corresponds to the threshold value on the loan that the firm can get. This constraint becomes binding if the rate of interest demanded by the lender on extra units of loan exceeds a certain threshold that the firm is unable to meet. Consequently, the firm would not be able to meet its required R&D investment level. The rate of interest corresponding to the threshold could be thought of as the interest rate on the maximum amount of debt a firm can incur. This threshold can differ from firm to firm depending on the financial position of the firm. Take the example of two firms that are equal in every respect except that one firm has a better financial position than the other. The firm that is in a better financial position is less likely to hit its debt limit than the firm whose financial position is not as sound. It should be noted that what is driving these results is the positive probability of bankruptcy. *Ceteris paribus*, the worse the financial position of the firm, the greater is the loan demanded, which implies that the fixed repayment obligation and the risk of bankruptcy are also greater.

10.4   The empirical model

Before we set up our econometric model we would like to note that the observed R&D expenditure corresponds to R_{op}, the optimal R&D capital demanded under the optimal/standard debt contract, but the observed outcome is closer to the first best level if the firm does not report that it is financially constrained. Our objective here is to assess how the observed outcome/R&D expenditure behaves under the presence of financial constraint.

We hypothesize that:

$$DFIN = I[fin - F > 0], \tag{5}$$

where *DFIN* is the binary variable that takes value 1 if the firm reports that it is financially constrained and value 0 otherwise, and I is the indicator function that equals one if its argument is true and zero otherwise.

For our empirical analysis of the effects of financial constraints on R&D investment we now seek to set up a model whose estimation will help us judge the effects of financial constraint on R&D investment. Any such empirical model would have to take into account the sample selection that arises in our data set. Also, in a model of sample selection, common unobservables may affect both the outcome (R&D investment) and the probability of selection (the decision to innovate) in unknown ways. To handle endogeneity in a model of sample selection we use Lewbel's (2006) estimator, which takes the form of simple weighted averages, GMM or two-stage least squares. Lewbel shows that the distribution function of potential outcomes, conditional on covariates, can be identified given an observed variable V, called a very exogenous variable, that affects the selection probability in certain ways and is conditionally independent of the error terms in a model of potential outcomes. The nice thing about this estimator is that it is semiparametric and there are no stringent assumptions as to the error terms.[4]

We specify the model below. Equation (6) is our main regression equation in which we seek to establish our determinants of R&D intensity, equation (7) is our innovator selection equation, and equation (8) is the indicator function given in equation (5).

Let LR_i be log of R&D intensity of a plant i, where R&D intensity is defined as a level of R&D investment in a year divided by the year value of plant I's sales:

$$LR_i = (SINV_i\beta_1 + DFIN_i\beta_2 + X_i\beta_3 + V_i\beta_4 + \varepsilon_i)D_i \tag{6}$$

$$D_i = I[0 \leq V_i + M(SINV_i, DFIN_i, X_i, e_i)] \tag{7}$$

$$DFIN_i = I[fin_i - F_i > 0], \tag{8}$$

where D_i equals one if the firm i is an innovator and zero otherwise. If $D_i = 1$ we observe some R&D expenditure which may also be zero. In our estimation we use log of R&D intensity instead of R&D expenditure. For those firms that are innovators and for whom R&D intensity is zero,[5] log of R&D intensity is taken to be a little lower than the lowest R&D intensity for a firm with positive R&D expenditure. We do this because logarithmic transformation of zero is not defined and therefore such an exercise prevents us from losing any data during estimation.

Our variable V,[6] the very exogenous regressor, is the size of firms measured in terms of employment. The assumption with V is that it is an observed, continuously distributed covariate (or known function of covariates) with large support. The coefficient on V has been normalized to 1. In the Schumpeterian tradition, it makes sense to include size as an explanatory variable in the main as well as the selection equation. It can also be argued that if there are fixed costs of investing, then, as Cohen and Klepper (1996) argue, large firms have more incentive to engage in innovative activities because they can amortize these costs by selling more units of output.[7]

M is an unobserved latent variable which is a function of explanatory variables other than size. We also assume M to be linear function of its arguments. I is the indicator function that equals one if its argument is true and zero otherwise.

SINV is the share of sales with innovative products in total sales of the firm. Analogous to the literature on physical investment, *SINV* could be thought of as a proxy for q which is the expectation of the marginal contribution of new capital goods to future profit. We also experimented with alternative proxies for q, such as lagged values of share of innovation.[8] Mulkay, Hall and Mairesse (2001) assess the impact of cash flow or profits on R&D and physical investment. The share of sales with innovative products in total sales could be a more accurate measure of the value accruing from R&D investment than cash flow or profits are.

Below are listed the other explanatory variables included in X in equations (6) and (7):

DOTH: This variable carries the effect of other hampering factors. This is a dummy variable that takes value one if a firm is constrained because of one of the following factors: a) internal organization; b) market uncertainties; or c) regulation. The primary aim of constructing this variable is to see the effect of other hampering factors such as uncertainty or institutional factors such as regulation and organizational rigidities on R&D intensity and to see the effect of financial constraint in the presence of such factors.

DCOOPERATION: The literature on cooperation and R&D activities is not sparse. The crux of the issue lies in knowledge spillover and its effect on investment. Spillovers increase the relative profitability of R&D cooperation once spillovers are sufficiently high. But higher spillovers also increase the incentives to cheat by partner firms and the profits to be gained from free riding. Firms can increase the effectiveness of incoming spillovers by investing in 'absorptive capacity'. Cohen and Levinthal (1989) show that external knowledge is more effective for the innovation process when the firm engages in its own R&D. Increased absorptive capacity through investments in internal R&D efforts thus increases the effectiveness of incoming information. Also, when firms are not direct competitors but market independent or produce complementary goods, cooperation is associated with higher R&D investment levels independent of the amount of spillovers.

AGE:[9] In our specification we also include the age of the firms. CIS data do not provide this information. The birth date of the firm was obtained from the Business Register.

LOG(MKTSHARE): This variable is a logarithmic transformation of the market share, defined as the ratio of sales of the firm to the total sales of the industry. It is a proxy for concentration or the degree of monopoly. Schumpeter (1942) argues that a firm is incited to innovate if it enjoys a monopoly position to prevent entry of potential rivals.

Innovating firms are asked if they have introduced new products or processes into the market, and if so, if the new products or processes are: a) developed by the enterprise; b) developed in alliance with third parties; or c) developed mainly by third parties.

PDOTH is a dummy equal to one if the new products were developed mainly by third parties.

PDALOTH is a dummy equal to one if the introduced new products were developed in alliance with third parties.

PCOTH is a dummy equal to one if the introduced new processes were developed mainly by third parties.

PCAOTH is a dummy with value one if the new process were developed in alliance with third parties.

The rationale for including these dummies in the specification can be found in Table 10.1. It is evident from this table that the R&D intensity monotonically decreases with the degree of alliance. However, it should be mentioned that this is not the same as cooperation in R&D activities with other institutions. Summary statistics reveal (see Table 10.2) that the mean R&D intensity is higher for those firms that have entered into cooperative arrangements with other institutions than for those that have not, but also that the R&D intensity monotonically decreases with the degree of alliance in the introduction of new products or processes.

Table 10.1 Mean distribution of R&D intensity along alliance in the introduction of new products and process

	Mainly by your enterprise	**Cooperation with third parties**	**Mainly by third parties**
Product	1.45	0.68	0.35
	(1363)	(679)	(296)
Process	1.70	0.77	0.24
	(643)	(601)	(441)

The figures in parentheses are the number of observations.
These numbers are from the full sample of CIS 3.5, which has 10,628 observations.

Table 10.2 Descriptive statistics of the variables of interest

	Mean	**St. Dev.**	**Min**	**Max**
Variables for innovating firms				
LR	−5.09	3.80	−19.70	4.84
SINV	17.15	22.61	0	100
DCOOPERATION	0.41	0.49	0	1
PDALOTH	0.21	0.41	0	1
PDOTH	0.08	0.28	0	1
PCALOTH	0.16	0.36	0	1
PCOTH	0.08	0.28	0	1
Variables for all the firms				
DFIN	0.04	0.21	0	1
DOTH	0.11	0.32	0	1
*DFIN*DOTH*	0.04	0.18	0	1
LOG(MKTSHARE)	−8.88	2.27	−18.26	−0.48
SIZE	218.34	1014.91	2.67	39591.50
DSINPL	0.44	0.50	0	1
AGE	22.37	11.59	2.00	35.00

In our specifications we also include a dummy variable *DSINPL*, that takes value one if the enterprise does not belong to a group headed by a company that has more than one enterprise working for it. It could be quite possible that the firm in question, if faced with financial distress, could be bailed out by the company to which it belongs. It is also possible that the company to which this enterprise belongs engages in diverse activities and produces diverse products which reduces its risk of going bankrupt, thus enhancing its ability to borrow more.

Earlier we explained the construction of our binary variables *DFIN*. In our bid to explain what causes financial constraint we use Lewbel's (2000, 2004) semiparametric estimator to estimate a binary-choice model. For our estimation we choose a simple functional form for the function, *fin-F*, which is given by:

$$fin_i - F_i = V_i + R(X_i, \varepsilon_i),\tag{9}$$

where V and X include variables that parameterize the arguments in the function *fin*. R is a latent variable, which we assume to be a linear function of variables other than V, the very exogenous regressor, and the error term [epsilon]. Thus, the estimation equation is given by the following equation:

$$DFIN_i = I[0 \leq V_i + R(X_i, \varepsilon_i)]\tag{10}$$

V in our model is the size of firms measured in terms of employment. The coefficient on V has been normalized to 1. The assumption on V is that it is an observed, continuously distributed covariate (or known function of covariates) with large support.[10] It is known that small firms may be more tightly constrained because they have less access to internally generated funds for the financing of an innovation project and therefore have to approach outside financiers. These considerations imply that the size of the firm has a bearing on the financial wealth of the firm, especially with respect to the financing of R&D investment from internal funds. Problems arising from information asymmetries may also be more severe for small firms and may affect their ability to raise outside finance. Moreover for smaller, newer firms there may be no track record upon which to base a case for funding and/or there may be fewer realizable assets to use as collateral. Thus size may have an effect of raising the required rate of return independently of the financial position of the firms.

For the same reason as stated in the model on R&D intensity we use $SINV_i$, the share of sales with innovative products in total sales of the firm, as a proxy for future expected profitability.

As mentioned earlier, a proper explanation of a firm being financially constrained necessitates information on the balance sheet of the firms. But since we do not have such information we use the age of the firm, the log of market share, and a dummy if a firm belongs to a group, as proxies for wealth. We include the age of the firm since it might be the case that long-established firms that have survived exit are in financially better shape than new entrants. Age carries a reputation effect which can have a bearing on the accessibility of outside funds.

10.5 Results

This section has two subsections. The first discusses the results of the sample selection model in which we establish the determinants of R&D intensity and the second discusses the result of the binary-choice model, where we seek to explain the probability of a firm being financially constrained.

10.5.1 R&D intensity

In this subsection, we discuss the results of the effect of the financial variable, *DFIN*, after controlling for the effect of other variables that influence the choice of R&D investment.

Table 10.3 presents the result for R&D intensity. The estimates in the columns differ only in the choice of instruments. The common set of instruments for the two columns are the age of the firm (*AGE*); the logarithm of market share (*LOG(MKTSHARE)*), the lagged dummy variable for being financially constrained (*DFIN$_{-1}$*); the lag of the share of innovative sales in the total output of the firm (*SINV$_{-1}$*); the lag of the dummy equal to 1 if the firm cooperated with others in its R&D endeavours (*DCOOPERATION$_{-1}$*); the lag of the log of market share (*LOG(MKTSHARE)$_{-1}$*); the dummy set equal to one if the firm did not belong to a group (*DSINPL*); the dummy indicating if the firm also did non-technological innovation (*DNONTECH*) and its lag (*DNONTECH$_{-1}$*); the dummy that is equal to one if new products were developed in alliance with third parties (*PDALOTH*); the dummy that takes value 1 if new processes were developed in alliance with third parties (*PCALOTH*); the dummy variable that takes value 1 if non-technological reasons or market oriented reasons were important in driving innovation activities (*NONTECHR*); the dummy variable that takes value 1 if technological reasons were important in driving innovation activities (*TECHR*); total investment of the firm during the last period (*INVT$_{-1}$*); and industry dummies. The instrument set in column (a) includes an additional variable *PDOTH,* which is a dummy set equal to one if the new products were developed mainly by third parties. Some of the variables in the list of instruments, such as TECHR and NONTECHR, turned out to be insignificant and were therefore not included among the explanatory variables.

The number of over-identifying restrictions (number of instruments minus number of estimated coefficients) is equal to 2 in column (a) and 3 in column (b). The specifications in both columns satisfy the Sargan test that the over-identifying orthogonality restrictions are not significantly different from zero.

The results from the estimates suggest that, once other factors are controlled for, a firm is adversely affected in its pursuit of R&D activities, as measured by the R&D intensity, by the presence of financial constraints. The large negative sign on *DFIN* is testament to this fact. From our discussion of the model we know that, given the uncertainty, the risk of bankruptcy is large

Table 10.3   Determinants of R&D intensity
Very exogenous variable: size in 100
Dependent variable: log of R&D intensity

	(a)	(b)
DFIN	−41.65***	−41.66***
	(11.44)	(11.45)
*DFIN*DOTH*	44.44***	44.45***
	(11.44)	(11.45)
DOTH	−1.77***	−1.74***
	(0.59)	(0.62)
DCOOPERATION	0.75***	0.74***
	(0.19)	(0.20)
SINV	0.04***	0.04***
	(0.01)	(0.02)
AGE	0.04***	0.04***
	(0.01)	(0.01)
LOG(MKTSHARE)	−0.18***	−0.17***
	(0.04)	(0.04)
DSINPL	−0.29*	−0.28*
	(0.17)	(0.17)
PDOTH	3.05***	2.97***
	(0.45)	(0.73)
PDALOTH	−0.20	−0.20
	(0.42)	(0.42)
PCOTH	−9.57***	−9.63***
	(1.24)	(1.31)
PCALOTH	−1.04***	−1.05***
	(0.40)	(0.40)
Sargan Test	6.04	6.02
Degrees of Freedom	3	2
P-Value	0.11	0.05
F-stat	3.86	3.65
P-Value	0.049	0.056

Significance levels: *: 10%, **: 5%, ***: 1%. Industry dummies are controlled for. For list of instruments, see Section 10.1

for firms that are not financially healthy. This risk plays an important part in reducing the amount of R&D investment. We include *DOTH* to assess the effect of other constraints. The results of our analysis suggest that such factors on their own also have a negative effect on the amount of R&D capital a firm wishes to use. The effects of the other constraints are much weaker than the financial constraints; this suggests that, if there are any major hampering factors, then these are financial constraints. To capture the effect of financial constraints in the presence of other hampering factors, we include the interaction of *DFIN* and *DOTH*, *DFIN*DOTH*. Our results imply that financial constraints are less binding if market uncertainties or institutional or other hampering factors are also present (the coefficient of *DFIN*DOTH* is positive and statistically significant). The effect of financial constraints in the presence of other constraints is captured by the sum of the coefficients of *DFIN*, *DFIN*DOTH*, and *DOTH*. The F-statistic corresponding to the test of the null hypothesis that the sum of these coefficients is equal to zero is reported at the bottom of Table 10.3. The restriction is marginally rejected in column (b) but not in column (a). The estimated coefficients are rather similar in both columns. We can thus conclude that the total effect of all constraints is not significantly different from zero, but that the financial constraints alone are quite prominent and negatively affect the R&D intensity.

Our results suggest that R&D intensity reacts strongly to *SINV*, which is the share of sales with innovative products in the total sales of the firm that we assumed to be a proxy for future expected profitability. The strong positive sign on *SINV* suggests that the higher the future expected profitability, the higher the R&D intensity. However, we find that firms that have a higher market share also have a lower R&D intensity. Not surprisingly, the sign of this coefficient is positive when we use the logarithm of R&D expenditure instead of the logarithm of R&D intensity as the dependent variable. These findings are not new; they only suggest that a monopoly firm does indeed invest more than a firm in a more competitive industry but proportionately less as it increases in size, as measured by sales.[11] Our results suggest that, controlling for other factors, older firms tend to have a higher R&D intensity than younger firms and that the spillover effects of cooperation lead to higher R&D intensity. They could also suggest that the cooperative arrangements are made with non-rivals or with firms that are engaged in producing complementary goods.[12] The negative sign of variable *DSINPL* indicates that firms that do not belong to a group have a lower R&D intensity than those that do belong to a group. Enterprises belonging to a group could be special units, set up with the purpose of carrying out R&D activities for the whole group.

10.5.2 Financial constraint

This section discusses the results of the binary-choice models with which we seek to explain the determinants of the financial constraint itself. Our dependent variable is *DFIN* which is the binary variable that takes value one if the firms finds itself being financially constrained and zero otherwise. As stated earlier, to handle the potential endogeneity of the regressors we use Lewbel's (2000, 2004) semiparametric estimator.

To estimate the binary-choice model we construct another dependent variable DFIN*, which is $DFIN\text{-}I(V \geq 0)$ weighted by the inverse of the conditional density function of the negative of the logarithm of the size of the firm, measured in terms of employment, the very exogenous variable V, to use the

Table 10.4   Determinants of financial constraint
Very exogenous variable: log of size
Dependent variable: DFIN, binary variable indicating if the firm was financially constrained or not

	(a)	(b)	(c)	(d)
SINV	0.36	−0.06		
	(0.35)	(0.59)		
SINV$_{-1}$		22.61	20.6	20.87
		(25.9)	(15.18)	(15.1)
DOTH	−15.25*	−13.09	−13.46	−13.31
	(9.36)	(9.67)	(8.87)	(8.84)
AGE	−0.96***	−0.94***	−0.95***	−0.95***
	(0.24)	(0.24)	(0.24)	(0.24)
LOG(MKTSHARE)	0.16	0.27	0.25	
	(1.38)	(1.38)	(1.36)	
DSINPL	17.45***	17.65***	17.62***	17.54***
	(5.54)	(5.53)	(5.53)	(5.51)
Sargan Test	13.23	12.51	12.52	12.55
Degrees of Freedom	10	9	10	11
P-value	0.21	0.19	0.25	0.32

Significance levels: *: 10%, **: 5%, ***: 1%. Industry dummies are controlled for. For list of instruments, see Section 5.2

same notation as in Lewbel's (2000, 2004) papers. *I* is an indicator variable that takes value 1 if the argument in parentheses is true. The conditioning variable is the union of all the explanatory variables and the instruments. We take the negative of the logarithm of size because one of the assumptions of the model is that, as *V* decreases, the probability of *DFIN* being zero increases (refer to footnote 9). In Lewbel's method, the division by the conditional density of V, converts V to a uniform distribution.

The results of the binary-choice model with which we seek to explain the determinants of financial constraint are presented in Table 10.4. The set of instruments in all columns contains *DOTH, DOTH*$_{-1}$*, AGE, DSINPL, LOG(MKTSHARE), LOG(MKTSHARE)*$_{-1}$*, DCOOPERATION*$_{-1}$*, PDOTH, PDALOTH, PCALOTH, PCOTH, SINV*$_{-1}$*, DNONTECH, DNONTECH*$_{-1}$*,* lagged size, and sectoral dummies.

The more striking results of this part of our analysis are the coefficient estimates that we obtain on age and DSINPL. The results suggest that the older a firm is, the less likely it is to be financially constrained, and significantly so. This is understandable, since older firms, having survived preemption, are more likely to be financially stable than new firms. Also, older firms have a better reputation than younger firms, and therefore they have greater access to external funds. Secondly, the estimation results indicate that a firm is more likely to be financially constrained if it does not belong to a group. This could suggest that if it belongs to a group, then it has at its disposal some alternative avenues of financing its projects that are closed to firms that do not belong to a group. The fact that it belongs to a group may be an indication that the group is engaged in diverse activities and thus less prone to risk than a single enterprise engaged in a single activity. As explained earlier, *DFIN* is a function of the financial state variables. In the absence of information on the balance sheets, the effect of financial state variables is included in the error term. Hence, the instruments that are supposed to be correlated with the regressors are also correlated with the error term. But since the results of the test of over-identifying restrictions do not lead to rejection, we conclude that age and the dummy indicating that the firm belongs to group are picking up the effects of financial variables.

As explained earlier the binary variable *DFIN* is an indicator of the firm's willingness to undertake R&D activity as well as of its financial position. As a proxy for future expected profitability we experiment both with the current value of the share of innovative sales *SINV* and with its lag. Our results suggest that controlling for other variables, the higher a firm's future expected profitability, as proxied by *SINV* or its lag, the higher the probability of it being financially constrained, but not significantly so.

The results in Table 10.4 also suggest that a firm facing *a priori* hampering factors other than financial constraints is less willing to undertake R&D activities and thus less likely to be hit by financial constraints. The results on over-identification restrictions do not suggest that there is simultaneity in the determination of *DOTH* and *DFIN*, since *DOTH* is included in the instrumental variables.

10.6   Conclusions

In this paper we have empirically investigated the determinants of R&D and investment. In particular, our aim was to see how financial constraints affect a firm's R&D intensity. We found that a firm that reports that it is financially constrained but not otherwise constrained is adversely affected in its pursuit of R&D activity. Financial constraints have a large and a significant impact in affecting R&D investment.

However, financial constraints are less binding if the firm runs into other hampering factors or other constraints that are not a function of financial constraint itself. We obtained this result both by looking at the effect of financial constraint on R&D intensity in the presence of other constraints, such as market uncertainty, institutional constraints and organizational rigidities, and looking at the probability of a firm being financially constrained in the presence of other than financial constraints. We also found that the effect of these other constraints is much weaker than that of financial constraint, which confirms the findings of many papers that financial factors are the major stumbling block to the pursuit of any activity. However, this does not diminish the fact that institutional and organizational rigidities also reduce the amount or R&D investment. As well as taking into account the hampering factors that inhibit R&D activities, policy-makers should also consider such factors. Also, since financial constraint seems to be the most important factor that inhibits R&D activities, policy-makers should consider setting up institutions that would allow economically sound projects to get the required finance to enable them to be carried out. In particular, care should be taken with young firms and firms that do not belong to a group, since these firms are more susceptible to the exigencies of nature, as was well reflected in our analysis. Finally, as a comment on financial constraint, we noted that age and group membership, as proxies for the financial wealth of a firm, appear to be significant predictors of a firm being financially constrained.

One of the shortcomings of our paper is that we have not used financial information from the balance sheet of the firms, but instead used proxies for financial-state variables. As a part of our future research agenda we would like to enrich our model by using data from the balance sheets of firms in the explanation of financial constraint. Also, for our future research we plan to carry out our investigation of financial constraint on R&D investment in a dynamic setting by using more waves of CIS data. This would also necessitate a dynamic model of financial constraint and investment.

Appendices

Appendix 10.1   A model of financial constraint

In this appendix we present a model of financial constraint and study the decision of a firm to innovate and how much to invest in R&D in the presence of financial constraints.[13] Firms wish to undertake risky ventures but lack the necessary resources, so they turn to investors, banks or other deposit-taking financial institutions for external finance. Venture capital and other types of non-deposit private equity are not considered in our analysis. The firm's initial net wealth is $W_0 = A_0 - R_0$, where A_0 is the firms's initial liquid assets and R_0 the firm's initial indebtedness. Assume that the firm's need of R&D expenditure R is greater than W_0. The firm is assumed to be risk-neutral; it maximizes the expected present value of its 'wealth'. The returns to the risky venture are described by a revenue function f: an investment of R units produces a revenue of $f(s, R)$ units in state s, s being the state of nature. The revenue function is also assumed to exhibit decreasing returns to scale. Assume that $f(s, R) = s\phi(R; .)$, '.' represents other parameters characterizing the firm. A crucial assumption is that agents have asymmetric information. The firm observes the states free of charge, but the lender can only observe the states by paying some observational cost. Gale and Hellwig (1985) have shown that the optimal contract between the firm and the lender is a standard debt contract, which involves a fixed repayment obligation $\overline{R}_l$, and a declaration of bankruptcy if and only if the repayment obligation cannot be met, and a confiscation of whatever wealth remains in the event of bankruptcy.

Under an optimal contract the firm takes into account the possible chances of bankruptcy. If the firm declares bankruptcy its revenue is reduced to $\alpha s\phi(R; .)$, where $0 \leq \alpha \leq 1$, and it suffers a fixed nonpecuniary penalty whose monetary equivalent is $K \geq 0$. Under an optimal contract the firm solves the following problem:

$$\max_{R,\overline{R}} E[s\phi(R; FC, CON) - \overline{R}_l]^+ - \Pr[s\phi(R; FC, CON) < \overline{R}_l] \tag{A.1}$$

subject to

$$E\widetilde{R}_l \geq (1 + ir)(R - W_0) \tag{A.2}$$

$$R \geq 0,$$

where $[X]^+ \equiv \max\{X, 0\}$, $\Pr[.]$, denotes a probability, the expectation is taken over the states of nature, ir is the risk-free rate of return, FC is firm characteristics, CON is other constraints such as institutional factors that deter firms from taking up R&D activities and $\widetilde{R}_l$ is given by:

$$\widetilde{R} = \overline{R} \qquad \text{if } s\phi(R; .) \geq \overline{R}_l, \text{ and}$$

$$\widetilde{R} = \alpha s\phi(R; .) \qquad \text{if } s\phi(R; .) < \overline{R}_l. \tag{A.3}$$

$\widetilde{R}_l$ is a random variable, which is the lender's gross return under a standard debt contract. $\overline{R}_l$, under the standard debt contract is the fixed payment to the lender when the firm is solvent. In the event of bankruptcy, that is, if $s\phi(R; .) < \overline{R}_l$, the revenue is reduced to $\alpha s\phi(R; .)$, and since the lender is allowed to recoup whatever he/she can of the lender's revenue in the state of bankruptcy is $\alpha s\phi(R; .)$. One can interpret $(1 - \alpha)s\phi(R; .)$ as the cost borne by the lender for investigation in the event bankruptcy. Equation (11) is the zero profit condition of the lender, which states that the expected return from lending to the firm should be at least equal the amount he/she can earn from lending the same amount at the risk-free rate of interest ir. Let R_{op} be the solution to (A.1) and (A.2).

To invoke the notion of financial constraint let us now see what happens under the assumption that both the lender and the firm can directly observe the state of nature. In such a situation, which is termed first best, since the firm and the lender share the same information about the nature of the project and the lender can costlessly observe the states of nature, the problem of the firm as well as the lender is the same. This can be written as

$$\max_{R} E\{sf(R,.) - (1+ir)(R - W_0)\}. \tag{A.4}$$

Let, R_{fb} be the solution to the above problem. Gale and Hellwig (1985) have shown that $R_{fb} \geq R_{op}$ and that $R_{fb} \geq R_{op}$ if $\Pr[s\phi(R,.) < \overline{R}_l] > 0$ and $\alpha < 1$, that is to say that the amount of R&D capital demanded in the first best situation is at least as great as the amount lent under an optimal contract and is strictly greater if there is a positive probability of bankruptcy and if the cost borne by the lender $(1-\alpha)s\phi(R;.)$ is positive.

Let r be the equilibrium rate of interest that the firm pays so that the lender's zero-profit constraint is satisfied. This rate of interest r in (A.5) is the interest rate actually paid by the firm when it is not bankrupt and is given by:

$$(1+r)(R_{op} - W_0) = \overline{R}_l. \tag{A.5}$$

This implies that:

$$r = r(R_{op}, \overline{R}_l). \tag{A.6}$$

However, it should be noted that both R_{op} and $\overline{R}_l$ are determined simultaneously and are functions of the distribution of the states of nature, which we denote here by $h(s)$; firm characteristics, FC; the organizational and the institutional constraints that the firm faces and which deters a firm from taking up R&D activities, CON; the liquid wealth W_0 that the firm has at its disposal and the risk-free rate of interest ir. Hence:

$$R_{op} = R_{op}(E(\pi), FC, CON, ir), \tag{A.7}$$

and:

$$\overline{R}_l = \overline{R}_l(E(\pi), FC, CON, ir). \tag{A.8}$$

Here we seek to capture the distribution of the states of nature on which a firm bases its expectation with a single variable, $E(\pi)$, the expected future profitability; this is given by $E(\pi) \equiv E[s\phi'(R)] = \int s\phi'(R)h(s)ds$.

Gale and Hellwig (1985, 1986) and Gomes, Yaron and Zhang (2006) show that $R'_{op_{ir}} < 0$, $R'_{op_W} > 0^{14}$, where "'" denotes the derivative of the variable with respect to the subscript variable. It can also be shown that $R'_{op_E} > 0$ and $R'_{op_{CON}} < 0$. In words this means that: as the risk-free rate of interest rises the demand for R&D capital decreases; as the liquid wealth of the firm increases the demand for R&D capital decreases; and as the future expected profitability, $E(\pi)$, increases the demand for R&D capital increases. Also, since the fixed payment to the lender when the firm is solvent, $\overline{R}_l$, increases with the amount lent, the effect of ir, W_0, $E(\pi)$, and CON on $\bar{R}_l$ are qualitatively the same as those on R_{op}.

Equation (A.7) and (A.8) imply that:[15]

$$r = r(E(\pi), FC, CON, ir). \tag{A.9}$$

Since the demand for R&D capital increases in expectation of future profitability it can be shown that $r'_E > 0$ and since the demand decreases due to presence of institutional factors that hamper R&D activities, $r'_{CON} < 0$. Also, since the demand for external sources of funding decreases with the increase in the internal wealth of the firm, this implies that $r'_{W_0} < 0$. Define the function *fin* as:[16]

$$fin = fin\{(E(\pi), FC, CON, ir), \varepsilon\}, \tag{A.10}$$

where ε is an idiosyncratic disturbance term. The inequalities discussed above imply that $fin'_E \geq 0$, $fin'_{CON} \leq 0$, and $fin'_{W_0} \leq 0$. We say that a firm is financially constrained if:

$$fin \geq F \tag{A.11}$$

that is, if the rate of interest demanded by the lender on an extra unit of loan exceeds a certain threshold that the firm is unable to meet. Consequently the firm would not be able to meet its required R&D investment level. The rate of interest corresponding to the threshold could be thought of as the interest rate on the maximum amount of debt a firm can incur. This threshold can differ from firm to firm depending on the financial position of the firm. For example, consider two firms that are equal in every respect except that one firm has a better financial position than the other. The firm that is in a better financial position is less likely to hit its debt limit than the firm whose financial position is not as sound. It should be noted that what is driving these results is the positive probability of bankruptcy. *Ceteris paribus*, the worse the financial position of the firm, the greater the loan demanded and therefore the higher the fixed repayment obligation and thus the greater the chances of bankruptcy.

Appendix 10.2   A note on estimation

Given our estimation model equations (6) and (7) in the main text:

$$LR = (SINV\beta_1 + DFIN\beta_2 + X\beta_3 + V\beta_4 + \varepsilon)D \tag{6}$$

$$D = I[0 \leq V + M(SINV, DFIN, X, e)] \tag{7}$$

where LR, the log of R&D intensity is the outcome and D is the decision variable to innovate. D takes value $= 1$ if the firm chooses to innovate and zero otherwise. Define:

$$U^* = Z(LR^* - (SINV\beta_1 + DFIN\beta_2 + X\beta_3 + V\beta_4)), \qquad (A.12)$$

where Z is the vector of instruments and LR^* is the unobserved R&D intensity for firms which report to be non-innovators and therefore do not report their R&D intensity. In such a situation the coefficients of the model could be estimated by two-stage least squares or a GMM technique using the moment condition $E(U^*) = 0$. But what we observe in fact is U, which is given by:

$$U = Z(LR - (SINV\beta_1 + DFIN\beta_2 + X\beta_3 + V\beta_4))D. \qquad (A.13)$$

In the presence of selection, GMM or two-stage least squares is infeasible because we only observe LR and not LR^*, and unobservables that determine the selection such as M, the unobserved latent variable, are correlated with LR^* and U^*. But the estimation of the required coefficients could become feasible given a consistent estimator of $E(U^*)$. Define the weighting scalar W by $W = D/f(V|Y)$ where f is the conditional probability density function of V, introduced earlier, given Y, which is the union of the set of instruments and the other covariates, that is, $DFIN$, $SINV$ and X, that appear in equation (6). Lewbel (2006) shows that:

$$E(U^*) = p\lim_{n\to\infty} \frac{\sum_{i=1}^{n}(U_i W_i)}{\sum_{i=1}^{n} W_i}. \qquad (A.14)$$

The main assumptions required for equation (19) to hold are that the support of $V|Y$ contains the support of $-M|Y$ (these could all equal the real line, for example), and that:

$$V|Y, U^*, M \sim V|Y \qquad (A.15)$$

that is, V is conditionally independent of the unobserved latent variables of the model, conditioning on the set of covariates X. Given the above, our estimates are based on the moment conditions:

$$E[ZW(LR - (SINV\beta_1 + DFIN\beta_2 + X\beta_3 + V\beta_4))] = 0. \qquad (A.16)$$

We estimate the above by using the method of two-stage least squares. To estimate the conditional density of V given Y, $f(V|Y)$, we employ the nonparametric density estimator described in Lewbel and Schennach (2007). To obtain estimated standard errors we use the formulas derived by Lewbel. As suggested by Lewbel (2004), we also applied the bootstrap to obtain standard errors. The results appeared to be similar to those obtained using analytical formulas for the asymptotic variances of the estimators. Therefore, we do not report them here.

Appendix 10.3   Part of the CIS 2000–2002 questionnaire asking respondents for information on hampering factors

8. Hampering factors general

a. During 2000–2002, did your enterprise encountered hampering factors leading to seriously delayed, abandoned, not started innovation projects?

Yes   go to question 9

No   go to question 10

b. In question 2 you have stated that your enterprise did not engage in activities aimed at technological improvements. What was the reason for this?

For our enterprise it was not necessary to engage in such activities in 2000–2002

go to question 10

Such activities were needed, but hampered and therefore NOT started

go to question 9 (last column)

9. Hampering factors and consequences for innovation projects

Tick the consequences of the hampering factors your enterprise experienced in innovation projects in 2000–2002

Consequences hampering factors: innovation projects are

		seriously delayed	abandoned	not started
No financing	Lack of appropriate sources of finance			
Cost too high	Innovation costs were/became too high			
Economic risks	Too much uncertainty of future benefits and costs			
Shortage personnel	Lack of *qualified* personnel			
Shortage knowledge	Lack of knowledge on technologies needed			
Internal organization	Organizational rigidities within the enterprise			
Market uncertainties	Future market developments uncertain			
Regulation				
Other reason	Namely:			

Source: Community Innovation Survey (CIS) 3: Statistics Netherlands

Acknowledgement

The authors would like to thank the referees and the editors of this volume for their suggestions. We would also like to thank the seminar participants at the workshop on Innovation Systems and Firm Performance, in particular the discussant of this paper, Hans Lööf, for their valuable comments.

Notes

1. The data collected through CIS are at the enterprise level and not at the company level. Here we use the term firm and enterprise exchangeably.
2. See Gale and Hellwig (1985) for a detailed discussion.

3. We now ignore the risk free rate of interest *ir*, since it should stay constant for a single period of survey.
4. See Appendix 10.2: 'A note on the estimation'.
5. Out of 1531 innovating firms, 107 or about 7 per cent of them do not have R&D expenditure for the period of the survey.
6. To make sure that V or the log of size has a large support we demean it. With this exercise, we make sure that V takes negative as well as positive values.
7. Nilsen and Schiantarelli (2003) find strong statistical evidence of this relationship, including much greater incidences of zero investments in small versus large plants. They attribute this relevance of plant size both to the presence of absolute as well as relative fixed costs and to potential indivisibilities in investment.
8. See Nilsen and Schiantarelli (2003).
9. The age-of-firms data are available from 1967 onwards.
10. An implication of the large support assumption for V is that, for any value X [and epsilon] may take on, it is possible for V to be small enough to make $D=0$, with probability one, or large enough to make $D=1$ with probability one.
11. See Cohen, Levin and Mowery (1987) and Geroski (1990).
12. See De Bondt, Slaets and Cassiman. (1992) and Röller, Tombak and Siebert (1997).
13. See Gale and Hellwig (1985) for a detailed discussion.
14. However, Gale and Hellwig (1986) show it is not generally true that a reduction in the firm's internal funds leads to a reduction in investment. They show that the relation between the firm's net wealth and investment is exceedingly complicated. Formally, this complexity is due to the nonconvexity that arises from the possibility of bankruptcy. Conceptually, the difficulties arise from the strategic interaction between the borrower's interests and the lender's interests. To understand the basic difficulty, consider the situation when the firm has some prior debt so that its liquid net wealth is negative. A lender may be willing to roll over the prior debt if he receives an appropriate claim on the surplus that the enterprise generates. In this situation, the lender is likely to insist on an investment level that is sufficient to generate a substantial surplus. If the marginal returns to investment are unaffected by the costs of bankruptcy, for example if the cost of bankruptcy is a fixed nonmonetary cost falling on the borrower, then for very low (negative) levels of the firm's net wealth, the chosen investment level will actually be close to the first best level, because that maximizes the expected surplus that can be made available to the lender. At this point, the marginal bankruptcy cost of investment to the firm becomes irrelevant because the firm only has the choice between an immediate default on its prior debt and an investment policy that is acceptable to the lender.

    Thus it may happen that investment is close to the first best level both if the firm's net wealth is very high so that little outside capital is needed and if the firm's net wealth is very low so that lenders are barely willing to roll over the firm's prior debts.

    However, for intermediate wealth levels, investment will be strictly less than the first best level because the firm takes account of the marginal bankruptcy costs of increased borrowing. In this chapter we assume that the wealth level of the firm lies in the region that Gale and Hellwig (1986) characterize as intermediate wealth levels. There are three reasons for this assumption. Firstly, R&D activities are mostly taken by firms that have a reasonably sound financial position; secondly, for our analysis we take only those firms that appear both in CIS3 and CIS3.5, that is those firms who since the last survey have survived until the current survey and hence are either likely to be large or growing firms; and thirdly, if there is a situation where the lender is likely to insist on an investment level that is sufficient to generate a substantial surplus and the firm only has the choice between an immediate default on its prior debt and an investment policy that is acceptable to the lender then there would be no financial constraint.

15. In fact the rate of interest r does not have an independent meaning in the context of the model. It is just another characterization of the fixed repayment obligation of the firm, $\bar{R}_i$. We only introduce it here so that we can write the model to be estimated.

16. We now ignore the risk-free rate of interest $i r$, since it should stay constant for a single period of survey.

References

Aydogan, A. (2003) 'How Sensitive is Investment to Cash Flow when Financing is Frictionless?', *Journal of Finance*, 58, pp. 707–22.

Bond, S. and C. Meghir (1994) 'Dynamic Investment Models and the Firm's Financial Policy', *Review of Economic Studies*, 61, pp. 197–222.

Bond S., J. Elston, J. Mairesse and B. Mulkay (1997) 'Financial Factors and Investment in Belgium, France, Germany and the UK: A Comparison Using Company Panel Data', Institute for Fiscal Studies Working Papers, W97/08.

Cleary, S (1999) 'The Relationship between Firm Investment and Financial Status', *Journal of Finance*, 54, pp. 673–92.

Cohen W. M., R. C. Levin and D. C. Mowery (1987) 'Firm Size and R & D Intensity: A Re-Examination', *Journal of Industrial Economics*, 4, pp. 543–65.

Cohen, W. M. and D. Levinthal, (1989) 'Innovation and Learning: the Two Faces of R&D', *Economic Journal*, 99, pp. 569–96.

Cohen W. M. and S. Klepper (1996) 'A Reprise of Size and R&D', *The Economic Journal*, 106, pp. 925–51.

De Bondt, Raymond, P. Slaets and B. Cassiman (1992) 'The Degree of Spillovers and the Number of Rivals for Maximum Effective R&D', *International Journal of Industrial Organization*, 10, pp. 35–54.

Dow, J., G. Gorton and A. Krishnamurthy (2005) 'Equilibrium Asset Prices with Imperfect Corporate Control', *American Economic Review*, 95: 3, pp. 659–81.

Fazzari S. M, R. G. Hubbard, and B. C. Petersen (1988) 'Financing Constraints and Corporate Investment', *Brookings Papers on Economic Activity*, pp. 141–195.

Gale, D. and M. Hellwig (1985) 'Incentive-Compatible Debt Contracts: The One-Period Problem', *Review of Economic Studies*, 52, pp. 647–63.

Gale, D. and M. Hellwig (1986) 'The Optimal Debt Contract: A Comparative Static Analysis', CARESS Working Paper, 86–06.

Geroski, P. A. (1990) 'Innovation, Technological Opportunity and Market Share', *Oxford Economic Papers*, 42, pp. 586–602.

Gomes, J. F. (2001) 'Financing Investment', *American Economic Review*, 91, pp. 1236–85.

Gomes, J. F., A. Yaron and L. Zhang (2006) 'Asset Pricing Implications of Firms' Financing Constraints', *Review of Financial Studies*, 19, pp. 1321–56.

Harhoff D. (1998) 'Are there Financing Constraints for R&D and Investment in German Manufacturing Firms?', *Annales d'Economie et de Statistique*, 49/50, pp. 421–56.

Himmelberg C. and Petersen B. (1994) 'R&D and Internal Finance: A Panel Study of Small Firms in High-Tech Industries', *Review of Economics and Statistics*, 76, pp. 38–51.

Jensen, M. C. and W. H. Meckling (1976) 'Theory of the Firm: Managerial Behavior, Agency Costs and Ownership Structure', *Journal of Financial Economics*, 3, pp. 305–60.

Kaplan, S. and L. Zingales (1997) 'Do Financing Constraints Explain why Investment is Correlated with Cash Flow?', *Quarterly Journal of Economics*, 112, pp. 169–216.

Kaplan, S. and L. Zingales (2000) 'Investment-Cash Flow Sensitivities are not Valid Measures of Financing Constraints', NBER Working Paper 7659.

Lewbel, A. (2000) 'Semiparametric Qualitative Response Model Estimation with Unknown Heteroscedasticity and Instrumental Variables', *Journal of Econometrics*, 97, pp. 145–77.

Lewbel, A. (2004) 'Simple Estimators for Hard Problems: Endogeneity in Discrete Choice Related Models', Unpublished Manuscript, available at: www2.bc.edu/lewbel/.

Lewbel, A. (2006) 'Endogenous Selection or Treatment Model Estimation', *Journal of Econometrics*, 113: 2, pp. 231–63.

Lewbel, A. and S. Schennach (2007) 'A Simple Ordered Data Estimator for Inverse Density Weighted Functions', *Journal of Econometrics*, 136, pp. 189–211.

Mairesse J., B. H. Hall and B. Mulkay (1999) 'Firm-Level Investment in France and the United States: An Exploration of What We Have Learned in Twenty Years', *Annales d'Economie et de Statistique*, 55–56, pp. 27–63.

Modigliani, F. and M. H. Miller (1958) 'The Cost of Capital, Corporation Finance, and the Theory of Investment', *American Economic Review*, 48, pp. 261–97.

Mulkay B., B. H. Hall and J. Mairesse (2001) 'Firm Level Investment and R&D in France and in the United States', in Deutsche Bundesbank (ed.) *Investing Today for the World of Tomorrow* (Springer Verlag).

Myers, S. C. and N. S. Majluf (1984) 'Corporate Financing and Investment Decision When Firms Have Information that Investors Do Not Have', *Journal of Financial Economics*, 13, pp. 187–221.

Nilsen, O. A. and F. Schiantarelli (2003) 'Zeros and Lumps in Investment: Empirical Evidence on Irreversibilities and Nonconvexities', *The Review of Economics and Statistics*, 85: 4, pp. 1021–37

Röller, L., M. Tombak and R. Siebert (1997) 'Why Firms Form Research Joint Ventures: Theory and Evidence', CEPR Discussion Paper Series, 1654.

Ross, S. A., R. W. Westerfield and B. D. Jordan (1993) *Fundamentals of Corporate Finance*, 2nd edition (Boston: Irwin Press).

Savignac, F. (2005) 'The Impact of Financial Constraints on Innovation: Evidence from French Manufacturing Firms', ERUDITE, Université Paris, Working Paper.

Schumpeter, J. A. (1942) *Capitalism, Socialism, and Democracy* (New York: Harper and Brothers) (Harper Colophon edition, 1976.)

Whited, T. M. (1992) 'Debt, Liquidity Constraints and Corporate Investment: Evidence from Panel Data', *Journal of Finance*, 47, pp. 1425–60.

Whited, T. M. and G. Wu (2006) 'Financial Constraint Risk', *Review of Financial Studies*, 19, pp. 531–59.

Part III
External Organization

11
Technology Diffusion and Innovation: The Importance of Domestic and Foreign Sources

Hans Lööf

11.1 Introduction

Recent work in economic growth using aggregate data suggests that variation in cross-country productivity is at least as much due to foreign as to domestic innovation (Keller and Yale, 2003). At the same time, a vast majority of scholars now agree that proximity afforded by locating in large urban regions creates an advantage for firms by facilitating information and knowledge flows for innovation activities, according to arguments presented earlier by Vernon (1962), later by Glaesner (1999) and Feldman and Audretsch (1999).

The question of whether technological knowledge is mainly global or local has been examined at various levels of aggregation within different branches of the literature, with mixed findings. To summarize, there is robust evidence of strong influence of global sources of knowledge at the national level. The global influence becomes weaker at the industry level and the evidence for global ideas versus proximity is somewhat mixed when micro-data is used.

Traditionally, foreign direct investment (FDI) and trade have been suspected to be major sources of international technology transfer. Recent data on corporate spending indicates an overall altered research and development (R&D) strategy of multinational enterprises (MNEs) implying both increased total R&D intensity and more dispersed R&D engagements across borders (more FDI in research and development).

According to the Boston Consulting Group's annual management survey of 2006, innovation is ranked among the top three strategic imperatives by over 70 per cent of 1070 executives in the world's largest corporations (Boston Consulting Group, 2006). Moreover, about 41 per cent reported that the expenditures on research and development will increase between 2005 and 2006 (McGregor, 2006). The survey confirms the recent trend that research and development are becoming central activities of MNEs. Between 1991 to 1996 research and development (R&D) expenditures in multinational enterprises increased by 4.4 per cent annually and by 2.8 per cent annually between 1996 and 2002 (UNCTAD, 2005).

Recent research also suggests that MNEs are increasingly investing in R&D activities in their foreign subsidiaries (Persson, 2006). For instance, the share of R&D in the Swedish private sector that is carried out by foreign-owned firms increased from 41 per cent in 2001 to 45 per cent in 2003 (ITPS, 2003). Correspondingly, the share of R&D by the 20 largest Swedish MNEs that was accounted for by subsidiaries abroad increased from 22 per cent in 1995 to 43 per cent in 2003 (UNCTAD, 2005).

The increasing dispersion of resources for research and development in MNEs as well as the lack of robust empirical evidence on knowledge spillovers motivates further research on the importance of domestic or foreign sources for innovation. This paper estimates the elasticity of innovation output with respect to knowledge transfer via collaboration, FDI and imports.

Using a sample of approximately two-thirds of Swedish firms with at least 10 employees and by accounting for selectivity and simultaneity biases, sector-specific effects and firm-specific effects, we find robust evidence for import spillover. The presence of FDI expressed as foreign-owned firms is neutral with respect to innovation output. Among a sub-sample consisting only of multinational firms there is support for knowledge transfer to the local multinational firms from innovation arrangements that include foreign scientific partners and foreign sub-units. We find only some weak association between proximity to local partners and innovation. The most influential aspect of the local milieu on innovation is skilled labour.

The outline of our study is as follows: Section 11.2 presents a theoretical framework and elaborates on findings in previous studies. The discussion is focused on access to embodied foreign technology in the form of intermediate goods and disembodied technology diffusion in the form of direct communication through FDI and collaboration. The data is described in Section 11.3. Section 11.4 introduces the methodological approach. Section 11.5 presents an assessment of econometric results. Section 11.6 outlines the conclusion.

11.2   Knowledge spillovers

The increasingly central role of across-border transactions of goods, services, capital, labour and knowledge has brought about a surge in interest in understanding the external sources of variance for the firm's innovation and productivity performance. In particular, research in this area has come to focus on trade, FDI and flow of ideas through innovation collaboration and patent citations.

An implication of the endogenous growth models (Romer, 1990) is the importance of spillover from the existing stock of knowledge through intermediate products. A simplified and general possibility implies that all research outcomes enter a common global pool, which individual firms and countries can tap. The main contributors to this pool are a very small number of countries – the so-called G7 – that account for more than 90 per cent of global GDP. Examining aggregate productivity growth since the Second World War in five of these leading research economies (West Germany, France, the UK, Japan and the US) and assuming the presence of a global stock of knowledge, Eaton and Kortum (1995) find that growth is primarily the result of research performed abroad. Eaton and Kortum show that even the world's leading R&D nation, the US, obtained over 40 per cent of its growth from foreign innovations.

When exploiting disaggregated data the spillover from global knowledge is found to be somewhat smaller but still of importance. For instance, using US industry data, Keller (2001) estimates a strong productivity effect both from in-house R&D spending and R&D conducted elsewhere. The contribution of R&D in the industry itself was about 50 per cent in the sample. Domestic R&D in other industries was the source of 30 per cent of the productivity increase and the remaining 20 per cent was due to R&D in foreign industries.

How is global knowledge transferred across borders? It has been suggested that FDI and imports are the major channels. Traditional FDI models (Vernon, 1966) assume that firm advantages can be derived from favourable home-country institutional conditions (such as the National System of Innovations). These technological and managerial advantages of a firm are subsequently transferred to foreign sub-units where they are exploited. Importing technologically advanced intermediate goods is another channel available to a country to get access to foreign knowledge.

With a sample of about 1100 US firms for the years 1987 to 1996, Keller and Yeaple (2003) find robust evidence for substantial FDI spillovers, but also weak support for import-related technology spillover. They estimate that FDI spillovers accounted for about 14 per cent of US productivity over that period. Using USPTO patent citations, Branstetter (2006) tests the hypothesis that FDI is a channel of knowledge spillover for Japanese MNEs undertaking FDI in the United States. In conformity with Keller and Yeaple (2003), he finds that FDI is a significant channel of knowledge spillover both from investing firms to indigenous firms and from indigenous firms to investing firms.

On the one hand, as opposed to markets, multinational enterprises have been identified as a superior institutional form for the international transfer of knowledge (Kogut and Zander, 1993). On the other, difficulties in achieving knowledge transfer within multinationals have been recognized not only within the academic community (see for instance Gupta and Govindarajan, 2000), but also in the business community. In a survey by Ernst & Young, it was found that only 13 per cent of 471 corporate executives indicated that their organization was adept at transferring knowledge (Persson, 2006). Exploiting evidence from Belgian CIS-survey data, Veugelers and Cassiman (2004) suggest that foreign subsidiaries are not necessarily effective R&D partners for knowledge spillover. What seems to be more important for the local firm is having an international network of collaborators that provides access to international technology.

In spite of the increasing global flows of ideas and the increasing dispersion of R&D activities across borders, many authors claim an increased importance for the proximity to sources of knowledge for innovation and make a distinction between knowledge that can be codified into transmittable information and knowledge that is difficult or even impossible to codify. Knowledge that is difficult to codify has been termed 'complex' by Beckmann (1994), 'tacit' by Polanyi (1966) and 'sticky' by von Hippel (1994). While 'complex' directly refers to non-codified knowledge, 'sticky' refers to knowledge that is strongly attached to given persons or groups of individuals. As argued by Antonelli, Marchionatti and Usai (2003), this may imply that knowledge can be shared by firms in a local environment with little risk that the knowledge is spread outside the local context. A general assumption is that face-to-face contacts facilitate communication and transfer of complex knowledge.

Supporting the basic ideas launched by Marshall (1890), a growing body of empirical studies using patent citation data suggests the importance of geographical proximity for innovation. Investigating US patent citation data, Sonn and Stolper (2003) find that investors increasingly use domestic knowledge more than foreign knowledge, in-state knowledge more than out-of-state knowledge and knowledge from the same metropolitan area more than knowledge from outside.

We now revisit the issue of local and global sources of innovation and whether the most recent internationalization of R&D has influenced the importance of MNEs as a network of different subsidiary units spread geographically across vast distances.

11.3   Models and estimation framework

The theoretical framework for our study is a production function explaining variation in innovation performance by different categories of knowledge sources and a number of control variables that can be represented schematically by the following equation,

$$y_i = \beta_0 + \beta_x x_i + \beta_k k_i + u_i \tag{1}$$

Where i denotes log of variables expressed in per-employee terms, the left-hand variable y is the innovation sales in firm, x is a vector of standard control variables such as R&D, size as physical capital, employment and industry dummies, and k is the various sources of knowledge or technology spillovers that might influence innovation. β_x is the elasticity of output with respect to changes in the control variables, β_k is the elasticity of output with respect to knowledge and technology spillovers, and u is the random-error term representing all disturbances that prevent (1) from holding exactly.

Let us first consider the OLS linear model:

$$y = X\beta + u \tag{2}$$

where, in matrix form, y is innovation sales, and X is a matrix of different categories of possible influences on firm performance: 1) knowledge sources within the firm; 2) knowledge sources within the local/national systems of innovation; 3) global knowledge sources within the group, and scientific, vertical and horizontal partners; 4) international knowledge spillovers via imports and FDI; and 5) other firm and industry characteristics.

The key assumption in regression model (2) is that the unobserved factors involved in the production function are not related systematically to the observed factors X; that is, that the u processes have a zero-conditional mean. However, we suspect a non-random sample of firms with observed innovation output as well as simultaneous determination of some exogenous variables and the endogenous innovation output; here the basic statistical assumptions do not hold and we have to make a departure from the linear model.

11.3.1 Sample-selection regressions

A regression estimated from the subpopulation of innovative firms, that is, firms with positive R&D and innovation sales, will yield coefficients that are biased without correction for non-random selection from the population at large. In this paper, we will employ Heckman's two-step estimator from the Heckman selection model (Heckman 1979) in order to make such a correction by estimating an omitted regressor $\lambda(x_1'\beta_1)$, labelled the inverse Mills ratio (IMR). Formally, this can be described as follows:[1]

Let y_1^* denote a latent variable and the outcome y_2^* is observed if $y_2^* > 0$, that is, if the observed firm is classified as innovative. For example, y_1^* determines whether or not the firm is classified as innovative, and y_2^* determines the firm's innovation performance. The variable y_1^* is different from y_2^* since firm size or corporate structure, for instance, are more important in determining engagement in innovation activities than the size of innovation sales per employee. The sample selection model then comprises the following participating or selection equation and resulting outcome equation:

$$y_1 = \begin{cases} 1 & \text{if } y_1^* > 0, \\ 0 & \text{if } y_1^* \leq 0 \end{cases} \tag{3}$$

$$y_2 = \begin{cases} y_2^* & \text{if } y_1^* > 0, \\ - & \text{if } y_1^* \leq 0 \end{cases} \tag{4}$$

The standard model specifies a linear model with additive errors for the latent variables:

$$y_1^* = x_1'\beta_1 + \varepsilon_1$$
$$y_2^* = x_2'\beta_2 + \varepsilon_2 \tag{5}$$

Where β_2 is our primary interest, but a problem will arise estimating β_2 if ε_1 and ε_2 are correlated. Is this case OLS regression of y_2 on x_2 using only the observed positive variables on y_2 results in inconsistent estimates.

By including an estimate of IMR, Heckman's two-step procedure can be written as:

$$y_{2i} = x_{2i}'\beta_2 + \sigma_{12}\lambda(x_{1i}'\hat{\beta}_1) + \upsilon_i \tag{6}$$

Where υ is an error term, $\hat{\beta}_1$ is obtained by first-step probit regression of y_1 on x_1.

The Heckman model performs a test of whether or not the error terms ε_1 and ε_2 in equation (5) are correlated and whether the sample selection correlation is needed.

In addition to the selection model, we will exploit the predicted IMR in the model dealing with the issue of simultaneity bias, which is presented below.

11.3.2   Generalized method of moments

Consider the linear regression model (2), where each component of x is acting as an exogenous regressor if it is uncorrelated with the error in the model and a variable x is endogenous if it is correlated with the disturbance. In the first case, the OLS estimators can be used; otherwise, the OLS estimators are inconsistent for estimating β.

In order to derive consistent estimates of equation (2) in the presence of endogeneity among the regressors, we must find variables that satisfy two properties: they must be uncorrelated with u but must be as highly correlated with x as possible. A variable that meets those two conditions can serve as an instrument for the correlation of the regressor and the error term.

In the case of simultaneous determination of response variables and regressors, or endogeneity, there are several instrumental-variable options; the IV and two-stage least squares (2SLS) as well as the generalization to generalized method-of-moments (GMM) estimators. In this paper, we will employ the GMM estimator.

11.3.3   Model specifications

Consider first the selection equation of the Heckman two-step model. The empirical challenge here is to find a single or a set of variables that strongly affects the probability of being an innovative firm but not necessarily the size of innovation output. The determinants in the first step of the model (selection equation) are firm size, physical capital, capital structure and market (a dummy variable indicating whether the firm is mainly focused on the global market). Ten industry dummies are also included.

Our primary interest variables in the outcome equation are R&D collaboration, FDI and imports. The dependent variable innovation output is measured as sales income from new products per employee. The control variables in the outcome equation are R&D, skill (approximated by wage sum per employee), the firm's size measured by employment, investment in machinery and equipment, and capital structure and industry indicators.

All variables are expressed as logarithms and are in per-employee terms, with the exception of capital structure, human capital, market and the indicator variables for collaboration on innovation, which are given as percentages.

The GMM estimation is split into two parts. First, we consider a vector of determinants that is almost the Heckman set of variables, with the exception that we have included and instrumented for export. The instruments are (in logs and intensity) gross investment, export value/export weight and import value/import weight and the dummy variable that indicates whether the firm exports more than 50 per cent of its production. Second, we extend the analysis of collaboration on innovation by considering 50 different combinations of cooperation arrangements, reflecting complementarities between various innovation partners.

11.4 Data

The empirical analyses in this study are based on data from the Community Innovation Survey (CIS) IV for Sweden. The survey was conducted in 2005 and covers the period 2002–2004. The rate of response was close to 70 per cent. It covers both manufacturing and business-service sectors. The original sample contains 3094 firms. The information on innovation activities from the survey has been supplemented with register data on sales, value added, wages, physical capital, human capital, employment, exports, imports and corporate structure from Statistics Sweden for the firms in question.

In order to ensure that the data are suitable for our estimation purposes, we have imposed restrictions on the sample. First, we removed all observations which the total sales in both the survey data and in the register data remained zero even after the data treatment (see below). A second restriction was the elimination of all observations for which the value added and wage cost were zero. In total the restrictions applied to 10 observations. A third restriction was the removal of 113 public utility firms (Nace 40 and 41) and six financial intermediates (Nace 66–69). In the present analysis, these industries are not considered 'innovative industries'. The result was 2962 complete observations of firms with more than 10 employees.

11.4.1 Definition of innovative firms

Aiming to distinguish firms by their innovative nature, we selected a sample consisting of only innovative firms. There is, however, no general agreement in the literature on how to classify a firm as 'innovative' or as to what distinguishes innovation from technical changes. Schmookler (1966) suggests that when an enterprise produces new goods or services or uses a method that is new to it, it is introducing technical changes.

The enterprise that is first to make a given technical change is an innovator. However, Hall (1994) noticed that the distinction between an innovator and its followers – the imitator firms – often is unclear. In their attempts to imitate, firms often do things differently (unintentionally or by design) from the way they were done by the first firm and thus become innovators in their own right. The Oslo Manual (OECD, 2005), which sets out the guidelines for collecting and interpreting innovation data in the CIS surveys, defines an innovation as products, services and methods new or significantly improved in respect to the market.

The CIS survey also provides an opening for a softer definition of innovation by aiming questions at products that are new or significantly improved with respect to the market as a whole as well as to the firm only. Together these two aspects will probably reflect the findings of Geroski et al. (1993) who indicate that the importance of innovation lies not only in the innovation in itself, but also in the learning process associated with the innovation. These CIS classifications of innovation can either be analysed jointly or separately. In this paper we will choose the former.

We then define an innovative firm according to the following criteria: a firm is innovative if its total sum of research and development expenditures on: 1) intramural R&D; 2) extramural R&D; 3) acquisition of machinery; and 4) other external knowledge is positive, and if it also has positive sales of goods and services according to the joint classification of innovation.

The CIS survey also allows us to distinguish between products developed: 1) mainly by the firm; 2) by firms in collaboration with others; and 3) mainly by others. Interestingly, all three categories are associated with about the same average innovation expenditures as a fraction of sales (7 to 9 per cent). Moreover innovation sales as a fraction of sales are on average largest among firms that reported that their innovative products were mainly developed by others (24 per cent versus 19 per cent and 17 per cent respectively for the two other categories of firms). Based on this information we consider a firm as innovative irrespective of whether it mainly developed the new product itself or not. We end up with a sub-sample of 1091 (36.8 per cent) innovative firms.

11.4.2 Cleaning data

Finally, we defined a 'clean' dataset according to the following criteria. First, we censored any observation for which R&D was more than two times larger than sales. This means that for 21 observations with R&D expenditures reported to be more than 200 per cent bigger than sales the R&D expenditures are replaced by observations equal to sales times two. Second, if the reported sales were zero or missing in the survey data, these have been replaced by the figures from the register data and vice versa. There are 33 such observations and all concern non-innovative firms. Third, we made value added identical to sales if value added was larger than sales. This resulted in 21 changes, all concerning non-innovative firms. Finally, for all observations for which employment was zero or missing in the register data, we replaced these with the information from the survey data (16 observations of non-innovative firms and five of innovative firms). In total, the 'cleaning process' resulted in 150 changes for non-innovative firms and seven for firms belonging to the innovative sample. The censoring eliminates the influence of extreme observations and yet allows us to retain the observations in the estimation procedure.

The non-innovative firms, according to our definition, consist of firms: 1) with neither positive R&D nor positive innovation sales: 2) firms with positive R&D but no positive innovation sales, and: 3) firms with positive innovation sales but no R&D. The non-innovative firms are retained in the total sample and are used in the selection equation for estimating a correcting variable which Heckman (1979) refers to as the inverse of Mills' ratio (IRM). We will also employ the IRM in the GMM estimations predicted from the Heckman model.

11.4.3   Variables

Innovative product sales. The Schumpeterian branch of economic literature, a branch characterized as explicitly focusing on innovation as a distinct economic activity with distinct economic causes and effects, has shown that R&D is a main determinant of productivity. A serious limitation of many studies on R&D and productivity is that they only investigate the relationship between R&D coefficients that are biased, and other input factors on the one hand, and productivity on the other. The neglected link is what Pakes and Griliches (1984) labelled 'the knowledge production function', a production of commercially valuable knowledge or innovation output. The explanation for this 'ignorance' is the lack of data on this commercially valuable knowledge. Although they are not perfect, the CIS surveys, which now have been introduced in the majority of OECD countries, offer an observation on the firm's assessment of their annual income from new products introduced to the market during the most recent three-year period. Our analysis will use this variable as the left-hand side variable and it is measured as the logarithm of innovative product sales per employee.

Our set of explanatory variables consists both of those that have commonly been documented as affecting innovation performance in the Schumpeterian

Table 11.1   Variable definition and expected sign of the correlation with innovative product sales

Variable	Definition
Innovative firms	Firms with positive R&D expenditures and positive innovative product sales.
Innovative product sales	Log sales income from innovate products per employee
FDI	Dummy variable indicating whether the firm is foreign-owned
Import value	Log import value (in monetary terms) per employee
FOR GRO	R&D collaboration, RDC, with foreign partners within the group
DOM GRO	RDC with domestic partners within the group
FOR SCI	RDC with foreign scientific partners (universities, research institutes)
DOM SCI	RDC with domestic scientific partners
FOR VER	RDC with foreign vertical partners (suppliers and customers)
DOM VER	RDC with domestic vertical partners
FOR HOR	RDC with foreign horizontal partners (competitors and consultants)
DOM HOR	RDC with domestic horizontal partners (suppliers and customers)
Import value/weight	Log import value (in monetary terms)/import weight per employee
Market	Dummy variable indicating whether export/sales > 50 percent
Skill	Log wage sum per employee
Size	Log employment
Gross investment	Log gross investment in physical capital per employee
Machinery investment	Log investment in machinery per employee
Export value	Log export value (in monetary terms) per employee
Export value/weight	Log export value (in monetary terms)/export weight per employee
Capital structure	Total debt/(Total debt + equity)

Note: Table 11.1 displays the variables included in the Heckman selection model in the GMM-estimation.

literature (our controls) and those that are supposed to capture the importance of positive externalities. The following variables are included in the analysis:

- *R&D.* Since the objective of the paper is to investigate the importance of external knowledge on firms' innovation performance we need to control for variation in (log) R&D intensity.
- *Skill.* In the specifications of the econometric models we have to account for factors that can cause problems in the estimation procedure. Along

with the two main problems discussed in Section 11.3, multi-collinearity among the explanatory variables and difficulties in identifying their effect is another issue. Two simple ways of checking for the presence of multi-collinearity are to look at the correlation coefficients among the explanatory variables and the R2 from regression of each explanatory variable on the remaining explanatory variables. Table 11.A1 in Appendix 11.1 below reveals a strong association between log R&D per employee and human capital, partly due to the fact that R&D personnel are a fraction of human capital. Since our data do not distinguish between R&D personnel and other kinds of human capital, we will exploit wage sum per employee as a proxy for human capital in order to avoid double-counting of R&D. The assumption is that the wage sum includes a skill premium. We therefore label this variable as 'skill'.

- *Firm size and physical capital.* The Schumpeterian literature has suggested the importance of controlling for variation in firm size and physical capital investment, which might be associated with innovation activities. Firm size is measured as log of employment. For physical capital we employ two different measures – gross investment and investment in machinery and equipment. The former is employed in the first step of the Heckman equation and the latter as an instrument in the GMM estimation.

- *Market.* In order to better isolate the importance of spillover effects, we include a variable that might pick up the importance of global export markets. It is a dummy variable indicating if the firm is selling more than 50 per cent of its production outside Sweden.

- *Capital structure.* Since the seminal paper by Modigliani and Miller (1958), several theories have been proposed to explain the variation in debt ratios across firms. There is, however, a broad agreement in the corporate finance literature that firms prefer to draw on internal financing from retained profits and seek external financing by issuing shares or corporate bonds when there are insufficient funds for internal financing. Recent literature suggests that small firms and R&D firms are financially constrained. (See Tiwari, Mohnen, Palm and Schim van der Loeff in Chapter 10 of this book.) While there is an extensive literature investigating how financial constraints affect a firm's R&D intensity, the issue of how the firm's capacity to leverage (increase the ratio between debt and equity) affects its innovation performance has been far less scrutinized. Assuming that the firm's innovation output signals growth opportunities, Harris and Raviv (1991) report that there is consensus in the literature the leverage should increase. If the innovation performance is related to profitability the evidence from the literature is mixed. Discussing the effect of profitability on leverage, Jensen (1986) predicts a positive correlation if the market for corporate control is effective and a negative correlation otherwise. The negative relationship is explained by the management's preference for internal financing while efficient corporate control forces the firm to pay out cash by leveraging up. Including information asymmetry among market imperfections, as Razin, Sadka and Yuen (2001) have done in their analysis, suggests that debt financing is preferred to equity since a choice of equity finance signals that the firm's shares are overvalued.

- *Knowledge transfer via collaboration on innovation.* Eight different indicators are used for measuring the importance of transmission of technology and knowledge via collaboration on innovation. We focus on collaboration within the group, with scientific partners (universities and research institutes), with vertical partners (suppliers and customers), and with horizontal partners (competitors and consultants). Since the data on collaboration contains information on national as well as global collaboration we hope to identify both local and global spillovers. In total, 50 different network combinations of R&D collaborations are investigated.

- *Knowledge transfer via FDI and trade.* Following Veugelers and Cassiman (2004) and others we use the presence of foreign-owned MNEs in the host country (Sweden) as an indicator of international knowledge spillovers. We are interested to know whether foreign-owned firms *ceteris paribus* have superior innovation performance in comparison to local firms. International trade is another common method of measuring knowledge diffusion across borders and among two alternatives – the ratio of import value to import weight. We use the latter in the equations and the former as an instrument in the GMM estimation. There is also a possibility that the firm's exports can be associated with knowledge transfer to customers. However, in this study we include exports among the control variables. A problem with this variable is that it can be assumed to be determined together with the endogenous variable, that is, innovation sales, and a possible result of this is that the estimation suffers from simultaneity bias. Therefore, in equation (4) we instrument for the export variable (export value) and make use of the ratio of export value to export weight as an instrument in the GMM regressions.

Industry classifications: In order to control for any industry-specific effects that may not be captured by the variables above, we also include ten industry dummies. Table 11.2 provides mean values for some key variables distributed over the 10 industry classes. There are large differences across industries. For instance, there are four industries for which the proportion of innovative industries is about 50 per cent or more (electrical and optical equipment 48 per cent; machinery and equipment 50 per cent; transport equipment 51 per cent; and pharmaceutical, plastics and other 55 per cent). In contrast, in the transport and communication sector, only 16 per cent of firms can be classed as innovative.

The average ratio of R&D to sales is 5.2 per cent in our sample, with a variation from 1.9 per cent (food, textiles and leather) to 11.9 per cent (business activities). Firms in the business activities category have the largest average innovation output when innovation sales are measured as a fraction of sales

Table 11.2   Summary statistics: key variables distributed over industry classes. Number of observations: 2962

Industry	Obs	Innovative[a]	R&D[b]	Innovation sales[b]	Human capital[c]	FDI[d]	Market[e]
1. Food, textiles, leather	506	0.312	0.019	0.070	0.120	0.144	0.113
2. Pulp and paper	231	0.346	0.031	0.075	0.243	0.173	0.117
3. Pharmaceuticals and plastics	199	0.547	0.071	0.119	0.218	0.306	0.215
4. Mineral and metals	317	0.343	0.039	0.060	0.123	0.208	0.144
5. Machinery and equipment	194	0.500	0.058	0.120	0.216	0.231	0.253
6. Electrical and optical equipment	251	0.478	0.095	0.155	0.293	0.211	0.190
7. Transport equipment	154	0.512	0.034	0.127	0.155	0.233	0.158
8. Wholesale and retail	197	0.355	0.014	0.099	0.269	0.406	0.044
9. Transport and communication	392	0.155	0.015	0.040	0.220	0.178	0.006
10. Business services	521	0.399	0.119	0.132	0.548	0.166	0.025
Mean		0.368	0.052	0.095	0.258	0.206	0.107
Min		0.155	0.019	0.040	0.120	0.144	0.006
Max		0.547	0.119	0.132	0.548	0.406	0.253

Notes: Table 10.2 reports summary statistics for the 10 industry classes included in the study.
  1 Manufacture of food products, beverages and tobacco; textile and textile products; leather and leather products; manufacturing NEC.
  2 Manufacture of pulp, paper and paper products: publishing and printing
  3 Manufacture of pharmaceutical products; plastic and rubber products, of coke, refined petroleum products and man-made fibres.
  4 Manufacture of other non-metallic mineral products; basic metals and fabricated products
  5 Manufacture of machinery and equipment
  6 Manufacture of electrical and optical equipment
  7 Manufacture of transport equipment
  8 Wholesale and retail (service industry)
  9 Transport, storage and communication (service industry)
10 Business services (service industry)
[a] Fraction of the firms
[b] Fraction of total sales
[c] Employment with a university education as a fraction of total employment
[d] Foreign-owned firms as a fraction of all firms in the sample
[e] Fraction of firms with export more than 50 per cent of sales.

(12 per cent), while another service industry, transport and communication, has a fraction of only 4 per cent.

The most human-capital-intensive industry is business services. The average share of university-educated employees is 55 per cent. The corresponding figure for food, textile and leather is only 4 per cent. There is a substantial presence of foreign ownership in the Swedish economy. One out of five firms in the sample is foreign-owned. The proportion of foreign ownership is highest in wholesale and retail (40 per cent) and pharmaceuticals, plastics and rubber (31 per cent). Finally, Table 11.2 shows that for 11 per cent of the firms in the sample, exports constitute more than half of their total sales. The most export-oriented industries are machinery and equipment (25 per cent), pharmaceuticals, plastics, rubber and petroleum (22 per cent), and electrical and optical equipment (19 per cent). Not unexpectedly, the service industries in the sample are highly focused on the home market.

Table 11.3 provides summary statistics for all the variables used in the analysis. We make a special distinction between multinational firms and non-multinational firms. The descriptive statistics are restricted to the innovative sample and we have transformed all observations into logarithms of intensity terms (per employee) or percentages. The monetary variables are measured in thousands of Swedish crowns. Column 1 shows statistics for the full sample, while columns 2 and 3 give statistics for MNEs and non-MNEs respectively. The most interesting findings are the large differences between the average MNE and non-MNE in almost all variables. Looking first at collaboration on innovation, not surprisingly it is shown that the typical MNE has a fairly broad network of national and global partners within and outside the group. The most important collaboration partners for non-MNEs are customers and suppliers both in Sweden and abroad, and domestic universities. We then see that close to one out of two MNEs in Sweden is foreign-owned and, not surprisingly, that only MNEs have extensive trade. Among the controls, the most striking differences concern firm size. The average employment is almost ten times higher among MNEs (about 440) compared to non-MNEs (about 50). The large difference between these two categories of firms supports our split of the sample into two groups and the choice to focus on the MNE group in our final analysis.

11.5   Empirical analysis

In the study, we investigate three main categories of external knowledge transfer: 1) through collaboration on innovation; 2) through the presence of foreign affiliates; and 3) through imports. The firms' collaboration on innovation is local/national as well as global. Tables 11.4 and 11.5 present results for the importance of eight different collaboration partners separately, while Table 11.6 reports estimates for collaboration within various networks. Only the significant estimates are displayed. Table 11.A3 in Appendix 11.1 presents all the 50 different combinations of collaboration arrangements analysed.

We have tried two estimators that differ in correction for selectivity and simultaneity bias. Table 11.4 gives the results from the Heckman two-step selection model. Tables 11.5 and 11.6 display results from the GMM model

Table 11.3 Summary statistics

	Full sample n = 1091				MNE only n = 611				Non-MNE only n = 480			
	Mean	SE	Min	Max	Mean	SE	Min	Max	Mean	SE	Min	Max
Performance variable												
Log innovative. products sales/emp	12.27	1.31	5.88	16.50	12.44	1.34	5.99	16.50	12.05	1.26	5.88	15.95
Knowledge transfer via collaboration												
FORGRO	0.21	0.41	0.00	1.00	0.36	0.48	0.00	1.00	0.00	0.00	0.00	1.00
DOMGRO	0.15	0.366	0.00	1.00	0.23	0.42	0.00	1.00	0.08	0.26	0.00	1.00
FORSCI	0.11	0.31	0.00	1.00	0.16	0.36	0.00	1.00	0.04	0.20	0.00	1.00
DOM SCI	0.31	0.46	0.00	1.00	0.39	0.49	0.00	1.00	0.22	0.41	0.00	1.00
FORVER	0.33	0.47	0.00	1.00	0.41	0.49	0.00	1.00	0.23	0.42	0.00	1.00
DOMVER	0.45	0.50	0.00	1.00	0.49	0.50	0.00	1.00	0.39	0.49	0.00	1.00
FORHOR	0.16	0.31	0.00	1.00	0.23	0.42	0.00	1.00	0.08	0.27	0.00	1.00
DOMHOR	0.32	0.56	0.00	1.00	0.38	0.48	0.00	1.00	0.24	0.43	0.00	1.00
Knowledge transfer via FDI and import												
FDI	0.25	0.43	0.00	1.00	0.45	0.49	0.00	1.00	0.00	0.00	0.00	0.00
Log import/emp	14.39	7.50	0.10	23.54	17.13	6.09	0.10	23.28	10.91	8.32	0.10	21.68
Controls												
Log R&D/ emp	10.47	1.79	1.70	14.84	10.59	1.79	3.55	14.84	10.31	1.78	1.70	14.61
Skill[1]	5.74	0.27	5.00	7.99	5.79	0.26	5.00	7.05	5.67	0.28	5.00	7.99
Human capital	0.32	0.26	0.00	1.00	0.33	0.24	0.00	1.00	0.30	0.27	0.00	1.00
Log firms size	4.10	1.50	2.30	9.87	4.78	1.51	2.30	9.87	3.22	0.91	2.30	8.25
Log mach. inv/emp	9.38	2.87	0.00	17.12	9.63	2.70	0.00	14.09	9.07	3.05	0.00	17.12
Log gross. inv/emp	11.13	1.95	0.00	17.47	11.41	1.80	0.00	15.16	10.78	2.07	0.00	17.52
Log [import value/ import weight]/emp	5.91	3.79	0.10	14.16	6.17	3.15	0.10	14.16	5.58	4.45	0.10	13.80
Market [2]	0.19	0.33	0.00	1.00	0.27	0.37	0.00	1.00	0.08	0.24	0.00	1.00
Log export value/emp	14.53	8.06	0.00	23.28	17.41	6.09	0.00	14.09	10.88	8.76	0.00	22.49
Log [export value/ export weight]/emp	5.89	3.91	0.00	15.06	6.28	3.28	0.00	13.66	5.39	4.46	0.00	15.06
Capital structure	0.68	0.23	0.01	1.00	0.66	0.23	0.01	1.00	0.70	0.22	0.02	1.00
Industry dummies	Yes				Yes				Yes			

Notes: Table 11.3 reports summary statistics for the performance variable, the variables used for investigating knowledge transfer via R&D collaboration, FDI and import, and the control variables. The abbreviations FORGRO, FORSCI, FORVER, FORHOR correspond to foreign collaboration on innovation with partners within the group, scientific partners, vertical partners and horizontal partners. The abbreviations DOMGRO, DOMSCI, DOMVER, DOMHOR correspond to domestic collaboration on innovation with partners within the group, scientific partners, vertical partners and horizontal partners. Skill (1) is measured as log wage per employee, and the variable market is a dummy variable indicating whether export/sales > 0.5

Table 11.4 Regression results of selection equation, Heckman two-step model
Dependent variables: outcome equation: log innovation sales per employee
(only innovative firms). Selection equation: propensity to be engaged in product
innovation

	All firms		MNE only		Non-MNE only	
	Coeff.	S.E.	Coeff.	S.E.	Coeff.	S.E.
Outcome equation						
Knowledge transfer via FDI and import						
Inward-FDI	0.124	0.097	0.075	0.106	–	–
Log import/emp	0.034***	0.005	0.030***	0.011	0.038***	0.007
Knowledge transfer via collaboration						
FORGRO	0.113	0.118	0.136	0.132	–	–
DOMGRO	−0.058	0.111	−0.148	0.132	–	–
FORSCI	0.057	0.150	0.264	0.171	−0.690**	0.311
DOMSCI	−0.045	0.106	−0.148	0.138	0.105	0.160
FORVER	0.199	0.105	−0.030	0.141	0.474***	0.152
DOMVER	0.079	0.099	0.111	0.141	0.070	0.131
FORHOR	−0.201	0.132	−0.105	0.158	−0.385*	0.231
DOMHOR	−0.111	0.104	0.004	0.137	−0.238	0.156
Controls						
Log R&D/emp	0.157***	0.022	0.168***	0.030	0.143***	0.032
Skill[1]	0.588***	0.154	0.586***	0.213	0.567**	0.222
Log firms size	−0.138***	0.043	−0.089	0.051	−0.237***	0.074
Log gross investment/emp	0.025*	0.015	0.046**	0.021	0.009	0.021
Capital structure	0.694***	0.176	1.152***	0.263	0.278	0.242
10 Industry dummies	Yes		Yes		Yes	
Selection equation						
Log firm size	0.146***	0.018	0.100***	0.025	0.133***	0.037
Market[2]	0.751	0.097	0.617***	0.120	0.832	0.182
Capital structure	−0.110	0.112	−0.303*	−0.303	0.087	0.153
Log gross investment/emp	0.030***	0.008	0.023*	0.013	0.037	0.101
Industry dummies	Yes	Yes	Yes	Yes	Yes	Yes
Mills, lambda	−0.713**	0.285	−0.989**	0.453	−0.470	0.433
Number of observations	2,962		1,249		1,713	
Censored observations	1,871		638		1,233	
Uncensored observations	1,091		611		480	

Notes: Standard error between brackets, ***$p < 0.01$, **$p < .005$, *$p < 0.10$. (1) Log wage per employee, (2) Log investment in machinery per employee, (2) Export/sales > 0.5. The table reports the parameter estimates of the correlation between innovation sales (i) FDI, (ii) import, (iii) and eight indicator variables for collaboration on innovation respectively, using the Heckman two-step estimator. In the regression 15 control variables are included. In the selection equation all observations are included, while the outcome equation contains only innovative firms.

Table 11.5   Regression results: GMM estimations
Dependent variables: log innovation sales per employee

	Full sample n = 1091		MNE only n = 611		Non-MNE only n = 480	
	Coeff.	S.E.	Coeff.	S.E.	Coeff.	S.E.
Knowledge transfer via FDI and import						
Inward-FDI	0.117	0.100	0.054	0.111	–	–
Log import/emp	0.028***	0.008	0.033**	0.016	0.029***	0.009
Knowledge transfer via collaboration						
FORGRO	0.119	0.118	0.140	0.138	–	–
DOMGRO	−0.029	0.118	−0.152	0.139	–	–
FORSCI	0.089	0.167	0.273	0.181	−0.635*	0.348
DOMSCI	−0.020	0.107	−0.125	0.140	0.070	0.150
FORVER	0.184*	0.105	−0.214	0.144	0.461***	0.147
DOMVER	0.048	0.103	0.100	0.149	0.052	0.135
FORHOR	−0.209	0.132	−0.106	0.167	−0.369*	0.147
DOMHOR	−0.105	0.105	0.012	0.143	−0.242	0.149
Controls						
Log R&D/emp	0.149***	0.024	0.163***	0.034	0.124***	0.033
Skill[1]	0.625***	0.175	0.616**	0.251	0.575**	0.225
Log firms size	−0.147***	0.041	−0.114**	0.022	0.248***	0.073
Log gross investment/ employee	0.032**	0.015	0.049**	0.022	0.018	0.020
Log export/emp	0.010	0.010	−0.009	0.017	0.020*	0.011
Capital structure	0.718***	0.172	1.030***	0.232	0.474**	0.232
Inverse Mills ratio, IMR	−0.629**	0.264	−0.844**	0.340	−0.362	0.443
10 industry dummies Test statistics	Yes		Yes		Yes	
Hansen J statistics. Overidentification	7.879	0.048	3.431	0.329	3.667	0.299
Anderson canon. Corr. identification	1310.118	0.000	544.471	0.000	693.643	0.000

Notes: The table reports the parameter estimates of the correlation between innovation sales (i) FDI, (ii) import, (iii) and eight indicator variables for collaboration on innovation respectively, using the GMM estimator. In the regression, 16 control variables are included. Standard error between brackets. ***: $p < 0.01$, **: $p < .005$, *: $p < 0.10$. (1) Log (w/l). Instrumented: Log export value per employee. Included instruments: All variables reported in the table above. Excluded instruments: Log gross investment per employee, Export/sales > 0.5, Log export value/export weight per employee, Log import value/import weight per employee. FDI is foreign-owned firms $ Test statistics in agreement with results reported in Table 11.3, column 2. The identification test (Andersson) and the overidentification test (Hansen) are both satisfactory.

Table 11.6 Regression results: GMM estimations. Collaboration with foreign partners.
Dependent variables: log innovation sales per employee. MNEs only: number of observations: 611

Equation	1	2	3	4	5	6	7	8	9
Knowledge transfer via FDI and imports									
FDI	0.087	0.102	0.091	0.080	0.102	0.094	0.091	0.093	0.080
	(0.102)	(0.102)	(0.102)	(0.101)	(0.102)	(0.101)	(0.101)	(0.101)	(0.102)
Log import/emp	0.033**	0.034**	0.033**	0.032**	0.033**	0.033**	0.033**	0.033**	0.032**
	(0.015)	(0.015)	(0.015)	(0.016)	(0.016)	(0.015)	(0.015)	(0.016)	(0.016)
Knowledge transfer via collaboration									
FORGRO + FORSCI	0.365**								
	(0.183)								
FORGRO + FORSCI + FORVER		0.385**							
		(0.195)							
FORGRO + FORSCI + FORHOR			0. 452**						
			(0.208)						
FORGRO + FORVER + FORHOR				0.302*					
				(0.162)					
FORSCI + DOMVER					0.321*				
					(0.175)				
FORGRO + FORSCI + DOMSCI						0.389*			
						(0.199)			
FORGRO + FORSCI + DOMVER							0.393**		
							(0.189)		
FORGRO + FORSCI + DOMHOR								0.376*	
								(0.211)	
FORGRO + FORHOR + DOMVER									0.287*
									(0.166)
Other controls	Yes	Yes	Yes	Yes	Yes	Yes	Yes	Yes	Yes
Industry dummies	Yes	Yes	Yes	Yes	Yes	Yes	Yes	Yes	Yes
Selection equation	Yes	Yes	Yes	Yes	Yes	Yes	Yes	Yes	Yes
Test statistics	$	$	$	$	$	$	$	$	$

Notes: The table reports the parameter estimates of the correlation between innovation sales (i) FDI, (ii) import, (iii) and eight indicator variables for collaboration on innovation respectively, using the GMM estimator. In the regression 16 control variables are included. Standard error between brackets. ***: $p < 0.01$, **: $p < .005$, *: $p < 0.10$. (1) Log (w/l). Instrumented: Log export value per employee. Included instruments: All variables reported in the table above. Excluded instruments: Log gross investment per employee, Export/sales > 0.5, Log export value/export weight per employee, Log import value/import weight per employee. FDI is foreign-owned firms
$ Test statistics in agreement with results reported in Table 11.3 column 2. The identification test (Andersson) and the overidentification test (Hansen) are both satisfactory

including the inverse Mills ratio (IMR), which implies that we attempt to control for both selectivity and simultaneity bias. Tables 11.4 and 11.5 show coefficient estimates for the full sample of innovative firms, innovative MNE firms and innovative non-MNE firms respectively. In Table 11.6 we report coefficient estimates for only FDI, imports and network of R&D collaborators.

From the economic theory, we would expect that the propensity to be innovative is an increasing function of firm size, gross investment and export market. Yet firms who are highly dependent on bank loans are less likely to be engaged in innovation activities compared to firms that finance their R&D investments through retained profits or the stock market. Given that the firms are classified as innovative, our *a priori* assumption is that the influence on innovation output exerted by R&D, skill and coefficients that are biased, physical capital and the capacity to leverage is positive. Regarding our key variables, Ebersberger and Lööf (2005) suggest that FDI is neutral with respect to innovation output when the observed firms are MNEs and positive when compared to non-MNEs. The importance of imports on innovation output has been overlooked in the empirical innovation literature analysing firm-level data, but based on work studying the correlation between import and productivity, a positive effect can be expected. The literature provides mixed results on the importance of R&D collaboration in relation to innovation output.

Consider first the selection equation results reported in Table 11.4. The benefit of using a selection model is to correct for a non-representative sample. In order to reduce possible endogeneity problems we have excluded the export variable from this equation but it will be used in the GMM equation. The columns correspond to different samples. The first column corresponds to the full sample, where we include all observations in the selection equation and only innovative firms in the outcome equation. The second column reports results only for MNEs. In the third column we report estimates for firms with no affiliates abroad, that is, non-MNEs. There is data for 2962 firms in the full sample, of which 1091 are uncensored. The corresponding figures for the MNE sample and the non-MNE sample are 1249 (611) and 1733 (480) respectively.

Recent research has addressed the involvement of foreign companies in domestic economies – the relative engagement of foreign-owned companies in R&D activities and embeddedness in various national innovation systems and the relative output performance from R&D in terms of innovation and productivity – with some mixed findings (Pavitt and Patel, 1999; Pfaffermayr and Bellak, 2002; Dachs, Ebersberger and Lööf, 2007). As displayed in columns (1) and (2) we find that the presence of inward FDI *per se* is neutral with respect to innovation output; that is, we find no difference between foreign and domestic MNEs with respect to innovation sales. When considering the coefficients on imports, a pattern emerges in these coefficients showing that spillovers from imports contribute significantly to innovation productivity. Note also that the estimated impact is highly significant for MNEs as well as for non-MNEs.

The point elasticities for knowledge transfer through collaboration on innovation are estimated to be non-significant for the full sample and MNEs only (columns (1) and (2)). When looking at non-MNEs in column (3) it shows that the estimate for global scientific collaboration is highly significant and negative. However, as reported in the summary statistics (Table 11.2), only a small percentage of these firms has global scientific collaboration arrangements. The typical innovative non-MNE is considerably less oriented towards the global market than its MNE counterpart. More interesting is the positive and significant correlation between innovation sales and customers and suppliers. Our interpretation is that these firms, which are smaller and less knowledge-intensive in terms of human capital and R&D than the MNEs, are more dependent on external knowledge received through market transactions.

The weak association between R&D collaboration and innovation output is fully consistent with the findings of Brouwer and Kleinknecht (1996). It is surprising that R&D collaborators do not have higher innovation output than non-collaborators. This is a motivation for further analysis, which we will return to in the subsequent discussion.

We now consider the control variables. The coefficients for R&D and physical capital are statistically significant and show a close association with innovation sales. The results are also consistent with the literature. Due to the strong correlation between innovation sales and human capital, we are using wage per employee as a proxy for human capital. The coefficient estimate is highly significant and the order of magnitude is close to 0.6. The capital structure variable controls for the firm's access to external financial resources. The estimate is significant and quite sizable, indicating the importance of the link between debt funding and innovation performance.

The selection equation confirms previous findings that the propensity to be engaged in innovation activities is an increasing function of firm size for both our categories of firms. However, the results for the other three variables are somewhat mixed. As expected, the firms focusing on the export market have a large likelihood of being innovative (MNEs only). In accordance with our *a priori* assumption, debt financing is negatively correlated to the likelihood of being an innovative firm (MNEs only). The coefficient estimate for investment intensity is positive and significant (full sample and MNEs). Finally, it is shown that the inverse Mills ratio (IRM) is significant.

Table 11.5 reports the innovation elasticities using the GMM estimator and an IMR variable predicted from the Heckman equation. The estimation results are supposed to have been corrected for both simultaneity bias and selection bias. The J statistics (over-identification) and the identification statistics are satisfactory for the two sub-samples, whereas the statistics for the four instruments are not entirely satisfactory when the full sample is considered.

Table 11.5 includes instrumented export intensity among the regressors, but it is found to have a weak influence on innovativeness. Comparing the results presented in tables 11.4 and 11.5 we find only marginal differences in the coefficient estimates. The summary finding is that imports is the main channel of technology diffusion when MNEs are considered whereas imports and vertical collaboration with domestic partners is important in the case of non-MNEs.

We will now consider the effect of R&D collaboration in some detail and investigate 50 possible network arrangements between the local firm and various innovation partners. There are 30 possible arrangements between the local firms and networks including both foreign and domestic partners and 10 collaboration networks with only domestic innovation partners. In order to properly include foreign sub-units in the analysis we will limit the discussion to MNEs only.

The results presented in Table 11.6 show the correlation between innovative product sales and our three categories of knowledge transfer using the same controls and industry dummies as those displayed in Table 11.5. The analysis is limited to the sub-sample of MNEs and we will report only the estimates for the key variables. The estimator is GMM-augmented with an inverse Mills ratio among the explanatory variables.

Three overall findings emerge from the analysis displayed in Table 11.6 and Table 11.A3 in Appendix 11.1. First, the results for the FDI variable and the imports variable are almost identical to those reported in tables 11.4 and 11.5. We can therefore concentrate our discussion on the effects of network collaboration. Foreign-owned firms do not have a different innovation performance than domestically owned MNEs and innovative product sales are an increasing function of import intensity. Second, when the aspect of network collaboration is taken into account it is shown that R&D collaborators have higher innovation inputs than non-collaborators in about one out of five collaboration combinations (nine out of 50 investigated networks).

Interestingly, there is a fairly robust pattern of collaboration arrangements that affects innovation performance. When the network is restricted to local (domestic) partners, no spillover effect can be established. When the network includes a foreign sub-unit and a scientific partner, the likelihood of successful technology transfer increases considerably. In fact, all six networks that include the local multinational firms, a foreign subsidiary and a foreign scientific partner correlate positively with innovation performance. It is also shown that the benefit of collaborating with local scientific, vertical and horizontal partners increases considerably when a foreign sub-unit and a foreign university are included in the arrangement. Finally, the possibility of spillover from foreign customers, suppliers, competitors and consultants is entirely dependent on assistance of a foreign firm within the group.

Concluding the results from this section, it is clear that multinational enterprises are in a special position for handling knowledge transfer. However, recent research in this area has identified difficulties in transferring knowledge across networks consisting of sub-units and innovation partners. Our results indicate that what seems to be important for the local MNE is to involve its foreign sub-units when collaborating on R&D internationally. Hence, it looks like the technology transfer is not necessarily a flow from one subunit to another, but rather one from different R&D collaborators to the local firm via the foreign sub-unit. In this collaboration arrangement foreign scientific partners also play a crucial role.

In a growing number of recent studies, research universities have been identified as location factors of growing importance (Henderson, Jaffe and Trajtenberg, 1998; Zucker, Darby and Brewer, 1998; Adams, 2002; Hall, Link and Scott, 2003; Brennenraedts, Bekkers and Verspagen, 2006). It has been suggested that regions with strong research universities have better opportunities to attract and support innovative industries than other regions. Our study suggests that such universities contribute not only to regional spillover but also to spillover across borders.

11.6　Conclusions

In our investigation of the importance of domestic and foreign sources for local firms' innovation performance, several main points emerged:

1. There is robust evidence that FDI, observed as foreign-owned firms, is neutral with respect to innovation output. No difference can be found in innovation output between foreign-owned MNEs and domestically owned MNEs.
2. Technology transfer through imports correlates highly significantly with innovation product sales among both MNEs and non-MNEs.
3. The evidence for spillover from R&D collaboration with domestic innovation partners is weak when bilateral arrangements are considered. Only non-MNEs collaborating with local, regional or national suppliers and customers benefit from the collaboration.
4. When multilateral R&D arrangements are taken into account it is shown that R&D collaborators have higher innovation inputs than non-collaborators.
5. When the network includes a foreign sub-unit and a scientific partner, the likelihood of successful technology transfer increases considerably.

We believe that our work suggests several lines of future research on domestic and foreign sources of knowledge for innovation. First, a deeper understanding is necessary of why a network, including both foreign units within the group and a foreign scientific partner, is superior to other collaboration arrangements. Second, much remains to be done in order to better understand how both imports and exports influence local firms' innovation performance. In particular, information on the geographical destination of exports and the geographical origin of imports, together with the technology classification of traded goods and a distinction between intra-firm trade and other trade, would improve the quality of the analysis considerably. Third, in order to assess the importance of FDI, it is desirable to investigate how local firms are related to foreign-owned firms in terms of suppliers, customers or collaborators. Fourth, the CIS data on R&D collaboration is limited. It informs us only whether collaboration exists or not. A proper analysis requires information on the scope of the collaboration in terms of expenditures, the time period and characteristics of the innovation projects. Finally, one must note that there are several other sources of spillover than those considered in this paper – these include patents, patent citations and strategic alliances.

Appendix 11.1

Table 11.A1   Regression results of explanatory variables
Dependent variable: log R&D per employee

Variables	Innovative sample n = 1091		
	Coefficient	S.E.	P-value
Human capital	1.862	0.247	0.000
Skill	0.592	0.224	0.009
Market	0.498	0.169	0.003
Global collaboration on innovation with scientific partners	0.456	0.188	0.016
Domestic collaboration on innovation with scientific partners	0.003	0.136	0.977
Global collaboration on innovation with vertical partners	0.205	0.137	0.137
Domestic collaboration on innovation with vertical partners	0.310	0.129	0.017
Global collaboration on innovation within the group	−0.091	0.149	0.546
Domestic collaboration on innovation within the group	0.023	0.158	0.883
Log import value per employee	−0.001	0.009	0.883
Log export value per employee	0.029	0.009	0.002
Log investment in machinery per employee	0.054	0.017	0.002
Capital structure	−0.070	0.225	0.754
FDI	−0.378	0.128	0.003

Table 11.A2   Test of appropriate instruments

Variables	Corr	Sig
Log (export value per employee/export weight) per employee	0.682	0.000
Log (import value per employee/import weight) per employee	−0.126	0.000
Log gross investment per employee	0.303	0.000
Fractions of firm with export/sales >0.5	0.423	0.000

Note: Partial correlation of log export per employee with the following variables. Innovative firms. Number of observations: 1091

Table 11.A3   50 different combinations of network collaborations

Foreign collaborators	Foreign and domestic collaborators	Domestic collaborators
FORGRO + FORSCI +	FORGRO + DOMSCI	DOMGRO + DOMSCI
FORGRO + FORVER	FORGRO + DOMVER	DOMGRO + DOMVER
FORGRO + FORHOR	FORGRO + DOMHOR	DOMGRO + DOMHOR
FORSCI + FORVER	FORSCI + DOMSCI	DOMSCI + DOMVER
FORSCI + FORHOR	FORSCI + DOMVER +	DOMSCI + DOMHOR
FORVER + FORHOR	FORSCI + DOMHOR	DOMVER + DOMHOR
FORGRO + FORSCI +	FORVER + DOMSCI	DOMGRO + DOMSCI +
FORVER + FORGRO +	FORVER + DOMVER	DOMVER
FORSCI + FORHOR +	FORVER + DOMHOR	DOMGRO + DOMSCI +
FORGRO + FORVER +	FORHOR + DOMSCI	DOMHOR
FORHOR + FORSCI +	FORHOR + DOMVER	DOMGRO + DOMVER +
FORVER + FORHOR	FORHOR + DOMHOR	DOMHOR
	FORGRO + FORSCI + DOMSCI +	DOMSCI + DOMVER +
	FORGRO + FORSCI + DOMVER +	DOMHOR
	FORGRO + FORSCI + DOMHOR +	
	FORGRO + FORVER + DOMSCI	
	FORGRO + FORVER + DOMVER	
	FORGRO + FORVER + DOMHOR	
	FORGRO + FORHOR + DOMSCI	
	FORGRO + FORHOR + DOMVER +	
	FORGRO + FORHOR + DOMHOR	
	FORSCI + FORVER + DOMSCI	
	FORSCI + FORVER + DOMVER	
	FORSCI + FORVER + DOMHOR	
	FORSCI + FORHOR + DOMSCI	
	FORSCI + FORHOR + DOMVER	
	FORSCI + FORHOR + DOMHOR	
	FORVER + FORHOR + DOMSCI	
	FORVER + FORHOR + DOMVER	
	FORVER + FORHOR + DOMHOR	

Notes: The table displays the different combinations of collaborative R&D networks investigated. The '+' sign indicates a significant correlation with innovation product sales using the GMM estimator and control variables. The sample consists of 611 innovating MNE firms.

Notes

1. Here we are partly following Baum (2006) and Cameron and Trivedi (2005).

References

Adams, J. (2002) 'Comparative Localization of Academic and Industrial Spillovers', *Journal of Economic Geography*, 2: 3, pp. 253–78.

Antonelli, C., R. Marchionatti and S. Usai (2003) 'Productivity and External Knowledge: The Italian Case', *Rivista Internazionale di Scienze Economiche e Commerciali*, 50, pp. 69–90.

Baum, C. F. (2006) 'An Introduction to Modern Econometrics Using Stata', *Stata Corop LP*, College Station, Texas.

Beckmann, M. J. (1994) 'On Knowledge Networks in Science: Collaboration among Equals', *Annals of Regional Science*, 28, pp. 233–42.

Boston Consulting Group (2006) *Innovation 2006*, available at www.bcg.com.

Branstetter, L. (2006) 'Is FDI a Channel of Knowledge Spillovers: Evidence from Japanese FDI in the United States', *Journal of International Economics*, 13 pp. 53–79.

Brennenraedts, R., R. Bekkers and B. Verspagen (2006). 'The Different Channels of University-Industry Knowledge Transfer: Empirical Evidence from Biomedical Engineering', paper presented at the DIME workshop on technology transfer from universities: a critical appraisal of patents, spin-offs and human mobility, 29–30 September 2006, EPFL, Lausanne, Switzerland.

Brouwer, E. and A. Kleinknecht (1996) 'Determinants of Innovation: a Microeconometric Analysis of Three Alternative Innovation Output Indicators', in A. Kleinknecht (ed.) *Determinants of Innovation. The Message from New Indicators* (London: Macmillan and New York: St. Martin's Press), pp. 99–124.

Cameron, A. Colin and P. K. Trivedi (2005) *Microeconometrics, Methods and Applications* (Cambridge: Cambridge University Press).

Dachs, B., B. Ebersberger and H. Lööf (2007) 'The Innovative Performance of Foreign-owned Enterprises in Small Open Economies', *Journal of Technology Transfer*, forthcoming.

Eaton, J. and S. Kortum (1995) 'Engines of Growth: Domestic and Foreign Sources of Innovation', *NBER*, No. 5207.

Ebersberger, B. and H. Lööf (2005) 'Multinational Enterprises, Spillover, Innovation and Productivity', *International Journal of Management Research*, 4, pp. 7–37.

Feldman, M. P. and D. B. Audretsch (1999) 'Innovation in Cities: Science-Based Diversity, Specialisation and Localised Competition', *European Economic Review*, 43, pp. 409–29.

Geroski, P. (1995) Markets for Technology: Knowledge, Innovation and Appropriability', in P. Stoneman (ed.) *Handbook of the Economics of Innovation and Technological Change* (Oxford: Blackwell), pp. 90–131.

Geroski, P., S. Machin and J. van Reenen (1993) 'The Profitability of Innovating Firms', *Rand Journal of Economics*, 24: 2, pp. 198–211

Glaeser, E. (1999) 'Learning in Cities', *Journal of Urban Economics*, 46, pp. 254–77.

Gupta, A. K. and V. Govindarajan (1994) 'Organizing for Knowledge Flows within MNCs', *International Business Review*, 3: 4, pp. 443–57.

Hall, P. (1994) *Innovation, Economics and Evolution, Theoretical Perspectives on Changing Technology in Economic Systems* (New York: Harvester Wheatsheaf).

Hall, B. H., A. N. Link and J. T. Scott (2003) 'Universities as Research Partners', *Review of Economics and Statistics*, 85: 2, pp. 485–49.

Harris, M. and A. Raviv (1991) 'The Theory of Capital Structure', *Journal of Finance* 46: 1, pp. 297–355.

Heckman, J. (1979) 'Sample Selection Bias as a Specification Error', *Econometrica*, 47, pp. 153–61.

Henderson, R., A. B. Jaffe and M. Trajtenberg (1998) 'Universities as a Source of Commercial Technology: A Detailed Analysis of University Patenting 1965–1988', *Review of Economic and Statistics*, 80: 1, pp. 119–27.

Jensen, M. (1986) 'Agency Costs of Free Cash Flow, Corporate Finance Takeovers', *American Economic Review*, 76: 2, pp. 323–39.

Keller, W. (2001) 'Trade and Transmission of Technology', *Journal of Economic Growth*, 7: 1, pp. 5–24.

Keller, W. and S. R. Yeaple (2003) 'Multinational Enterprises, International Trade and Productivity Growth: Firm Level Evidence from the United States', *National Bureau of Economic Research Working Paper*, No 9504.

Kogut, B. and U. Zander (1993) 'Knowledge of the Firm and the Evolutionary Theory of the Multinational Corporation', *Journal of International Business Studies*, 24: 4, pp. 625–45.

Marshall, A. (1920) *Principles of Economics*, 8th edition (London; Macmillan).

McGregor, J. (2006) 'The World's Most Innovative Companies', *Business Week*, 24 April.

Modigliani, F. and M. H. Miller (1958) 'The Cost of Capital, Corporation Finance and the Theory of Investment', *American Economic Review*, 48, pp. 261–97.

OECD (2005) *Oslo Manual: Guidelines for Collecting and Interpreting Innovation Data*, 3rd edition (Paris: OECD).

Pakes, A. and Z. Griliches (1984) 'Patents and R&D at the Firm Level: a First Look', in Z. Griliches (ed.) *R&D, Patents and Productivity* (Chicago: University of Chicago Press), pp. 55–72.

Pavitt, P. and Patel, K. (1999) 'Global Corporations and National Systems of Innovation: Who Dominates Whom', in D. Archiburgi, J. Howells and J. Michie (eds) *Innovation Policy in a Global Economy* (Cambridge: Cambridge University Press), pp. 94–119.

Persson, M. (2006) *Unpacking the Flow, Knowledge Transfer in the MNCs*, PhD dissertation, Uppsala University.

Pfaffermayr, M. and C. Bellak (2002) 'Why Foreign-owned Firms are Different: A Conceptual Framework and Empirical Evidence for Austria', in R. Jungnickel (ed.) *Foreign-owned Firms, Are They Different?* (Basingstoke and New York: Palgrave Macmillan), pp. 13–57.

Polanyi, M. (1966) *The Tacit Dimension* (London: Routledge & Kegan Paul).

Razin, A., E. Sadka and C. W. Yuen (2001) 'Why International Equity Inflows to Emerging Markets are Inefficient and Small Relative to International Debt Inflows', NBER Working Paper 8659.

Romer, P. (1990) 'Endogenous Technological Change', *Journal of Political Economy*, University of Chicago Press, 98: 5, pp. 1002–37.

Schmookler, J. (1966) *Invention and Economic Growth* (Cambridge, MA: Harvard University Press).

Sonn, J.W. and M. Stolper (2003) 'The Increasing Importance of Geographical Proximity in Technological Innovation, An Analysis of US Patent Citations, 1975–1997' Paper presented at the conference: What Do We Know about Innovation? In Honour of Keith Pavitt, Sussex 13–15 November, 2003.

Swedish Institute for Growth Policy, ITPS (2003) 'Forskning och utveckling i internationella företag' (Stockholm).

UNCTAD (2005) *World Investment Report: Transnational Corporations and the Internation-alization of R&D* (New York and Geneva: UNCTAD).

Vernon, R. (1962) *Metropolis 1985* (Cambridge, MA: Harvard University Press).

Vernon R. (1966) 'International Investment in International Trade in the Product Cycle', *The Quarterly Journal of Economics*, 80: 2, pp. 190–207.

Veugelers, R. and B. Cassiman (2002) 'R&D Cooperation and Spillovers: Some Empirical Evidence from Belgium', *American Economic Review*, 92: 4, pp. 1169–84.

Veugelers, R. and B. Cassiman (2004) 'Foreign Subsidiaries as a Channel of International Technology Diffusion, Some Direct Firm Level Evidence from Belgium', *European Economic Review*, 48: 2, pp. 455–76.

von Hippel, E. (1994) 'Sticky Information and the Locus of Problem Solving: Implications for Innovation', *Management Science*, 40, pp. 429–39.

Zucker, L. G., M. R. Darby and M. B. Brewer (1998) 'Intellectual Human Capital and the Birth of U.S. Biotechnology Enterprises', *American Economic Review*, 88, pp. 290–306.

12
Industry Specialization, Diversity and the Efficiency of Regional Innovation Systems

Michael Fritsch and Viktor Slavtchev

12.1   Industry specialization and innovation activity

Innovating firms are not isolated, self-sustained entities but rather are highly linked to their environment. This embeddedness can have a considerable effect on innovation processes, and it is not very far-fetched to assume that not all kinds of environment are equally well suited to a certain type of research and development (R&D) activity. There are two prominent hypotheses that pertain to the sectoral structure of the regional environment. One of these hypotheses states that the geographic concentration of firms that belong to the same industry or to related industries is conducive to innovation. The other hypothesis assumes that it is the diversity of industries and activities in a region, not the concentration of similar industries, that has a stimulating effect.

In this chapter we test these two hypotheses by linking sectoral specialization of a region to the performance of the respective regional innovation system (RIS). The next two sections (12.2 and 12.3) elaborate on the theoretical background of the two hypotheses and review the empirical evidence attained thus far. Section 12.4 introduces our concept of efficiency of the RIS and section 12.5 deals with data and measurement issues. We then give an overview on the efficiency of the German RIS (Section 12.6) and investigate the relationship between sectoral concentration and the RIS efficiency (section 12.7). The final section (12.8) presents our conclusions.

12.2   Why should sectoral specialization of a region stimulate or impede innovation?: the theoretical background

Innovation activity is characterized by the interaction and transfer of knowledge between people and institutions. It can be regarded as a collective learning process. The main actors involved in this learning process are private firms, customers, universities and other public research institutions, technology-transfer bureaus, industry associations as well as public policy-makers. If these actors are located in the same region they then participate in the same RIS.

The specialization of a certain region in a particular industry is believed to be conducive to innovation activities of firms affiliated with this industry for a number of reasons. Accordingly, the co-location of a large number of firms operating in similar technological fields may induce localization advantages because:

- the aggregate demand of a relatively large amount of firms of an industry may result in a pool of regional workers or employees with certain industry-specific skills that can be utilized by all firms belonging to that particular industry and located in the region (Marshall, 1890; Ellison and Glaeser, 1999);
- this aggregate demand of the regional firms can also induce a rich regional supply of other relevant inputs such as specialized business services, banks and credit institutions or certain kinds of infrastructure (Bartelsman, Caballero and Lyons, 1994);
- the sectoral specialization of a region may stimulate R&D cooperation between the firms which are sharing the same knowledge base and thus may promote a high level of knowledge spillovers (Mowery, Oxley and Silverman, 1998);
- tacit knowledge and geographically bounded knowledge spillovers may be conductive for local collective learning processes (Lawson and Lorenz, 1999; Maskell and Malmberg, 1999).

These benefits of specialization within a certain industry are external to the firm belonging to that industry but remain largely internal to the particular region. Such effects that result from the specialization of regional economic activities in the same industry are labeled Marshall-Arrow-Romer externalities[1] (MAR externalities) according to the authors who created this concept (Glaeser et al., 1992).

However, the concentration of several firms of the same industry in a region can also be disadvantageous if it leads to 'lock-in' effects. Such effects may occur if the specialization of the regional knowledge and resources deter the emergence and evolution of other technological fields (Grabher, 1993). In particular, specialization may hamper the exchange between heterogeneous actors with different, but complementary, types of knowledge. As argued by Jacobs (1969), many ingenious ideas are born in the exchange process which occurs between different fields of knowledge. In economic terms, this means that diversity may lead to advantages of innovation activity which are comprised of different technological fields. Hence, it may be the industrial variety in a region that is conducive to innovation activity. Such economies are external to the firms and industry but internal to the respective geographical location. Moreover, as pointed out by Jacobs (1969), these effects can be expected to be greater in densely populated regions. Therefore, regions with diverse kinds of activities and a high degree of agglomeration, particularly cities, may have a comparative advantage over less densely populated areas which are usually characterized by a lesser variety of actors, institutions and industries. Such effects of industrial diversity are labelled 'Jacobs externalities'. However, as Henderson (1997) showed for the US, agglomerations and cities not only tend to be more diversified but also more specialized in certain industries.

12.3   Empirical evidence

The answer to the question as to whether specialization or diversity in a region is conducive to innovation activity is still largely unclear. For example, Glaeser et al. (1992) found that diversity rather than regional specialization had a positive impact on employment growth in US cities in the 1956–1987 period. This study is, however, not directly linked to innovative activities. Feldman and Audretsch (1999) analysed the effect of sectoral specialization on innovative output on the basis of innovation counts which were attributed to four-digit SIC industries at the city level. They found that the innovative output of an industry tends to be lower in cities which are specialized in that particular industry. This result supports the idea that it is diversity rather than specialization that plays a major role (Jacobs, 1969). In an earlier study for the US, the authors found that the spatial concentration of certain industries (MAR externalities) is not an important determinant for explaining innovative output (Audretsch and Feldman, 1996a, 1996b). Obviously, Jacobs' thesis seems to hold for the US and can, according to Duranton and Puga (2000), be regarded as a stylized fact.

Many of the respective studies for European regions explicitly tested for both types of externalities. Paci and Usai (2000a) provide clear evidence for a significantly positive relationship between sectoral specialization and innovative output at the level of European NUTS-1 regions. The authors conclude that innovations simply occur in locations with pronounced manufacturing activities. However, there are typically a number of different knowledge sources (such as universities and other public R&D labs) and other supporting facilities in such locations that are not included in their analyses. In the case of Italy, Paci and Usai (1999, 2000b) found evidence for both Jacobs' externalities and MAR externalities. With respect to the latter, the authors conclude that innovative activities in a certain industry, as measured by the number of patents, tend to be higher in geographic locations which are specialized in that particular industry. In a more recent study, Greunz (2004) tested the impact of sectoral specialization on the number of patents at the level of European NUTS-2 regions and clearly confirmed these results. Van der Panne and van Beers (2006) argue that MAR and Jacobs' externalities may both be relevant for innovation; however, they occur at different stages of the process. According to their analysis for the Netherlands, MAR externalities have stronger positive effects in the early phases of innovation activity while Jacobs' externalities are more supportive for the marketing of an innovation.

Overall, previous analyses could not provide an unambiguous answer to the question of whether sectoral specialization or diversity in a region stimulates innovation activities. In contrast to previous studies which focused on the impact of MAR and Jacobs externalities on the number of innovations or patents, we use the efficiency of RIS in generating new knowledge as a performance indicator. Moreover, our analysis focuses not only on the role of specialization or diversity but it also accounts for other key determinants of the efficiency of RIS.

12.4   Assessing the efficiency of RIS

The term efficiency is used in a variety of ways. Our understanding of the efficiency of RIS corresponds to the concept of technical efficiency as introduced by Farrell (1957). Technical efficiency is defined as the generation of a maximum output from a given amount of resources. A firm is regarded as being technically inefficient if it fails to obtain the maximum possible output. Reasons for technical inefficiency can be manifold and comprise all kinds of mismanagement such as inappropriate work organization and improper use of technology (Fritsch and Mallok, 2002), bottlenecks in regard to certain inputs as well as the 'X-inefficiency' described in Leibenstein's (1966) seminal work. Applying that definition to the concept of RIS means that a region is technically efficient if it is able to produce the maximum possible innovative output from a given amount of innovative input. Accordingly, the inefficiency of a RIS results from the failure to meet the best practice of conducting innovation activity.

Our measure of efficiency is based on a regional knowledge production function that describes the relationship between innovative input and output (Griliches, 1979; Jaffe, 1989). The basic hypothesis behind the knowledge production function is that inventions do not 'fall from heaven' but result predominantly from systematic R&D efforts, that is:

$$\text{R\&D output} = f(\text{R\&D input}) \tag{1}$$

Adopting the Cobb-Douglas form of a production function, the basic relationship between regional R&D output and input can be written as

$$\text{R\&D output} = A * \text{R\&D input}^{\beta} * e^{\varepsilon} \tag{2}$$

with the term A representing a constant factor, β providing the elasticity by which R&D output varies with the input to the R&D process and ε as an additional *iid* distributed statistical noise component.

The output of the R&D process for regions may differ because of two reasons: the output elasticity of R&D input, β and the constant term, A. The output elasticity may be interpreted as a measure of the marginal productivity or efficiency of the input to the innovation process. If, for example, the quality of inputs to the R&D process is improving or if spillovers from the R&D activities of other actors in the region become more pronounced, the input elasticity of R&D output may increase. Differences between regions in regard to the constant term indicate higher innovative output at any level of input. Such differences in the constant term may be explained by all kinds of characteristics of RIS that influence average productivity of R&D input but do not necessarily affect marginal returns. An illustrative example of such differences that pertain only to the average productivity of R&D input and not to marginal productivity could be innovations that are not entirely based on current R&D but also on the existing stock of 'old' knowledge. Moreover, the presence of informal networks and 'milieux' may mainly affect average productivity. Due to the fact that, in practice, we are only able to assess the relevant knowledge stock rather incompletely, differences in regard to the constant term may also reflect a misspecification or incomplete measurement of the input variable. We therefore restrict ourselves here to the assessment based on the marginal productivity of R&D input. Analyses of the two measures show that they lead to a quite similar assessment of the quality of RIS (Fritsch and Slavtchev, 2006). Based on the estimates of the marginal productivity of R&D input in each region, the efficiency E_r of the region r is then calculated as:

$$E_r = (\hat{\beta}_r / \max \hat{\beta}_r) * 100 \, [\%] \tag{3}$$

According to this approach, at least one region will meet the benchmark value and the remaining regions will have efficiency values between 0 and 100 per cent of this benchmark value.

12.5   Data and measurement issues

In this study we use the number of disclosed patent applications as an indicator for the innovative output of the regional innovation processes. Information on the yearly number of disclosed patent applications is available for the 1995 to 2000 period from Greif and Schmiedl (2002). A patent application indicates that an invention has been made which extends the existing pool of economically relevant knowledge. However, using patents as an indicator for new knowledge has some shortcomings (Brouwer and Kleinknecht, 1996; Acs, Anselin and Varga, 2002; Griliches, 1990). On the one hand, patents may underestimate the output of R&D activity because the results of basic research cannot be patented in Germany. The actual R&D output may also be overestimated in the case of blocking patents, which are typically applied around one core invention in fairly new technological fields, where there may be many potential applications which are not yet known. Although the use of patents has some shortcomings, this paper follows previous studies in this field by assuming that patents are appropriate indicator of innovative output.

A patent is assigned to the region in which the inventor has his main residence. If a patent has more than one inventor, the patent is divided by the number of inventors and the respective shares are assigned to the regions in which the inventors have their residence. Therefore, in event of the inventors being located in different regions, the number of patents per region may not always be a whole number. We have rounded up the number of patents per region assuming that innovations are randomly occurring discrete events that typically follow a Poisson distribution. Hence, econometric methods that account for the discrete nature of the dependent variable appear more appropriate than the least square estimation technique, which is based on the assumption of a normal distribution of the residuals. However, as the distribution of patent records shows pronounced skewness to the left (over dispersion), we apply negative-binomial regression as an estimation technique for assessing the efficiency of RIS.[2]

In an analysis of the knowledge sources of innovation for West German districts[3] (*Kreise*) as well as for the German planning regions (*Raumordnungsregionen*) with the number of patent applications as the dependent variable, we found a dominant effect for the number of private-sector R&D employees in the region (Fritsch and Slavtchev, 2005, 2007). Further knowledge sources that had a significant effect on innovative output of a region were the number of R&D employees in adjacent regions indicating the presence of spatial knowledge spillovers as well as the amount of external research funds attracted by public research institutions. In this paper, we omit other input variables and limit the analysis to the number of private sector R&D employees as the main knowledge source in the knowledge production function. The main reason for this approach is that knowledge spillovers from adjacent regions as well as the presence of public research institutions can be regarded as determinants of the efficiency of private-sector R&D input and should, therefore, not be used for measuring it. The numbers for R&D employment in the private sector stems from the German Social Insurance Statistics (*Statistik der sozialversicherungspflichtig Beschäftigten*) as described and documented by Fritsch and Brixy (2004). Employees are classified as working in R&D if they have a tertiary degree in engineering or in natural sciences.

The estimation of a knowledge-production function at the level of planning regions (Table 12.1) shows a strong impact of the number of private-sector R&D employees on the number of patents. The production elasticity of

Table 12.1   The knowledge-production function

Variable	
Private sector R&D employees (ln)	0.885**
	(0.051)
Intercept	−1.773**
	(0.441)
N	388
Alpha	0.365
	(0.045)
Wald χ^2 (1)	306.46**
Log pseudo likelihood	−2,466.15
Pseudo R^{2adj}	0.916

Results of robust (cluster) negative-binomial regression; robust standard error in parentheses; **statistically significant at the 1% level.

private-sector R&D employment is 0.885, indicating that an increase of R&D employment by 1 per cent leads to an increase in the number of patents of nearly 0.89 percent. According to the constant term of the model, there are only 0.17 patents in the average planning region per year that cannot be attributed to private-sector R&D efforts as measured by R&D employment.

When relating knowledge input to innovation output we have to assume that there is a time-lag between the respective indicators for two reasons. Firstly, R&D activity requires time for attaining a patentable result. Secondly, patent applications are published only about 12 to 18 months after submission. This is the time necessary for the patent office to verify whether an application fulfils the basic preconditions for being granted a patent (Greif and Schmiedl, 2002). Thereafter, each patent application has to be disclosed (Hinze and Schmoch, 2004). Hence, at least two or three years should be an appropriate time-lag between input and output of the R&D process.[4] However, because reliable data on R&D employment in eastern Germany are only available for the years 1996 onwards, a time-lag of two or three years would lead to too few observations per region for estimating a region-specific effect. In order to have more observations available, we reduce the time-lag between R&D input and the patent application to a period of one year.[5] In other words, R&D output in the period 1997–2000 is related to R&D input between 1996 and 1999. This appears justified because there are no great fluctuations of both innovation input and innovation output over the years. Moreover, the differences between an estimated knowledge-production function with a time-lag of one year and with a time-lag of three years are negligible (Fritsch and Slavtchev, 2005, 2007).

The spatial pattern to be used for the analysis is given by the 97 German planning regions.[6] The spatial concept of planning regions focuses on commuter distances; therefore, they account for travel to work areas and are well suited to represent functional spatial economic entities. In general, planning regions consist of several districts and include at least one core city as well as its surroundings. For historical reasons, the cities of Berlin, Hamburg and Bremen are defined as planning regions even though they are not functional economic units. In order to create functional units, we merged these cities with adjacent planning regions for the analysis. Berlin was merged with the region Havelland-Flaeming, Hamburg with the region Schleswig-Holstein South, Bremen with Bremerhaven and with the region Bremen-Umland. Hence, the estimation approach applied in this paper is based on observations for 93 regions over four years.

To estimate the productivity of RIS in terms of the marginal return to R&D input, we include a binary dummy variable for each region which is multiplied by the respective number of private-sector R&D employees. This dummy variable assumes the value one for the respective region and otherwise has the value zero. The constant term, A, is assumed to be the same for all regions. Hence, equation (2) can be rewritten as:

$$\text{Patents}_r = A \prod_r \text{R\&D priv}_r^{\beta_r} * e^{\varepsilon_r} \tag{4}$$

with β_r as a measure of the marginal productivity of private-sector R&D employment in the rth region $(r = 1, \ldots, 93)$. In order to partly relax the assumption of independency of the observations for a particular planning region, we adjust the standard error for intragroup correlation by clustering the observations for each region. Applying the clustering procedure is equivalent to a White-corrected standard error in the presence of heteroscedasticity (White, 1980). The efficiency measure is computed according to equation (3). The results are reported in Table 12.A1 in Appendix 12.1.

12.6 The distribution of RIS efficiency across German regions

There is a wide dispersion of technical efficiency of RIS among the planning regions that reflects the marginal productivity of R&D input. The values for technical efficiency range between 53 per cent and 100 per cent, meaning that productivity of private R&D input in the best practice region is about twice the productivity in the least efficient region (see table 12A.1 in Appendix as well as Fritsch and Slavtchev, 2006, for details).

Generally, the values for the technical efficiency of RIS tend to be higher in regions with large, densely populated agglomerations such as Munich, Stuttgart, Cologne and Frankfurt. The lowest efficiency estimates

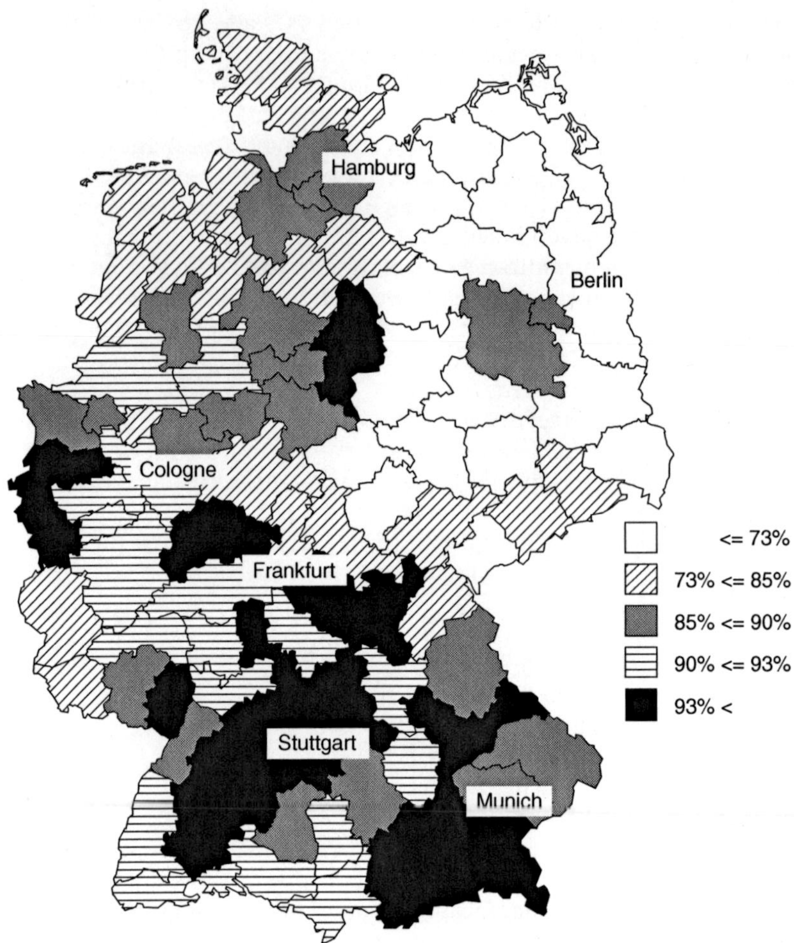

Figure 12.1   The distribution of efficiency of RIS in German planning regions

are found for regions in the northeast such as Mecklenburgische Seenplatte, Vorpommern and Altmark located in eastern Germany, the former German Democratic Republic (GDR). The Berlin region, showing a relatively high RIS efficiency, is an exception in the eastern German innovation landscape. The relatively low values for technical efficiency in eastern Germany indicate that the RIS in this part of the country is rather inefficient. Most of the regions with a relatively high level of technical efficiency of RIS are located in the southern and in the western part of the country. We find evidence for spatial clustering of regions with similar levels of RIS efficiency (see Fritsch and Slavtchev, 2006 for details). This indicates that some of the determinants of the efficiency of RIS apply to larger geographical units than planning regions.

12.7   Sectoral concentration and the efficiency of RIS

To estimate the relative impact of different determinants of the technical efficiency of RIS a robust OLS cross-section regression technique was applied.[7] Although the main focus of this study is on the relationship between sectoral concentration in a region and marginal productivity of R&D employment, a number of further important determinants of RIS efficiency as well as a number of control variables are included. Table 12.2 gives an overview of the definition of variables and respective data sources. Descriptive statistics presented in tables 12.3 and 12.4 show the regression results. Correlation coefficients for the relationship between the variables are given in Table 12.A2 in Appendix 12.1.

A significantly positive impact of RIS on technical efficiency can be found for the share of private-sector R&D employment. The estimated coefficient provides clear evidence for scale economies. This means that an increase of the share of private-sector R&D employment at a certain location may make innovation processes more efficient. The sources of such scale economies could be increasing opportunities for a division of innovative labour that is related to a high level of knowledge spillovers. However, if more detailed measures for regional specialization in R&D-intensive industries are included (models 4–8 in Table 12.4), the impact of the share of R&D employment becomes somewhat weaker or is no longer statistically significant (model 8 in Table 12.4).

The average amount of external research funds from private sector sources per university professor has a positive impact on the efficiency of RIS. This suggests that the intensity of university-industry linkages is conducive to the efficiency of regional innovation activity presumably as a result of the knowledge flows that are indicated by the money that private firms pay for the R&D that the universities perform for them.

The industrial diversity index is the inverse value of the Gini coefficient calculated on the basis of the number of employees in 58 different industries. The positive sign for the industrial diversity index (models 2–8) suggests that the efficiency of regional innovation activity increases with the variety of industries in the region and that interaction of actors with different knowledge endowments stimulates the generation of new ideas rather than specialization. The results favor Jacobs externalities. However, the negative sign for the squared value of the diversity index indicates a nonlinear relationship with the efficiency of the RIS that has the shape of an inverse 'U' which is truncated close behind the maximum value. Indeed, the same

Table 12.2 Definition of variables and data sources

Variable	Description	Definition	Source
Patents	Number of disclosed patent applications in the region, 1997–2000		German Patent and Trademark Office (*DPMA*)
$R\&D_{PRIV}$	Number of private-sector R&D employees in the region, 1996–9	Number of employees with tertiary degree in engineering and natural sciences in the region	German Social insurance Statistics
Efficiency of RIS	Marginal productivity of private sector R&D employees in the region, 1997–2000	See Section 12.4	See Section 12.4
$R\&D_{PRIV}$[share]	Share of private sector R&D employees in the region, 1996–9 average	Number of employees with tertiary degree in engineering and natural sciences in the region/number of employees in the region	German Social Insurance Statistics
SERVICES	Service sector relative size in the region, 1996–9 average	Share of employment in services in the region divided by the share of employment in services in the entire economy. This index is standardized in [−1; 1] according to Paci and Usai (1999).	German Social insurance Statistics
POPden	Population density in the region, 1996–9 average	Number of inhabitants per sq km	Federal Office for Building and Regional Planning
Ø FSIZE	Average firm size in the region, 1996–9 average	Number of employees in the region/number of firms in the region	German Social Insurance Statistics
ERF_{IND} per professor	Universities external research funds per professor in the region, 1996–9 average	Volume of external research funds that universities in the region gain from private sector actors [1000 Euro]/Number of professors at universities in the region	German University Statistics available at the Federal Statistical Office

DIV	Regional index of industrial diversity, 1996–9 average	Inverse of the Donaldson-Weymark relative S-Gini coefficient on basis of 58 industries (industrial classification WZ58)	German Social insurance Statistics
TRANSPORT_ENG	Share of employment in transportation engineering in the region, 1996–9 average	Number of employees in transportation engineering in the region/number of regional employees	German Social insurance Statistics
ELECTR_ENG	Share of employment in electrical engineering in the region, 1996–9 average	Number of employees in electrical engineering in the region/number of regional employment	German Social Insurance Statistics
OPTICS	Share of employment in measurement engineering and optics in the region, 1996–9 average	Number of employees in measurement engineering and optics in the region/number of regional employees	German Social Insurance Statistics
CHEMISTRY	Share of employment in chemistry in the region, 1996–9 average	Number of employees in chemistry in the region/number of regional employees	German Social Insurance Statistics
Dummy West	Region located in West Germany	Regions in former German Federal Republic = 1; regions in former GDR and Berlin = 0	
Dummy South	Region located south of Frankfurt (Main)	Regions located south of Frankfurt (Main) = 1, otherwise dummy = 0	
Dummy Periphery	Region located at the border of Germany	Regions located at the border of Germany = 1, otherwise dummy = 0	

Table 12.3 Descriptive statistics

Variable	Obs.	Mean	Std. Dev.	Min	Max	Median
Patents[a]	372	395.50	508.60	11.778	3,652.7	245.75
R&D$_{PRIV}$[a]	372	6,674.0	8,724.1	649.00	48,968	3,690.0
Marginal productivity of R&D$_{PRIV}$ [$\hat{\beta}$]	93	0.6513	0.0893	0.4119	0.7779	0.6768
Efficiency of RIS [%]	93	83.717	11.480	52.941	100.00	87.005
R&D$_{PRIV}$ [Share]	93	0.0223	0.0089	0.0089	0.0528	0,0200
ERF$_{IND}$ per professor	93	11.062	14.735	0	97.067	7.1950
DIV	93	1.4979	0.0825	1.3076	1.6785	1.5023
TRANSPORT_ENG	93	0.0428	0.0375	0.0096	0.2259	0.0308
ELECTR_ENG	93	0.0354	0.0233	0.0038	0.1227	0.0292
OPTICS	93	0.0086	0.0086	0.0022	0.0553	0.0055
CHEMISTRY	93	0.0167	0.0227	0.0009	0.1795	0.0100
Ø FSIZE	93	13.204	1.6957	8.5294	18.2661	13.308
SERVICES	93	−0.0481	0.0818	−0.2255	0.1999	−0.0556
POPden	93	336.99	507.56	53.425	3,886.9	180.67

Note: [a]pooled yearly values

pattern can be directly observed in the data (Figure 12.2).[8] This pattern implies that an optimum degree of industrial diversity exists and that a further increase beyond this level has an unfavourable effect. Obviously, at both extremes broad diversity as well as narrow specialization may be unfavourable to the performance of a RIS. Even after introducing a number of additional variables in order to control for further effects, the estimated pattern for industrial diversity remains remarkably stable.

Our results suggest that externalities of both the Marshall and Jacobs type affect the efficiency of regions in producing innovative output. This confirms the previous results of Paci and Usai (1999, 2000b), who used the Herfindahl index as a measure of industrial diversity, and it also parallels the findings of Greunz (2004), who tested the impact of the industrial structure on innovation in European regions by means of Gini coefficients.

In order to control for the relative impact of regional specialization in certain industries with a relatively high level of patenting, we include the share of employees in transportation engineering, electrical engineering, measurement engineering and optics. These are, according to Greif and Schmiedl (2002), the technological fields in which most of the patent applications in Germany are generated.[9] Due to the fact that the available data do not allow the identification of the exact number of employees in the biochemical industry, which is another field with a relatively high share of patenting, we include the percentage of people employed in chemistry as an indicator for the region's specialization in that particular sector. However, only regional

Table 12.4 Determinants of efficiency of RIS

	Dependent variable: Efficiency of RIS [Equation (3)]							
	(1)	(2)	(3)	(4)	(5)	(6)	(7)	(8)
R&D$_{PRIV}$ [Share] (ln)	0.026*	0.048*	0.067**	0.066**	0.056**	0.064**	0.060*	0.028
	(2.21)	(2.62)	(2.89)	(2.79)	(2.44)	(2.69)	(2.60)	(1.19)
ERF$_{IND}$ per professor (ln)	0.022*	0.012	0.015**	0.015**	0.014*	0.015**	0.015*	0.016*
	(1.99)	(1.92)	(2.65)	(2.67)	(2.54)	(2.65)	(2.63)	(2.62)
DIV (ln)		8.540**	4.210*	4.027*	3.884*	4.216*	4.130*	3.306*
		(3.71)	(2.54)	(2.45)	(2.51)	(2.54)	(2.45)	(2.05)
DIV^2 (ln)^2		−8.760**	−4.727*	−4.449*	−4.425*	−4.755*	−4.646*	−3.730
		(2.97)	(2.31)	(2.19)	(2.33)	(2.33)	(2.22)	(1.88)
TRANSPORT_ENG (ln)				0.008				0.012
				(0.80)				(1.25)
ELECTR_ENG (ln)					0.023*			0.032*
					(1.96)			(2.48)
OPTICS (ln)						0.005		0.005
						(0.46)		(0.49)
CHEMISTRY (ln)							0.005	0.013
							(0.61)	(1.37)
ØFSIZE (ln)	−0.441**	−0.224*	−0.248**	−0.253**	−0.244**	−0.239**	−0.234**	−0.206**
	(2.98)	(2.03)	(2.89)	(2.99)	(2.84)	(2.81)	(2.86)	(2.67)
SERVICES	−0.637**	−0.239	−0.473**	−0.453**	−0.436**	−0.468**	−0.478**	−0.401**
	(3.10)	(1.42)	(5.26)	(4.97)	(4.68)	(5.12)	(5.36)	(4.46)
POPden (ln)	0.137**	0.064**	0.069**	0.070**	0.068**	0.069**	0.068**	0.065**
	(4.65)	(3.51)	(4.63)	(4.61)	(4.93)	(4.61)	(4.37)	(4.53)
Dummy West (1 = yes)			0.155**	0.147**	0.148**	0.154**	0.150**	0.122**
			(5.92)	(5.65)	(5.62)	(5.86)	(5.08)	(3.81)
Dummy South (1 = yes)			0.080**	0.078**	0.074**	0.080**	0.081**	0.069**
			(5.23)	(4.98)	(4.98)	(5.15)	(5.31)	(4.49)
Dummy Periphery (1 = yes)			−0.028*	−0.029*	−0.023	−0.027*	−0.027*	−0.019
			(2.04)	(2.11)	(1.72)	(1.98)	(1.96)	(1.46)
Intercept	4.845**	2.811**	3.837**	3.869**	3.856**	3.807**	3.799**	3.783**
	(10.94)	(4.79)	(9.02)	(9.25)	(9.79)	(9.18)	(8.90)	(10.16)
R-squared	0.33	0.66	0.86	0.86	0.86	0.86	0.86	0.87
R-squared adj.	0.29	0.63	0.84	0.84	0.85	0.84	0.84	0.85
F	5.40	44.60	61.08	57.19	58.01	54.52	59.00	52.62
Prob > F	0.000	0.000	0.000	0.000	0.000	0.000	0.000	0.000

Note: Results of OLS, Huber-White estimation. Robust t-statistics in parentheses; * significant at 5% level; ** significant at 1% level. Number of observations (regions): 93.

specialization in electrical engineering seems to have an effect on the efficiency of RIS. The service sector may provide important support for the R&D activities in diverse ways such as counselling, technical services, provision of venture capital, and so on. This is particularly true for knowledge-intensive business services (KIBS), which also may produce and diffuse knowledge that is crucial for innovation processes (Muller and Zenker, 2001; Anselin, Varga and Acs, 2000). One could, therefore, expect a positive impact from

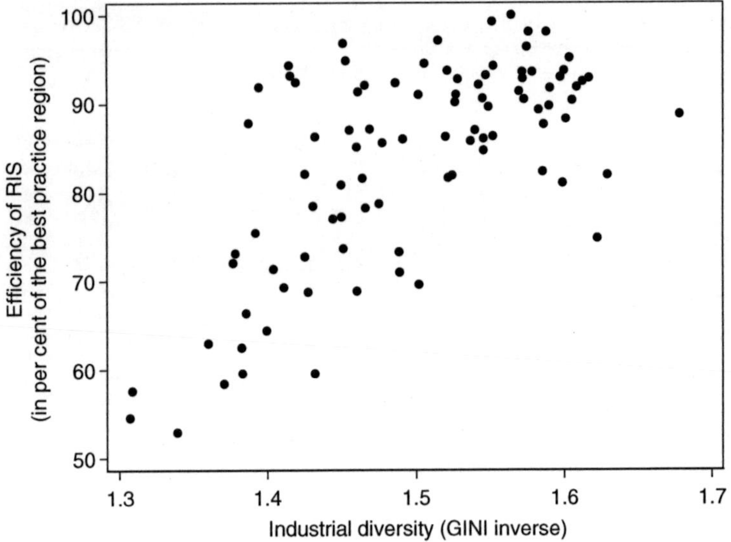

Figure 12.2 Industrial variety and technical efficiency of RIS at the level of the German planning regions

the share of the regional service sector on RIS efficiency. However, a high share of the service sector in the region may have a negative effect on the number of regional patents due to the relatively low propensity to patent in this sector. Hence, the overall effect of services on the efficiency of RIS is *a priori* not clear. In order to test the impact of the service supply in a region on the marginal patent productivity of private-sector R&D, we introduce the relative size of that sector (in terms of employment) into the model (SERVICES). Our results indicate that the share of the service sector has a negative impact on the efficiency of RIS. This means that despite their supporting function, resources allocated to the service sector are less efficient in terms of patenting. This corresponds to the relatively low share of patents in services.

As indicated by the significantly negative coefficient for average firm size, patenting efficiency tends to be lower in regions that are dominated by industries in which economies of scale play an important role. This confirms other studies which find that the number of patents per unit of R&D input is higher in smaller firms than in larger ones (Acs and Audretsch, 1990; Cohen and Klepper, 1996).

The positive coefficient for population density indicates the presence of urbanization economies. This suggests that a location in a densely populated region which provides a variety of opportunities for interaction in addition to often abundant supplies of input as well as a rich physical, institutional and communication infrastructure may be advantageous for innovation activity.

The results of the analysis also suggest that regions located in the west of Germany as well as in the south of the country are more efficient in producing innovative output per unit of innovative input than regions located in the north and in the east. Regions located on the periphery tend to be relatively inefficient in comparison to the nonperipheral areas. However, if the share of employment in electrical engineering is included (models 5 and 8), the estimated coefficient for location in the periphery becomes statistically insignificant, indicating that this industry is not present in this spatial category. The dummy variables for location in the western and in the southern part of Germany remain quite robust, providing clear evidence of the presence of region-specific factors which are not captured by the other variables.

12.8 Conclusions

This paper investigated the effect of a region's specialization in certain industries on the efficiency of RIS in producing knowledge. Our answer to the question 'Is regional specialization in a certain industry conducive to the performance of RIS in terms of efficiency?' is 'Yes, but only to a certain degree'. In fact, the data suggest that the relationship between sectoral specialization and the performance of RIS takes the form of an inverse 'U'. This means that if a certain level of specialization is reached any further concentration in the respective industry tends to be unfavourable for the efficiency of RIS. A high concentration as well as great diversity of the sectoral structure in a region is associated with a relatively low level of RIS efficiency. The results suggest that a region's specialization in a certain industry may increase the efficiency of the region in producing innovative output. However, this does not hold for all industries but seems to be the case for high-tech manufacturing industries such as electrical engineering.

The results of this paper raise some important questions for further research. First, the determinants of knowledge spillovers within the private sector as well as industry-universities relationships should be more illuminated because such interchanges seem to be conducive to regional innovative performance. Second, additional research is required in order to answer the question of what the forces are that determine the industrial structure of regions. Moreover, regarding the positive impact of industrial diversity on innovation, more information about the ways in which knowledge spills over between industries should be helpful in deriving reasonable policy implications.

Appendix 12.1

Table 12.A1   The distribution of technical efficiency in the German planning regions

Planning region		Estimated production elasticities		Technical efficiency [%]	Rank
Code	Name	$\hat{\beta}$	robust std. error	$\dfrac{\hat{\beta}}{\max\hat{\beta}} * 100$	
1	Schleswig-Holstein North	0.5685	0.3012	73.07	75
2	Schleswig-Holstein South-West	0.5412	0.2919	69.57	80
3	Schleswig-Holstein Central	0.6104	0.2408	78.46	67
4	Schleswig-Holstein East	0.5991	.0.2639	77.02	70
5 & 6	Schleswig-Holstein South & Hamburg	0.6657	0.1995	85.57	55
7	Western Mecklenburg	0.4634	0.2534	59.57	88
8	Central Mecklenburg/Rostock	0.5163	0.2524	66.37	84
9	Western Pomerania	0.4479	0.2558	57.58	91
10	Mecklenburgische Seenplatte	0.4119	0.2737	52.94	93
11 & 13 & 15	Bremen & Bremerhaven & Bremen-Umland	0.6123	0.2170	78.71	66
12	East Frisian	0.5866	0.2777	75.41	71
14	Hamburg-Umland-South	0.6778	0.2669	87.12	46
16	Oldenburg	0.6008	0.2683	77.22	69
17	Emsland	0.5823	0.2705	74.85	72
18	Osnabrück	0.6767	0.2550	86.99	48
19	Hanover	0.6691	0.2136	86.01	53
20	Suedheide	0.6290	0.2780	80.85	65
21	Luneburg	0.5726	0.3003	73.60	73
22	Brunswick	0.7250	0.2178	93.19	18
23	Hildesheim	0.6713	0.2566	86.29	50
24	Göttingen	0.6817	0.2601	87.62	45
25	Prignitz-Obehavel	0.4859	0.2630	62.46	87
26	Uckermark-Barnim	0.4542	0.2716	58.38	90
27	Oderland-Spree	0.4899	0.2574	62.98	86
28	Lusatia-Spreewald	0.5389	0.2314	69.28	81
29 & 30	Havelland-Flaeming & Berlin	0.6833	0.1915	87.83	44
31	Altmark	0.4247	0.3065	54.59	92
32	Magdeburg	0.5550	0.2300	71.34	78
33	Dessau	0.4634	0.2474	59.56	89
34	Halle/Saale	0.5604	0.2273	72.04	77
35	Muenster	0.7112	0.2255	91.42	31
36	Bielefeld	0.7150	0.2233	91.91	28
37	Paderborn	0.6673	0.2556	85.78	54
38	Arnsberg	0.6692	0.2516	86.03	52
39	Dortmund	0.6403	0.2276	82.31	58
40	Emscher-Lippe	0.6768	0.2413	87.01	47

(*Continued*)

Table 12.A1   (Continued)

Planning region		Estimated production elasticities		Technical efficiency [%]	Rank
Code	Name	$\hat{\beta}$	robust std. error	$\dfrac{\hat{\beta}}{\max\hat{\beta}} * 100$	
41	Duisburg/Essen	0.6714	0.2077	86.31	49
42	Düsseldorf	0.7335	0.1964	94.29	12
43	Bochum/Hagen	0.7171	0.2215	92.18	26
44	Cologne	0.7018	0.2008	90.21	38
45	Aachen	0.7237	0.2235	93.02	19
46	Bonn	0.7149	0.2418	91.90	29
47	Siegen	0.7049	0.2571	90.61	35
48	Northern Hesse	0.6353	0.2399	81.66	62
49	Central Hesse	0.7282	0.2366	93.61	15
50	Eastern Hesse	0.6306	0.2843	81.07	64
51	Rhine-Main	0.7107	0.1920	91.36	32
52	Starkenburg	0.7185	0.2141	92.35	25
53	Northern Thuringia	0.5008	0.2697	64.37	85
54	Central Thuringia	0.5658	0.2296	72.74	76
55	Southern Thuringia	0.5698	0.2540	73.24	74
56	Eastern Thuringia	0.6349	0.2354	81.61	63
57	Western Saxony	0.5347	0.2171	68.74	83
58	Upper Elbe Valley/Eastern Ore Mountains	0.6387	0.2132	82.10	59
59	Upper Lusatia-Lower Silesia	0.5356	0.2440	68.85	82
60	Chemnitz-Ore Mountains	0.6087	0.2254	78.25	68
61	South West Saxony	0.5520	0.2446	70.96	79
62	Middle Rhine-Nahe	0.7033	0.2385	90.40	37
63	Trier	0.6370	0.2847	81.89	61
64	Rhine-Hesse-Nahe	0.7220	0.2427	92.81	22
65	Western Palatinate	0.6619	0.2659	85.08	56
66	Rhine Palatinate	0.7339	0.2229	94.34	11
67	Saar	0.6591	0.2354	84.73	57
68	Upper Neckar	0.7084	0.2137	91.06	33
69	Franconia	0.7292	0.2348	93.73	14
70	Middle Upper Rhine	0.6975	0.2158	89.66	40
71	Northern Black Forest	0.7631	0.2490	98.09	3
72	Stuttgart	0.7556	0.1869	97.13	5
73	Eastern Wuertemberg	0.7631	0.2459	98.09	4
74	Danube-Iller (BW)	0.6950	0.2373	89.34	41
75	Neckar-Alb	0.7295	0.2390	93.77	13
76	Black Forest-Baar-Heuberg	0.7498	0.2501	96.39	7
77	Southern Upper Rhine	0.7141	0.2344	91.80	30
78	High Rhine-Lake Constance	0.7226	0.2397	92.88	20
79	Lake Constance-Upper Swabia	0.7198	0.2282	92.53	23

(Continued)

Table 12.A1 (Continued)

Planning region		Estimated production elasticities		Technical efficiency [%]	Rank
Code	Name	$\hat{\beta}$	robust std. error	$\dfrac{\hat{\beta}}{\max\hat{\beta}} * 100$	
80	Bavarian Lower Main	0.7254	0.2604	93.24	17
81	Wurzburg	0.7083	0.2495	91.05	34
82	Main-Rhone	0.7531	0.2603	96.81	6
83	Upper Franconia-West	0.7407	0.2558	95.21	8
84	Upper Franconia-East	0.6377	0.2599	81.97	60
85	Upper Franconia-North	0.6868	0.2669	88.28	43
86	Industrial Region Central Franconia	0.7167	0.2021	92.13	27
87	Augsburg	0.7281	0.2885	93.60	16
88	Western Central Franconia	0.6910	0.2305	88.83	42
89	Ingolstadt	0.7189	0.2545	92.40	24
90	Regensburg	0.7354	0.2384	94.53	10
91	Danube-Forest	0.6984	0.2658	89.78	39
92	Landshut	0.6713	0.2702	86.29	51
93	Munich	0.7379	0.1868	94.85	9
94	Danube-Iller (BY)	0.7223	0.2578	92.85	21
95	Allgaeu	0.7041	0.2612	90.51	36
96	Oberland	0.7779	0.2693	100.00	1
97	Southeast Upper Bavaria	0.7723	0.2441	99.27	2

Results of robust (cluster) negative-binomial regression.

Table 12.A2 Correlation of variables

Variable	1	2	3	4	5	6	7	8	9	10	11
1 Patents[a]											
2 R&D$_{PRIV}$[a]	0.92										
3 Efficiency of RIS		1.00									
4 R&D$_{PRIV}$ [Share]		0.22	1.00								
5 SERVICES		0.08	0.44	1.00							
6 POPden		0.17	0.38	0.47	1.00						
7 Ø FSIZE		0.08	0.58	0.19	0.46	1.00					
8 ERF$_{IND}$ per professor		0.23	0.33	0.20	0.04	0.20	1.00				
9 DIV		0.66	−0.09	−0.12	−0.05	−0.05	0.10	1.00			
10 TRANSPORT_ENG		0.29	0.12	−0.12	−0.05	0.16	0.13	−0.05	1.00		
11 ELECTR_ENG		0.55	0.26	−0.11	0.02	0.18	0.21	0.44	0.06	1.00	
12 OPTICS		0.34	0.02	−0.19	−0.08	−0.11	−0.04	0.31	0.00	0.36	1.00
13 CHEMISTRY		0.31	0.23	0.17	0.09	−0.01	−0.08	0.07	0.04	−0.08	0.02

[a]pooled yearly values.

Notes

1. Based on Marshall (1890), Arrow (1962) and Romer (1986).
2. See Greene (2003, pp. 931–9). As we find at least one patent per year for each district in our data, the problem of having 'too many zero values' does not apply.
3. The German districts (*Kreise*) coincide with the NUTS-3 regional classification.
4. Fritsch and Slavtchev (2005, 2007) relate patenting activities in West Germany between 1995 and 2000 to R&D activities three years ago. Acs, Anselin and Varga (2002) report that US innovation records in 1982 resulted from inventions that had been made 4.3 years earlier. Fischer and Varga (2003) used a two-year lag between R&D efforts and patent counts in Austria in 1993. Ronde and Hussler (2005) linked the innovative output – the number of patents between 1997 and 2000 – to R&D efforts in 1997.
5. Bode (2004) also uses a time-lag of one year when relating patent output to R&D employment across German planning regions.
6. For this definition of the planning regions, see the *Bundesamt für Bauwesen und Raumordnung, BBR* (Federal Office for Building and Regional Planning), 2003.
7. Since the dependent variable, the estimated marginal elasticity of private-sector R&D, is bounded between zero and 100 per cent, we also applied (two-limit) tobit regressions in order to check for robustness of the results. As the results of the tobit analyses are identical with the results of the OLS regressions, they are not reported here.
8. High values indicate high levels of industry diversification.
9. In the 1995–2000 period about 9.6 per cent of all patent applications were submitted in the field of transportation engineering, 13 per cent in electrical engineering and 7.4 per cent in measurement engineering/optics (Greif and Schmiedl, 2002).

References

Acs, Z. J. and D. B. Audretsch (1990) *Innovation and Small Firms* (Cambridge: Cambridge University Press).

Acs, Z. J., L. Anselin and A. Varga (2002) 'Patents and Innovation Counts as Measures of Regional Production of New Knowledge', *Research Policy*, 31: 7, pp. 1069–85.

Anselin, Luc, Attila Varga and Zoltan J. Acs (2000) 'Geographic and Sectoral Characteristics of Academic Knowledge Externalities', *Papers in Regional Science*, 79, 435–43.

Arrow, J. K. (1962) 'The Economic Implications of Learning by Doing,' *Review of Economic Studies*, 29, pp. 155–73.

Audretsch, D. B. and M. P. Feldman (1996a) 'R&D Spillovers and the Geography of Innovation and Production', *American Economic Review*, 86, pp. 631–40.

Audretsch, D. B. and M. P. Feldman (1996b) 'Innovative Clusters and the Industry Life Cycle', *Review of Industrial Organization*, 11, pp. 253–73.

Bartelsman, E. J., R. J. Caballero and R. K. Lyons (1994) 'Customer- and Supplier-Driven Externalities', *American Economic Review*, 84, pp. 1075–84.

Bode, E. (2004) 'The Spatial Pattern of Localized R&D Spillovers: an Empirical Investigation for Germany', *Journal of Economic Geography*, 4, pp. 43–64.

Brouwer, E. and A. Kleinknecht (1996) 'Determinants of Innovation: a Microeconomic Analysis of Three Alternative Innovation Indicators', in Alfred Kleinknecht (ed.) *Determinants of Innovation: The Message from New Indicators* (Basingstoke: Macmillan).

Bundesamt für Bauwesen und Raumordnung – BBR (2003): *Aktuelle Daten zur Entwicklung der Städte, Kreise und Gemeinden*, Band 17 (Bonn: BBR).

Cohen, W. M. and S. Klepper (1996) 'A Reprise of Size and R&D', *The Economic Journal*, 106, pp. 925–51.

Duranton, G. and D. Puga (2000) 'Diversity and Specialization in Cities: Why, Where and When Does It Matter?', *Urban Studies*, 37, pp. 533–55.

Ellison, G. and E. L. Glaeser (1999) 'The Geographic Concentration of Industry: Does Natural Advantages Explain Agglomeration?', *American Economic Review Papers and Proceedings*, 89, pp. 301–316.

Farrell, M. J. (1957) 'The Measurement of Productive Efficiency', *Journal of the Royal Statistical Society*, 120, pp. 253–82.

Feldman, M. P. and D. B. Audretsch (1999) 'Innovation in Cities: Science-base Diversity, Specialization and Localized Competition', *European Economic Review*, 43, pp. 409–29.

Fischer, M. M. and A. Varga (2003) 'Spatial Knowledge Spillovers and University Research: Evidence from Austria', *Annals of Regional Science*, 37, pp. 303–22.

Fritsch, M. and J. Mallok (2002) Machinery and Productivity – A Comparison of East and West German Manufacturing Plants', in L. Schätzl and J. Revilla Diez (eds) *Technological Change and Regional Development in Europe* (Heidelberg/New York: Physica), pp. 61–73.

Fritsch, M. and U. Brixy (2004) 'The Establishment File of the German Social Insurance Statistics', Schmollers Jahrbuch/*Journal of Applied Social Science Studies*, 124, pp. 183–90.

Fritsch, M. and V. Slavtchev (2005) 'The Role of Regional Knowledge Sources for Innovation – An Empirical Assessment', Working Paper 15/2005, Faculty of Economics and Business Administration, Technical University Bergakademie Freiberg.

Fritsch, M. and V. Slavtchev (2006) 'Measuring the Efficiency of Regional Innovation Systems – An Empirical Assessment', Working Paper 8/2006, Faculty of Economics and Business Administration, Technical University Bergakademie Freiberg.

Fritsch, M. and V. Slavtchev (2007) 'Universities and Innovation in Space', *Industry and Innovation*, 14, pp. 201–18.

Glaeser, E. L., H. D. Kallal, J. A. Scheinkam and Andrei Shleifer (1992) 'Growth in Cities', *The Journal of Political Economy*, 100, pp. 1126–52.

Grabher, G. (1993) 'The Weakness of Strong Ties: the Lock-in of Regional Developments in the Ruhr Area', in G. Grabher (ed.) *The Embedded Firm – On the Socioeconomics of Industrial Networks* (London: Routledge), pp. 255–77.

Greene, W. H. (2003) *Econometric Analysis*, 5th edition (New York: Prentice Hall).

Greif, S. and D. Schmiedl (2002) *Patentatlas Deutschland* (Munich: Deutsches Patent- und Markenamt).

Greunz, L. (2004) 'Industrial Structure and Innovation – Evidence from European Regions', *Journal of Evolutionary Economics*, 14, pp. 563–92.

Griliches, Z. (1979) 'Issues in Assessing the Contribution of Research and Development to Productivity Growth', *Bell Journal of Economics*, 10, pp. 92–116.

Griliches, Z. (1990) 'Patent Statistics as Economic Indicators: a Survey', *Journal of Economic Literature*, 28, pp. 1661–707.

Henderson, V. (1997) 'Medium Size Cities', *Regional Science and Urban Economics*, 27, pp. 583–612.

Hinze, S. and U. Schmoch (2004) 'Analytical Approaches and Their Impact on the Outcome of Statistical Patent Analysis', in H. F. Moed, W. Glänzel and U. Schmoch (eds) *Handbook of Quantitative Science and Technology Research: The Use of Publication and*

Patent Statistics in Studies of S&T Systems (Dordrecht: Kluwer Academic Publishers), pp. 215–36.

Jacobs, J. (1969) *The Economy of Cities* (New York: Vintage).

Jaffe, A. (1989) 'Real Effects of Academic Research', *American Economic Review,* 79, pp. 957–70.

Lawson, C. and E. Lorenz (1999) 'Collective Learning, Tacit Knowledge and Regional Innovative Capacity,' *Regional Studies*, 33, pp. 305–17.

Leibenstein, H. (1966) 'Allocative Efficiency vs. "X-efficiency"', *American Economic Review*, 56, pp. 392–415.

Marshall, A. (1890) *Principles of Economics* (London: Macmillan).

Maskell, P. and A. Malmberg (1999) 'Localized Learning and Industrial Competitiveness', *Cambridge Journal of Economics*, 23, pp. 167–85.

Mowery, D. C., J. E. Oxley and B. S. Silverman (1998) 'Technological Overlap and Interfirm Cooperation: Implications for the Resource-based View of the Firm', *Research Policy*, 27, pp. 507–23.

Muller, E. and A. Zenker (2001) 'Business Services as Actors of Knowledge Transformation: the Role of KIBS in Regional and National Innovation Systems', *Research Policy*, 30, pp. 1501–16.

Paci, R. and S. Usai (1999) 'Externalities, Knowledge Spillovers and the Spatial Distribution of Innovation', *GeoJournal*, 49, pp. 381–90.

Paci, R. and S. Usai (2000a) 'Technological Enclaves and Industrial Districts: An Analysis of the Regional Distribution of Innovative Activity in Europe', *Regional Studies*, 34, pp. 97–114.

Paci, R. and S. Usai (2000b) 'The Role of Specialization and Diversity Externalities in the Agglomeration of Innovative Activities', *Rivista Italiana degli Economisti*, 2, pp. 237–68.

Romer, P. M. (1986) 'Increasing Returns and Long-run Growth', *Journal of Political Economy*, 94, pp. 1002–37.

Ronde, P. and C. Hussler (2005) 'Innovation in Regions: What Does Really Matter?' *Research Policy*, 34, pp. 1150–72.

van der Panne, G. and C. van Beers (2006) 'On the Marshall-Jacobs Controversy: it Takes Two to Tango', *Industrial and Corporate Change*, 15, pp. 877–90.

White, H. (1980) 'A Heteroskedasticity-consistent Covariance Matrix Estimator and a Direct Test for Heteroskedasticity', *Econometrica*, 48, pp. 817–38.

Index